Imagining Antiquity in Islamic Societies

Imagining Antiquity in Islamic Societies

Edited by Stephennie Mulder

Bristol, UK / Chicago, USA

Imagining Antiquity in Islamic Societies is the seventh book in the Critical Studies in Architecture of the Middle East series. The series is edited by Mohammad Gharipour (Morgan State University, Baltimore) and Christiane Gruber (University of Michigan, Ann Arbor).
Critical Studies in Architecture of the Middle East is devoted to the most recent scholarship concerning historic and contemporary architecture, landscape and urban design of the Middle East and of regions shaped by diasporic communities more globally. We invite interdisciplinary studies from diverse perspectives that address the visual characteristics of the built environment, ranging from architectural case studies to urban analysis.

First published in the UK in 2022 by
Intellect, The Mill, Parnall Road, Fishponds, Bristol, BS16 3JG, UK

First published in the USA in 2022 by
Intellect, The University of Chicago Press, 1427 E. 60th Street,
Chicago, IL 60637, USA

Copyright © 2022 Intellect Ltd

All rights reserved. No part of this publication may be reproduced, stored in a retrieval system or transmitted, in any form or by any means, electronic, mechanical, photocopying, recording or otherwise, without written permission.

A catalogue record for this book is available from the British Library.

Cover designer: Aleksandra Szumlas
Cover image credit: The entrance to the Mosque of Tadmur. From *Views and Panoramas of Beirut and the Ruins of Palmyra (1865-67)* by Louis Vignes, printed by Charles Nègre, Palmyra, Syria, albumen print. Getty Research Institute, Los Angeles (2015.R.15).
Production editor: Laura Christopher
Series: Critical Studies in Architecture of the Middle East
Series editors: Mohammad Gharipour and Christiane Gruber
Typesetting: NewgenKnowledge Works

Print ISBN: 978-1-78938-548-9
ePDF ISBN: 978-1-78938-549-6
ePUB ISBN: 978-1-78938-550-2
Series ISSN: 2059-3562

Printed and bound by Shortrun, UK.

Contents

Introduction: Imagining Localities of Antiquity in Islamic Societies   1
    Stephennie Mulder

PART 1: Imagining Antiquity in Medieval Islam   33

1. 'Return to Origin Is Non-existence': Al-Mada'in and Perceptions of Ruins in Abbasid Iraq   35
    Sarah Cresap Johnson

2. Medieval Reports of the Preservation and Looting of Pre-Islamic Burials in South Arabia   63
    Daniel Mahoney

3. The Wisdom to Wonder: *Ajā'ib* and the Pillars of Islamic India   81
    Santhi Kavuri-Bauer

PART 2: Imagining Antiquity in Ottoman Lands   111

4. Explosions and Expulsions in Ottoman Athens: A Heritage Perspective on the Temple of Olympian Zeus   113
    Elizabeth Cohen

5. Spoils for the New Pyrrhus: Alternative Claims to Antiquity in Ottoman Greece   135
    Emily Neumeier

6. Claiming the Classical Past: Ottoman Archaeology at Lagina   163
    Amanda Herring

PART 3: Imagining Antiquity in Modernity — 191

7. Destruction as Layered Event: Twentieth Century Ruins in the Great Mosque of Gaza — 193
   Eli Osheroff and Dotan Halevy

8. *In Situ*: The Contraindications of World Heritage — 219
   Wendy M. K. Shaw

PART 4: Imagining Antiquity in the Contemporary World — 247

9. The Masjid al-Haram: Balancing Tradition and Renewal at the Heart of Islam — 249
   Muhsin Lutfi Martens

10. ISIS's Destruction of Mosul's Historical Monuments: Between Media Spectacle and Religious Doctrine — 265
    Miroslav Melčák and Ondřej Beránek

11. The Radicalization of Heritage in Tunisia — 291
    Virginie Rey

12. Heritage Crusades: Saving the Past from the Commons — 311
    Ian B. Straughn

Notes on Contributors — 332
Index — 337

Introduction: Imagining Localities of Antiquity in Islamic Societies

Stephennie Mulder

Imagining Antiquity at Palmyra

> At the way stations
>   stay. Grieve over the ruins.
> Ask the meadow grounds,
>   now desolate, this question.
> Where are those we loved,
>   where have their dark-white camels gone? [1]
>
> <div align="right">Ibn ʿArabi (<i>d.</i>1240)</div>

The publication of this edited volume comes as the Syrian war concludes its tenth gruelling year. With tens of millions dead or displaced, the war in Syria now ranks alongside the ongoing conflict in Yemen as among the worst human rights crises since World War II. Yet, among the countless tragic spectacles of human and heritage violence to emerge from this grim decade in Syria, few events focused the attention of the world in May of 2015 like the conquest of Palmyra by the so-called Islamic State (ISIS; also known as Daʿesh). Palmyra, an ancient city in the Syrian desert that grew prosperous on trade in the third century CE, is one of the most notable and visually magnificent sites of standing ruins from antiquity and Syria's most famous archaeological site. In the early summer of 2015, as ISIS moved into the area around the ancient city, news reports breathlessly followed the advance of the militia. Desperate accounts of the hurried evacuations of both local residents and archaeological objects issued from the city, culminating in terrified dispatches from museum workers, many of whom spent nights in the museum in an attempt to safeguard the objects. One of these was the site director at Palmyra Dr Khaled al-Asʿad, a venerable academic specialist on the city who served at Palmyra for some forty years. His shocking death later that summer would again bring the ancient city into the headlines and underscore the dangers faced by Syrian archaeologists, many of whom, like Dr al-Asʿad, worked to protect museums and archaeological sites from the beginning of the conflict.[2] This volume, and the questions raised within it, are dedicated to the scholarship and personal integrity of Dr al-Asʿad.

Despite the global outcry, and in fact, because of it, ISIS proceeded to do as they had done at the museum in Mosul and at hundreds of other lesser-known churches, mosques and shrines in the areas under their control.[3] Between August and October of 2015, ISIS actors placed explosives in and around three of Palmyra's most prominent monuments: the Temple of Baalshamin, the Temple of Bel, and the monumental Triumphal Arch that had formed the entrance to the city. The monuments' destruction was performed before a captive global audience as it was rapidly disseminated in photographs and videos on YouTube and social media.[4] The unprecedented response to this highly mediatized performance treated it as an act of image-breaking. Yet the proliferation of media around it made it into an act of image-making.[5] Nearly every major newspaper in the world featured the destruction of Palmyra on its cover, with headlines in bold font declaring that civilization itself was under attack. Palmyra, prior to the war a site hardly known to the average person outside Syria, became a household name overnight. Its ancient, bracketed columns were suddenly synonymous not with the unique and local achievements of the Eastern Mediterranean world out of which they had arisen, but with the now-threatened triumph of Western European civilization itself. Specialists in Syrian history and archaeology, myself among them, found their previously obscure interest landing them as newly minted 'experts' on major news programmes, struggling with the ethical implications of our role in the media replication of these acts of destruction.[6]

As the crisis unfolded, the media narrative was increasingly dominated by a dialectic of 'civilized versus barbaric' encounters with antiquity; in the popular imagination, ISIS came to embody something prototypically 'Islamic' about the relationship between the world's Muslims and the past. This popular notion was reinforced by a pattern of uncritical media repetition of ISIS's own explanations for their actions. With some exceptions, news media tended to follow the interpretive lead of ISIS's Twitter posts, YouTube videos, and articles published in their glossy recruitment magazine *Dabiq* as though they were legitimate sources on Islamic belief and practice, instead of the complex, carefully-orchestrated, propagandistic media products of hypermodern criminal actors. Tending to take the words directly from ISIS's mouth, news sources reported the destruction as a characteristically 'Islamic' attempt to stamp out idolatry, or as the expression of a fundamentalist desire to revive and enforce a return to a purified monotheism.

Yet, these same media accounts paid little attention to the simple question of how the monuments in question had been sustained and preserved during the more than 1,400 years of Islamic presence and governance in the region before the arrival of ISIS. Instead, a Western narrative about the inevitability of Islamic iconoclasm came to bear on sites of antiquity in Syria, a view initially established following the Taliban's destruction of the Bamiyan Buddhas in 2001 and further developed and reinforced during the *Jyllands-Posten* cartoon controversy in 2005 and the *Charlie Hebdo* massacre in 2015.[7]

The narrative recounted above is well known to many. Yet, hidden within the monumental embrace of the Temple of Bel's fortified temenos is another history of destruction, though it is rarely framed as such.[8] This is the story of the French creation of Palmyra as a heritage locale, which took place nearly a century prior to ISIS's performative encounter with the site. Here, instead of adherents to a fringe sect of Islam, the protagonists were members of the *Service des Antiquités de Syrie et du Liban* (the French Antiquities Service), established shortly after the declaration of the French Mandate in Syria in 1920. Their objective was, to their mind, noble: the restoration of Palmyra to its ancient state and the ostensible conservation and preservation of

Introduction: Imagining Localities of Antiquity in Islamic Societies

the site. Beginning in 1929, French archaeologists, working under the direction of Henri Seyrig, laid out an ambitious programme of restoration. Their efforts included the consolidation of the site, and the restoration of the interior cella of the famous temple, which had been dedicated to the ancient triad of deities worshipped at Palmyra. They also strengthened the entrance portal to the temple with reinforced concrete – there is no doubt that this is one reason it still stands as the sole remnant of the building, today soaring forlornly above the shattered ashlar blocks that are all that remain after ISIS's acts of destruction [Figure I.1].

Absent from this story is a simple fact: in order to preserve, the Antiquities Service had to destroy. When the French arrived at the site in 1929, the area of Palmyra and the vast temenos surrounding the Temple of Bel were not features of the long-abandoned, empty ruin pictured in the numerous paintings, engravings, and publications produced by the European imaginary over the previous 236 years, but a living town:[9] Tadmur, a site of near-continuous habitation since antiquity, one that still bears the ancient name its inhabitants used before the temple site was christened Palmyra by the first European visitors in the eighteenth century.[10] Indeed, the famous Temple of Bel, dedicated in 32 CE, most likely

Figure I.1: The monumental portal to the Temple of Bel, Palmyra, Syria, 2016. A general view taken on March 31, 2016 shows a photographer holding his picture of the temple taken on March 14, 2014 in front of the remains of the historic temple after it was destroyed by ISIS. Joseph Eid, Getty Images.

served as a temple for no more than two brief centuries of its nearly 2,000-year history, yet it was that brief era that the French set out to recreate.

What was the Temple of Bel for the rest of its history if not a temple? What was this locality of holiness for the people of Tadmur over the long course of the subsequent 1,800 years? From about the fourth century CE, the town of Tadmur flourished to the west of the temple, in the area known as the Camp of Diocletian. At some point in later centuries, following the Christianization of the eastern Mediterranean, the town began to develop inside the vast ancient temple temenos itself, following a pattern seen in other cities throughout the region, including Damascus and Baalbek [Figure I.2]. Just as the shrine for the head of Saint John the Baptist was incorporated by early Muslims into the Great Mosque of Damascus, the Christian inhabitants of Tadmur converted the temple at its heart, one of the largest in the Roman Empire, into a monumental Byzantine church.[11] Prior to its destruction by ISIS, one

Figure I.2: The earliest photograph of the town of Tadmur inside the precinct of the Temple of Bel by Louis Vignes, who passed through Palmyra in 1864. From *Views and Panoramas of Beirut and the Ruins of Palmyra* (1865–1867) by Louis Vignes, printed by Charles Nègre, Palmyra, Syria, albumen print. Getty Research Institute, Los Angeles (2015.R.15).

Figure I.3: Remains from the large Christian figurative scene on the interior of the west wall of the Temple of Bel, representing the Mother of God holding the divine child on her knees, surrounded by an angel and two saints, Palmyra, Syria, sixth century. Andreas Schmidt-Colinet.

could still see traces of the paintings of saints and martyrs that once graced the interior walls of the temple during its time as a church [Figure I.3].[12]

Following the Umayyad (661–750) takeover of the city in 634, rather than destroy the church or tear it down, the Umayyad governors may have chosen to reuse the magnificent temple-church by converting it into a mosque.[13] We will likely never know precisely when the conversion occurred, in part because the Christian and Islamic history of the site was largely erased in the process of resurrecting the temple. An early plan of the mosque, drawn by the French architect Louis-François Cassas and published in 1799, does survive [Figure I.4]. The research of Dr al-Asʿad and others has demonstrated that, during the Umayyad era, the old city centre outside the temple site continued to flourish; major infrastructure projects like the construction of congregational mosque and a *suq* (market) showcased the wares of the still-vibrant Silk Route trade that passed through the city as it had in antiquity.[14] The town continued to thrive as one of the main stopping points on the Syrian desert trade route, and in 1132, the Burid (1104–1154) governor Yusuf ibn Firuz built fortifications for the temenos and the town that then surrounded the mosque. The Arab geographer Yaqut (d.1229), who passed through Palmyra in the early thirteenth century, described Palmyra's

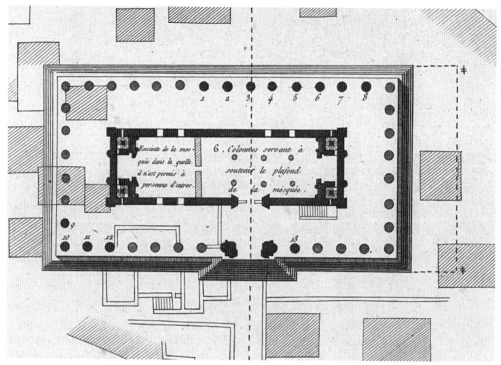

Figure I.4: An early plan of the Mosque of Palmyra, Palmyra, Syria. Detail of Charles-Nicolas Varin after Louis-François Cassas, etching, plate mark, 19.7 × 15.3 in. (50.2 × 39 cm). From *Voyage pittoresque de la Syrie, de la Phoénicie, de la Palestine, et de la Basse Egypte*, vol. 1 (Paris, Imprimerie de la République, c.1799), plate 28. Getty Research Institute, Los Angeles (2015.R.15).

residents as living in 'a castle surrounded by a stone wall'.[15] Around the same time, in 1230, the local Ayyubid (1171–1260) ruler, al-Mujahid Shirkuh, a nephew of the great Muslim general Salah al-Din, built the magnificent, still-extant castle on a hill overlooking the site [Figure I.5].[16] The city continued to be occupied into Ottoman (1299–1922) times.[17] In the late nineteenth century, in an act of cultural heritage preservation, the local governor Fakhr al-Din ibn Ma'an II carried out extensive renovations of the castle, fortifying it so well that it lasted into the contemporary era.[18] Over a period of one thousand years of Islamic history at Tadmur, Muslims and Christians lived, traded, worshipped, and carried out important expansions, additions, and acts of preservation at the Palmyra site. The erasure of these pasts means that when the French set out on a mission of restoration, they also embarked on a mission of selective destruction, one that would demolish a site of near-continuous habitation stretching back to Roman times, in order to privilege the symbolic spaces of antiquity.

What sort of town was Islamic Tadmur? What sort of place, locality, home? What sort of lives were lived here? Syrian archaeologist Salam al-Kuntar, whose mother was born in

Figure I.5: Distant view of the castle at Palmyra, built in the thirteenth century by al-Mujahid Shirkuh on a hill overlooking the Great Colonnade, Palmyra, Syria, 2005. Stephennie Mulder.

Palmyra, remembers the intimacy with which the residents of the town engaged with the site of antiquity in which they lived, observing that '[p]eople were integrated in this fabric of inhabited heritage […] This is the meaning of heritage – it's not only architecture or artefacts that are representing history, it's these memories and ancestral connection to the place.'[19] Al-Kuntar's childhood memories serve as a reminder that the clearing of the town and the dismantling of the mosque irretrievably diminished the complexity of our knowledge of not only the town, its history and its ways of life, but also of its central religious monument: a church and a mosque that had served the town's inhabitants for over a millennium. Given the enduring centuries of the Islamic presence in Tadmur, the dismemberment of the town and the relocation of its inhabitants under the French proceeded with astonishing rapidity, executed in just three short years between 1929 and 1932 [Figure I.6].

Figure I.6: The entrance to the Mosque of Tadmur. From *Views and Panoramas of Beirut and the Ruins of Palmyra* (1865–1867) by Louis Vignes, printed by Charles Nègre, Palmyra, Syria, albumen print. Getty Research Institute, Los Angeles (2015.R.15).

Aerial imagery from 1929 shows the town intact, its winding streets and small courtyard houses arrayed about the central mosque, the dwellings built in mud brick, which was the traditional medium of vernacular architecture throughout Syria until the present. Surrounding the mosque, two roads can be discerned: one, clearly visible, runs at the midpoint between the temple and the medieval fortified wall, while another, less discernible, runs near the outer wall. Two streets bisect the town from the east and the west, converging slightly off-centre to the front and back of the mosque. The eastern road leads directly from the medieval-era fortified gate of the town to the entrance to the mosque under the great portal of the Roman temple. The gate can be seen soaring above the simple mudbrick structures of the town in the earliest photographs from the site, taken in 1864 by the French Naval Officer Louis Vignes [Figure I.7]. In the aerial photo from 1929, the roof of a courtyard-style mosque is clearly visible.

Introduction: Imagining Localities of Antiquity in Islamic Societies

Figure I.7: Aerial images of the *temenos* of the Temple of Bel, Palmyra, Syria, 1929–2015. Thierry Fournet.

Figure I.8: The excavation house for the French excavations led by Henri Seyrig, formerly the home of the mayor of Palmyra, Palmyra, Syria. Institut français du Proche-Orient, Beirut.

Just a year later, in 1930, the town was half cleared, but the mosque was still intact. The villagers were relocated to a new, modern town built on the outskirts of the archaeological site. By 1932, the destruction of the town inside the temple precinct was complete. The photographs show the temenos emptied and vacated, the temple cleared of any sign of the mosque and ready for exploration by Seyrig. Just one house from the village remains, that of the Mayor of Tadmur, which was retained as an excavation house and storage depot for Seyrig's expedition [Figure I.8]. In executing their restoration, the French expedition disinterred, reimagined and privileged a structure that had served its population as the 'Temple of Bel' for a mere 240 years. In doing so, they erased over 1,300 years of ongoing ritual and religious life inside the structure, a building that had served as a church for 330 years and served as the Mosque of Tadmur for a millennium. Why, then, do we call it a temple at all? The answer can only be that the French *created* a temple. Yet it is a replica, an illusion, a vacant site cleared of living memory and history, generated with the aim of serving the needs of modern heritage values.

This, too, was a performance, an act of image-breaking and image-making, one no less powerful and no less generative of meaning, no less actively self-fashioning than ISIS's harkening back to an imagined caliphate. In the case of the French project, this resulted in the European appropriation and reanimation of an imagined, continent-crossing classical past. Instead of a caliphate freed from polytheist ties, the French created a Roman-era site from a past Christian and a living Islamic one. Instead of the revival of an imagined Islamic past, the French pursued the revival of a different, but no less idealized, history. This process, when we consider what it selectively preserves and destroys of that past, is not so ideologically different from ISIS's ostensible desire to revive and enforce a return to an imagined time of purified monotheism. At Palmyra, we have two imaginings of the past: that put forward by the French and that of ISIS. But we also have two belief systems: contemporary heritage values and the values of a contemporary revivalist Salafi movement. Both, it would seem, brought destruction to the identity, lifeways and historic integrity of the people of Tadmur. What is missing from these two tales of destruction is an understanding of the value, the lived experience, and the imagining of antiquity embraced by the people of the village of Tadmur and by other inhabitants of the city over time. For it was this imaginary that was, in every respect, the very vision that enabled the site to survive until Seyrig's arrival in 1929.

Heritage Values: Cosmopolitan or Local?

> One could say that, in its world-forming capacity, architecture transforms geological time into human time, which is another way of saying it turns matter into meaning. That is why the sight of ruins is such a reflexive and in some cases an unsettling experience. Ruins in an advanced state of ruination represent, or better they literally embody, the dissolution of meaning into matter.[20]
>
> Robert Pogue Harrison

It is often remarked that archaeology is an inherently destructive field, and it is true that, though we can know of the existence of the church and the mosque of Tadmur through drawings and photographs, no amount of archival research can bring them back to life. The aim of this volume is therefore to bring to life the voices of Muslims and others in Islamic lands who once engaged with and continue that engagement with ancient Palmyra as well as with other localities of antiquity, and to address the questions too often left unanswered in popular media accounts and in scholarly work on Palmyra and many other sites of antiquity in Islamic lands. How are and were ancient places and localities used in Islamic societies to create a sense of the past, and what are and were the routes, rituals and performances by which the past was inscribed on the landscape? How are holy sites, sites of memory, and sites of ancient heritage construed as places and spaces of the present moment in contemporary Islamic societies? How does heritage use the past to create the future?[21] These questions build on the history of the region that the Muslims set out to conquer in the seventh century. At the moment of the Islamic conquest, this was a region rich in antiquities, which in some places dated back to the Neolithic era and even to the times of our earliest known human ancestors. Syria was ruled in turn by numerous local dynasties and was colonized or conquered by the ancient Egyptians, the Akkadians and Assyrians, the Greeks, the Romans and various Persian dynasties including the Achaemenids and Sassanians. It was also a region marked by long episodes of autonomy under various local groups, as Palmyra was, for example, under Queen Zenobia in the third century. A similarly complex ancient history defines Islamic lands, from Spain to North Africa, from Iran to India. Thus, the early Islamic conquests brought Muslims into contact with the copious remains of ancient civilizations in almost every region they encountered.

This volume, an expansion of a special issue of the *International Journal of Islamic Architecture* published in 2017, engages the question of how Muslims have experienced and continue to encounter, interpret and imagine localities of antiquity.[22] Despite the long history of colonial archaeological encounters with ancient sites in many areas of the Islamic world, research on how Muslims themselves have engaged with such sites in the past and how they do so today has, until recently, been limited.[23] With their insistent focus on local, Islamic interpretations of the past, the authors in this volume raise questions that contribute to the rapidly developing critique of the globalized heritage discourse, the very discourse that informed the French justification for the destruction of the town of Tadmur. Often understood by many European and American observers to be ethical, inclusive and benign, it is this discourse that is here called to account for its frequent promotion of the heritage agendas of groups unrelated to the site, or for the promotion of hegemonic nationalist agendas at the expense of local actors. Anthropologist Laurajane Smith named these globalized heritage norms the 'Authorized Heritage Discourse', and she and others have shown that, while heritage today is a pervasive concept embraced across a number of sectors, it is frequently employed in ways that privilege certain groups and certain pasts at the expense of others.[24] UNESCO has been a crucial actor in developing a cosmopolitan heritage discourse and in spreading heritage consciousness around the world, but not without controversy. Recent work has emphasized the nationalist and exclusionary origins and present applications of Western heritage values. UNESCO World Heritage List models encourage this trend by prohibiting requests from localized, infranational actors and sanctioning claims for recognition only if made from within the nation-state model.[25] Such national claims are often linked to tourism and promote nationalist agendas that, ironically, serve to undermine UNESCO's stated goals of universalizing cosmopolitanism.[26]

Despite the claim that it presents a timeless and universal vision of the past, 'heritage' is 'a term of the present and works by mobilizing selected pasts and histories in the service of present day agendas and interests'.[27] As with nationalism itself, these interests are often quasi-religious in nature. Carol Duncan, Finbarr Barry Flood, Elliot Colla and others have pointed to the ways in which museum culture and the heritage discourse more broadly create cultural icons that are revered in ways that are not dissimilar to religious veneration.[28] Further, as noted previously, the parallel between modern secular heritage fetishism and religious idolatry was an inherent part of ISIS's critique of Western heritage 'worship' and was a propagandistically deployed motivating factor for their acts of iconoclasm. Historian Steven Hoelscher has argued that '[h]eritage […] is a faith, and like all faiths it originates in the deeply rooted human need to give meaning to contemporary chaos, to secure group boundaries, and to provide a symbolic sense of community and certainty that is often lacking in everyday life'.[29]

Colla has echoed that sentiment, arguing that ISIS's vision of museum objects as akin to religious idols arises directly from the world view inherent in Western heritage values:

> Most museum goers and appreciators of ancient artifacts do not think of their practices as a form of religion. But it is not so hard to see how the iconoclasts of ISIS imagine 'false religion' when [they] see the trappings of veneration that pervade museums. Nor are they entirely wrong to cry 'religion' when they hear absolutist claims about transcendent value, even those made by secularists and self-professed atheists.[30]

One way of interrupting the claims of iconoclasts and antiquity fetishists alike is to ask how contemporary heritage values compete with other values.[31] Or, with respect to our focus in this issue, we might ask what were and are the many meanings of objects of antiquity for Muslims, and how can they inform and enrich the contemporary heritage discourse?

Antiquity and the Islamic Imaginary

> When you pass by the Pyramids, say:
>   'How many are the lessons they have
> for the intelligent who would gaze at them!'[32]
>
> <div align="right">Ahmad ibn Muhammad (<i>d.</i>1482)</div>

Long before the emergence of ISIS and other so-called Islamist iconoclasts, long before European explorers and archaeologists like Henri Seyrig arrived at sites like Palmyra, perhaps as early as the rise of Islam itself, Muslims imagined Islamic and pre-Islamic antiquity and its localities in myriad ways. They were sites of memory, spaces of healing, or places imbued with didactic, historical, and moral power. Ancient statuary served as talismans, paintings were interpreted to foretell and reify the coming of Islam, and temples of ancient gods and churches devoted to saints were converted into mosques in ways that preserved aspects of their original meaning and sometimes even their architectural ornament and fabric. Often, such localities were valued simply as places that elicited a sense of awe and wonder, or of reflection on the present relevance of history and the greatness of past empires. This theme was so prevalent that it created the distinct *'aja'ib* (wonders) and *fada'il* (virtues) genres of Arabic and Persian literature. Sites like Ctesiphon, the ancient capital of the Zoroastrian Sassanians, or the Temple Mount, where the Jewish temple once stood, were embraced by early companions of the Prophet Muhammad and incorporated into Islamic notions of self-identification. Various Islamic, Jewish and Christian interpretive communities sometimes shared holy places and had similar haptic, sensorial and ritual connections that enabled them to imagine place in similar ways.[33] These engagements were often more dynamic and purposeful than can be accounted for by conventional scholarly notions of 'influence' and 'transmission'. Muslims also sometimes destroyed ancient places or powerfully reimagined them to serve their own purposes, as for example in the aftermath of the Crusader presence in the Holy Land or in the occasional destruction, reuse and rebuilding of ancient Buddhist and Hindu sites in South Asia. In contrast to the modern segregation of past from present upon which the isolation of ruins is based, Muslims and others in Islamic lands have often simply lived with ruins, incorporating elements of the past into their daily lives in ways that illuminate their value for people in Islamic lands across time.

Significantly, this volume does not aim to give a precise definition for 'Islamic' heritage and instead seeks to nuance what is meant by 'Muslim' experience or 'Islamic' approaches to antiquity. It thus assumes the premises argued in the monumental work of Shahab Ahmed, whose book *What Is Islam?* has transformed our understanding of the vast interpretive possibilities of the experience of being 'Islamic'.[34] For Ahmed, Islam has not been defined historically as orthodoxy, nor has it been lived or experienced primarily as a body of laws or religious rules. Rather, Islam has multiple manifestations which can appear as contradictory if one assumes that religions consistently adhere to an unchanging ideology; a standard that would be unrealistic for any practice with the geographic range and longevity of Islam. Thus, the range of Islamic discourses includes legal proscriptions against the drinking of wine; image-making and the visitation of tombs and shrines. These often belie the common and widespread lived activities of image-making, wine-drinking, and tomb and shrine visitation, which have often been sought out as essential social and spiritual practices by Muslims despite scholarly censure. Ahmed does not segregate such practices into categories of 'licit' or 'illicit', and 'orthodox' or 'popular' religion. Instead, he argues for the simultaneous embrace of these practices and their complexities and contradictions as part of an ongoing discourse on what it means to be 'Islamic'. Similarly, the chapters in this volume reveal that Islamic responses to localities of antiquity are and have always been diverse, varied and context-dependent. The work of the contributors points to a broadly pluralistic, multivalent range of responses to antiquity and reveals a variety of practices not limited to notions of religious 'orthodoxy' or 'orthopraxy'.

The contributors' responses have emerged from a range of interpretive framings, including local tradition, the affective impact of and response to encountering localities of antiquity, and the historical, spiritual, haptic, perceptual, and didactic significance of such localities for Muslim observers. These diverse interpretive framings reveal a critical challenge to the assumed universality of Western heritage values inherent in the logic that justified the French destruction of the Islamic past at Palmyra, and argue for greater attention to, and valuation of, local and community-specific ways of encountering and embracing the past. By engaging these approaches, the volume aligns with recent scholarship in critical heritage studies that envisions heritage as 'a contemporary product shaped from history' and that aims to de-privilege contemporary heritage values by elevating diverse local, non-expert, and non-hegemonic stakeholders and their heritage values.[35] This volume also understands heritage as a processual and discursive practice that produces the continual re-articulation, dynamic engagement, and embodied production of underlying systems of knowledge and meaning.[36]

Within this complex landscape of ideas, Islamic encounters with localities of antiquity can be interpreted as belonging to a number of broad categories, although it should be emphasized that they represent only a subset of Islamic lived and discursive engagements with traces of the past. Here, I propose the following general frameworks for thinking about these processes, while leaving open the possibility for other interpretive framings: 'Ajab (Wonder); 'Ibar (Lessons [of the Past]); Talismanic or Apotropaic Veneration or Reuse; Sacred Histories; and Modern and Contemporary Heritage Discourses.

'Ajab (Wonder)

Particularly in the medieval and early modern eras, Islamic discourses on localities of antiquity were frequently perceived as sites of 'ajab (wonder). The notion of 'ajab, experienced as a visceral and sometimes sensorially-overpowering feeling of astonishment and awe upon encountering things that are strange, ancient, extraordinarily beautiful, or marvellous, had, by about the tenth century, developed into a distinct genre of Arabic and Persian literature called the 'aja'ib. This genre had its roots in the geographical treatises of the classical world, and eventually came to include descriptions of wondrous ancient sites, natural phenomena, and strange flora and fauna, particularly those in far-off places. However, in its initial literary manifestation in the tenth century, the term appears in treatises describing the monuments and buildings of classical antiquity, and of ancient Egypt, Persia and Mesopotamia.[37] A related genre of Arabic literature, the *fada'il* (praise) treatises, arose simultaneously and focused on the excellence of things, places, people, qualities and regions. A prominent subset of the *fada'il* literature was dedicated to the virtues of cities and provinces, the excellence of which was often described as resting in their antiquity and their possession of ancient monuments and works of art.

The notion of ruins as sites of wonder was also a primary theme in pre-Islamic poetry within the oral tradition of the ancient Arabian Peninsula. In odes (*qasidas*) from the pre-Islamic period, wonder is evoked primarily as a response to the encounter with ruins in the form of the traces (*atlal*) of the encampment of one's beloved.[38] The notion of wonder is also a prominent matter in the Qur'an, which emphasizes the marvels of God's creation and enjoins believers to approach them with an attitude of wondrous admiration as a form of worship.[39] 'Ajab later became an important epistemological frame for the justification of the making of art and the preservation of ruins, and a key theme within the 'aja'ib literature was the idea that the skills and arts of the ancient world were more advanced than those of the present.[40]

'Ibar: The Lessons of the Past

Perhaps no less prominent than the notion of wonder, and directly arising from it, is the concept of 'ibar (lessons [of the past]), powerfully evoked and contained within ruins and ancient sites. The idea that ancient sites and the stories they bear can serve as lessons of history is also found within the Qur'an, where the story of the Pharaoh is presented in particular as a cautionary tale about the perils of overweening vanity and arrogance.[41] In these *suras*, the passage of time, the experience of which was incumbent upon even the greatest of men and creations, was meant to serve as a reminder of God's transcendence over the material world. As a result, Muslim philosophers, historians, and geographers gave ancient sites a prominent place within their writings, using them to indicate the futility of human efforts to transcend the passage of time. In this discourse, ruins, ancient statues, paintings, and writings served important roles for consideration and contemplation on the place of humanity within the cosmos.

Ancient sites are also revered because they contain practical lessons. The scientific and technical knowledge of ancient builders, artists, and scientists was admired and emulated throughout Islamic history, and long treatises on the builders and descriptive narratives in which there were attempts to measure such sites were common, a focus shared with early European travel narratives.[42] Certain traditions within Islamic thought occasionally made arguments in favour of iconoclasm, but Muslim scholars and rulers generally sought to emphasize the value of ancient localities for both contemplation and scientific knowledge, thereby placing value on leaving the monuments standing. In other examples, monuments may have employed spolia, parts of ancient buildings, as signs or lessons on the value of antiquity. The bimaristan (hospital) of the great Zangid (1127–1251) ruler Nur al-Din in Damascus, built in 1154, has an antique pediment reused as a lintel, which supports the cascading forms of a *muqarnas* (stalactite-ornamented) half vault [Figure I.9]. This building appears to have reused spolia from the nearby ancient Roman temple of Jupiter, either for purely aesthetic reasons or for purposes of allusion and propagandistic appropriation of the historical achievements of classical antiquity. The thirteenth century in northern Syria is described as having been graced by a period of 'classical revival' in stonecutting and ornamental techniques.[43]

Talismanic or Apotropaic Veneration and Reuse

Ancient sites and objects are also cared for, venerated, and visited because they are believed to have talismanic or apotropaic qualities. Historically, spolia from ancient sites were reused for practical reasons of ease of access to building materials, and because they were believed – precisely because of their antiquity – to have protective value. In Syria and the eastern Mediterranean in the medieval period and into the modern era, it was common for ancient paintings, sculptures, sculptural reliefs, and stone pillars to be reused and incorporated into new architectural constructions because they were talismans against rodents, reptiles, snakes or scorpions.[44] These practices of powerful selective reuse and re-appropriation often carried on the beliefs and understandings passed on from Byzantine or earlier times, and frequently resulted in the preservation of ancient objects into the modern era, during which

Figure I.9: Antique pediment over the door of the Bimaristan of Nur al-Din, Damascus, Syria, 1154. Bernard O'Kane, Alamy Stock Photo.

time many of the same associations prevailed. Re-use of ancient materials for apotropaic purposes is therefore an example of an important heritage belief.

The famous bronze Serpent Column with three heads from the Temple of Apollo at Delphi was placed in the centre of the former hippodrome (horse-racing arena) in Constantinople in the fourth century, on display near an ancient Egyptian obelisk originally made for Thutmose III in the fifteenth century BCE, and other ancient and Byzantine monuments [Figure I.10]. The sculpture came to be valued by Muslims during the medieval period and is mentioned in geographical treatises and city descriptions as early as the tenth century.[45] The Serpent Column was an ancient Greek votive offering taken from the most important Greek ritual site, and brought to Constantinople by the Christian Roman emperor as a symbol of his universal rule. By the late Byzantine era and in Ottoman times, it was revered as an apotropaic

Figure I.10: The Serpent Column (left of centre) as depicted in the Ottoman era Surname i Hümayun ('Imperial Festival Book') of Intizami, c.1588. Wikimedia Commons.

talisman believed to protect the city from poisonous snakes.[46] Such protective attributes were associated with countless pre-Islamic monuments, including the statuary visible in many cities in the Middle Ages. These monuments are described in the 'aja'ib literature and associated with sites from Syria and Yemen to India. Statuary often guarded the entrances to mosques, in a seeming contradiction of the Islamic proscription of figural imagery in religious spaces, serving instead as an indication of the broad flexibility regarding image presentation that always prevailed in Islamic contexts.[47] For example, the al-Azhar Mosque in Cairo (begun 970) featured two reused column capitals bearing carved images of birds that were meant to deter pigeons. The Wikala (caravanserai) of Qawsun (1341), also in Cairo, includes a reused threshold slab with ancient hieroglyphics dating to the era of Pharaoh Ramses II (d.1213 BCE) that remain intact [Figure I.11]. The hieroglyphics could easily have been removed by an iconoclast over the centuries since the caravanserai was built, or the slab could have been installed in such a way that the hieroglyphics would not be visible, but the fact that they were not suggests purposeful intentionality in the ancient object's placement in this liminal space

Figure I.11: Granite monolith bearing a thirteenth-century BCE hieroglyphic text of Ramses II, reused as a threshold for the entrance to the Wikala of Qawsun al-Nasiri, Cairo, Egypt, 1326–1341.

of passage between outside and inside.[48] The antiquity of these objects added to their efficacy to form a crucial aspect of their heritage value. These associations and values were also the direct mechanism for these ancient objects' preservation.[49]

Sacred Histories

This chapter began with a discussion of Palmyra, an example that reveals how Muslims esteemed and frequently reused ancient holy sites like temples, shrines, and churches both because of the inherent sacredness that adhered to them and because their antiquity was an important heritage value that further enhanced their holiness. Such sites were sometimes transformed as part of strategies of conquest, as at the temple and church foundations on which the main mosques of Jerusalem, Damascus, and Cordoba were built. The value attributed to them was not merely dominance-oriented and was inseparable from Muslim perceptions of the antiquity of these sites, which was believed to add to their religious power. At Jerusalem, the Dome of the Rock (691–92) was built as a triumphal monument as well as because the site was previously associated with Jewish and Christian beliefs about Abraham and Solomon.⁵⁰ The mosque built by the Umayyads in Damascus (715) was intentionally constructed on a site that had previously been occupied by a Roman temple and a Christian church, possibly also the case for the Umayyad Mosque in Cordoba (987). Both buildings were considered *'aja'ib* and were praised by Muslim geographers and other scholars, who consistently noted their antiquity as an attribute of their sanctity.⁵¹ In Damascus, Baalbek and Palmyra, reuse largely preserved the ancient buildings fully intact.

As noted previously, Muslims valued objects of antiquity for their ability to serve as signs (*'ibarat*) of a holy person's presence in a particular locality. Between the eleventh and thirteenth centuries in Syria, such sites frequently proliferated following a dream in which a holy figure might appear to indicate an ancient, inscribed stone as proof of a long-lost holy site. Such was the case with the Mashhad al-Muhassin, a lost shrine to a grandson of al-Husayn b. 'Ali that was revealed in a dream to the ruler of Aleppo, Sayf al-Dawla (*r*.944–67). In the dream, Sayf al-Dawla saw lights descending on the Jebel Jawshan outside of Aleppo, and when he went to the spot and began to dig, an inscribed stone bearing the name of al-Muhassin was found, indicating his tomb.⁵² Hundreds of new holy sites were 'rediscovered' in this way during this period, including the burial places of biblical prophets and other holy figures. This phenomenon created a new sacred landscape in the aftermath of the Crusades and generated a new and expanded Islamic notion of an *ard al-muqaddisa* (Holy Land).⁵³ As I have argued elsewhere, such sites are associated with the inscription of history and antiquity on the land from the eleventh through the thirteenth centuries, forming a notion of Islamic sacred landscape that was deeply embedded in, and reificatory for, the material connection of Islam to the ancient past and its place in sacred history. Many of these sites continue to be venerated in the present.⁵⁴

Modern and Contemporary Heritage Discourses

In addition to the diverse relationships outlined above, Muslims and others living in Islamic lands had, and continue to have, more mundane, ordinary relationships with the ancient images, objects and sites among which they live.⁵⁵ Contemporary Muslims also actively practice, publish, and engage with modern secularist global heritage and preservationist discourses, and political and scientific interests are a crucial part of the story of modern and contemporary engagement with the past in the Islamic world. Indeed, an important way that Muslims and people of many other faiths residing in predominantly Islamic lands have encountered the past since the late nineteenth century is through nationalist narratives, which were built, enriched, and perpetuated through the modern field of archaeology. Since the nineteenth century, Muslims and others have actively participated in archaeological excavations, museum curatorial and heritage work, and preservationist activities in accordance with the expectations of modern and contemporary academic and scientific norms. Such activities were pivotal in the process of nation building in the era of independence from colonial rule; in many regions, archaeological and heritage preservation work continues to serve that purpose.[56] Typically, the heritage of antiquity is positively valued in Islamic lands, but the process of nation-building and the archaeological and heritage discourses that lent weight to modern ideas of national identity often took a toll. Universalizing narratives were challenged and contested as increasingly monolithic national and religious identities led to the exclusion of those designated as 'others', who were outside the national or religious sphere. That process is still unfolding in many regions of the Islamic world.[57]

The chapters in this volume are organized into four parts, encompassing the medieval to the contemporary eras. The contributions in each section demonstrate that, across time, the power of ancient sites has resonated for diverse reasons as a reflection of changing and competing lived experiences and discourses. Part One explores medieval encounters with the pre-Islamic past. If the value of ancient localities resided in their apprehension as sites of wonder in the medieval period, it was often through their ability to enhance arguments about the virtues of place or the lineages of kingship. Sarah Cresap Johnson shows that respect for ancient sites was an inherent feature of Muslim engagements with the past from the very earliest years of the Islamic expansion. Johnson looks closely at textual accounts from the Abbasid (750–1258) era in Mesopotamia, when Muslims tended to build next to, not inside, ancient cities. Johnson reveals how the literary theme of meditating on ancient sites (*athar*) and responding with wonder or taking in their lessons (*'ibarat*) was integral to the Abbasid response to localities of antiquity across a range of literary genres. This same apprehension of the wondrous value of the past to solidify claims in the medieval present underpins the argument made by Daniel Mahoney. Mahoney explores a narrative by the tenth-century polymath Abu Muhammad al-Hamdani, whose compendium *al-Iklil* (The Crown), narrates the history of South Arabia from the pre-Islamic to the early Islamic period. One volume of al-Hamdani's compendium contains a collection of reports that describe the early Islamic uncovering of pre-Islamic burials. Mahoney claims that Hamdani anchors collective memory in a type of historical geography through these sites by using events of the deep and recent past to promote a distinct, South Arabian regional identity in the face of northern incursions. These accounts portray a vivid imagining of the ancient tombs and the stories of the buried, as well as the social, religious, and political uses to which the encounters with these burials were put. In a similar vein, Santhi Kavuri-Bauer takes us to medieval India, where the structuring principle of wonder reveals its origins in the Neoplatonic philosophy embraced by medieval Muslim scholars and rulers. Kavuri-Bauer focuses on two ancient Indian pillars: an iron pillar from the Gupta period (320–550 BCE) that was re-erected in the Quwwat al-Islam Mosque by Iltutmish (r.1211–36), and an Ashokan pillar (c.third century BCE) that was installed by Firuz Shah Tughluq (r.1351–88) in the fortress of Firuz Kotla. The abilities of these pillars to elicit wonder, to contain lessons about the proper order of divinely ordained kingship, and to serve apotropaic functions were employed as part of the cosmological arguments that enabled the legitimization of the authority of the sultan in the multi-religious sphere of medieval India.

Part Two of this volume explores four early modern and modern encounters with the localities of antiquity over the long span of the Ottoman era. Elizabeth Cohen examines the

Ottomanization and Islamization of Greece and its most famous city of Athens, which was ruled by the Ottomans for more than four hundred years. Yet, after the Revolution of 1821, the Ottoman period was reduced in Greek cultural memory to an occupation by an alien, outside force. It is only relatively recently that scholarly attention has turned toward Greece's nonconforming heritages, and there has been a growing understanding that Greek history is a palimpsest with an extraordinary variety of pasts. In a wide-ranging study that surveys examples from the fifteenth century and moves forward to the modern era, Cohen proposes diverse ways of experiencing and perceiving the many-layered memories of the iconic city of Athens, renowned for its antiquities. She approaches the city through a close reading of one its most famed monuments, the Temple of Olympian Zeus, which served as both a flexible site of wonder and one of Islamic and Christian worship. Cohen's demonstration of this ancient monument's remarkably varied uses provides for rich, cross-cultural definitions and applications of the modern concept of cultural heritage itself. Another approach to Islamic localities of antiquity prevalent during the Ottoman period is explored by Emily Neumeier in her chapter on Tepedelenli Ali Pasha, the nineteenth-century governor of the Morea in the Greek Peloponnese. Neumeier's reconstruction shows that Ali Pasha embraced local, Ottoman, and Islamic heritage values at the same time as he sought to participate in the 'scramble for the past' that characterized the nineteenth-century European encounter with antiquities in colonized lands. Remarkably, that relationship was avowedly local, and situated Ali Pasha not as a cosmopolitan Ottoman administrator or citizen of the world, but as the descendant of a local Hellenistic king. Amanda Herring takes us to the late Ottoman era, when the director of the Imperial Museum in Istanbul and 'father' of modern Ottoman archaeology Osman Hamdi Bey conducted the first archaeological excavations of the site of Lagina in western Anatolia. Building upon both European archaeological models and precedents established during his work at Nemrud Dağı (Mount Nimrod) and Sidon, Osman Hamdi established a new template for Ottoman archaeology. As part of a broader program of reform and modernization in the Ottoman Empire, the Ottoman state and many scientists and thinkers, including Osman Hamdi, turned their attention to the ancient societies whose ruins lay within their borders, and engaged with the classical past through the modern practice of archaeology.

Part Three explores the role of antiquity in defining modernity, particularly during the twentieth century, as the Islamic world struggled with the destabilizing forces of colonialism, independence, and nation-building. Eli Osheroff and Dotan Halevy analyse heritage contestation at the Great Mosque of Gaza (al-Jamiʿ al-ʿOmari al-Kabir) in twentieth-century Palestine in order to consider the varying contexts, motivations, and interpretations articulated through preservation and ruin. They examine two events of destruction: the shelling of the mosque during World War I, and a later intellectual debate over an engraving of a Jewish candelabrum on one of the mosque's pillars and its defacement. Osheroff and Halevy point away from religious motivations and ideology toward concrete, discursive, historically-grounded struggles over the identity of antiquities and their preservation in the modern Middle East. In a similar vein, Wendy M. K. Shaw explores three instances of rupture with historical, local imaginings of sites of antiquity engendered by modern heritage projects at four sites in the Islamic world. Shaw shows how, despite the claims by museums, UNESCO, and other heritage organizations that the Egyptian sites represent universal values, it has been local ways of interacting with such sites that have been wilfully erased in the process of the creation of contemporary heritage projects. Shaw presses us to question notions of 'civilization' and 'barbarism' that often underpin discussions of the modern, globalized heritage discourse.[58]

Part Four brings a range of viewpoints from the contemporary world. While many of the chapters in this volume explore the abundant evidence for the strong affective, scientific, and idealistic relationships that characterize the majority of interactions with the material traces of the ancient or premodern past, Muslims have also sometimes destroyed images, heritage objects and sites, or rebuilt them to serve contemporary needs.[59] Muhsin Lutfi Martens' chapter presents a history of the multiple building campaigns at the grand mosque in Makkah (Masjid al-Haram) over the past sixteen centuries. He places a particular focus on the extant arcade of the central courtyard, which was first initiated by sixteenth-century Ottoman Sultan Suleyman 'The Magnificent', rebuilt in the seventeenth century, and later dismantled and reconstructed by the Saudis between 2013 and 2015. Martens compares some of the historic and contemporary responses to the appropriation of land and the destruction and rebuilding undertaken by successive Muslim rulers in and around the sanctuary, attempting to ascertain recurrent and common themes and issues that characterize this dialogue across the last sixteen centuries. Martens invites us to consider the balance of ideological and practical considerations that underpin contemporary Saudi policies toward pre-Islamic and Islamic heritage in the heart of Islamic ritual practice.

Miroslav Melčák and Ondřej Beránek turn to the tragic framing event for this volume by analysing the destruction caused by ISIS in Mosul. Their work demonstrates that launching a challenge to the contemporary cosmopolitan heritage discourse was a powerful motivation behind ISIS's destruction at ancient World Heritage Sites like Palmyra. Yet Melčák and Beránek carefully analyse satellite imagery in which ISIS is shown, almost exclusively, to have targeted small and locally relevant sites largely unknown outside of Iraq. This evidence shows that ISIS employs multiple strategies of human, visual and material violence and reveals that, in addition to their desire to attack global heritage values through the performance of hypermodern spectacles of destruction, ISIS seems to have been motivated as well by a desire to inflict damage on local peoples' religious and heritage values and identities.

Two chapters in Part Four confront the globalist cosmopolitan heritage discourse and challenge many of its basic assumptions and values. In the process, they embrace a call for an alternative heritage discourse that brings non-expert and local heritage values to the fore. Virginie Rey's chapter explores the many contested forms of heritage in contemporary Tunisia, where a state-sponsored heritage discourse under the Ben Ali government in the middle of the twentieth century embraced an ostensibly universalizing European-style heritage regime that focused on the pre-Islamic Mediterranean classical past. This discourse excluded the many diverse communities that constituted modern Tunisia and devalued and deemphasized Islamic, Jewish, black African, and Amazigh heritages, leading to the alienation of many Tunisians from their heritage and the politicization of patrimonial practices and institutions. One high-profile outcome of this process was the 2015 attack, in which armed Salafi Islamists took hostages inside the Bardo Museum in Tunis, killing 24 and injuring 50. This violent event obscured many other more positive expressions of heritage reconfiguration and contestation in Tunisia, including attempts by Jewish and Muslim communities to undertake local and community-based heritage initiatives. Rey explores the struggle over who defines the meanings and uses of heritage in Tunisia, and the new challenges and opportunities Salafi attacks have created for the heritage sector since the Jasmine revolution, the campaign of civil resistance to the government of Zine El Abidine Ben Ali that took place between Dec 18, 2010 and Jan 14, 2011. Taking the idea of local and nonconforming heritages one step further, Ian Straughn's chapter presents several cases of vernacular heritage value and reuse in Egypt and Syria that remain undisturbed by—and often actively reject—an intervening globalized heritage discourse. Straughn's chapter also argues against moral and political attributions of local heritage values and makes a powerful call for an expansion of the ethical framework by which heritage is defined.

The twelve chapters in this volume illustrate the vibrancy and value of distinct, multivalent, and local Islamic responses to the material past, and they evoke the consistent presence of a rich spiritual, affective, practical, and discursive world around diverse notions of the value of antiquity in Islamic societies. The authors explore Muslim engagements with heritage, from the inception of this engagement during the earliest years of the growth of the Islamic community to the present, in numerous localities across the vast, continent-encompassing geographical span of the Islamic world. These studies reveal the multivalent ways Muslims engaged with antiquity in the past, and continue to do so in the present, and navigate the contours of diverse Islamic notions of heritage that emphasize the limits of the cosmopolitan heritage goals advocated by international heritage organizations. In some cases, as at Palmyra/Tadmur, those same heritage goals can be protective of that heritage, as they were under the care of archaeologists like Khaled al-Asʿad and the many other archaeologists, museum curators and other heritage workers in the Islamic world. Those heritage goals may also cause destruction, whether through biases against Islamic ways of engaging with the material past, or by inadvertently providing encouragement to the destructive impulses of groups like ISIS. Here, we argue that a heritage discourse that is rooted in local, community-centred ways of valuing and imagining the localities of antiquity must be part of any future engagement with ancient sites in the Islamic world. It is only then that heritage discourse will become truly cosmopolitan.

Acknowledgements

All scholarship is the combined effort of many minds, and I owe thanks to several people who assisted me with the images for this chapter, including Elizabeth Tuggle, Mark Doroba, Thibaud Fournet, Andreas Schmidt-Colinet, Omniya Abdel Barr and Emine Fetvacı. Thanks are also due to Wendy M. K. Shaw and Brian Daniels, who read and commented on drafts. I am grateful to Mohammad Gharipour, Director and Founding Editor of the *International Journal of Islamic Architecture* (*IJIA*), who invited me to edit the special issue on which this volume is based, and for the patient and careful eye of Assistant Editor Mehreen Chida-Razvi and the *IJIA* editorial team.

Notes

1. Muhyiddin Ibn 'Arabi, 'Poem 18 (Qif bi l-Manazil)', *The Translation of Desires*, quoted in Michael Sells, trans., *Journal of the Muhyiddin Ibn 'Arabi Society* 18 (1995), http://www.ibnarabisociety.org/articles/sellswaystations.html.
2. Salam al-Quntar [al-Kuntar] and Brian Daniels, 'Responses to the Destruction of Syrian Cultural Heritage: A Critical Review of Current Efforts', *International Journal of Islamic Architecture* 5.2 (2016): 381–97.
3. Salam al-Kuntar, a Syrian archaeologist who grew up in Palmyra, Assistant Professor of Classics at Rutgers and co-founder of Saving the Heritage of Syria and Iraq Initiative (SHOSI), confirmed during discussion at the conference 'Erasing the Past: Da'esh and the Crisis of Heritage Destruction', Wellesley College, September 24, 2015, that her contacts in Palmyra had told her that the international media coverage spurred by ISIS's takeover of the city encouraged the group to proceed with the destruction of the monuments.
4. ISIS also destroyed and looted sculptures inside the Tadmur Museum and damaged a well-known statue called the *Lion of Al-Lat* as well as demolishing several tower tombs in the vicinity of the city. In March of 2016, ISIS fled in advance of the Syrian Army's recapture of the city, dynamiting part of the thirteenth-century Fakhr-al-Din al-Ma'ani Castle that overlooks the site. After ISIS reconquered Palmyra in December of 2016, they destroyed part of the *scaenae frons* (stage backdrop) of the Roman theatre and the tetrapylon monument at the centre of the city. 'Isis Destroys Tetrapylon Monument in Palmyra', *The Guardian*, January 20, 2017. https://www.theguardian.com/world/2017/jan/20/isis-destroys-tetrapylon-monument-palmyra-syria.
5. This argument has been insightfully made by Ömür Harmanşah, 'ISIS, Heritage, and the Spectacles of Destruction in the Global Media', Special issue, 'The Cultural Heritage Crisis in the Middle East', *Near Eastern Archaeology* 78.3 (2015): 170–77. See also Finbarr Barry Flood, 'Idol-Breaking as Image-Making in the "Islamic State"', *Religion and Society: Advances in Research* 7 (2016): 116–38; Eckart Frahm, 'Mutilated Mnemotopes: Why ISIS Destroys Cultural Heritage Sites in Iraq and Syria', *European Union National Institutes for Cultures*, accessed July 19, 2021, https://www.academia.edu/19580732/Mutilated_Mnemotopes_Why_ISIS_Destroys_Cultural_Heritage_Sites_in_Iraq_and_Syria.
6. I am grateful to my friend and colleague Ömür Harmanşah for two spirited and enlightening debates that took place around this question on *Facebook*, the second of which occurred between September 24 and 27, 2015, http://bit.ly/2lVyBzE. Many of these same ethical challenges were explored in a rich and enlightening roundtable conversation with Zainab

Bahrani, Daniel Bertrand Monk, Nicolai Ouroussoff, Laurie Rush, and Ian B. Straughn (who has contributed a chapter to this volume) at Columbia University on October 29, 2015, Columbia Graduate School of Architecture Planning and Preservation (GSAPP), 'Culture and Heritage After Palmyra, Interdisciplinary Discussion', *YouTube*, November 24, 2015, https://www.youtube.com/watch?v=kLm3Uf6Xtvc.

7. The Danish or *Jyllands-Posten* Muhammad cartoons controversy began on 30 September 2005 when the Danish newspaper *Jyllands-Posten* published 12 editorial cartoons, most of which depicted Muhammad, as an ostensible "free speech" exercise. Their publication led to global protests, including violent demonstrations in some Muslim-majority countries. The *Charlie Hebdo* attacks, in which the French Muslim brothers Saïd and Chérif Kouachi killed 12 people in the offices of the satirical news magazine *Charlie Hebdo* in Paris on 7 January 2015, are also widely assumed to have been in response to satirical representations of the Prophet Muhammad.

8. Archaeologist Michael D. Press has written a series of important articles on the complex history of Palmyra. See 'Excavating the Popular History of Palmyra', *Hyperallergic*, April 22, 2016, http://hyperallergic.com/292461/excavating-the-forgotten-history-of-palmyra/; 'Why Do We Care About Palmyra So Much?', *Hyperallergic*, June 2, 2016, http://hyperallergic.com/299983/why-do-we-care-about-palmyra-so-much/; 'The Getty's Online Palmyra Exhibition Falls Into Orientalist Traps', *Hyperallergic*, February 28, 2017, http://hyperallergic.com/360675/the-gettys-online-palmyra-exhibition-falls-into-orientalist-traps/. See also Maira al-Manzali, 'Palmyra and the Political History of Archaeology in Syria', *Mangal Media*, October 2, 2016, https://www.mangalmedia.net/english//palmyra; Ingrid Rowland, 'Breakfast in the Ruins', *New York Review of Books*, September 17, 2016, http://www.nybooks.com/daily/2016/09/17/breakfast-in-the-ruins-palmyra-photographs/.

9. As Andreas Schmidt-Colinet has shown, the first known painting of Palmyra is a monumental panoramic view dated to 1693 and attributed to Gerarde Hofstede, now in the Allard Pierson Museum in Amsterdam. The earliest modern measured drawings, plans, views, and reconstructions of Palmyra were produced by English travellers Robert Wood and James Dawkins, who visited Palmyra in 1751. The publication of these drawings had a tremendous impact on late eighteenth-century European art and design, sparking further European exploration of the site, which culminated just thirty years later with the visit by architect and painter Louis-François Cassas in 1785 and the subsequent publication of a three-volume study containing over 100 of Cassas's meticulous drawings. See Andreas Schmidt-Colinet, *Kein tempel in Palmyra! Plädoyer gegen einen wiederafbau des Beltempels* (German with English translation) (Frankfurt am Main: Edition Fischer, 2020), 12–15; see also 'No Temple in Palmyra! Opposing the Reconstruction of the Temple of Bel' in *Syria Studies* 11.2 (1999): 63–85. For the works of Cassas, see Schmidt-Colinet, 'Antike denkmäler in Syrien: Die stichvorlagen des L.-Fr. Cassas (1756–1827) im Wallraf-Richartz-Museum in Köln', *Kölner Jahrbuch* 29, 1996 (1997): 343–548, figs. 1–358. I extend my gratitude to Prof. Schmidt-Colinet for generously sharing his publications with me.

10. See Wendy M. K. Shaw's chapter in this volume.

11. Elżbieta Jastrzebowska, 'Christianisation of Palmyra: Early Byzantine Church in the Temple of Bel', *Studia Palmyreńskie* 12 (2013): 177–91.

12. Andreas Schmidt-Colinet, *Kein tempel in Palmyra!*, 30, pl. XII. A concise but comprehensive summary of the full history of Palmyra was published by the: Caroline Durand, Thibaud Fournet and Pauline Piraud-Fournet, 'Bel est bien mort: In memoriam, Palmyre (6 avril – 28 août 2015)', *Les carnets de l'IFPO*, Institut français du Proche-Orient, October 10, 2015, http://ifpo.hypotheses.org/7020. An English translation is available: 'So long, Bel: In memoriam, Palmyra (6 April 32–28 August 2015)', November 6, 2015, updated December 25, 2015, http://ifpo.hypotheses.org/7101.
13. Jere Bacharach has speculated that, given the intensive restructuring of the *suq* during the Umayyad period, it seems reasonable that the conversion occurred at that time. Jere L. Bacharach, 'Marwanid Umayyad Building Activities: Speculations on Patronage', *Muqarnas* 13 (1996): 31. The archaeological sequencing of the mosque was apparently not recorded by Seyrig before its destruction, although he does credit the inhabitants of the village for the 'happy situation' of reuse that allowed the ancient building to be preserved so well. The Arabic inscriptions were recorded in 1931 and 1933 in Jean Sauvaget, 'Les inscriptions arabes du temple de Bel à Palmyre', *Syria* 12.2 (1931): 143–54. See also Manar Hammad, *Bel/Palmyra hommage* (Paris: Geuthner, 2016), xvii.
14. Excavations in 2006 led by Denis Genequand uncovered a congregational mosque dating to the Umayyad era south of the tetrapylon. Denis Genequand, 'An Early Islamic Mosque in Palmyra', *Levant* 40.1 (2008): 3–15. See also Khaled al-As'ad, 'Iktishaf suq min al-'ahd al-Umawi fi Tadmur', *Les Annales archéologiques arabes syriennes* 37–38 (1987–88): 121–40; Khaled al-As'ad and Franciszek M. Stepiniowski, 'The Umayyad Suq in Palmyra', *Damaszener Mitteilungen* 4 (1989): 205–23; Denis Genequand, *Les etablissements des élites omeyyades en Palmyrène et au Proche-Orient*, (Bibliothèque archéologique et historique) (Beirut: Institut français du Proche-Orient (IFPO), 2012), 51–52.
15. Yaqut al-Hamawi, *Kitab mu'jam al-buldan*, quoted in Guy Le Strange, *Palestine under the Moslems* (London: Palestine Exploration Fund, 1890), 541.
16. Oleg Grabar, Renata Holod, James Knustad, and William Trousdale, *City in the Desert: Qasr al-Hayr East* (Cambridge, MA: Harvard University Press, 1978), 161.
17. Zeynep Çelik, *About Antiquities: Politics of Archaeology in the Ottoman Empire* (Austin: University of Texas Press, 2016), 175–78.
18. Janusz Byliński, 'The Arab Castle in Palmyra', *Polish Archaeology in the Mediterranean* 2 (1991): 91.
19. Salam al-Kuntar, quoted in Kanishk Tharoor and Maryam Maruf, 'Museum of Lost Objects: The Temple of Bel', *BBC Magazine*, accessed July 15, 2021, http://www.bbc.com/news/magazine-35688943.
20. Robert Pogue Harrison, *The Dominion of the Dead* (Chicago: University of Chicago Press, 2003), 3.
21. Rodney Harrison, Caitlin DeSilvey, Cornelius Holtorf, Sharon Macdonald, Nadia Bartolini, Esther Breithoff, Harald Fredheim, Antony Lyons, Sarah May, Jennie Morgan, and Sefryn Penrose, *Heritage Futures: Comparative Approaches to Natural and Cultural Heritage Practices* (London: University College London Press, 2020).

22. Stephennie Mulder, ed., special issue, 'Imagining Localities of Antiquity in Islamic Societies', *International Journal of Islamic Architecture* 6.2 (2017). https://www.ingentaconnect.com/content/intellect/ijia/2017/00000006/00000002.
23. In the field of critical heritage studies, Nour Munawwar's recent work on heritagization processes in Syria stands out. See Nour Munawwar, 'Lifecycles of Cultural Heritage in Conflict: Destruction, Reconstruction and Representation in Syria and Iraq' (Ph.D. diss, University of Amsterdam, 2021); 'Competing Heritage: Curating the Post-Conflict Heritage of Roman Syria', *Bulletin of the Institute of Classical Studies* 62.1 (2019): 142–65. Trinidad Rico has published numerous articles on perceptions of heritage in Islamic societies and has recently launched the book series Heritage Studies in the Muslim World. The first volume appeared as an open-access publication. Trinidad Rico, ed., *The Making of Islamic Heritage: Muslim Pasts and Heritage Present* (Springer, 2017), https://link.springer.com/book/10.1007%2F978-981-10-4071-9.
24. On 'Authorized Heritage Discourse', see Laurajane Smith, *The Uses of Heritage* (London; New York: Routledge, 2006), 11–43; see also Bjarke Nielsen, 'UNESCO and the "Right" Kind of Culture: Bureaucratic Production and Articulation', *Critique of Anthropology* 31.4 (2011): 273–92. On the utilization of heritage, see Mads Daugbjerg and Thomas Fibiger, 'Introduction: Heritage Gone Global: Investigating the Production and Problematics of Globalized Pasts', *History and Anthropology* 22.2 (2011): 135–47.
25. See Marc Askew, 'UNESCO, World Heritage, and the Agendas of States', in *Heritage and Globalisation*, ed. Sophia Labadi and Colin Long (London; New York: Routledge, 2010), 19–44.
26. Lynn Meskill, 'UNESCO and the Fate of the World Heritage Indigenous Peoples Council of Experts (WHIPCOE)', *International Journal of Cultural Property* 20.2 (2013): 156.
27. Daugbjerg and Fibiger, 'Introduction', 136.
28. Flood, 'Idol-Breaking', 121; F. Barry Flood, 'Between Cult and Culture: Bamiyan, Islamic Iconoclasm, and the Museum', *Art Bulletin* 84.4 (2002): 641–59; Elliot Colla, 'On the Iconoclasm of ISIS', March 5, 2015, http://www.elliottcolla.com/blog/2015/3/5/on-the-iconoclasm-of-isis; see also Elliot Colla, *Conflicted Antiquities: Egyptology, Egyptomania, Egyptian Modernity* (Durham, NC; London: Duke University Press, 2007). For a foundational study on museums as sites of secular ritual, see Carol Duncan, *Civilizing Rituals: Inside Public Art Museums* (London; New York: Routledge, 1995).
29. Steven Hoelscher, 'Heritage', in *A Companion to Museum Studies*, ed. Sharon McDonald (Malden, MA: Blackwell, 2006), 216.
30. Colla, 'On the Iconoclasm of ISIS'.
31. I am indebted to Trinidad Rico for this question, which she posed in a panel chaired by Mirjam Brusius, 'Alternative Preservation Practices of "Cultural Heritage" in the Middle East', Middle East Studies Association, November 18, 2016. See also Trinidad Rico, 'Islamic Values as Heritage Subjects', *Material Religion* 10.4 (2014): 533–44.
32. Jalal al-Din al-Suyuti, *Kitab husn al-muhadara fi akhbar Misr wa al-Qahira*, quoted in Colla, *Conflicted Antiquities*, 80.

33. See the studies in Mohammad Gharipour, ed., *Sacred Precincts: The Religious Architecture of Non-Muslim Communities Across the Islamic World* (Leiden: Brill, 2014); Josef Meri, *The Cult of Saints among Muslims and Jews in Medieval Syria* (Oxford: Oxford University Press, 2002), 12.
34. Shahab Ahmed, *What Is Islam? The Importance of Being Islamic* (Princeton: Princeton University Press, 2015), 247–97.
35. John E. Turnbridge and Gregory J. Ashworth, *Dissonant Heritage: The Management of the Past as a Resource in Conflict* (Chichester, UK: John Wiley & Sons, 1996).
36. Wendy M. K. Shaw, 'From Postcoloniality to Decoloniality, From Heritage to Perpetuation: the Islamic at the Museum', in *Heritage, Islam, Europe: Entanglements and Directions. An Introduction*, ed. Katarzyna Puzon, Sharon Macdonald, and Mirjam Shatanawi (London: Routledge, 2021), 31-51.
37. The most important recent studies focus on the thirteenth-century *'aja'ib* treatise of Zakariya ibn Muhammad al-Qazwini (*d*.1283). See Persis Berlekamp, *Wonder, Image, and Cosmos in Medieval Islam* (New Haven, CT; London: Yale University Press, 2011); C. E. Bosworth and I. Afshar, "Aja'eb al-Makluqat', *Encyclopaedia Iranica* online, accessed July 19, 2021, https://iranicaonline.org/articles/ajaeb-al-makluqat.
38. See Ibn Sina's quote at the beginning of this chapter.
39. "Aja'eb al-Makluqat', *Encyclopaedia Iranica* online.
40. Colla, *Conflicted Antiquities*, 80–86.
41. Michael Cook, 'Pharaonic History in Medieval Egypt', *Studia Islamica* 57 (1983): 67–103.
42. Colla, 'The Measure of Egypt', *Postcolonial Studies* 7.3 (2005): 271–93.
43. Yasser Tabbaa, 'The Muqarnas Dome: Origins and Meaning', *Muqarnas* 3 (1985): 61–74; Terry Allen, *A Classical Revival in Islamic Architecture* (Wiesbaden: Reichert, 1986); J. M. Rogers, 'A Renaissance of Classical Antiquity in North Syria', *Annales archéologiques Arabes Syriennes* 21 (1971): 347–56.
44. F. Barry Flood, 'Image against Nature: Spolia as Apotropaia in Byzantium and the Dar al-Islam', *The Medieval History Journal* 9.1 (2006): 143–66; Julia Gonnella, 'Columns and Hieroglyphs: Magic *Spolia* in Medieval Islamic Architecture of Northern Syria', *Muqarnas* 27 (2010): 103–20.
45. Flood, 'Image against Nature', 147.
46. Rolf Strootman, 'The Serpent Column: The Persistent Meanings of a Pagan Relic in Christian and Islamic Constantinople', *Material Religion* 10.4 (2014): 432–51.
47. See Ahmed, *What Is Islam?*, 46–57, 408–25; Christiane Gruber, 'In Defense and Devotion: Affective Practices in Early Modern Turco-Persian Manuscript Paintings', in *Emotion and Subjectivity in the Art and Architecture of Early Modern Muslim Empires*, ed. Kishwar Rizvi (Leiden: Brill, 2017), 95-123.
48. David Lorand, 'A Block of Ramesses II Reused as a Threshold in the Wakala of Qawsun (Cairo)', *Journal of Egyptian Archaeology* 99 (2013): 270–71. There are dozens of examples of this type of reuse in Cairo. See Hasan Abd al-Wahhab, 'Al-athar al-manqula wa al-muntahila fi al-athar al-islamiyya', *Bulletin de l'institut de l'Égypte* 38 (1955–56): 243–83; Viktoria Meinecke-Berg, 'Spolien in der mittelalterlichen architektur von Kairo', in *Ägypten, Dauer und Wandel: Symposium anlässlich des 75-jährigen bestehens des Deutschen Archäologischen Instituts Kairo* (Mainz: Philipp von Zabern, 1985), 131–42.

49. Flood, 'Image against Nature', 155.
50. Nasser Rabbat, 'The Meaning of the Umayyad Dome of the Rock', *Muqarnas* 6 (1989): 12–21.
51. Nicola Clarke, 'Medieval Arabic Accounts of the Conquest of Cordoba: Creating a Narrative for a Provincial Capital', Bulletin of the School of Oriental and African Studies 74.1 (2011): 41-57; Nuha Khoury, 'The Meaning of the Great Mosque of Cordoba in the Tenth Century', *Muqarnas* 13 (1996): 80–98; Mattia Giudetti, 'Churches Attracting Mosques: Religious Architecture in Early Islamic Syria', in Gharipour, ed., *Sacred Precincts*, 11–27.
52. Stephennie Mulder, *The Shrines of the 'Alids in Medieval Syria* (Edinburgh: Edinburgh University Press, 2014), 68.
53. On the shrines of biblical prophets discovered in this period, see 'Ali ibn Abi Bakr al-Harawi, *A Lonely Wayfarer's Guide to Pilgrimage: 'Ali ibn Abi Bakr al-Harawi's Kitab al-isharat ila ma'rifat al-ziyarat*, trans. Josef Meri (Princeton: Darwin Press, 2004). On the expanded notion of a Holy Land in this period, see Zayde Antrim, *Routes and Realms* (Oxford: Oxford University Press, 2012).
54. Mulder, *Shrines*, 247–66.
55. On the current implementation of such values in the reconstruction of Aleppo, Syria, see Giulia Annalinda Neglia, *The Cultural Meaning of Aleppo: A Landscape of Recovery for the Ancient City* (Bristol, UK; Chicago: Intellect Publishers, 2020).
56. For recent research, see Çelik, *About Antiquities*; Colla, *Conflicted Antiquities*; Donald Malcolm Reid, *Whose Pharaohs? Archaeology, Museums, and Egyptian National Identity from Napoleon to World War I* (Cairo: American University in Cairo Press, 2002).
57. On the destruction of heritage in service to the aims of contemporary religio-nationalist identity-building in the recent example of Nakhichevan, Azerbaijan's Armenian Christian cemeteries and churches, see Simon Maghakyan and Sarah Pickman, 'A Regime Conceals Its Erasure of Indigenous Armenian Culture', *Hyperallergic*, February 18, 2019, https://hyperallergic.com/482353/a-regime-conceals-its-erasure-of-indigenous-armenian-culture/ See also Dale Berning Sawa, 'Monumental loss: Azerbaijan and "the worst cultural genocide of the 21st century"', *The Guardian*, March 1, 2019, https://www.theguardian.com/artanddesign/2019/mar/01/monumental-loss-azerbaijan-cultural-genocide-khachkars.
58. Smith, *Uses of Heritage*, 11.
59. Flood, 'Between Cult and Culture', 644–51; Gruber, 'In Defense and Devotion'.

Part 1

Imagining Antiquity in Medieval Islam

1

'Return to Origin Is Non-existence': Al-Mada'in and Perceptions of Ruins in Abbasid Iraq

Sarah Cresap Johnson

Ruins, it has been observed, are essentially features of modernity [...] It was in the imagination of the Renaissance spectator who regarded collapsed remains as some remove of space and time that the irresistible decay of a ruin first became differentiated from dilapidation.[1]

Ruins have been studied extensively from the European perspective, from the early-twentieth-century treatises of Georg Simmel and Alois Riegl to the 1997 Getty museum exhibition, *Irresistible Decay*, to Svetlana Boym's publications at the turn of the twenty-first century.[2] European scholars' perceptions of Middle Eastern ruins have also received attention from researchers and in the media, beginning with studies of orientalist painters in the nineteenth century and culminating in reactions to the recent occupation and destruction at Palmyra.[3] But is it true that a fascination with ruins is particularly European and modern? The abundance of Middle Eastern writings on ruins – from Imru' al-Qays's *Mu'allaqat* in the sixth century to the tenth-century *Book of Strangers* by al-Isfahani, which recorded poetic graffiti left by travellers on ruins – makes clear that encounters with, and responses to ruins were an important part of Middle Eastern cultural life.[4] As Svetlana Boym illustrates in her work, attitudes toward ruins are historically specific, wrapped up in the literary, cultural and linguistic traditions of the moment they were conceived.[5] By looking at Arabic writings from the early Abbasid period (750–1055) up to the Seljuq era (1040–1196), this chapter attempts to discern Middle Eastern attitudes toward ruins with greater historical specificity. These periods are particularly important for the study of ruins as they saw both the reconfiguration of the landscape, with the political centre shifting from Greater Syria to Iraq, and the flourishing of new forms of literature, which gave rise to new perspectives on ancient places. Through an examination of Abbasid texts, it is clear that ruins served as signs for a variety of often-conflicting cultural, social and political issues, including the impermanence of life, the strength of pre-Islamic empires and poetic wonder.

Changing Geographies

In Greater Syria during the Umayyad period (661–750), conquered cities were inhabited rather than abandoned, leaving the urban geography relatively intact from the pre-Islamic period. Alan Walmsley describes the occupation of Syria-Palestine by early

Figure 1.1: The Umayyad suq in the Great Colonnade, Palmyra, Syria. Dr Michal Gawlikowski.

Muslim populations as 'so indiscernible in the archaeological record that this historically momentous sequence of events has been appropriately termed the "Invisible Conquest"'.[6] Ruins held talismanic and aesthetic significance in the Umayyad period; the latter, for example, can be seen in the reuse of lintels and jambs from a gate in pre-Islamic Palmyra in the façade of the Umayyad desert palace, Qasr al-Hayr al-Gharbi (724–27).[7] Julia Gonnella has shown that in medieval Syria, such reuses of pre-Islamic spolia were not incidental and were often ascribed with magical properties.[8] Because of the continuous habitation that characterized life in post-conquest Syria, ruins were largely described as part of the urban fabric of Umayyad Greater Syria rather than as unoccupied, detached spaces. For example, the ruins of Palmyra (Arabic: Tadmur) were inhabited during the early Islamic period, and the town played an active role in Umayyad political and historical life [Figure 1.1]. One of the great myths associated with the pre-Islamic ruins of Palmyra was the Caliph Marwan II's discovery of the Tomb of Tadmur, said to be a descendent of Noah. Here, the story is connected to a rebellion during the Umayyad period and not with the town's status as an ancient ruin.[9] The discovery of the tomb of Tadmur is placed within the text as part

'Return to Origin Is Non-existence': Al-Mada'in and Perceptions of Ruins in Abbasid Iraq

of a legitimization of Marwan's position as caliph, not as part of the history of the pre-Islamic site.

Following the Abbasid conquest in 750, ruins in Iraq – such as al-Mada'in, a group of Parthian and Sassanian cities near present-day Baghdad – were also occupied. However, in Iraq, the pattern of founding new Islamic cities, such as Baghdad, Kufa and Samarra, next to, but not directly within older inhabited areas, led to the literary conceptualization of pre-Islamic settlements largely as abandoned ruins, even if in reality they frequently still

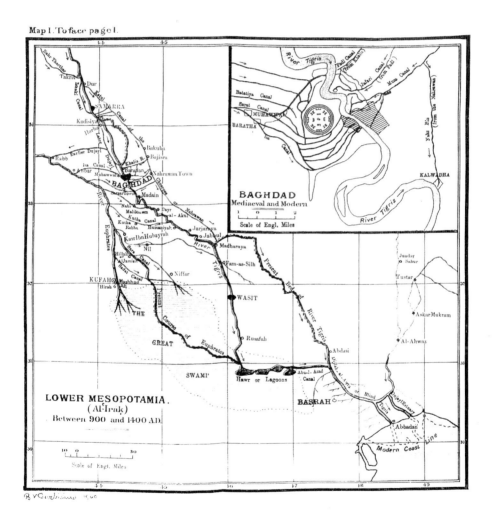

Figure 1.2: Map of Lower Mesopotamia during the Abbasid caliphate. G. le Strange, *Baghdad during the Abbasid Caliphate* (London: Humphrey Milford, 1924), Map 1.

contained settlements [Figure 1.2].¹⁰ Al-Mada'in and al-Hira were described in Abbasid writing not as part of the urban structure but as ruins in proximity to Kufa and Baghdad, respectively. Abbasid writing on ruins developed not only in reaction to pre-Islamic ruins, but also as a result of the ruination of many early Islamic cities and monuments within the Iraqi landscape due to political unrest. Literature provided intellectual discourse on, as well as emotional catharsis to, the ruin of the Abbasid landscape.

The Abbasid Texts

The theme of meditating on ruins (*athar*) is one of the most common tropes in Arabic literature. It first appears in poetry from the pre-Islamic period, where the ruins take the form of abandoned campsites. Meditations on the affective power and moral lessons of ruins persist well into the Abbasid era, when the theme can be found in a variety of literary genres. The theme, particularly in poetry, has been previously addressed by scholars.¹¹ However, there has been little attempt to connect the author's visualization of the physical ruins with the ruins' literary manifestations.

Three types of texts experienced significant development during the Abbasid period: history (*tar'ikh*), geography and poetry.¹² The early Abbasid period also saw the rise of *adab*, a complex conception of literature and of the values and mores of literary society, the prominence of which denoted a strong interest in literature among the educated classes.¹³ While Abbasid authors were not always clear in their opinions and often continued to claim that they were transmitting history directly from their predecessors, individualism became more accepted in writing during this period and individual perspectives are evident through variations in the texts.¹⁴ For example, whereas the seminal Abbasid historian Muhammad ibn Jarir al-Tabari (d.923) relays the wonder that Muslim armies felt when initially entering al-Mada'in, Ahmad ibn Yahya al-Baladhuri (d.892), a writer working in the Abbasid court, claims that it was only a pestilent swamp.¹⁵

In conjunction with these developing literary genres, diction and language also shaped Abbasid attitudes to ruins.¹⁶ The Arabic language created specific descriptive possibilities, and geographers, historians and poets used a variety of Arabic words to differentiate between different forms of ruins. By the time Abbasid writers – such as Abu al-Qasim ibn Hawqal (d.c.990) – were travelling through Iraq, many early Islamic cities consisted completely or partially of ruins. In terminology, historians and geographers often made a distinction between the ruins of contemporary Islamic civilization and the ruins of the pre-Islamic past. Ruins of Islamic cities were described as actively decaying or destroyed (*kharab*), and pre-Islamic ruins were described as traces and relics of the past (*athar*).¹⁷ In the Arabic etymology, pre-Islamic ruins were seen positively as what remained and Islamic ruins were seen negatively as what was disappearing. For example, Ibn Hawqal described the ruins of Samarra as a vanishing place of loss, but he described al-Mada'in a few pages later as having grand ancient monuments (*atharuha 'azima*).¹⁸ While the word used for the monuments of al-Mada'in does suggest ruin and decay in its etymology, Ibn Hawqal's description of the grandeur of its 'traces' signifies reverence for preservation rather than sadness at loss. It may be argued that this linguistic distinction indicates a visual perception of the past through ruins that is based on an Arabic etymology. More specifically, the Abbasid writer's terminology shows that he saw monuments as actively decaying or resisting decay rather than as static structures.

History

By the height of the early Abbasid period in the ninth century, there was a strong interest in historical writing, and works of history frequently described early Muslim encounters with ruins.[19] In his *History of Prophets and Kings*, al-Tabari describes early Muslim temporary habitation of pre-Islamic monuments, while at the same time being conscious of the monuments as having been considered ruins during his own time. Al-Tabari's long description of the conquest of al-Mada'in incorporates the physical structure of the city into its mytho-historic tradition. Al-Mada'in, literally 'the cities', was the Arabic name for a conglomeration of ancient cities near Baghdad, which included the Sassanian capital Ctesiphon, whose two royal palaces, the Taq-i Kisra and the White Palace, played an important role in early Islamic literature. Before Abbasid histories, the Taq-i Kisra existed in Islamic literature as a mythical place associated with Qur'anic history, a site that was ruined at the birth of Muhammad.[20]

Al-Tabari's descriptions of the Taq-i Kisra, which still stands today [Figure 1.3], and of the no-longer-extant White Palace, complicated the mythical Qur'anic ruination of the structures by describing the historical habitation of the city by early Muslim armies.[21] His description of the awe that Muslims felt when viewing the White Palace for the first time focuses on wonder rather than hatred or a desire for destruction:

> When the Muslims entered Bahurasir in the middle of the night, they saw something white. Dirar b. al-Khattab exclaimed, 'God is great, this white thing there must be the palace of the king, as God and His messenger have promised us.' The people never stopped shouting 'God is great!' until dawn.[22]

Al-Tabari does not ignore the Qur'anic prophecy cited by earlier authors. However, in the structure of his text, the exaltation of the Muslim newcomers at the fulfilment of the prophecy is directed toward the monument itself, as if worshiping an idol rather than preparing to ruin the structure. In a way, the celebration of the destruction here becomes its own form of idolatry, complicating the Qur'anic prohibition of idol worship.[23]

Al-Tabari's description of the occupation and conversion of the White Palace into a mosque does not insist on its complete transformation into an Islamic structure but rather on its dualism as an Islamic mosque and a Sassanian ruin. As Sa'd ibn Abi Waqqas (*d*.675), an early Muslim military leader, turns the White Palace into a Friday Mosque, al-Tabari inserts his own commentary by emphasizing its unlikely position as a prayer space, because

Figure 1.3: Ctesiphon, Iraq (c.1880–1930), photographic print. Antoin Sevruguin, Myron Bement Smith Collection: Antoin Sevruguin Photographs. Freer Gallery of Art and Arthur M. Sackler Gallery Archives, Smithsonian Institution, Washington, DC. Gift of Katherine Dennis Smith, 1973–1985, FSA A.4 2.12. Sm.65.

worship took place among plaster statues.[24] While nothing remains of the White Palace, a stucco figure from the church of Qasr bint al-Qadi at Ctesiphon gives an impression of the statues that Saʿd might have seen there [Figure 1.4]. For al-Tabari, the statues were potent symbols of a remaining Sassanian presence in an early Islamic ritual space.

Saʿd's recitation of a nostalgic Qur'anic passage upon entering the audience hall suggests that the abandoned state of the palace as a ruin was the very thing that had facilitated its transformation into a mosque:

> How many gardens and springs (flowing therein) have they abandoned, how many sown fields and noble habitats, how many comforts in which they took delight! […] Then he performed a prayer ritual commemorating the conquest; this was no congregational prayer meeting […] He adopted the Great Hall as a site for the prayer ritual. There were plaster statues there, of men and horses, but that did not prevent Saʿd, nor the other Muslims, [from praying there] and they were left as they were.[25]

'Return to Origin Is Non-existence': Al-Mada'in and Perceptions of Ruins in Abbasid Iraq

Figure 1.4: Ctesiphon, Iraq, painted stucco figure, Qasr bint al-Qadi, Sassanian period. Johannes Kramer, Museum für Islamische Kunst, Staatliche Museen zu Berlin, kt.W.292/1.7727.

The White Palace was not inhabited by Muslims until it was completely empty, or in other words, had become a ruin: 'The Muslim army did not enter [the city], however, until a Persian called out, "By God, there is no one here". Then they moved in.'[26] In al-Tabari's text, the abandonment of the monument inspires Sa'd to quote a Qur'anic passage, which in turn, leads to his personal moment of prayer. Sa'd's choice of this particular Qur'anic passage relates to a pre-Islamic Arabic poetic tradition of nostalgia for ruins in the form of abandoned campsites, and suggests that the unfamiliar Sassanian monument has the same power to elicit nostalgia as the ancient Arab campsites.[27]

Geographies and Founded Cities

As Muslims moved out of pre-existing structures into new Islamic cities, urban centres were configured within a landscape of pre-Islamic monuments, close enough to incorporate them into the Abbasid worldview but far enough to designate them as abandoned ruins. In the context of Iraq, and particularly of al-Mada'in, this structural change in the landscape should not be seen as a movement away from monuments of the pre-Islamic past, but instead as a reconfiguring of them within the Islamic worldview. Arab historians believed that al-Mada'in was called such because of the building of cities next to one another on the site. The continuous citation of nearly abandoned cities like al-Mada'in and Babylon in Abbasid literature when describing living cities indicates that a collective landscape was created between founded cities and ancient monuments.[28] Of course, this fact also shows that founding cities next to ruins was common practice in the region throughout antiquity.[29] The landscape of clustered cities was not new, but the lenses of new literary forms during the Abbasid period shifted the perception of these multilayered geographies.

The primary interest of geographers was to document territories, frontiers and roads, but ruins are also continually mentioned in relation to cities, indicating their importance to descriptions of the Abbasid landscape.[30] For example, Ibn Hawqal emphasized that the ruins of Nineveh were clearly visible from Mosul [Figure 1.5].[31] The continuous citation of ruins within geographical texts turned them into literary topoi, or formulaic conventions separate from their physical forms, which came to be habitually cited whenever discussing a nearby Islamic city. As the bureaucratic name of the Abbasid region where Baghdad was situated, Babylon (Babil) also delimited the entire region. Its physical presence was also used to legitimize new Abbasid cities. The geographer Ahmad ibn 'Umar ibn Rusta (active c.903–13) connects Baghdad to Babylon through the administrative terminology used to describe the cities:

Baghdad was the name of a place, which was on this site before, which, they claim, was a place of wooden images and idols in the old age. It is the *Ard Babil*, and Babylon is the oldest of all these places.[32]

'Return to Origin Is Non-existence': Al-Mada'in and Perceptions of Ruins in Abbasid Iraq

Figure 1.5: Ruins of Nineveh on the left bank of the Tigris opposite the city of Mosul, Iraq (*c*.1923), photomechanical print. A. Kerim, Special Collections, Fine Arts Library, Harvard University, HSM.86.004.055.

Here, Babylon's age gives importance to Baghdad.

Because few ruins were visible in Babylon during the Abbasid period, its extreme age, often associated with the Qur'anic figures of Noah and Daniel, added to its significance within geographical literature.[33] Frequently, geographers combined the Qur'anic stories with the physical ruins. For example, 'Ali ibn al-Husayn al-Mas'udi (*d*.957) notes: 'The traveller remarks that in this village [Babylon] are great ruins [*athar*] lying in rubble, antiquities and buildings which have become mounds [...] And many people go there because they believe that the two angels, Harut and Marut, are there.'[34] Al-Mas'udi's description shows his interest not only in Babylon's history and its impression on him as a traveller but also in the ritual interactions of everyday people with the site. In this case, the practice of visiting ruins extended beyond elite literary society. These layered stories in the Abbasid authors' texts show the pervasiveness of the power of ruins as a theme in various genres of literary production, including religious myths, travel accounts and bureaucratic administration.

Spolia and the Ruin

Despite these positive associations with ancient sites, the picture was not always so clear. For example, the predominance of the use of 'Babil' (Babylon) as an administrative term was also associated with a threat to the Islamic bureaucracy and society. There was an intellectual awareness of the power of the administrative term, Babil, to bring the pre-Islamic past into the Abbasid present. This awareness is attested to by a scholarly discourse that argued that the district name, Babil, distracted from the glory of the Islamic present. Muhammad ibn Ahmad Shams al-Din al-Muqaddasi (*d.*991) provides a concise summary of this argument:

> We scrutinized Islam, long and broad, and we did not hear the people say anything other than that this climate zone was Iraq, and most people do not even know where Babil is [...] Do you not take into account the answer of Abu Bakr to 'Umar [...] 'Never will God give me control over one foot of holy ground that is dearer to me than one of the subdistricts of Iraq': and he did not say 'of the subdistricts of Babil'.[35]

Here, al-Muqaddasi contrasts the nomenclature of an idealized Islamic past, that of the 'Rightly Guided' Caliphs Abu Bakr and 'Umar, with the nomenclature of a more distant and non-Islamic past of ancient Babylon. His discomfort with the name Babil suggests his belief that even toponyms separated from their ruined monuments held a problematic power to bring the pre-Islamic past into the landscape, one that threatened to overpower the Islamic present. Further, the name had talismanic associations: in many Abbasid texts, the name Babil is associated with magic and curses.[36] This magical association with Babylon's ruins is part of a larger tradition predominant during the Abbasid period on the theme of the talismanic attributes of ruins in treasure-hunting stories. To cite just one example, the tenth-century catalogue of Arabic graffiti, *The Book of Strangers*, relates a story about the discovery of treasure in a ruined building: '[T]he treasure had a mighty and fearsome talisman [...] we went inside, where we saw ancient and mighty buildings, awe-inspiring ruins and deadly snakes.'[37]

In a way, the name Babil functioned as a form of spolia, appropriated from the past into the current administrative and terminological structure. Indeed, the calculated use of physical spolia from pre-Islamic ruins to build Abbasid cities complicated the semiotic distinction between the traces of pre-Islamic monuments and decaying Islamic cities. On the one hand, spolia represented destruction of the past through ruin, but at the same time, they indicated a desire for citation of the transformed monument through reconstruction. The ruined monument, often overlooked in discussions of spolia, was an integral part of the Abbasids' discussion of the appropriation of material from pre-Islamic monuments to build their cities. The Abbasids were aware that their destruction of pre-Islamic monuments was a form of iconoclasm imbued with potent symbolism. Jas Elsner elucidates the way in which iconoclasm and spolia are integrally related:

The preserved damaged object, in its own material being, signals both its predamaged state – a different past, with potentially different cultural, political, and social meanings – and its new or altered state […] Like the Roman god Janus, such monuments face in two directions simultaneously.[38]

Historical and geographical writing from the Abbasid period allows the modern reader to see this Janus effect in Islamic monuments made from the material of pre-Islamic ruins. In Iraq, the proximity of Abbasid cities to pre-Islamic ruins underlined the relationship between spolia and their origins.

Abbasid consciousness of this dualism between spolia and ruination is illustrated in the story of Caliph al-Mansur's (*r.c.*709–14) decision to tear down al-Mada'in in order to build Baghdad.[39] Al-Mansur approached the destruction of al-Mada'in critically, calling together his advisers in order to weigh different theories. Khalid ibn Barmak, an adviser of Iranian heritage, argued that tearing down al-Mada'in would destroy a testament to the Muslim conquest of Iraq and early Islamic history.[40] Al-Mansur, however, suspected Khalid ibn Barmak of favouring the monument as a symbol of Iranian glory, and decided to tear it down against the suggestion of his advisers. When al-Mansur could not afford to tear down the monument, only managing to partially destroy the White Palace, Khalid ibn Barmak claimed that the ruined structure now symbolized al-Mansur's weakness and should be torn down completely. In this story, Khalid ibn Barmak recognized the Janus effect of spolia and understood that the state of the ruins of al-Mada'in would speak to the city of Baghdad.

Ibn Khaldun (*d.*1406) suggested an explanation for al-Mansur's philosophical dilemma regarding using building materials from the White Palace to build his city:

Al-Rashid had the intention of tearing it down but was unable […] [Later] dynasties are unable to tear down and destroy many great architectural monuments, even though destruction is much easier than construction, because destruction is a return to the origin, which is non-existence.[41]

While Ibn Khaldun was writing some five hundred years later, it is evident from his text that there was a long mytho-historic legacy of rulers attempting to destroy pre-Islamic monuments and failing to do so. In later periods, the ruler's uncertain relationship with ruins was often illustrated in the Iranian poet Nizami Ganjavi's (*d.*1209) *Khamsa* ('Quintet') in which the ruler Nushirwan is advised against war and destruction by the sage Buzurgmihr while contemplating ruins [Figure 1.6].[42] Ibn Khaldun does not suggest that rulers cannot tear down monuments because of lack of strength or because of a particular reverence for past civilizations; rather, he suggests that they are incapable because of more abstract notions of the impossibility of achieving a state of 'return to the origin' or 'non-existence'. In other words, history in its most abstract sense would be lost from both Islamic monuments and from the landscape in general if pre-Islamic ruins were destroyed completely. Al-Mansur's reuse of the bricks of al-Mada'in would lose its semiotic power if the ruins of al-Mada'in no

Figure 1.6: Nushirwan listens to the owls, folio from a manuscript of the Khamsa ('Quintet') by Nizami (c.1525), Tabriz, Iran, opaque watercolour, ink and gold on paper. Arthur M. Sackler Gallery, Purchase – Smithsonian Unrestricted Trust Funds, Smithsonian Collections Acquisition Program, and Dr Arthur M. Sackler, S1986.214.

longer existed, for they functioned to establish the connection between al-Mansur's city of Baghdad and the earlier Sassanian city.

Royal Power and the Ruin

As is evident in historical and geographic descriptions of al-Mada'in, ruins were defined in Abbasid literature by their emptiness and decay; even if they were in reality close to inhabited settlements, their portrayal as abandoned imbued them with mystery. In Abbasid literature, rulers are often recorded as having camped at ruins, because they provided physical markers of past rulers mythologized in Abbasid literature, and meditative spaces where current rulers could contemplate the fate of empires. Al-Mas'udi tells the story of caliphs leaving Kufa and going to the nearby pre-Islamic Lakhmid town of al-Hira because of its proximity to the palaces of Khavarnaq and Nadjaf.[43] The benefit associated with the caliph resting in the empty and peripheral palace may relate to the Abbasid royal architectural programme, which separated the palace from the city.[44] While no illustrations of these Abbasid stories remain, the Iranian legend of the ruler Darab sleeping under the ruined vault – recorded in the poet Firdawsi's *Shahnama* ('Book of Kings') (completed 1010) – was often illustrated [Figure 1.7]. It suggests a widespread Islamic belief in the connection between royal power and ruins and perhaps the pre-Islamic origins of this association.[45]

Whereas pre-Islamic ruins were often described as wondrous and empowering, Islamic ruins were threatening, symbolizing the possibility of the ultimate decay of Islamic civilization. Al-Muqaddasi saw the deterioration of Baghdad not as natural decay over time but as a consequence of corruption prevalent in other Islamic cities:

> It used to be the most beautiful possession of the Muslims, a most splendid city, far exceeding our description of it. However, the authority of the caliphs declined, the city deteriorated, and the population dwindled. The City of Peace is now desolate: the Mosque alone is frequented on Fridays, and otherwise the whole place is deserted [...] Day by day the town is going from bad to worse: truly, I fear it will become like Samarra, what with the corruption, the ignorance and immorality, and the outrageous oppression of the ruler.[46]

The hundreds of Islamic ruins that al-Muqaddasi described did not exist at a comfortable distance from the city and were not empty of inhabitants, but instead reflected the immorality and corruption of the Abbasids who once inhabited the structures.[47] As al-Mas'udi relates, even al-Hira, largely associated with its glorified pre-Islamic past, was in danger of falling into decaying ruin because of political and social corruption: '[T]he decadence of al-Hira increased significantly up to the reign of [Abbasid caliph] al-Mu'tadid, when it disappeared under its ruins (*kharab*).'[48]

The Book of Strangers makes clear the widespread association between physical ruin and political collapse. Al-Muqaddasi's lament at Samarra's ruin is echoed by an anonymous traveller,

Figure 1.7: Darab sleeping in the ruined vault, folio from *Shahnama* ('Book of Kings') by Firdawsi (*c.*1330–1340), Tabriz, Iran, opaque watercolour, ink and gold on paper. Freer Gallery of Art, F1930.78.

Figure 1.8: Ernst Herzfeld, *Balkuwara Palace: View of the Ruins* (1911–1913), Iraq, photographic print. Ernst Herzfeld, The Ernst Herzfeld papers. Freer Gallery of Art and Arthur M. Sackler Gallery Archives, Smithsonian Institution, Washington, DC, FSA A.6 04.PF.23.086.

whose poem – recorded in *The Book of Strangers* and written on the ruins of Samarra's Balkuwara Palace – states that the building is now emptied of 'glory, power, and rank' [Figure 1.8].[49] Another traveller, passing through the Abbasid ruins of Raqqa, records this poem on the palace ruins:

> Consider and you will see people in the
>   palace and feel how empty it is
> though it once had glory that rose sky-high.
>   It is as if government and sovereignty were never
> here only suffering.[50]

Poetry

Unlike historical and geographical texts, which tended to insist on a certain distance between the author's opinions and the information related, Abbasid poetry used pre-Islamic ruins for catharsis and to gain personal perspective on the ruins of contemporary civilization. The concept of the ruined abode was integral to the structure of the Arabic poem from the pre-Islamic period, and ruins in Arabic poetry have often been considered merely as literary tropes used to represent nostalgia, disconnected from the physical ruins themselves. However, it has less frequently been noted that some poems of the ninth and tenth centuries employ a description of the physical ruins within the poetic structure, directly connecting the ruins' phenomenology and aesthetics with the emotions of the poet.

The predominant form of Arabic poetry in this period, the *qasida*, was itself a form of ruin in early Islamic literary discourse. The *qasida* was part of a pre-Islamic Arab past and was often imitated in the early Islamic period, rather than updated.[51] The *qasida* poem was separated into three thematic sections: the *nasib*, or the sense of loss and yearning (nostalgia); the *rahil*, or the travel and setting out; and the *fakhr* or *madih*, or praise of self and others.[52] Of central importance to this chapter is the first theme of nostalgia, or the *nasib*. In pre-Islamic times, poetic ruins were impermanent traces called *atlal*, which were often toponyms with no description of a physical structure.[53] In this way, these poetic descriptions contrast with Abbasid descriptions of the more permanent brick and mudbrick constructions that characterized pre-Islamic *athar* in Iraq. The pre-Islamic poet Imru' al-Qays's (d.c.550) poem, the *Mu'allaqat*, a typical example of the *qasida*, connects the ruins of his abode (campsite) with the painful memory of the loss of his beloved:

> Halt, my two friends, and we will
> > weep For the memory of one
> > beloved
> And an abode at Siqt al-Liwa
> > between al-Dakhul, then Hawmal,
> Then Tudih, then al-Miqrat, whose
> trace
> > Was not effaced
> By the two winds weaving over it.[54]

The central ruins in al-Qays's poem are defined only by toponyms. He tells the reader that the traces (*atlal*) have not been effaced but the double negative gives no substance to the ruins.[55] His nostalgia comes from the absence rather than the presence of physical structures.

Later, as the Abbasids developed a stronger intellectual and emotional connection to cities and permanent monuments in their domain, poets dismissed the empty toponyms of the past and addressed the physicality and aesthetics of the ruins around them, in order to convey their nostalgia for a new conception of the past. Poets continued to use the pre-Islamic poetic form of the *qasida* to describe ruins, but new literary and physical ruins began to enter the poet's vocabulary. A new form of poetry, building on the traditional *qasida*, was created to accommodate new, physically more substantive city ruins. The city elegy, or *ritha' al-mudun*, developed both from the traditional *ritha'*, or elegy for a person, and the *nasib*, the nostalgia for the ruined Bedouin campsite.[56] For poets, new building material differentiated the Iraqi and Abbasid past from the past of the pre-Islamic *qasida*. In pre-Islamic poetry, stone was an enduring material:

> Then in the forenoon it was pouring
> > Its water down around Kutayfah,
> Overturning the lofty kanahbal
> > trees… In Tayma' it did not leave
> A single palm trunk
> > standing, Or a single
> > castle but
> Those built of stone.[57]

'Return to Origin Is Non-existence': Al-Mada'in and Perceptions of Ruins in Abbasid Iraq

By the ninth century, stone and brick structures had lost their indelibility. For Abbasid poets, stone was destructible and vulnerable. In Abu Ya'qub al-Khuraymi's (d.829) elegy to Baghdad, the stones are personified and bleed:

> It has become emptied of humankind.
>> Its stones have been made to
>> bleed.
> A desolate waste where dogs howl.
>> A traveller would not recognize the traces left behind.[58]

This personification of stone represents a departure from the early *qasidas* both in terms of structure and content. The nostalgia for the ruins expressed in this early *nasib* is likened to personal grief over the loss of a family member or loved one. In al-Khuraymi's poem, the loved one and the ruined structure merge so that the poet laments the ruined stones of Baghdad in the same way he would a loved one in a more traditional *qasida* structure.

Just as al-Mada'in figured prominently in the discussion of ruins in historical and geographical texts, they were also important in informing Abbasid poetic approaches to ruins. Many Abbasid poets found more in common with the awe-inspiring structure of al-Mada'in than the fleeting campsites of their Bedouin past. The poet Abu Nuwas al-Hasan ibn Hani' (c.757–814) stated: 'How far from the Bedouins is the palace of Kisra / How far from the parade grounds the livestock pens.'[59] Al-Walid ibn 'Ubayd al-Buhturi (d.897) is perhaps the most famous and most discussed early Islamic poet to write about al-Mada'in. In al-Buhturi's *Iwan Kisra*, the ruins do not just stand in as abstract symbols; rather, their physical appearance moves al-Buhturi through an emotional journey into the past.

In al-Buhturi's poem, the traditional *qasida* structure is modified so that the ruins of the Sassanian Palace are not the introductory lament (*nasib*), but are the main body or destination of the poem.[60] The opening lament for ruins is replaced with al-Buhturi's sadness at the contemporary situation in Iraq. The ruin, which usually represents the ultimate decay of civilization, becomes a sign of endurance and consolation:

> Cares attended my
>> mount; Therefore,
> I turned my strong she-camel
>> Toward the white [Palace] of al-
> Mada'in I am consoled
>> For my own bad luck
> As I grieve for the ruined
> abode
>> Of the Sassanians.[61]

Figure 1.9: Al-Hamra Temple, *c.*sixth century BCE, Tayma', Saudi Arabia. Sarah Johnson.

Al-Buhturi makes the distinction in his poem between the pre-Islamic Arabian campsite traces (*atlal*) and the enduring traces of the Sassanian palace (*mahal* or *hilal*):[62]

> But it [Taq-i Kisra]
>   shows Endurance,
> Even though the oppressive breast of
>   fate Weights down upon it.[63]

Like Khalid ibn Barmak, al-Mansur's adviser, he sees the ruin as a marker of the greatness of past civilization.

Al-Buhturi creates a calculated reconstruction of al-Mada'in within his poem in order to achieve his desired emotional and literary effect. From the empty and ruined façade of the structure, he takes the reader to a preserved painting, balancing the aesthetics of decay and preservation. Surprisingly, in the context of the traditional *qasida*, al-Buhturi describes a painting on the interior of al-Mada'in as so perfectly preserved that he believes it to be reality rather than art:

> When you see
> > The picture of Antioch
>
> You are in panic
> > Between the Byzantine and Persian [armies].
>
> The Fates
> > Are standing,
> While Anushirwan urges
> > On the ranks beneath his banner,
>
> In green robe
> > Over yellow
> Which seems dyed
> > With turmeric…
>
> The eye describes
> > them As really
> > alive,
> Signalling to one another
> > Like the dumb.
> My curiosity
> > Concerning them increases Until I
> explore
> > And touch them.[64]

While one cannot be sure of the state of the frescoes in al-Mada'in at the time al-Buhturi wrote his poem, they were certainly not perfectly preserved. Hardly any Sassanian wall paintings survive to allow for comparison, and perhaps the best illustration is the wall painting of the synagogue at Dura Europos on the border of modern Syria and Iraq, painted in the mid-third century, though it existed on the border between the Sassanian and Roman empires [Figure 1.10]. Al-Buhturi's surprise at their lifelike appearance and vivid paint did not come from a general ignorance of wall painting, which covered the walls of Abbasid palaces in Baghdad and Samarra [Figure 1.11].[65] Rather, his description is a conscious and poetic choice to move away from a state of ruin toward an imagined past through the painting. The painting's ability to elicit an emotional response from al-Buhturi in its vivid colours and illusion of reality alludes to a triumph over the depredations of time.

Al-Buhturi's treatment of al-Mada'in had a profound effect on subsequent authors' approaches to the ruins. For example, the historian al-Khatib al-Baghdadi (*d*.1071) insisted

Figure 1.10: Mordechai on horseback, mid-third century, Synagogue of Dura Europos, Syria. Art Resource, NY.

on the artistic and poetic quality of al-Mada'in, and he included almost all of al-Buhturi's poem in order to describe the ruins: 'I heard 'Abdallah ibn al-Mu'tazz said: "If al-Buhturi had no other poetry besides his *qasida* on the subject of the description of the Iwan of Chosroes, the Arabs would not have a *qasida* comparable to it."'[66]

Al-Buhturi's poem did not herald a celebration of ruins for all subsequent writers. Khaqani's (*d.*1199) poem in reaction to al-Buhturi's pessimistically eschewed aesthetic appreciation of ruins, as the decay of all things is inevitable:

Indeed, why should you marvel so? For in the world's pleasance
　The owl follows the nightingale; laments follow sweet songs
[…] You laugh at my eyes, as if to say, 'What does he weep for here?'
　　But in this place they weep at those eyes that are not moved to tears.[67]

Khaqani's pessimistic perspective was shared by many other poets, who were cautious of glorifying monuments too insistently. Abu Nuwas was perhaps the most dismissive of

'Return to Origin Is Non-existence': Al-Mada'in and Perceptions of Ruins in Abbasid Iraq

Figure 1.11: Fragment of a wall painting, ninth century, Dar al-Khilafa, Jawsaq al-Khaqani, Bayt al-Khalifah ('Harem'), Samarra, Iraq. Ernst Herzfeld, image provided by The Metropolitan Museum of Art, New York, Thomas J. Watson Library, Harris Brisbane Dick Fund, 1943, eeh1016.1-88.

the ruin elegy: 'Talk of the effete ruins is an affair for the dull / Your epithets must fit the daughter of the vine!'[68]

Indeed, later poets' dismissal of ruin elegies only confirms that the Abbasid association between poetry and the ruin was a common and widespread trope. Perhaps most tellingly, the practice of writing poems on physical ruins themselves, described in *The Book of Strangers*, underlines the pervasiveness of the connection in Abbasid society. One anonymous author notes: 'I passed through Surra Man Ra'a [Samarra] one day and went to the Friday Mosque; there I read the graffiti of people recording their presence on about a third of the minaret and marvelled at their number.'[69] The author records that people would also leave commentary on previous poems written on ruins, creating an ongoing public literary dialogue inscribed on the walls of the ruined structure itself.[70] Thus in Abbasid Iraq ruins themselves came to speak of the nostalgia, awe and admiration evoked by their ongoing physical presence.

Conclusions

A unifying feature of the Abbasid texts, from al-Muqaddasi to the anonymous scribblers in *The Book of Strangers*, is the inevitability of ruin. This, on the one hand, connects back to the shifting landscapes of Abbasid Iraq and new perspectives on physical ruins, but it also relates to the political and social instability of the period. By the time Abbasid authors were writing in the ninth and tenth centuries, the caliphate had undergone civil war, revolution and a shifting court that had moved from Baghdad to Samarra and back again, with a brief interlude in Raqqa.[71] These political realities, with their implication of the fragility of empire, must have been topical to writers such as al-Tabari as they wrote within the context of the Abbasid court, and the authors make evident the parallels they perceived between political and monumental decay. Further, attitudes toward pre-Islamic structures, such as al-Mada'in, shifted with the political climate. As Sarah Savant has noted, al-Mada'in existed in the Abbasid imagination not only as a monument to the Sassanian past but also as an 'Alid stronghold and as a competitor to Baghdad.[72] When the Buyids seized power in Baghdad in the mid-tenth century, they repeatedly tried to rebuild al-Mada'in to glorify their Iranian origins.[73] However, as Matthew Saba has shown, mutability and uncertainty – key features of ruins – were part of wonder ('*ajab*), and led to aesthetic appreciation in Abbasid culture.[74] Al-Buhturi is comforted by al-Mada'in both because of the political chaos of his own time and because of the uncertainty of the Sassanian period, which led to the creation of such wondrous ruins. The ruins, while perceived on the one hand as part of inevitable political decay, also imbued political uncertainty with aesthetic beauty, and the Abbasid writer with a means of hope and a mechanism of catharsis.

Notes

1. Claire Lyons, 'Archives in Ruins: The Collections of the Getty Research Institute', in *Irresistible Decay: Ruins Reclaimed*, ed. Lynne Kostman (Los Angeles: Getty Research Institute, 1997), 79.
2. See Georg Simmel, 'Die Ruine', in *Philosophische Kultur: Gesammelte Essays* (Leipzig: Alfred Kröner, 1919), 125–33; Alois Riegl, *Der modern Denkmalkultus: sein Wesen und seine Entstehung* (Wien: W. Braumüller, 1903); Lynne Kostman, ed., *Irresistible Decay: Ruins*

Reclaimed (Los Angeles: Getty Research Institute, 1997); and Svetlana Boym, *Architecture of the Off-Modern* (Princeton: Princeton Architectural Press, 2008).

3. See Philippe Julian, *Les Orientalistes: la vision de l'Orient par les peintres européens au 19e siècle* (Fribourg: Office du livre, 1977); and Melissa Gronlund, 'What Do We Want to Save in Palmyra?', *New Yorker*, June 12, 2015, accessed February 10, 2016, http://www.newyorker.com/news/ news-desk/what-do-we-want-to-save-in-palmyra.

4. Translated in Suzanne Stetkevych, *The Mute Immortals Speak: Pre-Islamic Poetry and the Poetics of Ritual* (London: Cornell University Press, 1993), 249–57; Patricia Crone and Shmuel Moreh, trans., *The Book of Strangers: Medieval Arabic Graffiti on the Theme of Nostalgia* (Princeton: Markus Weiner Publishers, 2000).

5. 'There is a historic distinctiveness to the "ruin gaze" that can be understood as the particular optics that frames our relationship to ruins.' Svetlana Boym, 'Ruinophilia: Appreciation of Ruins', in *Atlas of Transformation* (2011), accessed August 7, 2016, http://monumenttotransformation.org/atlas-of-transformation/html/r/ruinophilia/ruinophilia-appreciation-of-ruins-svetlana-boym.html.

6. 'Unlike Iraq, Syria-Palestine was not subjected to mass immigration by Arab tribes after the Islamic expansion […] Those who did move to Syria-Palestine during or immediately after the Islamic expansion […] found sufficient space in existing towns.' Alan Walmsley, *Early Islamic Syria: An Archaeological Assessment* (London: Duckworth, 2007), 77.

7. Rina Talgman, *The Stylistic Origins of Umayyad Sculpture and Architectural Decoration, Part I* (Wiesbaden: Harrassowitz Verlag, 2004), 76.

8. Julia Gonnella, 'Columns and Hieroglyphs: Magic "Spolia" in Medieval Islamic Architecture of Northern Syria', *Muqarnas* 27 (2010): 104.

9. Michal Gawlikowski, 'Palmyra in the Early Islamic Times', in *Transformation Processes between Late Antiquity and Early Islam in Bilad al-Sham*, ed. Karin Bartl (Rahden: Leidorf, 2009), 90–91.

10. Sarah Savant, 'Forgetting Ctesiphon: Iran's Pre-Islamic Past, *c*.800–1100', in *History and Identity in the Late Antique Near East*, ed. Philip Wood (Oxford: Oxford University Press, 2013), 169–86.

11. See Alexander E. Elinson, *Looking Back at al-Andalus* (Boston: Brill, 2009); Sarah Savant, 'Forgetting Ctesiphon', 169–86; Jaroslav Stetkevych, 'Najd and Arcadia: The Topology of Nostalgia', in *The Zephyrs of Najd* (Chicago: University of Chicago Press, 1993), 114–35; and Akiko Motoyoshi Sumi, *Description in Classical Arabic Poetry* (Boston: Brill, 2004).

12. See M. J. L. Young, J. D. Latham and R. B. Serjeant, eds, *Religion, Learning and Science in the 'Abbasid Period* (Cambridge: Cambridge University Press, 1990).

13. See Crone and Moreh, *Book of Strangers*, 170–76; and S. A. Bonebakker, 'Adab and the Concept of Belles-Lettres', in *Abbasid Belles Lettres*, eds Julia Ashtiany et al. (Cambridge: Cambridge University Press, 1990), 16–27.

14. Crone and Moreh, *Book of Strangers*, 9 and 173; Muhammad ibn Jarir al-Tabari, 'General Introduction' and 'From the Creation to the Flood', trans. Franz Rosenthal, in *The History of al-Tabari*, vol. 1, ed. Ehsan Yarshater (Albany: State University of New York, 1989), 170–71.

15. 'The Muslims found the place [al-Mada'in] too dirty and productive of pestilence.' Ahmad ibn Yahya al-Baladhuri, *Kitab futuh al-buldan*, trans. Philip Khuri Hitti (New York: Columbia University, 1916), 435–37.

16. Michael Greenhalgh has taken up this issue in relation to ruins in medieval Europe. Michael Greenhalgh, 'Spolia: A Definition in Ruins', in *Reuse Value: Spolia and Appropriation in Art and Architecture from Constantine to Sherrie Levine*, eds Dale Kinney and Richard Brilliant (Farnham: Ashgate Publishing, 2011), 75–97.
17. See Edward William Lane, 'Athar', in *An Arabic-English Lexicon* (London: Williams and Norgate, 1863), 19. Muhammad ibn Ahmad al-Biruni's (973–c.1052) treatise on past civilizations uses the word *athar* in the title to denote traces or signs of the past. Muhammad ibn Ahmad al-Biruni, *Kitab al-athar al-baqiyah 'an al-qurun al-khaliyah* (*The Remaining Signs of Past Centuries*), ed. Eduard Sachau (Leipzig: Brockhaus, 1878).
18. Abu al-Qasim ibn Hawqal, *Kitab surat al-ard* (Cairo: Sharikat Nawabigh al-Fikar, 2009), 232–33.
19. Tarif Khalidi, *Arabic Historical Thought in the Classical Period* (New York: Cambridge University Press, 1994); Fred Donner, *Narratives of Islamic Origins: The Beginnings of Islamic Historical Writing* (Princeton: Darwin Press, Inc., 1998).
20. Stefan Sperl, 'Crossing Enemy Boundaries: Al-Buhturi's Ode on the Ruins of Ctesiphon Re-read in the Light of Virgil and Wilfred Owen', *Bulletin of the School of Oriental and African Studies* 69.3 (2006): 369.
21. Al-Tabari's description has led later writers and scholars to imagine the Taq-i Kisra and the White Palace within the same complex, when in fact they were located in different parts of the city. E. J. Keall, 'Ayvan-e Kesra', *Encyclopaedia Iranica*, last modified August 18, 2011, http://www.irani-caonline.org/articles/ayvan-e-kesra-palace-of-kosrow-at-ctesiphon.
22. Al-Tabari, 'The Conquest of Iraq, Southwestern Persia, and Egypt', trans. Gautier H. A. Juynboll, in *The History of al-Tabari*, vol. 13, ed. Ehsan Yarshater (Albany: State University of New York, 1989), 12.
23. Finbarr B. Flood, 'Between Cult and Culture: Bamiyan, Islamic Iconoclasm and the Museum', *Art Bulletin* 84.4 (2002): 641–59. The Qur'an encourages viewing ruins as a lesson for non-believers and sinners, complicating the relationship between destruction and preservation. For example, see Qur'an, 29: 34–35.
24. Al-Tabari, 'Conquest of Iraq', 30–32.
25. Ibid., 30.
26. Ibid., 12.
27. Qur'an, 44:25–27.
28. Jacob Lassner, *The Topography of Baghdad in the Early Middle Ages* (Detroit: Wayne State University Press, 1970), 131.
29. Barbara Finster and Jürgen Schmidt, 'Sasanidische und Frühislamische Ruinen im Iraq', *Baghdader Mitteilungen* 8 (1976): 152.
30. Andre Miquel, 'Geography', in *Encyclopaedia of the History of Arabic Science*, ed. Roshdi Rashed (London: Routledge, 1996), 797.
31. Ibn Hawqal, *Configuration de la Terre*, trans. J. H. Kramers and G. Wiet (Paris: Editions G.-P. Maisonneuve et Larose, 1964), 226.
32. Ahmad ibn 'Umar b. Rusta, *Kitab al-a'laq al-nafisa*, quoted in Caroline Janssen, *Babil, the City of Witchcraft and Wine* (Ghent: University of Ghent, 1995), 41.
33. Ibn Hawqal, *Configuration de la Terre*, 237.

34. Ali ibn al-Husayn al-Mas'udi, *Les Prairies d'Or*, vol. 2, trans. and eds C. Barbier de Meynard and Pavet de Courteille (Paris: L'Imprimerie Impériale, 1864), 116.
35. Muhammad ibn Ahmad Shams al-Din al-Muqaddasi, *The Best Divisions for Knowledge of the Regions*, trans. Basil Collins (London: Garnet Publishing Limited, 2001), 97.
36. Janssen, *Babil, the City of Witchcraft and Wine*, 195–97.
37. Crone and Moreh, *Book of Strangers*, 63. On the topic of snakes and talismans, see Finbarr B. Flood, 'Image against Nature: Spolia as Apotropaia in Byzantium and the Dar al-Islam', *The Medieval History Journal* 9.1 (2006): 143–66.
38. Jas Elsner, 'Iconoclasm and the Preservation of Memory', in *Monuments and Memory, Made and Unmade*, eds Robert S. Nelson and Margaret Olin (Chicago: University of Chicago Press, 2003), 210.
39. Al-Tabari, 'Al-Mansur and al-Mahdi', trans. Hugh Kennedy, in *The History of al-Tabari*, vol. 29, ed. Ehsan Yarshater (Albany, State University of New York, 1989), 4.
40. Ibid., 4.
41. Ibn Khaldun, *The Muqaddimah*, trans. Franz Rosenthal (London: Routledge and Kegan Paul, 1958), 266–67.
42. Nizami Ganjavi, *The Treasury of Mysteries*, trans. Gholam Khan (London: Arthur Probsthain, 1945).
43. 'Several Caliphs from the house of Abbas […] enjoyed stopping and resting there [al-Hira], because of its climate, its beautiful sky, the healthy condition of its territory, and its proximity to Khavarnaq and Nadjaf.' Al-Mas'udi, *Les Prairies d'Or*, vol. 3, 213–14.
44. Gülru Necipoglu, 'Shifting Paradigms in the Palatial Architecture of the Pre-Modern Islamic World', *Ars Orientalis* 23 (1993): 5–6.
45. Abolqasem Firdawsi, 'The Story of Darab and the Fuller', in *Shahnameh: The Persian Book of Kings*, trans. Dick Davis (New York: Penguin, 2006), Google Play edition.
46. Al-Muqaddasi, *Best Divisions for Knowledge of the Regions*, 102. 47. Ibid., 97–102.
47. Al-Mas'udi, *Les Prairies d'Or*, 213.
48. Crone and Moreh, *Book of Strangers*, 25.
49. Ibid., 51.
50. Rina Drory, 'The Abbasid Construction of the Jahiliyya: Cultural Authority in the Making', *Studia Islamica* 83 (1996): 33–34.
51. Jaroslav Stetkevych, *The Zephyrs of Najd* (Chicago: University of Chicago Press, 1993), 2.
52. Ibid., 107.
53. Imru' al-Qays, *Mu'allaqat*, stanzas 1 and 2, translated in Stetkevych, *Mute Immortals Speak*, 249.
54. Stetkevych, *Zephyrs of Najd*, 107.
55. The *ritha' al-mudun* was originally created to mourn the destruction of Baghdad during the civil war between the sons of Harun al-Rashid. Alexander E. Elinson, *Looking Back at al-Andalus* (Boston: Brill, 2009), 19–20.
56. Imru' al-Qays, *Mu'allaqat*, stanzas 75 and 77, translated in Stetkevych, *Mute Immortals Speak*, 256–57.
57. Abu Ya'qub al-Khuraymi, *Diwan*, eds 'A. J. al-Tahir and M. J. al-Mu'aybid (Beirut: Dar al-Kitab al-Jadid, 1971); partially translated in Elinson, *Looking Back at al-Andalus*, 21–22.

58. Quoted in Richard Serrano, 'Al-Buhturi's Poetics of Persian Abodes', in *Neither a Borrower: Forging Traditions in French, Chinese and Arabic Poetry* (Oxford: Legenda, 2002), 76.
59. Serrano, 'Al-Buhturi's Poetics of Persian Abodes', 69–70.
60. Al-Buhturi, line 12, translated in Sumi, *Description in Classical Arabic Poetry*, 101–08 and 214–18.
61. Serrano, 'Al-Buhturi's Poetics of Persian Abodes', 81.
62. Al-Buhturi, line 39, translated in Sumi, *Description in Classical Arabic Poetry*, 106.
63. Ibid., lines 22–28, 104.
64. Crone and Moreh, *Book of Strangers*, 24.
65. Al-Khatib al-Baghdadi, *L'Introduction Topographique à l'Histoire de Bagdadh*, trans. Georges Salmon (Paris: É. Bouillon, 1904), 179–80.
66. Khaqani, 'Elegy on Mada'in', translated in Julie Scott Meisami, 'The Persian Qasida to the End of the 12th Century', in *Qasida Poetry in Islamic Asia and Africa*, vol. 1, eds Stefan Sperl and Christopher Shackle (Leiden: E. J. Brill, 1996), 173–81.
67. Abu Nuwas al-Hasan ibn Hani', *Diwan*, ed. Ahmad 'Abd al-Majid al-Ghazali (Cairo: Matba'at Misr, 1953), quoted in Stetkevych, *Zephyrs of Najd*, 57.
68. Crone and Moreh, *Book of Strangers*, 65–66.
69. Ibid., 87.
70. Hugh Kennedy, *The Early Abbasid Caliphate: A Political History* (London: Routledge, 2016).
71. Savant, 'Forgetting Ctesiphon', 179.
72. Lionel Bier, 'The Sasanian Palaces and Their Influence in Early Islam', *Ars Orientalis* 23 (1993): 61.
73. Matthew Saba, 'Abbasid Lusterware and the Aesthetics of 'Ajab', *Muqarnas*
74. (2012): 202–03.

2

Medieval Reports of the Preservation and Looting of Pre-Islamic Burials in South Arabia

Daniel Mahoney

In the first half of the tenth century, Abu Muhammad al-Hasan b. Ahmad b. Yaʿqub al-Hamdani compiled a ten-volume historical compendium, entitled *al-Iklīl* (The Crown), whose reports extolled the achievements and virtues of South Arabia. These books contain a rich variety of texts that provide different perspectives on the pre-Islamic history of the region, for example, ranging from straight historical narratives until the advent of Islam, to criticism of false traditions about South Arabia. Overall, *al-Iklīl* may be seen as an extended manifestation of the so-called 'Qahtan Saga', which previous Yemeni authors, such as ʿAbid b. Sharya al-Jurhumi of the seventh century and Wahb b. Munabbih of the eighth century, had already begun to develop in their own works.[1] Both authors are referenced by al-Hamdani in his work, in addition to Yemeni tribal scholars such as Abu Nasr Muhammad b. ʿAbd Allah b. Saʿid al-Yahari, Muhammad b. ʿAbd Allah al-Awsani, and Muhammad b. Yunis al-Abrahi.

Unfortunately, several of the volumes of *al-Iklīl* seem to have been destroyed during the medieval period, as attested by al-Qifti in his biographical entry for al-Hamdani.[2] Only four volumes are known to have been preserved. Three of them (volumes 1, 2, and 10) contain different parts of the genealogies of the South Arabian population, including one that goes back into the patriarchal period to Adam and his sons, and other sections that describe the tribes of the confederations of Hamdan, Qudaʿa, and Himyar. The other surviving book (volume 8) consists of three parts that respectively comprise: (1) reports about the ancient monuments of South Arabia, (2) the uncovering of pre-Islamic burials and the inscriptions found in them, and (3) elegiac poems of Himyar.[3] It is in this volume that al-Hamdani uses innovative narrative strategies to depict these ancient localities and the stories of the people connected to them.

Al-Hamdani put together *al-Iklīl* during a transitional period in South Arabia when new groups from the north were attempting to establish their dominance in the region as others withdrew. Since the beginning of the Islamic period, the Prophet Muhammad and his successors had attempted to develop their authority in South Arabia through various types of missionary and military expeditions. But already in March 632, just before the death of Muhammad, ʿAbhala b. Kaʿb al-ʿAnsi claimed his own prophethood in the region of al-Jawf and led an uprising that expanded across much of Yemen.[4] Rebellions continued throughout the caliphate's troubled occupation of South Arabia until the beginning of the tenth century, when the death of the final Abbasid governor of Sanaa led to the complete withdrawal of caliphal power. Even the local Ziyadid dynasty, which initially had been set up by the 'Abbasid caliph al-Ma'mun in 817 to settle local tribal revolts and prevent an anti-caliphal state from developing in the Tihama region along the Red Sea, stopped striking coins in the name of the caliph in the second half of the ninth century. Around the same time, new religious groups from the north associated with Zaydis and Isma'ilis arrived to South Arabia with the aim of establishing new sites from which to spread both their political influence and religious beliefs.

Biographical elements of al-Hamdani's conflicts with the Zaydi population in the northern city of Sa'da and his resulting imprisonment in Sanaa are found in scattered reports throughout *al-Iklīl*. It is in the eighth volume, however, that al-Hamdani illustrates his antipathy for the presence of the Zaydis, the Isma'ilis, and caliphate in South Arabia in a deeper historical perspective through his descriptions of forts, religious buildings, and dams. Through these sites, he anchors collective memory in a type of historical geography by using events of the deep and recent past to promote a South Arabian regional identity in the face of northern invaders.[5] For example, in his entry on the famed Ghumdan Palace, al-Hamdani combines layers of the history of its ancient construction and eventual demise at the beginning of the Islamic period with the contemporary invasions of Sanaa by the Zaydis and Isma'ilis.[6] He begins with the story of Sam b. Nuh's discovery of the site on which to build the fortress through divine intervention, and then continues by noting that the structure remained erect for over four thousand lunar years during the span of many kings' reigns until it eventually became the ruins opposite the Great Mosque of Sanaa. Al-Hamdani then almost seamlessly transitions into a discussion of the destruction of Sanaa during the years of conflict, which includes the sequential takeovers of the city by the Zaydi imam al-Hadi and the Isma'ili missionary Ibn al-Fadl at the beginning of the tenth century, but optimistically notes that scholars believe Sanaa will return to its previous size and continue to grow. Throughout the rest of this entry, al-Hamdani continues to make parallels between Ghumdan and Sana'a, for example, by speaking repeatedly about their spatial proximity and the stones of the former being used to construct houses of the latter.

At the end of the entry al-Hamdani discusses how early Muslims from outside South Arabia reacted to the Ghumdan Palace. Citing a Qur'anic verse referring to the problem of structures built by wrongdoers, he states that the Prophet Muhammad sent Farwa b. Musayk to destroy the site.[7] Thus, al-Hamdani argues that Muhammad himself, and not just the Muslims in general, considered what was perhaps the most highly symbolic monument of South Arabia's pre-Islamic past as a threat that needed to be demolished. This ideological statement becomes more remarkable in light of a tradition from Ibn Hisham in the ninth century that attributes the destruction of the Ghumdan Palace to the Ethiopian intruder Aryat in the pre-Islamic period.[8] Hence, al-Hamdani appears to have made a conscious choice to ascribe this destruction to the early Islamic period without indicating the earlier tradition. Nonetheless, the idea of Muslims in the early Islamic period condemning pre-Islamic monuments does not persist in this volume.[9] In its next section, a varied and nuanced set of reactions to pre-Islamic burials can be found.

The second section of the eighth volume of *al-Iklīl* consists of a group of about forty reports describing the uncovering and exploration of pre-Islamic tombs, usually accompanied by grave inscriptions that briefly provide details of the identities and lives of those interred. Most of these burials, often containing luxurious treasures in extravagant vaults, were located in South Arabia. But some stories also take place in other parts of the Near East, such as Iran, Syria, and Egypt. The chains of transmission of many of these reports begin with the Iraqi scholar Hisham b. Muhammad al-Kalbi, but the subsequent lists of transmitters often end with informants of South Arabian origin. Other reports start with specific Yemeni scholars, such as al-Sanʿani and Abu Nasr (indicating Abu Nasr Muhammad al-Yahari, who is referenced in other parts of *al-Iklīl*). Despite this source documentation, the veracity of various aspects of these reports may be put into question due to fantastical and improbable elements found within them, such as reanimated corpses and extensive tomb vaults, as well as the explicitly confessional style and content of many of the associated inscriptions.[10] Even al-Hamdani himself openly expresses scepticism in one of the reports, speculating that in an especially deep necropolis there would not be enough air supply for breathing or keeping a flame lit.[11] At the same time, the types of burials described in these reports generally reflect what is known from the archaeological record associated with funerary remains in pre-Islamic South Arabia, such as extensive necropolises and mausolea (e.g., the Hayd ibn ʿAqil cemetery outside of the town of Timnaʿ and the necropolis of the Temple of Awam in Marib), rock and cave tombs (largely in the northern and central highland regions), and subterranean pit burials covered with stones or mudbricks (e.g., Raybun Cemetery).[12]

On one level, these reports may be seen as a type of historical fiction containing various storytelling elements, with the excavation serving as a metaphor for an exploration of the region's pre-Islamic past.[13] That is, the tombs and their inscriptions reveal the Muslim imagination of certain features of the *Jahiliyya* (the period of supposed ignorance before Islam) in South Arabia and how this region fits into the wider narrative of Islamic history.[14] In particular, many of these reports focus on individuals involved in various sides of Yemen's early conversion to monotheism. At the same time, some of these pre-Islamic stories are also framed within a later historical context through references to early Islamic figures, including caliphs and governors of Yemen, who often serve as arbiters for what to do with the burials. Consequently, although these reports may not be taken entirely at face value, as they present colourful ideas about the tombs and those buried within them, the varied ways that individuals in the early Islamic period react to the tombs indicate the dynamic contradictions in their views of the pre-Islamic past. On the one hand, some of the interred, such as prophets or other significant religious figures, were revered and their graves were left alone and covered back up for their preservation.[15] This simple resealing of the burials does not seem to indicate an intention to forget, but rather suggests that the sites should not be transgressed out of respect for their sanctity. Only in a report about the tomb of Hud is there indication that at that point in time a site had become part of a sacred landscape connected to active pilgrimage.[16] On the other hand, other tombs, sometimes but not always containing polytheists, did not possess this sacred nature and instead became the object of intentional looting.[17] Notably, however, the destruction of funerary remains based on legal or moral grounds seems to be less of a motivation or justification in these reports.[18] Several examples of these different reactions to pre-Islamic burials will be examined below. Overall, the reports found in *al-Iklīl* may be read both as stories of embodied engagement with the pre-Islamic past and as strategic endeavours to link and situate South Arabia within broader narratives of Islamic history through themes of religious persecution and conversion. In this way, al-Hamdani moulds and bolsters the religious identity of South Arabia through narratives associated with these pre-Islamic burials, whether real or imagined.

Reports of Preservation

Some reports from *al-Iklīl* describe a pattern in which individuals from the early Islamic period encounter the tomb of a revered pre-Islamic figure. After inspecting the tomb and reading the inscription identifying the body, these individuals restore the covering of the burial in order to preserve it. One of these reports begins with the Prophet Muhammad discussing ancient tombs with a group of people when a man from Juhayna approaches with the intention of converting to Islam.[19] Adding to the conversation, the man speaks of a tomb that others had described to him: during a famine, a group of tribesmen had inadvertently stumbled upon a tomb while searching for animals in a cave. Within the cave there was a depression, where beneath a stone was a man wearing a woollen garment and a ring inscribed with the phrase 'I am Hanzala b. Safwan, a messenger of God'. Another inscription beside his head stated: 'God sent me to Himyar and to the Arabs of the people of Yemen, but they denied me and killed me.' After this discovery, the men placed the stone back in its place. Al-Hamdani concludes the report by stating that Hanzala b. Safwan was the *sahib* (companion) of al-Rass. This report clearly refers to the Qur'anic narrative of pre-Islamic messengers who are sent to spread the message of God to different groups, such as Thamud or 'Ad, but are refused by them. In this case, although the Qur'an explicitly mentions the people of the pre-Islamic Yemeni rulers, known as *tubba'*, alongside these other pre-Islamic groups,[20] the prophet Hanzala b. Safwan himself is not named. Rather, it was later on in the Islamic tradition that he became associated with the people of al-Rass.[21] Hence, with this report, al-Hamdani directly connects this prophet to an important Islamic narrative that shaped how the Muslim community viewed the ultimate emergence of their identity. Moreover, the report's frame, around which the prophet's story is told, further points to this religious process of conversion for Yemenis as specifically inspired by these pre-Islamic prophets. Not only did the visitors reseal the cave tomb, demonstrating the sanctity that was interpreted by and impressed upon them, but their story motivated another man to seek out Muhammad specifically for conversion.[22]

A similar report describes an encounter with the tomb of the pre-Islamic prophet Hud.[23] It begins with a man from the Yemeni region of Hadramawt approaching 'Ali b. Abi Talib during the caliphate of either Abu Bakr or 'Umar in order to convert to Islam. After his conversion, 'Ali asks the man about the Hadramawt, and he in turn describes his quest to visit the tomb of Hud, whom he and his companions held in high esteem. After a guide leads him to the cave containing the burial, he finds his corpse between two stones on a bier, next to an inscription in Arabic that reads: 'I am Hud who believed in God. I had compassion for 'Ad for their unbelief. But the command of God was not averted'.[24] Unlike the previous report, there is extensive discussion of Hud and his attempt to bring the message of God to the people of 'Ad the Qur'an,[25] which may explain the reason for the brevity of the inscription, and hence this report directly connects Yemen to the wider narrative of the denial of pre-Islamic prophets by communities across Arabia. Furthermore, the report indicates that the tomb was not only preserved, but had already become an important pilgrimage site within the South Arabian sacred landscape by the time of the early caliphate.[26]

Another report, which comes from Hisham b. Muhammad al-Kalbi, takes place during the period of 'Umar ibn al-Khattab.[27] In Sanaa, a pit was being dug for an unstated reason when the excavators came upon a clothed corpse of a man who had not decayed and whose hand was held to his head as if he were still alive. When the excavators removed the hand, blood spewed forth from an open wound. And when they put it back, the blood flow stopped. On the hand was a ring with the inscription 'I am 'Abd Allah b. Thamir'. 'Umar ibn al-Khattab inquired about this individual and was told that he was from the people who believed in the religion of Jesus. His friends were burnt by the king of Yemen in a trench of fire, as narrated in the Qur'an.[28] 'Abd Allah b. Thamir was then killed himself and buried the way he appears. In response to this information, 'Umar ordered that the man be returned exactly as he had been found and that his burial place be hidden so that enemies would not exhume him.

This report refers to a prominent member of the Christian community in Najran and their massacre in 523 at the hands of the last Himyarite king, Yusuf As'ar Ya'thar, also known in Islamic historiography as Dhu Nuwas. As in the previous report, a monotheist – in this case even a Christian – is treated with respect and reburied. This narrative, however, becomes more intriguing when compared to a very similar but more extensive report about 'Abd Allah b. Thamir in Ibn Hisham's recension of *Sirat al-nabi*.[29] In this text, it is said that 'Abd Allah, through his knowledge of God, developed the power to cure the infirm if they accepted monotheism or professed belief in the 'unity of God' (*tawhid Allah*). As a result, the king of Najran came to feel threatened, but was only able to kill 'Abd Allah b. Thamir if he himself converted. Consequently, as soon as the king did this, he struck a fatal blow to the head of 'Abd Allah b. Thamir with a staff. This event incited a mass conversion within the city of Najran. At this point in the narrative, the text of *Sirat al-nabi* continues with an account very similar to the one found in *al-Iklil*, except that the uncovering of the burial took place in Najran and the inscription of the ring stated: 'God is my lord'.[30] This discrepancy raises the question of why al-Hamdani relocates the burial to Sanaa. One interpretation may be that this relocation is a way to place a prominent narrative of pre-Islamic history into the centre of South Arabia rather than on its northern periphery. This decision would bolster the core region's importance in the sequence of events leading to the advent of Islam, as well as perhaps draw attention to its Christian population. Furthermore, the fantastical element of the blood flowing from the head may be an indication of still unsettled sentiments about the historical events surrounding these burials,[31] as supported by ʿUmar's order to restore the tomb so that enemies may not find and transgress against it.

Reports of Looting

Unlike the reports describing reverence for the buried, other accounts describe ambivalence toward pre-Islamic tombs, even if, at times, the burial inscriptions indicate that the interred had adhered to monotheistic beliefs. Accordingly, these reports often begin with a group of people setting out to loot the contents of the tombs for financial gain, although this occasionally occurs after the graves and their contents are uncovered due to natural causes. The perpetrators of this grave-robbing range from bands of local inhabitants to the members of expeditions ordered by the governors of South Arabia, such as the oft-mentioned Muhammad b. Yusuf al-Thaqafi, who was in power at the turn of the eighth century.

One example of looting by locals comes from a report by Muhammad b. Ibrahim b. Muhammad b. ʿAbd al-Rahman al-Sanʿani, an owner of the mint in Sanaa and Saʿda.[32] He states that in Wadi Dahr there is a vineyard called 'the woman's plot of land' (*qitʿat al-marʾa*). When he inquired about this name to the local inhabitants of the region, they told him about a cultural tradition of the Abara people.[33] When a daughter is born to a man, they blacken her face and hang a death shroud upon the door of her father's house. One time, however, the young men were told that a daughter had been born to one of them, but that the father was hiding the matter. In response, they first told the locals about the daughter and then later that night went to some of the sarcophagi of Dahr. Here they removed a corpse of a woman wrapped in a burial shroud and carried her to the house of the man, where they set her upright at its door. The next morning, when the man opened his door and found the corpse of the woman, he also spotted her wearing anklets of red gold, which he removed. After reburying the corpse, he weighed the anklets and discovered their value amounted to enough to purchase the plot of land on the vineyard. Beforehand, the man had been poor, but after this incident he became wealthy and lived well.

This rich report of apparent historical ethnography reveals various attitudes about gender, reproduction, death, and inheritance that may be interpreted in a multitude of ways. But as an example of looting pre-Islamic tombs, what is initially striking is that the report focuses on the activity itself more than the identity of the person buried, who remains unidentified other than limited information about her proximate place of burial and valuable jewellery. The ambivalence toward the ancient dead, expressed in this grave report perhaps more bluntly than in any other, seems to communicate a distinct disjuncture between the current living local community and the presumably ancient individuals buried in nearby graves.[34] At the same time, however, in this particular report, there does not seem to be any ill-will directed toward the corpse of the woman itself, despite its removal and placement at the door of the new father; she is reburied after her jewellery is stripped. Hence, the clearest and most enduring relationship between the living and the dead appears to be that of an economic transaction.[35] This transference of wealth resulting in a thriving vineyard leads, in the end, to the main purpose of the story: to explain the origin of the vineyard's name. Thus, this report of looting, or at least its effects, is presented as a local success story in which wealth generated by looting is a justified, if not celebrated, activity, thereby inscribing this specific instance into the landscape as a collective memory for the local community. It remains to be noted, however, that the original motivation for the extraction and delivery of the corpse by the young men remains ambiguous and not necessarily based on economic interests.

Other reports of local looting contain narratives that mirror those of the stories of reverence and preservation discussed above. These accounts, however, do not concern the burial sites of the prophets who came to South Arabia, but the graves of those who denied them. One example describes a Himyar expedition aimed at the excavation of the marble-cut necropolis of the kings of the Hadramawt.[36] Initially in their digging, the looters came down onto a stepped sequence of ledges covered with dirt and large boulders. After removing this debris, they arrived at trenches from which they were able to enter caverns that led to a group of vaults in which a king was buried with his treasures. The first vault contained a bald man lying on a bier with an inscription next to his head stating:

> I am Abu Malik 'Ammikarib b. Malkikarib. I lived for 800 years. I took power and was the dominant claimant. Shu'ayb al-Haduri called on us to believe, but we denied him. He undertook prayer with us, but we resisted him. So he called his lord upon us. And a harmful wind came, enflaming our nostrils and branding us. Each of us believed that death was coming. And in an hour, we became mortal remains and scraps.

The second vault contained weaponry and other implements of war, while the third was filled with jewels, gold, and silver. The looters then took what they could and restored the vaults to their previous state. They attempted to return to the tomb again but were not able to find its location.

This report continues to play upon the Qur'anic trope in which a pre-Islamic prophet is denied by the community to which he was sent. In this case, as further elaborated by al-Tabari and al-Hamdani in his *Sifat jazirat al-'Arab*, Shu'ayb was sent to preach in the mountainous region of Hadur, north of Sanaa, but was instead rejected by its inhabitants who were in turn exterminated.[37] Consequently, unlike the previous reports of preservation, here looting of the tomb of an unbeliever appears as an acceptable activity. A notable distinction remains, however, between this plundering for financial gain and the total destruction of funerary remains as a condemnation of the grave and its interred king by looters in the early Islamic period. In any case, the narrative of this tomb further situates South Arabia within the wider theme of unsuccessful missions by pre-Islamic prophets and their aftermath.

A second example of this type of narrative, however, begins to indicate a more complex process of conversion to monotheism as a result of the arrival of pre-Islamic prophets to South Arabia. Another report originating from a man from the Hadramawt region describes at length a man from al-Maʿafir who, along with the narrator, wanted to visit a cave that local people were afraid to enter.[38] Approaching the cave they repeated charms and verses from the Qurʾan, and upon entering it, they called upon the name of God. Therein they found numerous chambers. In one lay three men on golden biers. The inscription in Himyarite next to the first stated: 'I am ʿAd b. Iram. I conquered the lands, ruled over humanity, anchored my (tent-)poles, and fathered many children. A messenger came to us, but we denied him. He forbade, but we didn't believe him. So a wind, stripping of scalps, came to us, and left us extinct.' The inscription of the second stated: 'I am Murthad b. Qaf of the winding sand-hills (al-ahqaf).[39] Hud called on me to contradict my people, but I denied him and did not believe his message. What struck my people from the punishment of God, struck me.' The inscription next to the third stated: 'I am Mansak b. Luqaym, treasurer of ʿAd.' Afterward, the intruders located a room full of treasure and took as much as they could. This report clearly serves as a mirror to that describing the burial of Hud, except now the narrative of the pre-Islamic prophet is told through the perspective of a community that was punished because it rejected his message. In the context of the early Islamic period, both of the necropolises are in the Hadramawt, yet al-Hamdani describes Hud's burial as a place of visitation, while the tombs under consideration here were avoided by locals.

Another notable aspect of this report emerges from a section in which the looters first find the tomb of a woman before proceeding on to the other graves.[40] They came upon a marble sarcophagus containing the corpse of a woman adorned with many jewels. A marble slab beside her head inscribed in the Himyarite language stated:

> I am Rawʿa, Bint ʿAd b. Iram. My father was haughty, proud, and evil. So God killed him with a barren wind. But I believe in God and what descended from Him. Whoever sees me: pay no mind to what is upon me, continue to that which is more wondrous than me, and beware that if he takes what is not his, then he will be killed.

Frightened, the looters closed the lid of the sarcophagus and continued to other chambers. Taken within the larger context of the report, this section highlights the grave of a convert in contrast to those that rejected the calls to monotheism. Hence, in this sense, the looting of the latter and not the former may be interpreted as a symbolic act of judgement over the religious beliefs of the interred.

The grave inscription of Rawʿa, however, also contains a line cursing those who take from her, to which the looters themselves seem to have directly responded. In *al-Iklīl*, there is only one other example of such an admonitory curse in a grave in Yemen,[41] but there is no indication of a specific reaction to the malediction itself. Al-Hamdani also provides another report from Syria that contains a curse. It describes the looting of Tadmur (Palmyra) by the Umayyad caliph Marwan b. Muhammad, during which he encounters the sarcophagus of a woman whose inscription warned him: 'I am Tadmur, the daughter of Hissan b. Udhayna, the king. May God destroy the house of whoever destroys my house'.[42] Shortly thereafter, Marwan b. Muhammad was killed.[43] Along with the report featuring Raw'a, these curses do not appear as something to be taken lightly by those that encounter them. As a result, the uncertainty of whether the grave of Raw'a was not looted due to her curse or because of her monotheism perpetuates ambiguity about the perspectives of early Muslims regarding the looting of graves of those that profess their belief in one god. Overall, this report not only further connects South Arabia to wider Islamic narratives about pre-Islamic prophets, but also reveals the gradual process of conversion to monotheism over generations.

The looting of graves is also described in *al-Iklīl* as an activity of the governors of Yemen who treated its antiquities as goods to be plundered for financial gain. One report from a man from Hamdan recounts the tale of Majalid b. Sa'id, who during his time in Mecca notices a sword decorated with gold and asks the owner about its origins.[44] The man replies that he acquired the sword when he served in the retinue of the governor of Yemen. At this time, a man came and asked the governor if he would like to be guided to treasure. The governor accepted and then sent a group that included his companion. The group dug in a location until they reached the door of a cave in which they found a coffin filled with gold. An inscribed tablet on the coffin stated: 'This is a grave of a *tubba'* who died as a believer in the true religion (*'ala al-hanifiyya*) testifying that there is no god but God.' They stripped the gold and brought it to the governor, who in turn granted his companion 100 dinars that he used to decorate the sword that would later catch the attention of Majalid b. Sa'id. Consequently, this report provides a clear example of robbing a burial site in which the interred explicitly states that he possessed monotheistic beliefs, despite being a pre-Islamic Yemeni king. In this case, neither the identity nor time period of the governor is revealed, but another group of four reports about the exposure of ancient burials of monotheist sisters during the Umayyad period explores these issues in a more precise and nuanced manner.

When the caliph 'Abd al-Malik b. Marwan came to power, he appointed al-Hajjaj b. Yusuf al-Thaqafi as governor over the regions of the Hijaz, al-Yamama, and Yemen. In turn, al-Hajjaj assigned his relatives from the family of Abu 'Aqil al-Thaqafi to represent him in South Arabia. The first was his brother, Muhammad b. Yusuf al-Thaqafi, who served in the position during the years 692–710. Although this family was known for its harsh treatment toward its subjects,[45] the only evidence of his exploitation of the region from *al-Iklīl* is his association with the purposeful looting of its tombs. Four reports appear to recount the same looting event, despite some name changes, via different transmissions that provide varying details. The first, from a man from Himyar, states that Muhammad b. Yusuf specifically dispatched groups to graves and demanded the burial goods from them.[46] One of these groups forced themselves into something like a cave, where they found two women lying on a bier with an inscribed cane between them, stating: 'I am May, daughter of a *tubba'* and this is my sister Radwa. We died not associating anything with God and testify that there is no god but God and Muhammad is the messenger of

God.'[47] In a second report, Yahya b. Sinan states that when his grandfather was ruling over Yemen he would dig up tombs of the pre-Islamic period (*qubur al-jahiliyya*) and remove their grave goods.[48] While looting one those graves, he found two girls with a pillar at their heads inscribed: 'I am Radwa and this is my sister. We are daughters of a *tubbaʿ*. We believe in God and do not associate anything with him.' A third report, from Tawuf, states that he found a grave during the governorship of Muhammad b. Yusuf at a location in Yemen that had sunken in and exposed a door.[49] When he opened the door, he found a bier covered with clothing lined with silk brocades, two skulls of women, and a silver palm branch inscribed in gold, stating: 'I am Hayy, daughter of a *tubbaʿ* and this is my sister. We died not associating anything with God.' Taken altogether, to varying degrees, these first three reports set up stories of looting, but do not tell us what the looters actually did with the burial.

A fourth report, however, offers the most developed narrative of the fate of the tomb of the monotheist sisters, disclosing not only what actions were taken, but also precise opinions on the practice of looting the graves of monotheists in general. Originating from the Yemeni Abu Nasr, this final report states that during the governorship of Muhammad b. Yusuf some pre-Islamic graves (*qubur al-jahiliyya*) were found in Yemen with an inscription.[50] A gold coffin, in which there was a gold basket filled with a gold tablet and human bones, was taken from the site. The inscription in the Himyarite language stated: 'This is Shamsa and Lamis. We are daughters of a *tubbaʿ*. We died testifying that there is no god but God.' This discovery was brought to the attention of Caliph ʿAbd al-Malik through al-Hajjaj, and he responded with a letter containing explicit instructions: Wash the bones, pray over them, and rebury them; give the treasure to the treasury and do not return to what you did; the Commander of the Believers testifies that there is not god but God. In this report, ʿAbd al-Malik, although he accepts the graves goods into the treasury, is quite clear that he does not support the looting of the graves of those who at least profess monotheism, much like ʿUmar in the report about ʿAbd Allah b. Thamir. The caliph also advises a type of re-sacralization of the interred through the washing and praying over their bones. While the funerary ablution of corpses was performed on both Muslim and non-Muslims during the early Islamic period, the additional prayer over them suggests a ritual process of Islamization.[51] Thus, from this perspective, the order for ablution and prayer over the corpses of the monotheist sisters may be interpreted as an overt act of accepting and bringing them into (or confirming them within) the Islamic community. At the same time, however, this treatment of the monotheist sisters is far from venerating their remains as relics, as was the case for more prominent religious figures of the pre-Islamic period.[52]

Conclusion

Al-Hamdani's collection and retelling of these reports seem to serve multiple aims based on the varied attitudes of individuals in early Islamic South Arabia toward the pre-Islamic past. Through many of these reports it becomes clear that al-Hamdani wants to connect South Arabia to the wider Islamic narrative of conversion from polytheism, including the perspectives of the prophets, those who rejected them, and those who accepted monotheism. Al-Hamdani's focus on this narrative is striking because in the surviving volumes of *al-Iklīl* overall he only minimally elaborates on places associated with the arrival and existence of Islam in the region: mainly a brief list of ten mosques constructed in Yemen in the earlier 'monuments' section of the eighth volume, in contrast to the long entries on fortresses.[53] This reticence is also reflected in the ways al-Hamdani concentrates on the newly arrived groups of Zaydis and Isma'ilis more as destructive invaders who threaten the political dynamic of South Arabia rather than as carriers of new perspectives on Islam. Consequently, his focus on Islam in these burial texts is primarily expressed in terms of the arrival and eventual acceptance of its basic message in the region, rather than as a more strategic project emerging from a specific group within its community.[54]

Building on these core stories about the internment of pre-Islamic figures, al-Hamdani also aims to show how individuals were affected by these burial encounters. In some of the reports in which the tombs were restored to their previous states, the effect of exposure to the sacred burials of rejected pre-Islamic prophets continued this historiographic theme of conversion by inspiring people to personally seek out Muhammad and 'Ali for their own conversions to Islam. Moreover, the report on the tomb of Hud, in which the visitors were led to the location by a local guide, demonstrates that there was already a practice of pilgrimage to the site, which had only increased over the centuries. Other reports, however, indicate that many of the tombs were perceived by locals and foreign rulers as a source for financial gain through the looting of their contents. Consequently, the destruction of these tombs was justified by monetary gain through the collection of treasure and not by any type of moral condemnation against the beliefs of the pre-Islamic population in the vein of the attempt by Muhammad to raze the Ghumdan Palace. This is especially accentuated in the report about the vineyard woman – nothing is known about her beliefs – but also in the reports of those who accepted God, including a *hanif* (a person in the pre-Islamic period who maintained the pure monotheism of the prophet Ibrahim), whose tombs were still mostly plundered. Thus, there appears to be a grey area regarding the reaction to the tombs of monotheists and hence the level of their sanctity. This ambiguity emerges outright in the report about the discovery of the tomb of the two self-professed monotheist sisters, in which 'Abd al-Malik gives a mixed response in that the grave goods were to be sent to the treasury, but the bones put through a process of re-sanctification. Overall, through his collection of these reports, al-Hamdani seems to be trying to communicate a certain level of tolerance or at least ambivalence towards these localities of antiquity, whose ruins still dominated his tenth-century countryside and from which the diversity of the pre-Islamic past may be learned.

Notes

1. Michael Pitrovsky, 'Al-Hamdani and Qahtanide Epos', in *Al-Hamdani, Lisan al-Yaman*, ed. Yusuf Muhammad 'Abd Allah (Sanaa: Dar al-Tanwir li-l-Tiba'at wa-l-Nashr, 1986), 17–25. 'Abid b. Sharya al-Jurhumi wrote *Akhbar al-Yaman wa-ash'aruha wa-ansabiha* (*Reports of Yemen and Its Poetry and Genealogy*) and Wahb b. Munabbih wrote *Kitab al-muluk al-mutawwaja min Himyar wa-akhbarihim wa-qisasihim wa-quburihim wa-ash'arihim* (*The Crowned Kings of Himyar, their Narratives, Stories, Tombs, and Poems*). A likely later version of the second text, transmitted by 'Abd al-Malik b. Hisham but ascribed to Wahb b. Munabbih, is *Kitab al-tijan fi muluk Himyar wa-l-Yaman* (*The Books of Crowns about the Kings of Himyar and Yemen*). It is found along with al-Jurhumi's text in a 1928 edition by F. Krenkow (Hyderabad: Matba'at Majlis Da'irat al-Ma'arif al-'Uthmaniyya).
2. 'Ali b.Yusuf al-Qifti, *Inbah al-Ruwat 'ala Anbah Nuhat*, ed. M. A. Ibrahim, vol. 1 (Cairo: Dar al-Kutub al-Misriyya, 1950), 279–84.
3. Abu Muhammad al-Hasan b. Ah. mad b. Ya'qub al-Hamdani, *al-Iklīl*, ed. Muhammad b. 'Ali al-Akwa', vol. 8 (Sanaa: Ministry of Culture and Tourism, 2004).
4. Abd al-Muhsin al-Mad'aj, *The Yemen in Early Islam (9-233/630-847): A Political History* (London: Ithaca Press, 1988), 24–40.
5. Daniel Mahoney, 'Cultural Heritage and Identity Politics in Early Medieval South Arabia', in *Southwest Arabia across History: Essays to the Memory of Walter Dostal*, eds Andre Gingrich and Siegfried Haas (Vienna: Verlag der Österreichischen Akademie der Wissenschaften, 2014), 70–71.
6. Al-Hamdani, *al-Iklīl*, vol. 8, 26–49.
7. Qur'an 9:110. Incidentally, al-Hamdani states Farwa b. Musayk was only able to set the Ghumdan Palace on fire, and in another section of the entry he very briefly mentions that the building was completely destroyed in the days of 'Uthman.
8. 'Abd al-Malik Ibn Hisham, *Sirat al-Nabi* (Tanta, Egypt: Dar al-Sahaba li-l-Turath, 1995), 76. Noura Khoury has further documented the Ghumdan Palace's connection to the concept of pre-Islamic Arab kingship, which in the Umayyad period manifested in the Dome of the Rock:'The Dome of the Rock, the Ka'ba, and Ghumdan: Arab Myths and Umayyad Monument', *Muqarnas* 10 (1993): 60–63.
9. The architectural record of Yemen also contains many examples of pre-Islamic structures integrated into both sacred and secular buildings in the Islamic period: Barbara Finster, 'An Outline of the History of Islamic Religious Architecture in Yemen', *Muqarnas* 9 (1992): 124–33; Barbara Finster, 'Cubical Yemeni Mosques', *Proceedings of the Seminar for Arabian Studies* 21 (1991): 49–68.
10. Overall, very little is known about those who would have originally recorded these medieval reports, including their inscriptions, but there is indication of al-Hamdani's personal knowledge of the Himyarite language and script through his documentation of it in an earlier section of the eighth volume of *al-Iklīl* (154–55).
11. Al-Hamdani, *al-Iklīl*, vol. 8, 171–72.

12. For an overview of the types of burials, grave goods, and funerary stele found in South Arabia, see: Burkhard Vogt, 'Death and Funerary Practices', in *Caravan Kingdoms: Yemen and the Ancient Incense Trade*, ed. A. C. Gunter (Washington, D.C.: Smithsonian Institute, 2005), 80–9.
13. Franz Rosenthal, *A History of Muslim Historiography* (Leiden: Brill, 1968), 186–93. More recent work has pushed further the investigation of the function of texts focused on pre-Islamic rulers, such as Egyptian pharaohs: Konrad Hirschler, 'The "Pharoah" Anecdote in Pre-Modern Arabic Historiography', *Journal of Arabic and Islamic Studies* 10 (2010): 45–74.
14. The diverse imagination and construction of the *Jahiliyya* by medieval-period Muslims with their own agendas has been investigated recently by Peter Webb in *Imagining the Arabs: Arab Identity and the Rise of Islam* (Edinburgh: Edinburgh University Press, 2016), 255–69; and notably, for example, by Gerald Hawting in *The Idea of Idolatry and the Emergence of Islam* (Cambridge: Cambridge University Press, 1999) and Rina Drory in 'The Abbasid Construction of the Jahiliyya: Cultural Authority in the Making', *Studia Islamica* 83 (1996): 33–49.
15. The term 'preservation' in this chapter refers to the simple recovery of burials, as alluded to in the texts, and not any greater efforts at conservation or commemoration, with the exception of the examples of the tomb of the prophet Hud and the tomb of the two sisters, which will be discussed below.
16. Sacredness here refers to locations and objects through which social conventions prohibit and prescribe certain types of behavior related to them, such as restricted access or rituals like pilgrimage. This definition follows Brannon Wheeler in his discussion of relics, rituals, and prophet burials in the Islamic world in *Mecca and Eden: Ritual, Relics, and Territory in Islam* (Chicago: University of Chicago Press, 2006), 2–10. At the same time, the places encompassed and practices performed within a sacred landscape are given meaning through narrative frameworks that are embedded within the social memory of the inhabitants creating a more immediate relationship between past and present: Kathryn Reese-Taylor, 'Sacred Places and Sacred Landscapes', in *Oxford Handbook of Mesoamerican Archaeology*, eds Deborah L. Nichols and Christopher A. Pool, (Oxford: Oxford University Press, 2012), 755–56. In this case, visiting the tomb of Hud follows a practice of pilgrimage to sacred places that goes back millennia in the Near East, as documented by Joy McCorriston in *Pilgrimage and Household in the Ancient Near East* (Cambridge: Cambridge University Press, 2011).
17. Okasha el-Daly has similarly laid out the evidence for 'treasure hunting' in ancient graves within the context of medieval Egypt: *Egyptology: The Missing Millennium: Ancient Egypt in Medieval Arabic Writings* (London: UCL Press, 2005), 31–44. Unfortunately, there is not nearly the same amount nor diversity of evidence for looting in medieval Yemen. Yet el-Daly did briefly interpret the way that al-Hamdani describes the monu-ments and burials in *al-Iklīl* as a type of archaeological methodology akin to that of al-Idrisi in the thirteenth century (45–46).
18. Thomas Leisten has summarized the hadith and subsequent sharia that reference interdictions against funerary architecture, which is mainly based on concern for the structural threats against the corpse, as well as general opposition to the practices of

polytheists and unbelievers involved in the cult of the dead or the veneration of tombs, such as praying at cemeteries: 'Between Orthodoxy and Exegesis: Some Attitudes in the Shari'a toward Funerary Architecture', *Muqarnas* 7 (1990): 14–16. Nonetheless, the overall diversity of these legal views and wider political context allowed for the continued tolerance and construction of funerary architecture: Leisten, 18–22; and Leor Halevi, *Muhammad's Grave. Death Rites and the Making of Islamic Society* (New York: Columbia University Press, 2007), 165–95.

19. Al-Hamdani, *al-Iklīl*, vol. 8, 166–67.
20. Qur'an 50:14.
21. The *Ashab al-Rass* are mentioned alongside 'Ad and Thamud in the Qur'an (25:38).
22. The scholars of Sanaa state that the tomb of Hanzala b. Safwan is located in the Great Mosque of Sanaa (Al-Hamdani, ed. al-Akwa', *al-Iklīl*, vol. 8, 167–68, note 9), indicating that this reported site of the cave tomb was either fabricated, forgotten, or lost, possibly due to this act of preservation, and hence it is not part of the physical sacred landscape of Yemen.
23. Al-Hamdani, *al-Iklīl*, vol. 8, 161–63.
24. The description of the tomb of Hud in this report does not accord with what Brannon Wheeler has identified as the 'long tomb' type, i.e. a category of burial sizable in length and belonging to pre-Islamic prophets found throughout the Middle East and beyond, despite Wheeler citing later twentieth-century reports that do describe the tomb of Hud as being quite large in size: *Mecca and Eden*, 100–01, 212–13.
25. Qur'an 11:50–60.
26. The tomb of Hud continues to be a place of pilgrimage in Wadi Hadramawt. See R. B. Serjeant, 'Hud and other pre-Islamic prophets of Hadramawt', *Le Muséon* 47 (1954): 121–79; Shaykh 'Abd al-Qadir Muhammad al-Sabban, *Visits and Customs: The Visit to the Tomb of the Prophet Hud*, ed. and trans. Linda Boxberger and Awad Abdelrahim Abu Hulayqa (Ardmore, PA: American Institute for Yemeni Studies, 1998).
27. Al-Hamdani, *al-Iklīl*, vol. 8, 163–64.
28. Qur'an 85:4–5.
29. Ibn Hisha-m, *S-ı rat al-nab-ı*, 71–73.
30. Ibid., 74.
31. There are also similar reports in *al-Iklīl* concerning the uncovering of preserved corpses that bleed. These accounts seem to express similar attitudes towards other religious figures of undeserved violence. For example, one report states that the 'Umayyad caliph Sulayman b. 'Abd al-Malik was passing through Wadi al-Qura in the Hijaz, north of Sanaa (Al-Hamdani, *al-Iklīl*, vol. 8, 165). He ordered a hole dug for an unspecified reason, which his men did until coming upon a boulder. When they removed it, below was a man with two shirts and his hand over his chin. When Sulayman ordered his hand to be lifted, blood flowed, and when it was let go, this action stopped the spillage. The accompanying inscription stated: 'I am al-Harith b. 'Amr, messenger of the messenger of God Shu'ayb to the people of Madayn, but they denied me and then killed me'. Unfortunately, this report ends before stating if Caliph Sulayman b. 'Abd al-Malik reacted in the same way as 'Umar ibn al-Khattab and returned the burial to its former state.
32. Al-Hamdani, *al-Iklīl*, vol. 8, 179–80.

33. Al-Akwaʿ states in a footnote that the Abara are a group of Himyar that used to live in Dahr.
34. This idea of disconnection from local graves may also be the result of the movement of groups within South Arabia. Al-Hamdani provides examples of this type of movement earlier on in volume eight of *Al-Ikl-ıl* when describing the fortresses of a region being named after their predecessors (Dhu al-Mahfid) rather than the current group inhabiting the region (Dhu Khalil): Al-Hamdani, *al-Iklīl*, vol. 8, 84.
35. As a note of comparison, Patrick Geary has described the necessity of economic exchanges between the living and the dead in medieval Europe to be a balanced reciprocation, e.g. through prayer, out of concern for retribution from the dead: *Living with the Dead in the Middle Ages* (Ithaca: Cornell University Press, 1994), 77–83. His comments, however, were focused on the exchange of wealth through inheritance or the Church, and not through the looting of burials.
36. Al-Hamdani, *al-Iklīl*, vol. 8, 159–61.
37. See al-Tabari, *Taʾrikh al-rusul waʾl-muluk* (Cairo: 1960–69), vol. 1, 559 and vol. 6, 271; and Al-Hamdani, *Sifat jazirat al-ʾArab* (Riyadh: 1989), 210. A notable distinction between the narratives of these two authors is that while al-Hamdani describes the extermination of the people of Hadur due to a harmful wind, al-Tabari states that they are the victims of the army of Nebuchadezzar sent by God. Furthermore, Shuʿayb al-Haduri, whose genealogy is given by al-Hamdani, should be distinguished from the more well-known prophet Shuʿayb who is mentioned in the Qurʾan as having been sent to the 'People of the Thicket' or Maydan. Although not mentioned by al-Hamdani, a tomb and mosque of the Prophet Shuʿayb now lie on the highest peak of the region of Hadur, demonstrating the further extension of the sacred landscape of South Arabia through the construction of this later commemoration: J. Schleifer and A.K. Irvine, 'Hadur' in *Encyclopaedia of Islam*, 2nd ed.
38. Al-Hamdani, *al-Iklīl*, vol. 8, 168–171.
39. *Al-Ahqaf* is the specific region of the ʿAd referred to in the Qurʾan, 46:20.
40. Al-Hamdani, *al-Iklīl*, vol. 8, 169.
41. Ibid., vol. 8, 164.
42. Ibid., vol. 8, 156–57.
43. The meaning of this report has been interpreted in various ways. Antoine Borrut argues that this report, which is also found in the early tenth-century *Mukhtasar kitab al-buldan* of Ibn al-Faqih al-Hamadhani, indicates the consequences of the rupture of the pact between the Umayyad dynasty and Solomon after the resettlement of the capital in Harran instead of the Bilad al-Sham: *Entre memoire et pouvoir. L'espace syrien sous les derniers Omeyyades et les premiers Abbasides (v. 72-193/692-809)* (Leiden: Brill Press, 2011), 224–28. The narrative may also communicate more generally an overall condemnation of the ʿUmayyads by al-Kalbi who was closely associated with the ʿAbbasid caliphs. Or, if viewed from outside of its immediate political context, this report may simply document the belief that Muslims should not destroy or loot the antiquities that surround them. Further versions of this report have also been found in other texts including, for example, *Arabian Nights* via Yaqut: see David Pinault, *Story-Telling Techniques in the Arabian Nights* (Leiden: Brill, 1992), 202–08.
44. Al-Hamdani, *al-Iklīl*, vol. 8, 175–76.
45. Al-Madʿaj, *Yemen in Early Islam*, 162–63.

46. Al-Hamdani, *al-Iklīl*, vol. 8, 174.
47. The mention of Muhammad in this report is unique amongst the inscriptions of the monotheist tombs in these reports. Its significance either points to this tomb postdating Muhammad (which seems to contradict the identity of the daughters' father as an ancient ruler of South Arabia), or is a clear indication that this report, or at least the inscription, is fabricated to some extent.
48. Ibid., vol. 8, 173.
49. Ibid., vol. 8, 158.
50. Ibid., vol. 8, 173–74.
51. Leor Halevi, *Muhammad's Grave: Death Rites and the Making of Islamic Society* (New York: Columbia University Press, 2007), 43–84. Additionally, Halevi suggests that early Islamic pietists perceived 'death as a crisis that requires funerary prayers and other rituals to restore the social order and reestablish a sense of communal solidarity' (234).
52. For example, Nancy Khalek has shown how the institution of the relics of John the Baptist, along with the narratives surrounding him, worked toward making Damascus a new sacred landscape in the early Islamic period: *Damascus after the Muslim Conquest* (London: Oxford University Press, 2011), 85–134.
53. Al-Hamdani, *al-Iklīl*, vol. 8, 102–03.
54. This non-sectarian outlook sits in contrast to the tombs connected to a Hadrami population in Yemen associated with the 'Alawi way and the destruction of the tomb of one of its sixteenth-century saints in 1994, which Enseng Ho interprets as an attack not only on the saint but also the community surrounding him: *The Graves of Tarim: Genealogy and Mobility across the Indian Ocean* (Berkeley: University of California Press, 2006), 5–6.

3

The Wisdom to Wonder: *'Ajā'ib* and the Pillars of Islamic India

Santhi Kavuri-Bauer

The memoir of Firuz Shah Tughluq, *Sirat-i Firozshahi,* composed in Persian by an anonymous author in 1370, contains an account of an Ashokan pillar [Figure 3.1 and Figure 3.2] dating from the third century BCE being transported to Delhi and subsequently erected in the new city of Firuzabad. The description begins with a poem.

> Seen from a hundred *farsang* [the pillar] looks like a hillock of gold, as the Sun when it spreads its rays in the morning.
>
> No bird – neither eagle, nor crane – can fly as high as its top; and arrows […] cannot reach its middle.
>
> O God! How did they lift this heavy mountain; and in what did they fix it that it does not move from its place?

Figure 3.1: Reinstalled Ashokan pillar, Firuz Shah Kotla Fort, Firuzabad. Steve Browne.

Imagining Antiquity in Islamic Societies

Figure 3.2: Detail of Ashokan pillar. Patrick A. Rogers.

How did they carry it to the top of the building which almost touches the heavens and place it there in an upright position?

How could they paint it all over with gold, that it appears to people like the golden morning?[1]

The poem is followed by an awe-inspiring and detailed account of the Shah's discovery of this 13-metre-high, 27-ton Ashokan pillar, its excavation, its transport over 200 kilometres to Delhi from Ambala, Haryana and its final reinstallation near the congregational mosque, where it was prominently placed on a pyramidal structure. This medieval account is particularly notable for its emphasis on Firuz Shah's ingenuity in identifying the wondrous pillar as well as his intellectual faculties that were integral to the pillar's recovery and new emplacement. Just as noteworthy is the complete absence of any jihadi rhetoric framing the pillar's reuse as symbolic of an Islamic victory over the idolatrous Hindu past. Instead, the author of the *Sirat-i Firozshahi* focuses entirely on the wonderment effected by the ancient column and the king's singular perspicacity. This chapter examines the rhetorical logic through which pre-Islamic artefacts like the pillar in Firuzabad were displayed by rulers as cynosures of their new architectural projects. This logic, I argue, is centred on the unique potential of pre-Islamic forms to evoke an aesthetic response of wonderment. Such objects or phenomena, whose properties transcend common human comprehension, were known in medieval Islam as *'aja'ib* (sing. *'ajiba*), and the effect of wonderment emanating from them guided the order and meaning of certain architectural practices in Islamic India.

The fact that Islamic rulers of India should have venerated pre-Islamic architectural forms runs counter to the notion that they collected and displayed Hindu and Buddhist pillars solely to traumatize and humiliate non-believers. This theory, proposed by orientalist scholars and disseminated today by Hindu fundamentalists, has informed the popular conception of Islamic power in India as violently and eternally iconoclastic. Only in the past few decades have scholars like Robert Hillenbrand, William J. McKibben, Finbarr B. Flood, Richard M. Eaton and Phillip B. Wagoner, and Alka Patel challenged this representation.[2] Each of these writers has meticulously argued that when it comes to the reuse of pre-Islamic architectural elements within new buildings, Islamic rulers were acting not according to dictates established by a singular religious authority, but in response to local Indic power structures and practices of kingship, as well as to the practical matter of finding ready material for new building projects. In these readings, then, when architectural forms like pillars, gateways and temple parts were reused in Islamic spaces, their presence revealed a ruler's desire to signal the discontinuation (as in the case of 'conquest mosques') or continuation of Indian modes of rulership with the aim of establishing his place within the historical topography of India. In this chapter I do not argue against such an interpretation of the practice of reuse – i.e., in service to the political expediencies of the day – nor of its probable perception and interpretation by local populations. However, I wish to propose the prior existence of an Islamic predisposition toward certain kinds of ancient objects informed by medieval Islamic geographical and cosmological thought, and that this mindset prompted early Islamic Indian rulers to select Hindu and Buddhist architectural forms for reuse and prominent display.

While the primary aim of this chapter is to elaborate on how Islamic rulers reckoned with pre-Islamic architecture, it also questions the continued separation of Islam from its architectural expression in the discourse of Islamic architectural history. After the postmodern turn that sought to dismantle the orientalist generalizations of Islamic culture by focusing on the variations exhibited by Islamic builders, few scholars have returned to the possibility that there may have been unifying and underlying principles at work in the production of Islamic architecture. Wendy M. K. Shaw draws attention to the continued reticence about finding an 'intellectual substrate' in a field that would rather focus on local cultural-political contexts or the aesthetic effects of Islamic ornamentation than consider how both can be seen as articulations of an evolving but nonetheless deeply religious mindset, i.e., 'to see Islam as a substantive conceptual substrate through which to understand the multiple subjectivities of the Islamic world, past and present'.[3] I believe that ignoring such a substrate, whether due to the secularist mandate of art history that demands positivist analysis or the postmodern interest in variations produced by local contexts, prevents an interpretation of Islamic architectural practices as the materialization and spatialization of mystical and philosophical principles common to the Islamic world.[4] In order to achieve a 'deeper interpretation' of the reuse of pre-Islamic forms, larger theoretical Islamic fields of intellectual endeavour such as philosophy, cosmology and cosmogony, structured around the phenomenon of 'aja'ib, are brought to bear on the interpretation of these architectural acts.[5]

In order to achieve a deeper interpretation of the reuse of non-Islamic architectural forms by early Islamic rulers of the Delhi Sultanate, this chapter contextualizes the practice within the broader conceptual discourse of 'aja'ib, found originally in encyclopaedic texts of history and geography that were circulating in the Islamic world since the tenth century. More specifically, it focuses on two instances of reuse that I argue were textually and spatially framed as 'aja'ib and meant to reflect on the enlightened power of Delhi Sultanate-era kings. The first instance is the re-erection of the Gupta period (320–550 BCE) iron pillar found in the courtyard of the Quwwat al-Islam Mosque by Iltutmish (r.1211–36) [Figure 3.3], and the second is the abovementioned Ashokan pillar (third century BCE) re-erected by Firuz Shah Tughluq (r.1351–88), both found in Delhi. My analysis does not depend on positivist research alone to reconstruct the details of how the pillars were reused, as objective contemporary sources describing such activities are scarce. Instead, I draw on the discursive framework of 'aja'ib to extrapolate how Islamic Indian rulers approached, selected and re-erected ancient Indian architectural forms as they sought to reorder their Indian dominions and legitimize their authority over this topography.

Whence 'aja'ib?

Islamic rulers and intellectual elites from the Abbasid caliphate (750–1258) onwards supported the acquisition of knowledge of pre-Islamic and non-Islamic architectural monuments, especially those that sparked a sense of wonder. Topographical details and wondrous sites encountered by merchants, sailors, scholars and other travellers from Cordoba to the South China Sea were gathered into the Arabic geographical and topographical literature and

Figure 3.3: Iron pillar, Quwwat al-Islam Mosque, Delhi. Sujit Kumar.

disseminated across the Islamicate world. Embedded in these texts of factual geographical information were the *'aja'ib* or, more precisely, the 'real or imaginary phenomena in the physical world which challenged human understanding'.[6] Examples of *'aja'ib* were men with faces on their chests, Amazonian women and fantastical animals, such as a snake so large it could devour buffalos and elephants. Also counted among those things that challenged human understanding were 'man-made objects – prominently among them the great monuments of the pre-Islamic past'.[7] Since India contained both natural and man-made ancient wonders, it was featured in early *'aja'ib* literature. India as a land of wonders, in fact, enters the Islamic imagination through the *adab al-rihla*, or travel writing, which emerged fifty years after the Arab conquest of Sindh in 710.[8]

By the mid-eighth century, when Arab conquests of new lands had largely subsided and Islamic hereditary rule was on secure footing, the Abbasid caliphs turned their energies to establishing Baghdad as a centre of learning. To further these efforts, Caliph Harun al-Rashid (r.786–809) had Greek and Sanskrit texts of cosmography, philosophy, geography, medicine and history translated into Islamic 'spatial, conceptual and ethnic terms'.[9] The challenging process of translation required not only making sense of a foreign culture but also bringing its truths into accord with an Islamic world-view concerning man and the nature of existence. Rather than to a Qur'an and hadith-centred theology, scholars turned to Greek philosophy to accomplish this hermeneutical manoeuvre. The *'aja'ib* emerged at this time to frame inquiry and knowledge production, and to reconcile new discoveries with Islamic scripture.[10] In the context of the sciences, wonders like rainbows, Egyptian pyramids and fantastical animals functioned to mediate between one's own reasoning ability and the jarring effects of surprise, confusion, danger and chaos. The *'aja'ib* informed Islamic epistemology, which at this time sought to unite faith with philosophical reason.[11] *'Aja'ib* were thus not only a physical feature in Islamic geography and cosmography, but also an aesthetic effect that promoted philosophical speculation, which in turn led to knowledge. Wonder, in fact, was regarded by Aristotle as the root of all understanding: 'It is through wonder that men now begin and originally began to philosophize.'[12] In Islamic scholarly writing that features descriptions of *'aja'ib*, the Greek dialectical method of understanding was adapted to accommodate both Islamic philosophy and belief: by speculative looking (*nazar*) at the wondrous, one used reason to encounter God's design and existence.[13]

The final aspect of the *'aja'ib* that is crucial to the study of the reuse of ancient architectural forms by Indian Islamic rulers is that wonders, and especially ancient forms, were integrated into the metaphysics of Islamic philosophy and the theory of emanation, or *fayd*. Derived from Neoplatonism, emanation theory aims to explain the immaterial cause behind the physical world. While philosophers like al-Farabi writing in the tenth century and Ibn Sina in the eleventh century differ on certain points, most agree on several general aspects of this theory: God did not create the world but it emerged from him gradually; all things in the material and immaterial world can be ordered by their relative proximity to God (also referred to as the Perfect); the physical world is the least perfect; and between God and matter lies the celestial realm of the stars and planets. The material world is further subdivided according to the ability of its constituents to perceive Reason: the plant kingdom is the lowest, followed by the animal kingdom with its faculty for unconscious reasoning. Man, endowed with the ability to perceive the light of Reason through conscious thought, is elevated above them both. Unlike early Islamic conceptions of God the Creator, 'the God of emanationism' is not external to creation. All things are a necessary result of God's existence; just as a Möbius strip is devoid of boundaries between planes, God and the material world are seen as part of one and the same creative purpose. This is a radical idea in that it allows newly conquered lands on the Islamic frontier (*dar al-harb*), as well as the cultures antedating the arrival of Islam (in the period known as the *jahiliyya*) to be seen as emanations of the same God. Consequently, ancient monuments and relics that inspired a sense of wonder were seen as signs of God's cosmic order; moreover, because they also promoted reason, they were not seen as products of *shirk* (idolatry) and targeted for destruction. Instead, in this philosophically structured Islamic epistemology, they were regarded as worthy of reverence – along with the people who had produced them.

Islamic epistemology posits that as things move away from the Perfect, they become less perfect, degrading into lesser beings. Man's duty, like the philosopher's, is to use reason to find the way back to Perfection. If reason is the mode of finding the way to God, then Muslims and non-Muslims, pre-Islamic peoples and Islamic peoples all have the potential to attain the Perfect. The eleventh-century philosopher and scientist Abu Rayhan al-Biruni espoused this belief. In his study of ancient Indian philosophy and science, he saw Hindu thinkers on a par with Greek and Muslim scholars seeking truth in the abstract realm. This notion of propinquity informs his favourable description of Hindu ideas of God:

> The Hindus believe with regard to God that he is one, eternal, without beginning and end, acting by free will, almighty, all-wise, living, giving life, ruling, preserving; one who in his sovereignty is unique, beyond all likeness and unlikeness and that he does not resemble anything nor does anything resemble him.[14]

Al-Biruni could sit with Brahmin scholars and translate ancient Sanskrit texts because if God, as he believed, was the all-permeating wellspring of existence, unbounded by space and time, then His truth could be found in Hindu India no less than in the Islamic world. The intellectual's belief in emanation would later be adopted by Islamic rulers in India, who, like al-Biruni, would see in India's ancient past things worth preserving because they were the products of the same God and His ordering of the world.

By the thirteenth century, the *'aja'ib*'s epistemological function as the cause of inquiry enabling individuals to grasp the truth and order of this world was codified in texts dedicated specifically to this subject. It was for the latter purpose of bringing about an awareness of the divine order that the most famous and heavily copied illustrated manuscript within the *'aja'ib* literary tradition was written, the *'Aja'ib al-makhluqat wa ghara'ib al-mawjudat*, or the 'Wonders of Creation and the Curiosities of Existence', compiled by Zakariya ibn Muhammad al-Qazwini (*d*.1283) between the years 1260 and 1280.[15] In her discussion of the paintings of *'aja'ib* found within the text, Persis Berlekamp describes the role of wonder in its epistemological function:

> In these manuscripts [...] visual perception of eye-catching painted images of wonders could prompt aesthetic appreciation, so that viewers would engage with the wonders presented in these paintings not only with their eyes, but with their internal senses [imagination, common sense, estimation, memory, representation]. This could pave

the way for intellectual engagement with the wonders the images represented. That engagement in turn paved the way for awe at God's divinely ordered cosmos.¹⁶

Berlekamp's analysis of the pictorial *'aja'ib* as conducive to spreading the deeper truth of Islamic epistemology in thirteenth-century Islam is compelling. The encounter with the *'aja'ib*, however, was not reserved only for textual experience but was transposed to geographical experience as well. Using the definition and function of *'aja'ib* from Berlekamp's well-argued study, I propose that alongside pictorial representations of wonder, architectural wonders in the form of monuments such as mosques, minarets and ancient pillars also existed, and that they were meant to be sources of awe before God's divinely ordered cosmos and symbols of the just and wise rulers that had the foresight to build or reuse them.

The Quwwat al-Islam Mosque and Indian Islamic *'Aja'ib*

When al-Biruni completed his *Tarikh al-Hind* in 1030, it was for the purpose of providing information on India to 'any one [in Islam] who wants to converse with the Hindus, and to discuss with them questions of religion, science, or literature, on the very basis of their own civilization'.¹⁷ Al-Biruni did not refrain from chastising his patron Mahmud of Ghazni (r.997–1030) for destroying the Shiva temple in Somnath, Gujarat and humiliating its Brahmin caretakers. From his viewpoint, which is based on the epistemology of emanation, the Brahmins were intellectuals and part of a social hierarchy based not on religion, but on reason – and it was through reason that they reached God, not through the reviled practice of idolatry associated with Hindu temples.¹⁸ Al-Biruni, therefore, did not see Mahmud of Ghazni's incursions into India as advancing the cause of Islamic civilization, but rather as a source of distrust and animosity among the Hindu population, especially its intellectuals. Indeed, he did not mince words. Regarding Mahmud's conquest, he writes,

> Mahmud utterly ruined the prosperity of the country, and performed there [inconceivable] exploits, by which the Hindus became like atoms of dust scattered in all directions, and like a tale of old in the mouth of the people. Their scattered remains cherish, of course, the most inveterate aversion towards all Muslims. This is the reason, too, why Hindu sciences have retired far away from those parts of the country conquered by us, and have fled to places which our hand cannot yet reach, to Kashmir, Benares and other places. And there the antagonism between them and all foreigners receives more and more nourishment both from political and religious sources.¹⁹

Al-Biruni points out that kings and princes in the Islamic past (most likely a reference to Baghdad in the ninth and tenth centuries) honoured science and scholars with patronage. Rulers in his day were not the same:

They are the very opposite, and therefore it is quite impossible that a new science or any new kind of research should arise in our days. What we have of sciences is nothing but the scanty remains of bygone better times.[20]

In these passages, which are interspersed between his study and translation of Indian philosophy, astronomy, mathematics and geography, al-Biruni reveals a method of reckoning with Indian culture that was in keeping with the Islamic epistemology of emanation, where all religions and cultures could find their own way to God.

The theory of emanation went underground in the eleventh century due to a backlash led by al-Ghazali (*d*.1111) against the theory's conception of God, but it would later take root in the periphery of the Islamic world under the first free ruler of India, Qutb al-Din Aybek's son-in-law Shams al-Din Iltutmish (*r*.1210–36). At this time, a more refined intellectual and cultural expression of Islam began to emerge in India, as religious scholars, poets and Sufis migrating in the wake of Ghurid conquests or fleeing the Mongol conquests of Persia and Central Asia found new patronage in Delhi. Two such scholars that wrote histories of Iltutmish's reign were Sadid al-Din Muhammad 'Awfi (*d*.1233), originally from Bukhara, and Hasan Nizami of Nishapur (*d*.unknown). Their histories include high praise for Iltutmish's architectural projects and reveal how the rhetoric of *'aja'ib* came to signify his sovereignty as just, thereby in turn increasing India's prominence in the Islamic world.

'Awfi's and Nizami's historical writings were essentially paeans to Iltutmish and his accomplishments. They were written and read in the Islamic literary tradition of *adab* (manners and customs) that brought together a variety of subjects including history, geography, poetry, philosophy, religion and etiquette. *Adab* enabled an author to demonstrate his wide range of knowledge in support of his patron's authority. The rhetorical style, structure and contents of *adab* varied with context and depended upon both the needs of the patron (e.g., to legitimate their rule) and the skills of the writer.[21] In medieval India, *adab* could include Qur'anic verses, Arabic poetry, biographies of early Sufi saints and Persian literary traditions such as the Mirrors for Princes genre, which featured anecdotes of respected kings intended to steer their elite readership toward good practices of governance. The *adab* literary context is where *'aja'ib*, encountered in the writers' rhetorical descriptions of the built monuments of India, was first connected to an Islamic Indian sovereign's just and wise rule over his dominion. This connection is clearly made in 'Awfi's and Nizami's writings describing Iltutmish's expansion of the Quwwat al-Islam Mosque [Figure 3.4], built by his father-in-law, the Ghurid slave general Qutb al-Din Aybek, in 1192 after his conquest of Delhi, and Iltutmish's addition of three stories to the Qutb Minar [Figure 3.5] also started by his predecessor.

'Awfi's *Jawami' al-hikayat wa lawami' al-riwayat* ('Collections of Stories and Illustrations of Histories') of 1228 is an early example of Indian *adab*, and demonstrates one of the first interpretations of Delhi's monuments as wonders in the context of Iltutmish's sultanate. The text is divided into four books, with the last dedicated to 'Strange Occurrences, the Wonders of Seas and Lands, the Temperament of Animals and the Facetiousness of Eminent Persons'.

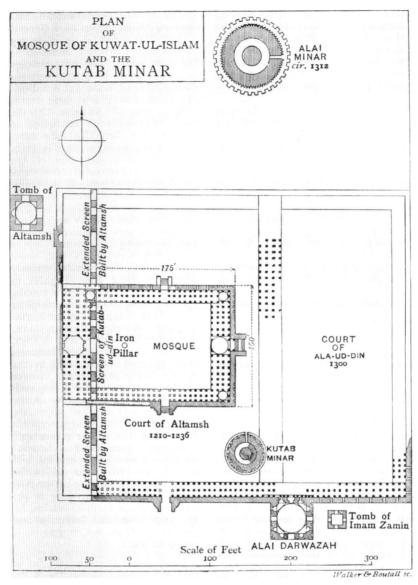

Figure 3.4: Plan of Quwwat al-Islam complex. John Murray, *A Handbook for Travellers in India, Burma, and Ceylon* (London, J. Murray: 1911), 371.

Figure 3.5: Qutb Minar, Delhi. Santhi Kavuri-Bauer.

In Chapter 19 of Book 4, titled 'Monuments and Remarkable Buildings', 'Awfi opens with an unattributed yet famous Arabic verse: 'These are our works which prove what we have done / Look, therefore, at our works when we are gone.'[22] Subsequently, 'Awfi describes ancient mythical wonders, among them the tower of Dhu al-Qarnayn in the port of Alexandria, with its mirror that could burn ships at sea; the relics of the marble-columned court built by

Divs for the Prophet Solomon at Alexandria; the column and statue at 'Ain Shams and the pharaonic pyramids in Egypt; the Ayvan-i Kisra, the famous Persian palace of Ctesiphon in Persia; and the round city of Baghdad of Caliph al-Mansur. In his description of Baghdad, 'Awfi mentions that Hindu engineers worked with Arabs in planning the caliphal city. This inclusion of Hindus follows al-Biruni's view that even in India there is scientific wisdom that was not only acknowledged but also allowed to participate in the founding of the wondrous round city of Baghdad. Finally, at the end of the chapter, 'Awfi produces a lyrical description of the Quwwat al-Islam Mosque and the Qutb Minar as part of a panegyric to Iltutmish, 'the liberator of the realms of the world, the propagator of the words of God, the refuge-giver to the men of faith, the heir to the kingdom of Solomon'.[23] While the two structures were conceived to meet the requirements of Islamic prayer, Iltutmish is described as going beyond these practical concerns by producing architecture that was so wondrous in nature that it was as though he'd 'constructed a Ka'ba in India'.[24] In his flowery description of the mosque, 'Awfi emphasizes its uncanny nature: 'The whole of the courtyard and the flooring of the mosque is made of white marble and the arches also have been constructed of stone in such a manner as to baffle the imagination.'[25]

He goes on to assert that the Qutb Minar – at 72 metres, the world's tallest minaret at the time – likewise beggars description.[26] By ending the chapter on famous ancient monuments with Iltutmish's contemporary works such as the Qutb Minar and expansions of the Quwwat al-Islam and using the rhetoric of *'aja'ib* to frame them all, 'Awfi creates equivalencies between new and ancient wonders. Iltutmish, through his patronage of new wonders, is aligned with the wise and just kings of the past, worthy of commendation as their equal: 'Praise be to the king, great as the first Mehdi and powerful as Alexander.'[27]

The rhetoric of *'aja'ib*, by which the Quwwat al-Islam and the Qutb Minar were introduced into the early historiography of Islamic India, allowed 'Awfi and his patron to encode the geography of India as *dar al-islam* (and no longer as *dar al-harb*). Perhaps more importantly, it helped establish Iltutmish, the first ruler of Islamic India, as a just king who ruled through the divine gift of reason. Travis Zadeh outlines this connection of reasoned rule to *'aja'ib* in his discussion of al-Qazwini's writings:

> al-Qazwini argues that the marvellous is recognized only by one who contemplates existence and develops the faculty of reason; the negligent, out of their ignorance, fail to perceive the marvellous design of nature, and thus readily reject that which they do not understand.[28]

In his *Taj al-Ma'athir*, or 'Crown of Glorious Deeds', Nizami cites Iltutmish's singular faculties of reason as the explanation for the success of all his endeavours:

> He restored the splendour of Hindustani dominions by good administration, without the help of which an empire cannot remain stable. He extinguished the fire of disturbance and put down the dust of rebellion with his pen without the support of which even the

sword cannot be effectively wielded. He put out [the] fire of harshness with the water of kindness and compassion with the help of *the light of reason* which is the mirror that shows everything in its true form. By exercising unusual patience, which is an adornment to reason and an ornament to art, he suppressed arrogance by showing humility.[29]

Prior to this description, Nizami compares Iltutmish's fame to four pillars: the minaret in Syria, the minaret in Yemen, the minaret in Iraq and the black stone in Mecca. All of these monuments were represented as *'aja'ib* in medieval Islamic geographies and cosmologies of the period. Mentioning them in relation to Iltutmish's rule would undoubtedly have evoked the Qutb Minar as a fifth pillar extending the reach of Islam to India. The Quwwat al-Islam too is likened by Nizami to the well-known wonders of Heruman and Alexander's fortresses.[30] Like 'Awfi, Nizami uses the rhetoric of *'aja'ib* to frame the new monuments of Iltutmish as the work of an enlightened king who brought to India the same reasoned authority found in the pre-Islamic and Islamic past. Since the rhetorical logic of *'aja'ib* was instrumental in producing the meaning of Iltutmish's early architectural projects, we may assume that it continued to influence and frame the projects he undertook after the above histories were written. Of these projects, the installation of the iron pillar in the central courtyard of the Quwwat al-Islam is among the most remarkable.

The expansion of the monumental screen [Figure 3.6] at the entrance of the prayer hall of the Quwwat al-Islam followed Iltutmish's investiture by the caliph in Baghdad in 1229. The historian Juzjani, who was in Delhi at the time, wrote in his *Tabaqat-i Nasiri* that Iltutmish had the residents of Delhi adorn the city streets and their houses to welcome the emissaries from Baghdad. He also writes that the sultan had domes and arches raised to mark the occasion of India's official inclusion in the *dar al-islam*.[31] Although the exact date of the installation of the iron pillar is unknown, it must have taken place at the same time, or shortly after. The placing of this pillar was the first example of an ancient pre-Islamic column being given a place of significance by an Islamic ruler. Standing at about 6 metres above ground, with a diameter of 43 centimetres and tapering to 30 centimetres at the top, the pillar is made of 6 metric tons of solid wrought iron. There are several inscriptions on its surface. The earliest [Figure 3.7] is of six lines in Sanskrit found on the pillar's western face that reveal the circumstances of its making: in the fourth century, after victory in battle against his enemies in the Vanga country (Bengal), King Chandra 'carried a beauty of countenance like (the beauty of) the full-moon, having in faith fixed his mind upon (the god) Vishnu, this lofty standard of the divine Vishnu was set up on the hill (called) Vishnupada'.[32] Where this hill was located is unknown; British archaeologists believed the iron pillar was brought to Delhi by later Hindu kings and then installed at the Quwwat al-Islam by Iltutmish.[33] In addition to constructing a new subterranean base that sits about 1 metre below ground, Iltutmish's builders must have removed the capital, which most likely contained an image of the god Vishnu or his eagle, Garuda [Figure 3.8]. Placed in the centre of the mosque's courtyard and aligned with the *mihrab* or directional marker of prayer, the pillar is framed by the arches of the eastern entrance gate [Figure 3.9] and monumental western screen [Figure 3.10]. This

Figure 3.6: Screen to prayer hall. Abhishek Joshi.

placement ensured that the pillar was an object of focus and contemplation, adding to the space of the mosque a new depth and dimension.

The unprecedented installation of an ancient iron pillar in the centre of the Quwwat al-Islam would have struck the community of the faithful as a certain curiosity, since this type of spatial arrangement had not been seen before. Moreover, the pillar possessed a singular characteristic never observed in other ancient iron works: it was resistant to corrosion. This unique property continues to be a source of wonder for modern tourists and scientists.[34] In Iltutmish's day, an incorruptible, 800-year-old iron pillar would most certainly have fit into the aesthetic and philosophical category of *'aja'ib*, a category that, as 'Awfi's text shows us, also framed his patron's other great project, the Qutb Minar. It is easy to see how building the tallest minaret ever seen would reflect favourably on any Islamic ruler. Given Iltutmish's well-documented propensity for rational thought and enlightened rule, the placement of the pillar within the mosque was hardly a demonstration of Muslim ascendancy, but rather the assembly of two wondrous constructions to be admired and pondered, one Islamic, one not – but both part of God's cosmic order and reflecting the wisdom and authority of the

Figure 3.7: Sanskrit inscription from Gupta period on iron pillar in Quwaat al-Islam Mosque. Santhi Kavuri-Bauer.

ruler. Here was an invitation to all his Muslim subjects, be they Sunnis or Shi'is, mystics or mullahs, newly converted or born into the faith, to come together in wonder and share in their sovereign's enlightened dominion. The pillar's specific placement within the mosque is important, as it further substantiates the assumption of its intended status as an *'ajiba*, a wonder, rather than a token of domination or submission. It was set off from the rest of the mosque and erected in the centre of the courtyard. No inscription was added, leaving it as an independent statement, different from the epigraphic and design programme of the rest of the mosque complex. Following conventional practices, the carved texts found on the mosque's screens and walls, on the Qutb Minar and on the interior walls of Iltutmish's highly ornamented tomb, were taken from the Qur'an and iterate the message of Islam's might and the punishment of infidels. Such a message would certainly have satisfied the traditional Islamic institutions and norms. However, once inside the mosque the cynosure must have been the curious pillar. Its isolated placement in the centre of the courtyard marks a very different treatment and attitude from that typically inflicted on non-Islamic spoils of war serving as symbols of Islamic triumph in India. The audience at the mosque must have been

Figure 3.8: Empty capital of iron pillar. Debbasish Das.

well aware of this, and an example of humiliating treatment of Hindu artefacts was certainly also present at the Quwwat al-Islam. In 1235, Iltutmish conquered Ujjain and sacked the temple of Mahakal. The *Tarikh-i Firishta* mentions that Iltutmish brought brass and stone idols from the temple back to Delhi, broke them and placed the pieces at the door of the Friday Mosque.[35] The iron pillar's placement, by contrast, was that of a reverent artefact to be read in quite a different light. Indeed, unlike the figurative idols that had to be destroyed, the pillar could be installed within the mosque without upsetting the sensibilities of the

Figure 3.9: Eastern entrance of the Quwwat al-Islam. Varun Shiv Kapur.

Muslim community. Placed inside the courtyard, it was resignified as an *'ajiba* instead of a sign of *shirk* or pagan worship. The effect of wonder rather than domination produced by the pillar is substantiated in later writings. In 1333, the traveller and scholar Ibn Battuta wrote of the mystery and wonder that the pillar continued to evoke one hundred years after its instalment:

> In the centre of the mosque is the awe-inspiring column of which [it is said] nobody knows of what metal it is constructed. One of their learned men told me that it is called Haft Jush, which means 'seven metals' [sic], and that it is composed of these seven. A part of this column, of a finger's length, has been polished, and this polished part gives out a brilliant gleam. Iron makes no impression on it. It is thirty cubits high, and we rolled a turban round it, and the portion which encircled it measured eight cubits.[36]

The full meaning of the iron pillar's placement in the Quwwat al-Islam will never be known, as no eye-witness accounts of its initial discovery or re-erection exist. However, when

Figure 3.10: Pillar framed by screen to prayer hall. Thomas Anzenhofer.

examined through the conceptual lens of *'aja'ib*, and in comparison with the rhetorical descriptions of the mosque and nearby minaret as well as similar pillar re-erections in later periods, it can be read as a radical gesture meant to bring India into alignment with the Islamic world, as well as a means to project the ruler's own qualities as a just and wise king. In the next example of pillar re-erection, Firuz Shah Tughluq's eulogistic chronicles reveal clearly how the rhetorical logic of *'aja'ib* produced not only a connection between the reuse of pre-Islamic architectural forms and kingship, but also a mystical basis for this kingship.

The Pillar of Firuz Shah

In the case of Firuz Shah's reinstallation of the ancient Ashokan pillar (third century BCE), Islamic histories are more forthcoming about the events and effects of its reuse. As the lines quoted in the introduction to this chapter show, the author of the *Sirat-i Firozshahi* used the rhetorical logic of the *'aja'ib* as a framing device to give meaning to both the ruler and

The Wisdom to Wonder

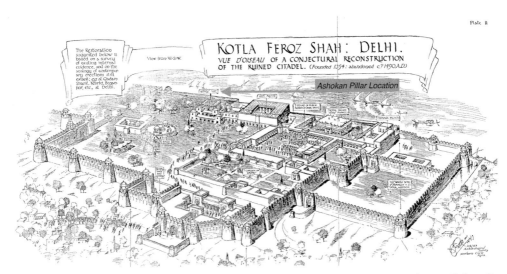

Figure 3.11: Conjectural drawing of the Firuz Shah Kotla Fort, Delhi. J. A. Page, 'A Memoir on Kotla Firoz Shah, Delhi with a Translation of Sirat-i Firozshahi', *Memoirs of the Archaeological Survey of India* 52 (1937), Plate II.

the wonder of Creation he brought to the centre of his new fort in Delhi. The pillar is one of an unknown number that were originally set up by the Mauryan Emperor Ashoka in the third century BCE to spread the Buddhist faith across India. Of the twenty that have been discovered, all were made of the same polished, buff-coloured sandstone. Some had animal capitals, such as lions, bulls and elephants. They weigh about 40 tons and are 14 metres in height. It was after the conquest of Sind that Firuz Shah decided to take possession of one of these wondrous columns (thought to have been 4,000 years old) and to bring it, without its animal capital, to the banks of the Jumna River, the site of his fort, the Firuz Kotla, in the newly built city of Firuzabad [Figure 3.11 and Figure 3.12]. In verse, in the *Sirat-i Firozshahi*, the singularity of the pillar is explained: 'None ever saw such a pillar under the canopy of the heavens which is unsupported by any poles.'[37] It is also important to note that the author believed that the pillar was beyond the grasp of reason – a true mark of an *'ajiba*:

> The sages and wise men of the time were simply astonished at the sight, and though they dived deep into the sea of thought they succeeded not in bringing out the pearl of the solution of these secrets – namely whence and how this heavy and lofty stone monolith was brought to this place [...] Verily such an achievement could hardly have been accomplished by human beings for the simple reason that it is beyond the powers of Man.[38]

The text goes on to remark that there was only one man endowed with the ability to reckon with the ancient pillar and perceive the truth of its existence. This man, of course, was Sultan

Figure 3.12: Ashokan pillar on pyramidal structure. Patrick A. Rogers.

Firuz Shah Tughluq. Consequently, the pillar would not only stand as an example of *'aja'ib*, but also as a reminder of Firuz Shah's unmatched reasoning powers.

In his account and illustrations [Figure 3.13 and Figure 3.14] of the transportation process, the anonymous author of the *Sirat-i Firozshahi* reiterates how wise men and scholars – who likened themselves to Ibn Sina, Plato and Aristotle – possessed insufficient powers of reason as they could not solve the many logistical problems of transporting and re-erecting the column:

> Thereupon His Majesty the King of Islam who has been adorned and amply endowed by God with all religious and worldly virtues and with sound knowledge and perfect wisdom, himself devised ingenious plans and methods of each operation connected with this achievement.[39]

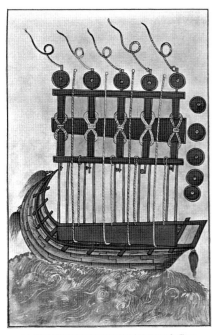 

(a). Removing wheels of the cart from one side and tying ropes and pulling up the pillar to place it in the boat.   (b). Arrival of boat with pillar at the bank of the Jamna, (near Delhi) tying ropes to the pillar to remove it from the boat and place it on the cart.

Figure 3.13: Illustration of the transportation by boat of the Ashokan pillar to Delhi. A. Page, 'A Memoir on Kotla Firoz Shah, Delhi with a Translation of Sirat-i Firozshahi', *Memoirs of the Archaeological Survey of India* 52 (1937), Plate VI, a–b.

The pillar was first taken down in a nail-biting and spectacular set of steps that required the manpower of twenty thousand men. It was then transported by land and river and re-erected on a pyramidal platform[40] by a complex system of pulleys. Paving stones of black, white and red stones from all over the realm were laid at the foot of the pillar. The column was gilded and capped with an elaborate copper finial. In its new position, the pillar was renamed Minar-i Zarin or the golden minaret. The gleaming gold and copper as well as the elevated placement of the pillar ensured its visibility from multiple vantage points. Boatmen on the Jumna, visitors coming to enjoy the gardens from older parts of the city, the faithful leaving the mosque after prayer, all would have beheld the pillar and connected it in their minds to Firuz Shah himself.

In the opening lines of his description of the pillar, the author of the *Sirat-i Firozshahi* reveals it to certainly have been an object of wonder, but he also points out that, in devising the process of its re-erection, the Shah made the pillar a token of the unequalled reasoning power he claimed to possess. After Firuz Shah's death, his intellect as

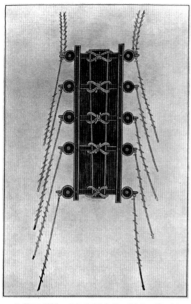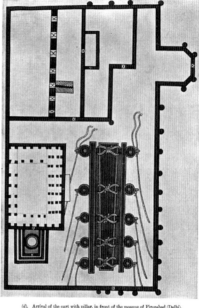

Figure 3.14: Illustration of the transportation by cart of the Ashokan pillar to the Firuz Shah Kotla Fort, Delhi. J. A. Page, 'A Memoir on Kotla Firoz Shah, Delhi with a Translation of Sirat-i Firozshahi', *Memoirs of the Archaeological Survey of India* 52 (1937), Plate VI, c–d.

exemplified by the pillar was reinterpreted as a mystical power that qualified him to be seen as the Perfect Man (*insan-i kamil*), as revealed in Shams Siraj 'Afif's panegyric history, *Tarikh-i Firuz Shahi*. Written after Timur sacked Delhi and thus after the death of Firuz Shah in 1388, 'Afif's account of the pillar's re-erection would be framed as an *'ajiba* and within the mystical terms of the *manaqib* idiom of writing.[41] The mystical turn did not mean the faculties of reason were transposed with magic. Instead, they were now mutually supportive of the ruler's power and ascendancy over his fellow man. Originally, *manaqib* literature recounted the miracles and merits of holy men, usually Sufi founders of mystic orders, for teaching purposes.[42] From within this textual discourse, the *'aja'ib* or wonders of Creation not only revealed God's work but that of his principal man, 'whose perfection consists in his distance from humanity'.[43] In the early fifteenth century, the *'aja'ib* were no longer a means for a ruler to show his reason, but they and the ruler were signified as indexical markers of God's cosmic order. Firuz Shah's discovery, removal and reinstallation of the Ashokan pillar were not acts based on contingency (political or social), but they were acts emanating from God who works through his shadow on earth: the Perfect Man.

Figure 3.15: Inscription in Brahmi of Buddhist edicts on the Ashokan pillar. Amit Bhatnagar.

In his writings about the reinstallation of the Ashokan pillar, 'Afif states that he saw the process as a boy of 12. This does not mean, however, that he is furnishing an eyewitness account nor that he is focused on researching the historical connection of the pillar to actual pre Islamic kings. Instead, he connects the pillar's origins to stories found in the ancient Sanskrit epic, the *Mahabharata*. The pillar that was brought with such dexterity to Delhi, 'Afif writes, was one of a pair that had been fashioned by the giant Bhim, the youngest of the mythical Pandava brothers, to function as his staff. When he died, Bhim left them in the vicinity of Delhi as his memorial. When Firuz Shah found the pillars, he was struck by their majesty; 'Afif uses the Persian word *'aja'ibat* to describe what the king saw.[44] The writer next describes the moving of one of the pillars to Delhi in much the same way as it is described in the *Sirat-i Firozshahi*. He ends the event with a note about the inscription on the pillar [Figure 3.15] to punctuate Firuz Shah's special and elevated status among men, both Hindus and Muslims:

Some said that some infidels had read this Indian script, and that it was written there that no one would move this pillar from its place by force, be *they Muslim Sultans or arrogant Rajahs*. Yet in later times a wise king was to come by the name of Firuz who would intend it, and remove this pillar from its place. For such favour springs from God's Grace that whatever Sultan Firuz intended, God in his Grace will grant him his wish.[45]

The ancient pillar as described by 'Afif was much more than a vehicle to test and reveal the reasoning power of the king. God put it on Earth for a future time when by providence Firuz Shah, whom he also put there, would come upon it. Firuz Shah was, in other words, always meant to move the ancient pillar to his city; 'Afif writes, 'some said some infidels had read' this future event that was written on the pillar itself!⁴⁶ Unlike in the *Sirat-i Firozshahi*, where the pillar is portrayed as a sign of Firuz Shah's uncommon reason, in 'Afif's history the *'ajiba* becomes an index of the ruler's status as God's shadow on Earth, or in Sufi terminology, the Perfect Man.

By the start of the fourteenth century, the *'aja'ib* in the form of ancient Hindu pillars functioned as both a sign of the Muslim ruler's rationality, as it did for Iltutmish and Firuz Shah in the *Sirat-i Firozshahi*, and as an index of his human perfection, as in 'Afif's panegyric. The Mughal rulers were later to adopt this function and meaning of the *'aja'ib* with zest. The architectural programmes of Akbar and Shah Jahan, in particular, utilized the symbolism of the pillar to signify their kingships based on Sufi ideals of the Perfect Man.⁴⁷

Conclusion

This study introduced the concept of *'aja'ib* as an organizing principle based in an Islamic epistemology, in order to better understand how Muslim rulers reckoned with the historical remains of pre-Islamic India. From this framework, we can now conclude that recent acts of desecrating the remains of ancient culture in Iraq and Syria were not reiterations of a unified past Islamic practice, as both the fundamentalists and the popular media would lead us to believe. While instances of temple desecration and destruction certainly did occur in the past, they did not define the whole of Islamic history, nor even the majority of Islamic history. From the Abbasid caliphate to the early modern era, Muslims practised a mode of interaction with ancient artefacts that signified them as objects of wonder, or *'aja'ib*, and as signs of God's cosmic order worthy of preservation and reverence. Another conclusion that can be drawn from the study of the *'aja'ib* is that Islamic architectural practices, such as the re-erection of ancient pillars, were embedded in an Islamic epistemological framework that was neither monolithic nor static. By examining the changing conceptions and uses of the *'aja'ib* category between the thirteenth and early fifteenth centuries, I have shown that there were a variety of interpretations of pre-Islamic artefacts, as well as a variety of subjectivities informing and informed by the *'aja'ib*. For example, the interpretation of the Indian pillar changed from a sign of the ruler's supreme reasoning powers to an index of his sacred kingship, as the Indian Islamic ruler transformed from a reasoning individual, like Iltutmish, into God's Perfect Man, like Firuz Shah. As Islamic rule spread further south, the *'aja'ib* category would be used by Islamic historians to take account of the new architectural and artistic curiosities that they confronted, such as the cave temples of Ellora (fifth–eighth centuries), in Maharashtra, India.⁴⁸ Later developments also include the Mughal use of the aesthetic effect of *'aja'ib*, i.e., wonderment, to design awesome architectural forms. The rhetorical logic of *'aja'ib* would thus be a reoccurring conceptual framework, used both in describing pre-Islamic architectural forms and in shaping Indian Islamic architectural practice.

Acknowledgements

I would like to express my profound appreciation to Henning Bauer for his fantastic editing skills and his assistance with the Arabic and Persian translations and transliteration. I am also grateful to Taymiya Zaman for her comments. I would also like to thank Stephennie Mulder and the anonymous reviewers for their careful reading of the early drafts of this chapter.

Notes

1. J. A. Page, *A Memoir on Kotla Firoz Shah, Delhi with a Translation of Sirat-i Firozshahi: Memoirs of the Archaeological Survey of India No. 52* (Delhi, 1937), 33.
2. See Robert Hillenbrand, 'Political Symbolism in Early Indo-Islamic Mosque Architecture: The Case of Ajmir *Iran* 26 (1988): 105–17; William J. McKibben, 'The Monumental Pillars of Firuz Shah Tughluq', *Ars Orientalis* 24 (1994): 105–18; Finbarr B. Flood, 'Pillars, Palimpsests, and Princely Practices: Translating the Past in Sultanate Delhi', *RES: Anthropology and Aesthetics* 43 (2003): 95–116; Richard M. Eaton and Phillip B. Wagoner, *Power, Memory, Architecture: Contested Sites on India's Deccan Plateau, 1300–1600* (New Delhi: Oxford University Press, 2014); Alka Patel, *Building Communities in Gujarat: Architecture and Society during the Twelfth Through Fourteenth Centuries* (Leiden: Brill, 2004).
3. Wendy M. K. Shaw, 'The Islam in Islamic Art History: Secularism and Public Discourse', *Journal of Art Historiography* 6 (2012): 10. Samer Akkach made this point earlier and further notes, 'the deconstruction of the Islamic has only complexified the question without offering viable alternatives'. See Samer Akkach, *Cosmology and Architecture in Modern Islam: Architectural Reading of Mystical Ideas* (Albany: State University of New York Press, 2005), xii.
4. Akkach's discussion of Oleg Grabar's psychological and aesthetic interpretation of Islamic art and architectural ornamentation explains why he remained adamant about keeping the mystical, symbolic, and epistemological influences of Islam out of the study of Islamic art and architecture. Grabar's interpretation was mainly due to the lack of textual sources that clearly outline this connection.
5. My understanding of 'deep interpretation' is loosely drawn from Arthur Danto's writings on the approach that demands larger conceptual frameworks to interpret a work of art, thus going beyond the physical object of art and the artist's stated intentions. See Arthur C. Danto, *The Philosophical Disenfranchisement of Art* (New York: Columbia University Press, 1986).
6. "Aja'ib', in *Encyclopedia of Arabic Literature*, eds Julie Meisami and Paul Starkey (London: Routledge, 1998), 65.
7. Ibid., 65.

8. The famous books of travel to India include Ibn Khordadbeh, *Kitab al-Masalik wa al-Mamalik* ('Book of Itineraries and Kingdoms') completed in 870; Abu Zayd al-Sirafi, *Silsilat al-Tawarikh* ('Chain of Histories') completed in 916; Buzurg Ibn Shahriyar, *Kitab Aja'ib al-Hind* ('Wonders of India') completed in 1009.
9. Travis Zadeh, *Mapping Frontiers across Medieval Islam: Geography, Translation and the 'Abbasid Empire* (London: I.B. Tauris, 2011), 1.
10. Ibid., 1.
11. For a discussion on this epistemological turn in Islamic history, see Travis Zadeh, 'The Wiles of Creation: Philosophy, Fiction, and the *'Aja'ib* Tradition', *Middle Eastern Literatures* 13.1 (2010): 21–48.
12. Aristotle, *Aristotle's Metaphysics*, ed. W. D. Ross (Oxford: Clarendon Press, 1924), section 982b, Perseus Digital Library, accessed March 16, 2017, http://www.perseus.tufts.edu/hopper/text?doc=Perseus%3Atext%3A1999. 01.0052%3Abook%3D1%3Asection%3D982b.
13. In his discussion of al-Qazwini's method of writing in the *'Aja'ib al-makhluqat*, Travis Zadeh writes that '[f]or al-Qazwini speculation [*nazar*] ultimately bears a theological dimension, which he aligns with a scientific pursuit of discovering the order of the natural world, based on an implicit teleological argument from design for the proof of God, as reflected through the marvels of creation'. Zadeh, 'Wiles of Creation', 29.
14. Edward Sachau, *Alberuni's India*, vol. 1 (London: Trübner & Co., 1910), 27.
15. Qazwini received information from travellers, folk tales and earlier geographical encyclopaedias like Yaqut's *Muʻjam al-buldan* (1224–28), from which he borrowed heavily when writing *Athar al-bilad*. Maria Kowalska, 'The Sources of Al-Qazwini's Athar Al-Bilad', *Folia Orientalia* 8 (1966): 41–88.
16. Persis Berlekamp, *Wonder, Image, Cosmos in Medieval Islam* (New Haven: Yale University Press, 2011), 21–22.
17. Edward Sachau, *Alberuni's India*, vol. 2 (London: Trübner & Co., 1910), 246.
18. Jamal J. Elias, *Aisha's Cushion: Religious Art, Perception, and Practice in Islam* (Cambridge, MA: Harvard University Press, 2012), 117–20; Yohanan Friedmann, 'Medieval Muslim Views of Indian Religions', *Journal of the American Oriental Society* 95.2 (1975): 214–21.
19. Sachau, *Alberuni's India*, vol. 1, 22.
20. Ibid., 152.
21. Zayde Antrim, *Routes and Realms: The Power of Place in the Early Islamic World* (Oxford: Oxford University Press, 2012), 12–13.
22. Muhammad Nizamuddin, *Introduction to the Jawami ul-Hikayat wa Lawami ul-Riwayat of Sadid ud-din Muhammad al 'Awfi* (London: Luzac & Co., 1929), 249.
23. S. H. Askari, *On Awfi's Jawami-al Hikayat* (Patna: Khuda Bakhsh Oriental Public Library, 1995), 40.
24. Ibid., 41.
25. Ibid., 41.
26. Ibid., 42.
27. Ibid., 42.
28. Travis Zadeh, 'Wiles of Creation', 35.

29. Hasan Nizami, *Tajud Din Hasan Nizami's Taj ul Ma'athir, Crown of Glorious Deeds*, trans. Bhagwat Saroop (Delhi: Saud Ahmad Dehlavi, 1998), 322 (emphasis added).
30. Finbarr B. Flood, *Objects of Translation: Material Culture and Medieval 'Hindu-Muslim' Encounter* (Princeton: Princeton University Press, 2011), 242.
31. Juzjani, *Tabakat-i Nasiri* (London: Gilbert & Rivington, 1881), 616, n.3.
32. The translation is taken from the panel next to the pillar at the Quwwat al-Islam.
33. Vincent A. Smith, 'The Iron Pillar of Delhi (Mihrauli) and the Emperor Candra (Chandra)', *The Journal of the Royal Asiatic Society of Great Britain and Ireland* 29.1 (1897): 1–18.
34. The material and molecular consititution of the iron pillar has been the subject of scientific study. For the recent research, see Matthew V. Veazey, '1,600 Years Young', *Materials Performance* 44.7 (2005): 16–19.
35. John Briggs, *History of the Rise of the Mahomedan Power in India*, vol. 1 (London: R. Cambray & Co., 1908), 211.
36. Quoted in Flood, 'Pillars, Palimpsests, and Princely Practices', 105.
37. Page, *Memoir on Kotla Firoz Shah*, 34.
38. Ibid., 35.
39. Ibid., 35.
40. The pyramid is stepped with three terraces that diminish from 36, to 25, to about 17 metres square.
41. The sense of wonder and magic with which 'Afif framed the installation of the Ashokan pillar within the mystical concept of the Perfect Man was also used in the Mughal period to frame the authority of emperors such as Akbar, Jahangir and Shah Jahan. See Azfar Moin, *The Millennial Sovereign: Sacred Kingship and Sainthood in Islam* (New York: Columbia University Press, 2012). For another discussion of the Sufi concept of the Perfect Man and its relationship to Indian Islamic rule and patronage of architecture, see Wayne Begley, 'The Myth and Meaning of the Taj Mahal', *The Art Bulletin* 61.1 (1979): 31–32.
42. P. Hardy, *Historians of Medieval India; Studies in Indo-Muslim Historical Writing* (London: Luzac & Co., 1966), 41.
43. Ibid., 51.
44. Shams Siraj 'Afif, *Tarikh-i Firuz Shahi* (Calcutta: Baptist Mission Press, 1891, repr. 2006), 308.
45. Ibid., 313 (emphasis added).
46. Ibid., 313.
47. A study of the *'aja'ib* in the early modern history of the Mughals will be the focus of a future article.
48. Carl W. Ernst, 'Ellora Temples as Viewed by Indo-Muslim Authors', in *Beyond Turk and Hindu: Rethinking Religious Identities in Islamicate South Asia*, eds David Gilmartin and Bruce B. Lawrence (Gainesville: University Press of Florida, 2000), 98–120.

Part 2

Imagining Antiquity in Ottoman Lands

4

Explosions and Expulsions in Ottoman Athens: A Heritage Perspective on the Temple of Olympian Zeus

Elizabeth Cohen

Ottomanization and Islamization in the Ottoman Empire

The Ottoman Empire developed as a culturally and socially complex space with already-extant built environments that were gradually Ottomanized and Islamized. Reconfiguring the landscape involved developing everyday spaces to accommodate the needs of local Muslims as well as incorporating structures that symbolized Islam and the sultan.[1] Ottomanization and Islamization involved converting churches into mosques, developing *mahalle* (neighbourhood) networks, and introducing necessary social, economic, religious, and educational facilities (such as hammams, *çeşme*s/fountains, *bedesten*s/ covered markets, *caravanserai*s, *medrese*s and *imaret*s/public kitchens); later developments included the Ottomanization of the Tanzimat period.[2] In the Ottoman Balkans this urbanization resulted in spaces that layered or fused ancient, Byzantine, and emergent Ottoman forms that were in turn shaped by Timurid and Turcoman aesthetics.[3] However, there are currently few analyses of how the Ottomans perceived their inherited cultural landscapes, landscapes that were replete with pre-Ottoman sites and buildings. In discussions of Ottoman Greece as well as other former Ottoman territories, Ottoman perspectives are sometimes overlooked or misrepresented, as past studies have perhaps somewhat uncritically relied on accounts by European travellers (including topographers, antiquarians, and diplomats). The travellers' philhellenic imperial gaze was largely fixed on the benchmark period of the classical era, and this perspective often shaped their perceptions and thus influenced their writings and drawings: they often overlooked other versions of Greece in search of classical originals, or deplored contemporary conditions as a 'fall from grace'. It is therefore important to understand that Ottomanization and Islamization involved not only spatial development, but also cultural interpretation, because urban spaces were viewed and imagined through many generations of Ottoman Muslim eyes.

Greece's built landscape underwent such processes of Ottomanization and Islamization for more than four hundred years.[4] Following independence, many stakeholder groups within modern Greece worked toward identifying, defining, and creating a nationscape capable of endorsing a national and cultural identity that presented an unmediated Helleno-Christianity. Greek identity largely perceived its Ottoman pasts as distinctly un-Greek, as taints on the nationscape that represented 'the Turkish yoke'. Nineteenth- and twentieth-century Hellenization and modernization all worked toward spatial and mental de-Ottomanization. While this was never fully achieved, the result was that Greece's Ottoman memories and heritages became marginalized, and these Ottoman pasts predominantly exist as passive remnants in a heritage-scape that promotes Greece's ancient and Byzantine pasts. It is only relatively recently that attention has turned toward Greece's nonconforming heritages, and there has been a growing understanding that its nationscape is a palimpsest with an extraordinary variety of pasts. New readings of Greece's cultural landscapes are increasingly uncovering the interweaving of perspectives and exploring their contradictions and differences.[5] This chapter will examine the renowned city of Athens, which was pivotal in the formation of modern Greece's identity and holds an almost unique position within the international imagination as the birthplace of the 'West' and 'Europe'. Incorporating Ottoman sources and re-reading European travellers' accounts together paints a picture of a less familiar Athens, but a story that is no less important a part of the city's urban biography. Particular attention will be paid to the Olympieion that, like many sites in Athens, has a layered complexity that reflects cross-cultural uses. Unlike many other ancient Athenian sites, the Olympieion is distinctive because its *in situ* interpretation more actively incorporates its Ottoman uses as a key part of the site's biography.

The Layering of Ottoman Athens's Complex Heritage

> In sum, nowhere on the face of the earth in all the seven climes are there such noteworthy wonders and sight-worthy marvels as this city of mild climate and ancient entrepôt of Athens and its surroundings.[6]

Athens surrendered to Turahanoğlu Ömer Bey in 1456. Ottoman rule, with the exception of two short periods of Venetian occupation (1466 and 1687–88), effectively lasted until 1830, and the garrison itself remained on the Acropolis until March 1833.[7] Following the visit of Sultan Mehmed II in 1458, Athens (Ottoman Atina) gained initial concessions[8] and became the centre of a *kadılık* (judicial district) within the Eğribos (modern Euboea) *sancak*.[9] Administrative changes occurred in the mid-seventeenth century when Athens was placed under the Kızlar Ağası (Chief Eunuch) who appointed a *voyvoda* (superintendent), and again in 1760 when the city and its environs entered the *malikane* tax-system (deed of lifetime ownership).[10] Athens was a significant town within the Ottoman Empire, although European accounts presented it as dilapidated and empty. Indeed, the city initially prospered and developed, and by the middle of the sixteenth century Athens's population was the fourth largest in the empire and had expanded beyond the city's walls by the late sixteenth century.[11] Athens continued as an important and sizeable urban centre within the late Ottoman Empire, with an active local market and a population of approximately 10,000 in 1817.[12] Athens's population was divided between Orthodox Greeks, Albanians, and Ottoman Muslims (who were in the minority), as well as a Frankish community and 'foreign' residents.[13] Although little is known about their specific organization,[14] roughly speaking the Athenian Muslims were divided between the garrison under the control of the *dizdar* (fortress commander), which was located on the Acropolis precinct, and those inhabiting the central areas of the lower town whom Athenian Panayis Skouzes (1776–1847) recollected as a mixture of '25 Muslim gypsy families, blacksmiths all, and some 30 families of Ethiopians [as well as] cobblers, tobacco-sellers, barbers, tailors [while] the rest followed no trade'.[15]

Ottoman Athens was divided into eight *platomata* (openings) and over thirty *mahalles* (neighbourhoods),[16] although the different communities were not strictly segregated within these areas.[17] Over the centuries, Athens developed into a distinctive Ottoman town with much of the administrative, mercantile, and socio-religious activities and their accompanying structures largely centred around the bazaar near the former Roman Agora.[18] Ottoman Athens boasted shops, warehouses, coffee houses, as well as a madrasa (seminary or college), the *Voyvodalık* (residence of the *voyvoda*), the *Kadılık* (residence of the judge),[19] the *Kousegeio* (town elders' congregation hall), and a prison, in addition to several mosques, *tekke*s (Sufi lodges), hammams, and *çeşme*s.[20] The Ottoman Athenian architectural make-up was a combination of newly built structures or converted and reused ancient buildings.

The Different Views of Ottoman Athens

It is almost a truism to point out that the city of Athens has long been renowned for its iconic classical architecture, literature, and art. Ottoman Athenian Muslims, however, were often accused by antiquarians, archaeologists, or classicists either of not being particularly interested in Athens or its ancient legacies,[21] or they were represented as being destructive or negligent. Many travellers would have agreed with the concern expressed by antiquarian Edward Dodwell (1767–1832) that Athens's antiquities were being threatened by the 'selfish rapacity of amateurs, and the destructive ignorance of the Mohamedans'.[22] Travellers' accounts are full of details of outright reuse of sites and materials, as well as of incorporation, destruction, and removal. Perhaps the most famous Ottoman-period reuse of ancient structures involved the garrison's occupation of the Acropolis. The Parthenon temple-turned-*basilica* functioned as a mosque, probably from the time of Mehmed II's visit, while the Ottoman garrison continued the Frankish-Crusader use of the Erechtheion and Propylaia as residences. Dodwell's drawings indicate that the space between the ancient structures was filled in with other dwellings, as well as shrubs and trees – a stark contrast to the brilliant white of today's stripped-back Acropolis [Figure 4.1]. Elsewhere in Athens, a part of the *voyvoda*'s residence occupied the portico of the Library of Hadrian; the Capuchin monastery used the Lysicrates Monument as a reading room; while the Tower of the Winds tower-turned-church functioned as a famous *tekke*.[23] Ancient sculptural and architectural components were also incorporated into new structures. Hadrian's Gate was worked into the wall built by the *voyvoda* Hacı Ali Haseki Ağa in 1787, and the pieces of the Temple of Nike were rebuilt into a bastion in 1686.[24] Classical scholar John B. S. Morritt (*c*.1772–1843) noted that '[o]ver almost every door is an antique statue or

Figure 4.1: View of west front of the Parthenon, plate. After Edward Dodwell, *Views in Greece*, from *Drawings by Edward Dodwell, ESQ. F. S. A & C.* (London: Rodwell and Martin, 1821), unnumbered plate. Wikimedia Commons.

basso-rilievo',[25] while Dodwell, antiquarian Richard Chandler (1737–1810), and politician Sir John Cam Hobhouse (1786–1869), observed the reworking of ancient stonework into Muslim tombstones.[26] Dodwell also observed the removal of an epistyle block (WW.AA.01) from the Erechtheion's western façade, which was then reinstalled over the entrance of the Acropolis bearing an Ottoman Turkish inscription dedicated 'in praise of the strong fortress and of the zeal displayed in its construction by Mustapha Effendi, the Voivode'.[27] Remonstrating with the *dizdar*, Dodwell claimed that the latter pointed at the Parthenon and Erechtheion and declared, 'What right have you to complain? Where are the marbles which were taken by your countrymen from the temples?'[28] Yet other Athenian antiquities were fully destroyed or removed from their original contexts, such as the Ilissos Bridge, which also met its fate during the building of Hacı Ali Haseki Ağa's wall, and of course Lord Elgin's infamous removal of the Parthenon/Elgin Marbles and Kore 'Maiden 3'.[29]

While western travellers reflected upon the fate of antiquities under the sultan and his subjects and worked them into homilies against the Ottoman Empire, visitors from Ottoman-ruled territories and the city's residents had their own perspectives. Accounts such as that by Skouzes provide some tantalizing glimpses as to local Greeks' perceptions of their contemporary environs.[30] Descriptions found in works by Ottoman travellers and the city's Muslim residents provide yet more impressions, although there are few such descriptions readily available and these are only recently being woven into urban biographies. Two key Ottoman texts are those by Evliya Çelebi and Mahmud Efendi. Evliya Çelebi (1611–1682) was a widely travelled and learned Ottoman writer whose *Seyahatname* ('Book of Travels') features a huge variety of descriptions of the lands and people that he visited during his voyages within the Ottoman realm and beyond. Less well known is the *Tarih-i Medinetü'l-Hukema* ('History of the City of the Philosophers') by Mahmud Efendi, whose family had lived in Greece and who became the *müfti* (jurisconsult) of Athens in 1698/99. Written with the aid of two Greek abbots, Mahmud Efendi's unique work fused ancient Greek texts and Ottoman and Arabic traditions with contemporary observations and conversations, resulting in an Ottoman and Islamicate account of Athenian history. Attending to such Ottoman perspectives provides new insights, as they indicate how local sites were reused and reinterpreted through processes of Ottomanization and Islamization. The Ottoman experience seems to have consisted of taking existing sites and weaving in local legends, ancient histories, and Qur'anic traditions, in a manner that was not strict imposition, but rather one of assimilation that made the spaces legible to different users and audiences.[31] Evliya Çelebi urged his readers that '[a]ll the Christian and Coptic chroniclers agree' that Athens was founded by Solomon and developed by his son Rehoboam.[32] Elizabeth Key Fowden has pointed out that there is a long tradition of Arab and Ottoman authors associating significant buildings with Solomon, and in this way their cultural surroundings are incorporated into Islamic and Ottoman histories.[33] Apart from Solomon, Ottoman authors also associated Athens and its buildings with Greek philosophers. Athens was known as 'city of the sages', divine Plato's place, the City of Illuminations or the City of Walkers.[34] Where Evliya Çelebi felt that the Tower of the Winds was known as Plato's pavilion, Mahmud Efendi associated it with Socrates the Wise.[35] Evliya Çelebi's account furthermore indicates how the Parthenon's sculptures were viewed through Ottoman eyes, as he perceived the figures as jinns, Satan, Azrael, and houris.[36] Through their (sometimes undiplomatic) encounters with Athenian Muslims, the western travellers also communicate local Muslim uses of place. Chandler and Hobhouse described how the cannon below the Erechtheion and above the Propylaia announced Ramadan; the same area was also used for the garrison women's promenade.[37] Athens's many caves were also spaces for local practices, and Dodwell described how he offended a group of Ottoman Muslim women and his Greek guide when he ate the women's fertility offerings that were left at the Tomb of Cimon near the Church of Agios Demetrios.[38]

Many Ottoman reuses were perceived more in terms of continuity of use, and it is important to remember that many ancient sites had been abandoned, destroyed, or reused during the intervening centuries since their initial construction. Adapting buildings, sites, and cultural landscapes – whether for pragmatic or symbolic purposes – is a common process in inherited built environments, and should not be thought of as a particularly Muslim phenomenon. Christianization and Byzantinization in Greco-Roman cities saw the reinterpretation of urban spaces through, for example, the carving of crosses onto statues and buildings, the use of spolia in churches, houses, walls, and fortifications, and the reorientation of internal spaces.[39] The Parthenon and the Erechtheion on the Athenian

Acropolis, as well as the Temple of Hephaistos (Theseion) in the Agora, were all converted into churches; indeed, the Christianized Parthenon became a site of pilgrimage.[40] During the Ottoman period, where holy sites were Islamized or Ottomanized, their ancient identities and Christian memories were sometimes venerated or respected. Ottoman Sultan Mehmed II (r.1444–46 and 1451–81), who visited Troy, identified with Alexander the Great and Julius Caesar and considered himself heir to Byzantium. He also visited Athens

> and was amazed, and he praised it, and especially the Acropolis as he went up into it. And from the ruins and the remains, he reconstructed mentally the ancient buildings, being a wise man and a Philhellene and as a great king, he conjectured how they must have been originally.[41]

The Parthenon was particularly considered miraculous. Archaeologist, historian, and author of *Christianity and Islam under the Sultans*, Frederick W. Hasluck, noted the seventeenth-century belief that light through the transparent marble window in the Parthenon was taken as a sign from the Prophet Muhammad to Mehmed II when the Parthenon *basilica* began to be used as a mosque, while an Ottoman Muslim allegedly fell down dead when he attempted to violate a Christian tomb, and another was supposedly killed by a ricochet after firing at an icon of the Virgin.[42] Other sites were similarly thought to be safeguarded by various otherworldly forces, as when Yusuf Ağa and his family were blown up after his attempt to bombard the Church of Agios Demetrios (henceforth known by the epithet 'the Bombadier').[43]

The Ottoman Olympieion and Its Multiple Presentations

The management of the Greco-Roman sanctuary of Olympian Zeus during the Ottoman period was similarly a mixture of reuse, reincorporation, and destruction, and this site also had many local traditions and tales associated with it.[44] Referred to by European travellers as the Temple of Olympian Jove or Hadrian's Temple, Evliya Çelebi described how it was magically built for Solomon by demons, and both Evliya and Mahmud Efendi called the site the Throne of Balqis (the Qur'anic name of the Queen of Sheba).[45] Indeed, Fowden has tentatively advanced the idea that the name given to the nearby Hadrian's Gate of Porta Vasilopoula (Gate of the Princess) could in fact be a Greek echo of the Ottoman Muslim association of the site with Balqis.[46] The Olympieion became an important religious site for all Ottoman Athenians as it was used as a common prayer ground, similar to the group who can just be discerned convening near the columns in Louis Dupré's drawing [Figure 4.2].[47]

Evliya Çelebi, referring to this phenomenon, wrote that

> [a]ll the Muslims of the city resort to it, fully armed, for the prayer of rain and for the two festivals […] It is a sight worth seeing, an open-air prayer-ground palace with soaring columns in praise of which the tongue falls short.[48]

Figure 4.2: 'Le Temple de Jupiter Olympien et l'Acropolis d'Athènes' ('The Temple of the Olympian Jupiter and the Acropolis in Athens'), plate. Louis Dupré, *Taxidi stin Athina kai stin Konstantinopoli* (*'Un voyage à Athènes et à Constantinople'*), ed. Manolis Vlachos (Athens: Olkos, [1825] 1994), plate 73. Aikaterini Laskaridis Foundation.

European travellers similarly described having witnessed rain prayers held during long-term droughts. Held over many days and accompanied by flocks of sheep, these prayers were conducted by Athenian Orthodox Christians and Muslims alike:

> prayers and holy rites were performed in [the Olympieion] for nine successive days, three of which were devoted to the Mahometans, three to the Christians, three to the strangers and slaves. [...] The Mahometan priest supplicated for all [...] but it was contrived by a little address that the animal creation should appear to second the entreaty of the Turks, for, just as the turbaned worshippers bowed themselves with one accord to the ground, and called upon the name of their god, the lambs of a large flock collected near the spot, who had just at the instant been separated from the ewes, began to bleat, and were answered by their dams. I know not that anyone was deceived by the scheme.[49]

Although this is a fascinating example of the reuse of an ancient site, research into the Ottoman Olympieion mosque is scarce. According to Hasluck, the use of the Olympieion site is unusual, because Ottoman Turkish rain prayer sites were marked by a *türbe*, dome, or pulpit and were normally located in the open air, on high ground, and outside the town proper.[50] One explanation as to why the Olympieion was used as an open prayer site can perhaps be found in historian Dimitris Karidis's comment that until the end of the nineteenth century it was almost as though the site was in the countryside because there was limited building activity around the Olympieion.[51]

Both Ottoman and European travellers mentioned the presence of elevated structures within the Olympieion. Evliya Çelebi described the Olympieion's 'vaults of Chosroes and lofty domes' while an array of European travellers – such as Dodwell, Chandler, Hobhouse, classical scholar Peter Edmund Laurent (1796–1837), admiral Charles Colville Frankland (1792–1876), diplomat William Turner (1792–1867), Captain Thomas A. Trant (1805–1832), American historian Henry M. Baird (1832–1906), and French historians Joseph-François Michaud (1767–1839) and Jean-Joseph-François Poujoulat (1808–1880) – all referred to an elevated residence of a hermit or saint.[52] Other more fantastical stories claimed that the temple supported a Flying Castle,[53] or contained a treasure with a supernatural guardian:

> the brick building is believed, by some of the superstitious inhabitants of the place, to be the repository of a great treasure, and the habitation of a supernatural black personage, who watches it all day, and at night amuses himself by jumping from one column to another.[54]

A similar story was related by Dodwell, who claimed that he was approached by an elderly Albanian woman named Cosmichi who informed him: '[y]ou know where the sequins are – but with all your magic you cannot conjure them into your box! For a black [personage] watches them all day; and at night jumps from column to column!' and that the 'building upon the architrave was the repository of the great treasure, and the habitation of a black [personage]'.[55] Hasluck disputed the presence of a hermitage, pointing out that most of the European travellers simply did not believe the story related to them, placed it in the distant past, or claimed that the hermit was long dead.[56] Instead, Hasluck suggested the structure in question was perhaps a cistern or clearing-chamber from an Ottoman aqueduct.[57]

However, it is important to not simply dismiss these stories as figments of the imagination or tall-tales told to the travellers. Often, these unreal features provide insight into how sites were mentally constructed and convey intriguing local perspectives on the ways in which local Muslims experienced their built environments and social and cultural landscapes. For example, Evliya Çelebi similarly claimed to have seen the non-existent mosque's dome on the Parthenon, as part of a process of imagining a more Ottoman view of the landscape.[58] These elaborate and fantastical stories, as well as tales of actual religious use, indicate that the Olympieion was not only used throughout the city's Ottoman period, but also had considerable local significance to both Ottoman Muslims and Orthodox Christians. Such re-readings of the European travellers and increased awareness and use of Ottoman texts reveal the ways in which we can understand how Athens's sites were Islamized and Ottomanized and how they developed their own folkloric traditions. Interpreting Athens's built environment with more varied and cross-cultural descriptions allows us to see the city as an evolving cultural landscape with various superimposed layers of meaning and memories, and not simply in terms of the original and 'authentic' classical structures.

This alternative approach to interpretive readings of Athens is of particular note for the Olympieion. The Olympieion is unusual in terms of contemporary heritage management as its Ottoman uses are clearly marked on a large interpretation panel titled Ολυμπιείον – Πύλη Αδριανού ('Olympieion – Hadrian's Gate') located within the modern archaeological site. This panel describes the open-air mosque during the time of the 'Turkish occupation'; mentions a hermitage or looking-post on top of the architrave at the temple's southeast corner; outlines how Hadrian's Gate was incorporated into 'the Turkish fortification, known as "Haseki's Wall"'; and features drawings by architects Stuart and Revett and German painter J. M. Wittmer.[59] The Olympieion's panel is notable within Athens because it is one of the few to significantly mention Ottoman histories. Thanks to the purifying zeal of architects, urban planners, and archaeologists attempting to create a de-Ottomanized capital city in the nineteenth century that would reflect Greece's unbroken and untainted Helleno-Christian identity, little of the Ottoman city now remains. The few Ottoman-period structures that still exist [Figure 4.3]

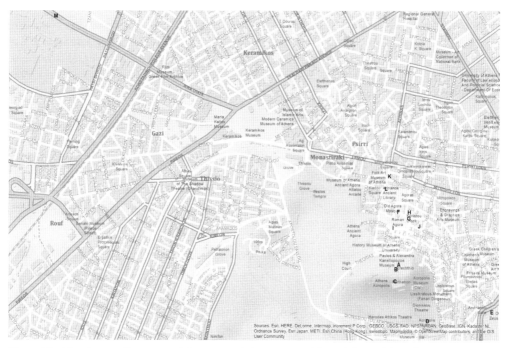

Figure 4.3: Athens's extant Ottoman-period structures: (A) WW.AA.01; (B) Erechtheion; (C) Parthenon; (D) remains of Hacı Ali Haseki Ağ a's wall; (E) Temple of Olympian Zeus; (F) Fethiye Mosque; (G) Tower of the Winds; (H) Medrese; (I) Kioutsouk Mosque; (J) Abid Efendi Hamam; (K) Tzisdarakis Mosque; (L) Library of Hadrian (Voivodalik); (M) remains of Hacı Ali Haseki's estate (Votanikos). Elizabeth Cohen.

include the Fethiye, Kioutsouk, and Tzisdarakis Mosques (near the Roman Agora site), the Abid Efendi Hamam (on Kirristou Street), and the Haseki Ali Ağa Fountain (on Iera Street within the Agricultural University).[60] The extant Ottoman-period sites generally feature minimal or no interpretation that describes their Ottoman pasts. Interpretation panels for the Acropolis or the Tower of the Winds, by way of comparison, either do not mention their Ottoman experiences or else focus on perceived negative histories such as Lord Elgin and Francesco Morosini. Thus, the panel produced for the Olympieion – which is a similarly ancient structure – is unusual in that it aims to provide a full site biography, while its use of European travellers' anecdotes and images injects life and character into its rendition of the site's post-Byzantine uses.

If the modern Olympieion site is relatively quiet compared with Athens's main archaeological tourist destinations, another local tale links it more explicitly with the Tzisdarakis (or Djistaraki) Mosque, a former mosque that stands minaret-less in the middle of the city's hubbub on the corner of Monastiraki Square and opposite the busy Monastiraki metro station. Now operating as the Museum of Greek Folk Art, this 'great mosque with a lofty minaret, and a broad shallow dome' was founded (according to its dedicatory inscription) in 1759 by the local *voyvoda* Mustafa Ağa Tzisdarakis.[61] The Tzisdarakis Mosque was an important urban mosque in the late-Ottoman Athenian period as it was located on two main streets next to the Kato Bazaar (Lower Bazaar), opposite a fountain (hence the building's other name of Kato Sintrivaniou, or the Mosque of the Lower Fountain), and near the *voyvoda*'s residence.[62] A persistent story connected with the Tzisdarakis Mosque is that the *voyvoda* exploded one of the Olympieion's columns so that it could be used for lime in the building's construction.[63] Chandler claimed that this column was 'over-turned with great difficulty',[64] while Dodwell wrote that it took four explosions to bring it down.[65] For having the temerity to use an ancient site as a source of building material, the *voyvoda* has been condemned by European travellers and classicists and this story has been used as evidence of the Ottomans' flagrant disregard for, or ignorance of, Greece's classical past as well as their complicity in its destruction. However, the event was also locally controversial at the time. The Pasha of Eğribos announced that the column was the sultan's property and not only fined the *voyvoda* seventeen or fifteen purses, but also brought about his expulsion from Athens.[66] Not content with these punishments, stories related how the three nearest columns at the Olympieion

> were heard [by the Athenians] at night to lament the loss of their sister! and these nocturnal lamentations did not cease to terrify the inhabitants, till the sacrilegious Voivode, who had been appointed governor of Zetoun, was destroyed by poison.[67]

The concept of the 'ensouled' statue (thought to contain a spirit or *arabim*) is common in tales of the use of antiquities in the Ottoman period, and a similar story was recorded about the Kore removed by Lord Elgin and other Acropolis marbles en route to the Piraeus for their exportation.[68] These tales have been woven into arguments to prove the continuity of

Greek identity and indicate proto-nationalist sentiments. Hobhouse, for example, was told that such statues would remain enchanted 'as long as the Turks are masters of Greece',[69] and while politician Frederic Douglas (1791–1819) doubted the *dızdar* (fortress commander) servant's claim to have heard the statue's cries, he felt that the Athenians in the lower town were not indifferent to these supposed laments.[70] However, Yannis Hamilakis has argued that local anger against the destruction of antiquities does not indicate the development of the modern concept of cultural heritage protection, but rather that locals were afraid of the retribution that would be enacted by these spirits once released.[71] Indeed, the idea of the ensouled statue has a much longer history in the Greco-Roman world,[72] but what is of interest here is that the tale of Tzisdarakis and his (alleged) exploding of a column from the Olympieion has long shadows, as this story of the destructive reuse of the Olympieion's material is sometimes woven into the nearby Fethiye Mosque's site biography as well.[73] The Fethiye Mosque was for a long time thought to have been built following Mehmed II's conquest of Athens because *fethiye* indicated 'victory', but it is now dated to 1668–70. However, the mosque is still popularly attributed to the period of Ottoman conquest, and thus is sometimes felt to represent Athens's shameful past under foreign rule. During the debate concerning the construction of an operational mosque for Athens's Muslims,[74] Tzisdarakis's destruction of the Olympieion column was sometimes conflated with the Fethiye Mosque's history. This conflation effectively emphasized the perceived problem of locating an operational mosque in direct sight of the 'Sacred Rock' of the Acropolis, and reiterated the pervading interpretation of the Ottoman period as traumatic and shameful and the Ottoman Turks as imperial oppressor and cultural vandal.

Discussion: The Inheritance of Ottoman Athens

Events such as the demolition of the Bamiyan Buddhas and Palmyra have functioned, at least in the West, to popularly define the relationship between Islam and cultural heritage as iconoclastic.[75] This perspective perpetuates the stereotypical notion of Islam as a monolithic culture that is inherently violent and anti-western, and overlooks scholarship into the developing complexity and diversity of cultures in the Islamic world. Instead, the Ottoman Empire's processes of Ottomanization and Islamization developed different ways of using their inherited urban environments. Eleni Bastea and Dimitris Karidis, for example, argued that Ottoman society tended to be flexible, practical, and adaptable, preferring to take advantage of the structures already present.[76] Athenian Muslim and Orthodox Christian inhabitants coexisted with the city's considerable antiquities, living in and around ancient structures as well as using them for building materials, and more recent research now highlights how sites and structures were imbued with different memories and identities through the interweaving of pagan, Christian, and Muslim stories.

The above examination of just some of the Ottomans' reuses of ancient sites in Athens has suggested the multiple ways in which Ottoman Greek Muslims imagined the past and

Figure 4.4: A view of Athens from the foot of Mount Anchesmus (now known as Mount Lykavitos); note the Olympieion pictured to the left, plate. John Cam Hobhouse, *A Journey through Albania, and other Provinces of Turkey in Europe and Asia, to Constantinople, during the Years 1809 and 1810,* vol. 1 (London: J. Cawthorn, 1813), unnumbered plate. Wellcome Library, London, L0045127.

perceived antiquities and cultural landscapes, and how western travellers' accounts and scholarship have directed our knowledge of these relationships. In the past, many western viewers tended to ignore anything unrelated to what was deemed Helleno-Christian, particularly anything perceived as 'Islamic'. With regard to the Olympieion, it is notable that many travellers' drawings of the site, such as those by Hobhouse [Figure 4.4]; or antiquarian and mineralogist Edward Daniel Clarke (1769–1822); or author and painter William Haygarth (1784–1825), show the sanctuary from afar and with few or no human figures, thus ensuring that the ancient structure culturally as well as physically dominates the scene, and that its Ottoman-ness is marginalized.

Likewise, even when Islamic or Ottoman presences and uses were cited in western sources, they were often viewed through a western lens. Within this framework, the Ottoman period is constructed as a time of stagnation and cultural violation and the Ottomans are represented as uncivilized, despotic, and cupidinous. In many ways, the 'West' has long defined itself in opposition to the 'Orient' and the 'East', and arguably Europe continues to imagine and represent the Islamic world as its binary opposite.[77] The perception of Ottoman indifference and negligence to antiquities also functioned as a colonial tool as it served to encourage the interpretation of the empire's territories as spaces that the West was justified in entering, and from which select antiquities could be removed because of Ottoman cultural inferiority.[78] Just as Greece was represented as a damsel in distress awaiting assistance and rescue, so was the 'logic' behind the removal of Greek statues related to 'liberating' captives from an occupied land.[79] The representation of the Ottoman people's purported disregard for their inherited antiquities was also a tool used to portray Ottoman spaces as requiring modernization, Hellenization, and westernization. Ottoman urban spaces were interpreted as unhygienic, dark, and winding and of little architectural value, and they could thus be stripped away to reveal the 'authentic' ancient sites underneath.[80] These processes of de-Ottomanization have thus largely silenced Ottoman imperial memories, making it difficult to read and understand Ottoman and Islamic concepts of space and time in contemporary landscapes. The disregard for Ottoman perspectives has in part been perpetuated by the isolation of Ottoman studies, married with a widespread ignorance of Islam and of the cultures of the Islamicate world.

Future Prospects for New Presentations of Complex Heritage

Despite the obscurantism described above, Ottoman studies is a growing field of research and the approaches that highlight alternative ways of imagining the Ottoman past and histories of cohabiting in inherited landscapes are now more widely disseminated. Increasingly Athens's Ottomanized and Islamized urban spaces are interpreted alongside depictions of the Ottoman city as underpopulated and neglected. The more widespread appreciation and circulation of studies on Islamic societies and the diversification of studies on Ottoman cultures in particular yields much more nuanced examinations that explore Ottoman perspectives in their own right, as well as attempts to set these perspectives into context regarding western interpretations. Works by Fowden on the history of the Ottoman Parthenon and Tunalı's research into Mahmud Efendi's perception and representation of Athens encourage alternative readings by providing translations of Ottoman texts and their different attitudes toward place, past, and legacy.[81] Other inroads – from the *Ottoman Athens, 1458–1833* conferences held by Gennadius Library (2015) and CIEPO (Comité International des Études Pré-Ottomanes et Ottomanes) in Rethymno (2012), the Ministry of Culture's landmark publication *Ottoman Architecture in Greece* (2008), and walking tours of Ottoman Athens organized by the crossmedia project Balkan Tales (2012), to the Greco-Turkish blog *One Day of a Turkish Merchant's Family in Athens in 1759*, and the recently restored seventeenth-century Venizelos mansion in the Plaka – all mark a change in how the material Ottoman Greek world is understood, as well as how Athens's Ottoman pasts are tangibly perceived and experienced.[82] Such approaches toward breaking down the archaeological gaze will allow for greater awareness of what we mean by 'local' when we speak of local attitudes toward antiquities. For example, as the above has indicated, it has hitherto been understood that 'locals' in Athens only includes the Greek

Orthodox population, but this is changing.[83] Understanding that there exists a multiplicity of perspectives also enables us to enjoy a more nuanced reading of Ottoman and European travellers' accounts, rather than only focusing on examples that provide details about 'original' and 'authentic' classical monuments, underline the perfidy of the Ottoman Turk, exemplify how the ancients were culturally superior, or that prove the continuity of the Greek spirit and its inherent identification with its 'national sacred heritage'. It would be interesting, for example, to see more subtle interpretations of the Ottoman Acropolis and the garrison's use and experience of this space. By way of contrast, the ancient Greeks' reuse of this space after the Persian sack in 480 BCE is interpreted in completely different ways – their incorporation of a segment of a Mycenaean wall or their use of temple fragments in a terrace wall on the north of the Acropolis are not seen in negative terms, but rather as providing insight into the Acropolis as a place of memory.[84] Such transformations in the built environment are seen as indigenous reuses of their rightful heritage, whereas the Ottoman presence and habitation of their Greek world is still largely viewed as a cultural violation and a period of outlandish destruction. Both, in reality, are intersecting layers in a cultural landscape, different chapters populated with a diversity of characters in a site's biography. Moreover, critical reappraisals of how the Ottomans or other communities in the Islamicate world imagined the past and used their varied cultural landscapes and inherited antiquities will also contribute to more cross-cultural definitions and applications of the modern concept of cultural heritage itself. Cultural heritage has often operated according to the traditional western 'Authorized Heritage Discourse', and has hitherto arguably acted as a colonial imposition that has marginalized non-western, nonelite, and non-material ways of engaging with the past and making meaning in the present.[85] Acknowledging, respecting, and balancing nonconforming and unofficial heritage approaches and traditions that emerge from a variety of cultural perspectives will hopefully stop the interpretation of 'dissonant' heritage as an inherently negative concept and will aid in our understanding that heritage is a constant cultural process that operates at different levels of society in manifold ways.

Notes

1. Irene Bierman, 'Ottomanization of Crete', in *The Ottoman City and Its Parts: Urban Structure and Social Order*, eds Irene Bierman, Rifa'at A. Abou-El-Haj, and Donald Preziosi (New Rochelle and New York: Caratzas, 1991), 53–75; Howard Crane, 'The Ottoman Sultan Mosques: Icons of Imperial Legitimacy', in *The Ottoman City and Its Parts: Urban Structure and Social Order*, eds Irene Bierman, Rifa'at A. Abou-El-Haj, and Donald Preziosi (New Rochelle and New York: Caratzas, 1991), 173–243.
2. Soner Cagaptay, *Islam, Secularism and Nationalism in Modern Turkey: Who Is a Turk?* (New York and London: Routlege, 2006), 94; Pierre Pinon, 'The Ottoman Cities of the

Balkans', in *The City in the Islamic World*, vol. 1, eds Salma K. Jayyusi, Renata Holod, Attilio Petruccioli, and André Raymond (Leiden and Boston: Brill, 2008), 143–58.

3. Pinon, 'Ottoman Cities of the Balkans', 143–58; see also Machiel Kiel for the pivotal role that the Balkans played in the early development of an imperial architectural style. Machiel Kiel, 'Introduction', in *Studies on the Ottoman Architecture of the Balkans: A Legacy in Stone* (Aldershot and Brookfield: Variorum, 1990), ix–xv.

4. Although it is popularly calculated to four hundred years, in reality it is difficult to provide a single date for the Ottoman Greek period as different areas of 'Greece' entered and left the empire at different points. Furthermore, some areas were never incorporated into the empire.

5. Among those pursuing this approach is Elizabeth Key Fowden in her forthcoming publications on the Parthenon mosque: Elizabeth Key Fowden, 'The Parthenon Mosque, King Solomon and the Greek Sages', to appear in *Ottoman Athens: Archaeology, Topography, History* (Athens: American School of Classical Studies at Athens/Gennadius Library, 2017) as well as *The Parthenon Mosque* (forthcoming); and Benjamin Anderson, '"An Alternative Discourse": Local Interpreters of Antiquities in the Ottoman Empire', *Journal of Field Archaeology* 40.4 (2015): 450–60.

6. Evliya Çelebi, *An Ottoman Traveller: Selections from the Book of Travels of Evliya Çelebi*, trans. Robert Dankoff and Sooyong Kim (London: Eland Publishing Limited, 2011), 278, 280.

7. Franz Babinger, *Mehmed the Conqueror and his Time*, ed. W. C. Hickman, trans. Ralph Manheim (Princeton: Princeton University Press, 1978); Eleni Bastea, *The Creation of Modern Athens: Planning the Myth* (Cambridge: Cambridge University Press, 2000), 101; John Travlos, 'Athens after the Liberation: Planning the New City and Exploring the Old', *Hesperia* 50.4 (1981), 395; K. M. Setton, *Athens in the Middle Ages* (London: Variorum Reprints, 1975); Donald M. Nicol, *The Immortal Emperor: The Life and Legend of Constantine Palaiologos, Last Emperor of the Romans* (Cambridge, New York, and Melbourne: Cambridge University Press, 1992); Machiel Kiel, 'Athens', in *Encyclopaedia of Islam* 3, BrillOnline, accessed September 4, 2013, http://www.brillonline.nl/entries/encyclopaedia-of-islam-3/athens-COM_26358; J. M. Hurwitt, *The Athenian Acropolis: History, Mythology, and Archaeology from the Neolithic Era to the Present* (Cambridge: Cambridge University Press, 1999), 298; M. Kardamitsi-Adami and M. Biris, *Neoclassical Architecture in Greece* (Athens: Melissa Publishing House, 2004), 74.

8. Nicol, *Immortal Emperor*, 397–98; Babinger, *Mehmed the Conqueror*, 160–61 (n. 1).

9. Kiel, 'Athens'; P. F. Sugar, *Southeastern Europe under Ottoman rule 1354–1804* (Seattle: University of Washington Press, 1977), 213 ff.; Dimitris N. Karidis, 'Town Development in the Balkans, 15th–19th Cent. The Case of Athens', *Études Balkaniques* 2 (1982): 50.

10. Raïna Pouli, 'Athens', *Ottoman Architecture in Greece*, ed. Ersi Brouskari, trans. Elizabeth Key Fowden (Athens: Hellenic Ministry of Culture, Directorate of Byzantine and Post-Byzantine Antiquities, 2008), 68; Dimitris N. Karidis, *Athens from 1456 to 1920: The Town Under Ottoman Rule and the 19th-Century Capital City* (Oxford: Archaeopress, 2014); Karidis, 'Town Development', 51–53; Sugar, *Southeastern Europe*, 213; Olga Augustinos, 'Eastern Concubines, Western Mistresses: Prévost's *Histoire d'une Grecque moderne*', in *Women in the*

Ottoman Balkans: Gender, Culture and History, eds A. Buturovic and I. C. Schick (London and New York: I.B. Tauris), 24.
11. Karidis, 'Town Development', 20, 51; Paul Sant Cassia and Constantina Bada, *The Making of the Modern Greek Family: Marriage and Exchange in Nineteenth-Century Athens* (Cambridge: Cambridge University Press, 1992), 22; Kiel, 'Athens'; 'Population Growth and Food Production in 16th Century Athens and Attica According to the Ottoman Tahrir Defters', in *Varia Turcica IV Comité International d'Études pré-Ottomanes, VIst Symposium Cambridge, 1st–4th July 1984*, eds J. L. Bacque-Grammont and E. van Donzel (Istanbul, Paris, and Leiden: Divit Press); Bastea, *Creation of Modern Athens*, 93.
12. Karidis, *Athens from 1456 to 1920*, 52; Karidis, 'Town Development', 50; Kiel, 'Athens'.
13. Kiel, 'Population Growth', 119; Edward Dodwell, *A Classical and Topographical Tour through Greece during the Years 1801, 1805, and 1806*, vol. 1 (London: Rodwell and Martin, 1819), 361; Karidis, *Athens from 1456 to 1920*.
14. Bastea, *Creation of Modern Athens*, 94.
15. Panayis Skouzes cited in *Athens Alive, or the Practical Tourist's Companion to the Fall of Man*, ed. Kevin Andrews (Athens: Hermes Publications, 1979), 118–19.
16. Karidis, *Athens from 1456 to 1920*, 128; Bastea, *Creation of Modern Athens*, 94; George Wheler, *A Journey Into Greece* (London: William Cademan, 1682), 346–47.
17. Çelebi, *Ottoman Traveller*, 287; Karidis, *Athens from 1456 to 1920*, 72.
18. Bastea, *Creation of Modern Athens*, 92, 94, 95.
19. See Nicole Saraga, 'Les monuments Ottomans d'Athènes au fil du Temps', in *Patrimoine culturels en Méditerranée: recherché scientifiques et enjeux identitaires. 3e atelier 26 Novembre 2009: Les héritiers de l'Empire ottoman et l'héritage refusé*, eds, Jean-Claude David and Sylvie Müller-Celka (Lyon: Recontres scientifiques en ligne de la Maison de l'Orient et de la Méditerranée), accessed November 11, 2021 http://www.mom.fr/sites/ mom.fr/files/img/Ressources_numeriques_et_outils/Documents_numerises/Colloques_texte_integral/ Patrimoines_culturels_en_Mediterranee_ orientale/3eme_atelier/Saraga_edite.pdf, 2.
20. Bastea, *Creation of Modern Athens*, 95; Saraga, 'Les monuments Ottomans', 4.
21. See for example, Michael Llewellyn-Smith, *Athens* (Oxford: Signal Books, 2004), 114.
22. Dodwell, *Classical and Topographical Tour*, 291.
23. Ibid., 378; Saraga, 'Les monuments Ottomans'; Karidis, *Athens from 1456 to 1920*, 73.
24. Richard A. McNeal, 'Archaeology and the Destruction of the Later Athenian Acropolis', *Antiquity* 65 (1991), 56.
25. George E. Marindin, ed., *The Letters of John B. S. Morritt of Rokeby, Descriptive of Journeys in Europe and Asia Minor in the Years 1794–1796* (London: John Murray, 1914), 179.
26. Richard Chandler, *Travels in Greece: or an Account of a Tour Made at the Expense of the Society of Dilettanti* (Oxford: Clarendon Press, 1776), 35; Dodwell, *Classical and Topographical Tour*, 305; John Cam Hobhouse, *A Journey through Albania, and Other Provinces of Turkey in Europe and Asia, to Constantinople during the years 1809 and 1810*, vol. 1 (Philadelphia: Carey and Son, 1817), 331; Yannis Hamilakis, 'Indigenous Archaeologies in Ottoman Greece', in *Scramble for the Past: Archaeology in Ottoman Lands, 1740–1914*, eds Z. Bahrani, Z. Çelik, and E. Eldem (Istanbul: SALT, 2011); Yannis Hamilakis and Fotis Ifantidis, 'Photo Essay: The Other Acropolises: Multi-Temporality and the Persistence of the

Past', in *The Oxford Handbook of the Archaeology of the Contemporary World*, eds P. Graves-Brown, R. Harrison, and A. Piccini (Oxford: Oxford University Press, 2013), 761.

27. Translated in Alexandra L. Lesk, 'A Diachronic Examination of the Erechtheion and its Reception' (Ph.D. diss., University of Cincinnati, 2004), 637; see also J. M. Paton, *The Erechtheum: Measured, Drawn and Restored by Gorham Phillips Stevens; text by Lacey Davis Caskey, Harold North Fowler, James Morton Paton, Gorham Phillips Steven* (Cambridge, MA: Harvard University Press, 1927), 71–72; Hamilakis and Ifantidis, 'Photo Essay', 763; Elizabeth Cohen, 'Managing and Interpreting Greece's Ottoman Heritage' (Ph.D. diss., University of Cambridge, 2015).
28. Dodwell, *Classical and Topographical Tour*, 352.
29. Jeanette Greenfield, *The Return of Cultural Treasures* (Cambridge, New York, and Melbourne: Cambridge University Press, 1989).
30. Panage-s Skouzes, *Chroniko tēs sklavōmenēs Athēnas sta chronia tēs tyranias tou Chatzalē* (Athens: Ekdose-A. Kololou, 1948). Chatzale is a contraction of Hacı Ali (Haseki Ağa). For a critical edition of the text, see Panagēs Skouzes, *Chroniko tēs sklavōmenēs Athēnas sta chronia tēs tyranias tou Chatzalē, 1772–1796*, ed. Thanase-s Ch. Papadopoulos (Athens: Kedros, 1975). On local perceptions of Ottoman rule, see also Johann Strauss, 'Ottoman Rule Experienced and Remembered: Remarks on Some Local Greek Chronicles of the Tourkokratia', in *The Ottomans and the Balkans: A Discussion of Historiography*, eds Fikret Adanır and Suraiya Faroqhi (Leiden: Brill, 2002), 193–221.
31. Fowden, 'Parthenon Mosque', n.pag.
32. Çelebi, *Ottoman Traveller*, 278.
33. Elizabeth Key Fowden, 'The Parthenon Mosque and Greek Philosophers: An Islamic Landscape with Figures' (paper presented at the Faculty of Classics, University of Cambridge, March 8, 2016).
34. Franz Babinger, 'Atīna', in *Encyclopaedia of Islam*, accessed September 4, 2013, http://www.brillonline.nl/entries/encyclopaedia-of-islam-2/atina-SIM_0849; Frederick W. Hasluck, *Christianity and Islam under the Sultan*, vols. 1 and 2, ed. M. Hasluck (Oxford: Clarendon Press, 1929), 15; K. W. Arafat, 'Ottoman Athens', in *Arts & the Islamıc World* 4.4 (1987–88), 25; Çelebi, *Ottoman Traveller*, 290.
35. Çelebi, *Ottoman Traveller*, 288; Gülçin Tunalı, 'Another Kind of Hellenism? Appropriation of Ancient Athens via Greek Channels for the Sake of Good Advice as Reflected in *Tarih-i Medinetü'l-Hukema*' (Ph.D. diss., Ruhr Universität Bochum, 2013), accessed November 11, 2021 http://www-brs.ub.ruhr-uni-bochum.de/netahtml/HSS/Diss/TunaliGuelcin/diss.pdf, 62.
36. Çelebi, *Ottoman Traveller*, 285.
37. Chandler, *Travels in Greece*, 46, 62, Hobhouse, *Journey through Albania*, 288, 290.
38. Dodwell, *Classical and Topographical Tour*, 396–97; Hasluck, *Christianity and Islam*, 221–22.
39. Helen Saradi, 'The Use of Ancient Spolia in Byzantine Monuments: The Archaeological and Literary Evidence', *International Journal of the Classical Tradition* 3.4 (1997), 395–423; Robert Coates-Stephens, 'Epigraphy as Spolia: The Reuse of Inscriptions in Early Medieval Buildings', in *Papers of the British School at Rome* 70 (2002): 275–96; John Bintliff, *The Complete Archaeology of Greece: From Hunter Gatherers to the 20th Century A.D.*

(Chichester: Wiley-Blackwell, 2012); Alison Frantz, *The Middle Ages in the Athenian Agora* (Princeton: American School of Classical Studies at Athens, 1961); Alison Frantz, 'From Paganism to Christianity in the Temples of Athens', in *Dumbarton Oaks Papers*, vol. 19 (Dumbarton Oaks: Trustees for Harvard University, 1965), 185, 187–205.

40. Anthony Kaldellis, *The Christian Parthenon: Classicism and Pilgrimage in Byzantine Athens* (Cambridge: Cambridge University Press, 2009).
41. Historian Kritoboulous (1410–1470) in Kevin Andrews, *Athens Alive, or the Practical Tourist's Companion to the Fall of Man*, ed. Kevin Andrews (Athens: Hermes Publications, 1979), 64.
42. Hasluck, *Christianity and Islam*, 13–14.
43. Julien-David Le Roy, *The Ruins of the Most Beautiful Monuments of Greece*, trans. David Britt (Los Angeles: Getty Publications, 2004), 258; Hasluck, *Christianity and Islam*, 28–29.
44. The Temple of Olympian Zeus is also known as the Olympieion (and formerly as the Palace of Hadrian), names that are applied to its much larger surrounding sanctuary complex.
45. Mahmud Efendi cited in Tunalı, 'Another Kind of Hellenism?', 63; see also Mary Beard, *The Parthenon* (London: Profile Books, 2002), 72; Çelebi, *Ottoman Traveller*, 288.
46. Fowden, 'Parthenon Mosque', n.pag.
47. C. W. J. Eliot described the place of worship as 'rudely converted into a church, and that it now lies abandoned in danger of further decay'. C. W. J. Eliot, 'Gennadeion Notes, III: Athens in the Time of Lord Byron', in *Hesperia: The Journal of the American School of Classical Studies at Athens* 37.2 (1968), 139.
48. Çelebi, *Ottoman Traveller*, 288.
49. Hobhouse, *Journey through Albania*, 268; see also John Galt, *Letters from the Levant; Containing Views of the State of Society, Manners, Opinions, and Commerce, in Greece and Several of the Principal Islands of the Archipelago* (London: Cadell and Davies, 1813), 228.
50. Hasluck, *Christianity and Islam*, 324–25.
51. Karidis, *Athens from 1456 to 1920*, 17 (Figure 4.3).
52. Hobhouse, *Journey Through Albania*, 268; Joseph-François Michaud and Jean-Joseph-François Poujoulat, *Correspondance d'Orient 1830–1831*, vol. 1 (Paris: Ducollet, 1833), 161; Dodwell, *Classical and Topographical Tour*, 389; Chandler, *Travels in Greece*, 77; Peter E. Laurent, *Recollections of a Classical Tour through Various Parts of Greece, Turkey, and Italy, Made in the Years 1818 & 1819* (London: Whittaker, 1821), 96; Charles C. Frankland, *Travels to and from Constantinople in the Years 1827 and 1828*, vol. 1. (London: Henry Colbrun, 1829), 302; William Turner, *Journal of a Tour in the Levant*, vol. 1 (London: John Murray, 1820), 379; Thomas A. Trant, *Narrative of a Journey through Greece in 1830* (London: Colburn and Bentley, 1830), 265; Henry M. Baird, *Modern Greece: A Narrative of a Residence and Travels in that Country, with Observations on its Antiquities, Literature, Language, Politics, and Religion* (New York: Harper & Brothers, 1856), 52; Çelebi, *Ottoman Traveller*, 288.
53. Hasluck, *Christianity and Islam*, 199.
54. William Bingley, *Travels in South Europe* (London: Harvey and Darton, 1821), 237.
55. Dodwell, *Classical and Topographical Tour*, 390.
56. Hasluck, *Christianity and Islam*, 638.
57. Hasluck, *Christianity and Islam*, 639–40.

58. Çelebi, *Ottoman Traveller*, 281–86; Fowden, 'Parthenon Mosque', n.pag.
59. See Dimitris Livianos, 'The Quest for Hellenism: Religion, Nationalism and Collective Identities in Greece (1453–1913)', for the problematic use of the appellations 'Turk' and 'Ottoman'. Dimitris Livianos, 'The Quest for Hellenism: Religion, Nationalism and Collective Identities in Greece (1453–1913)', in *The Historical Review/La Revue Historique* III (2006).
60. The Bath House of the Winds is managed by the Museum of Folk Art (accessed November 11, 2021, http://www.melt.gr/en/visit/the-bath-house-of-the-winds/the-monument/).
61. Dodwell, *Classical and Topographical Tour*, 378; Raïna Pouli, 'Tzisdarakis (or Kato Sintrivaniou) Mosque', in *Ottoman Architecture in Greece*, ed. Ersi Brouskari, trans. Elizabeth Key Fowden (Athens: Hellenic Ministry of Culture, Directorate of Byzantine and Post-Byzantine Antiquities, 2008), 74–76.
62. Karidis, *Athens from 1456 to 1920*, 82–83; Dimitris Kambouroglou, *Istoria ton Athinaion Tourkokratia periodos prote, 1458–1687*, vol. 3 (Athens: Sp. Kousoulinos, 1896), http://anemi.lib.uoc.gr/, 125.
63. Hobhouse, *Journey through Albania*, 267; Dodwell, *Classical and Topographical Tour*, 378. Raïna Pouli argues that the vague reference in the *Chronicle of Anthimos* to 'a column from those of Hadrian' could in fact refer to the adjacent Library of Hadrian. Pouli, Tzisdarakis, 74.
64. Chandler, *Travels in Greece*, 76.
65. Dodwell, *Classical and Topographical Tour*, 390.
66. Ibid.; Chandler, *Travels in Greece*, 74–76.
67. Dodwell, *Classical and Topographical Tour*, 390.
68. Frederic S. N. Douglas, *An Essay on Certain Points of Resemblance Between the Ancient and Modern Greeks* (London: John Murray, 1813), 85–86; Hobhouse, *Journey through Albania*, 288.
69. Hobhouse, *Journey through Albania*, 288.
70. Douglas, *Essay on Certain Points*, 85.
71. Yannis Hamilakis, 'Stories from Exile: Fragments from the Cultural Biography of the Parthenon (or "Elgin") Marbles', *World Archaeology* 31.2 (1999), 307.
72. Helen Saradi-Mendelovici, 'Christian Attitudes toward Pagan Monuments in Late Antiquity and Their Legacy in Later Byzantine Centuries', in *Dumbarton Oaks Papers* 44 (1990): 47–61.
73. Manos Meimarakis, 'Ftiakhnoun tzami stin Akropoli!', comment on *Gianniotis*, May 28, 2010, accessed November 11, 2021 http://gianniotis.blogs-pot.co.uk/2010/05/blog-post_8552.html.
74. Raïna Pouli, 'Fethiye (or Staropazarou) Mosque', in *Ottoman Architecture in Greece*, ed. Ersi Brouskari, trans. Elizabeth Key Fowden (Athens: Hellenic Ministry of Culture, Directorate of Byzantine and Post-Byzantine Antiquities, 2008), 70; Machiel Kiel, 'The Quatrefoil Plan in Ottoman Architecture Reconsidered in the Light of the"Fethiye Mosque"of Athens', *Muqarnas* 19 (2002), 109–22; Dimitris Antoniou, 'The Mosque that Was Not There: Ethnographic Elaborations on Orthodox Conceptions of Sacrifice', in *Orthodox Christianity in 21st Century Greece*, eds V. Roudometof and V. Makrides (Farnham, Surrey, and Burlington: Ashgate, 2010); Konstantinos Tsitelikis, *Old and New Islam in Greece: From Historical Minorities to Immigrant Newcomers* (Leiden: Martinus Nijhoff Publishers, 2011).

75. Finbarr B. Flood, 'Between Cult and Culture: Bamiyan, Islamic Iconoclasm, and the Museum', *The Art Bulletin* 84.4 (2002): 641–59; Clair Smith, Heather Burke, Cherrie de Leiuen, and Gary Jackson, 'The Islamic State's Symbolic War: Da'esh's Socially Mediated Terrorism as a Threat to Cultural Heritage', *Journal of Social Archaeology* 16.2 (2016): 164–88.
76. Bastea, *Creation of Modern Athens*, 9; Karidis, *Athens from 1456 to 1920*, 70.
77. Edward Said, *Orientalism* (London: Routledge, 1978); Zeynep Çelik, *Displaying the Orient: Architecture of Islam at Nineteenth-Century World's Fairs* (Berkeley, Los Angeles, and Oxford: University of California Press, 1992); Sharon Macdonald, 'Migrating Heritage, Networks and Networking: Europe and Islamic Heritage', in *Migrating Heritage: Experiences of Cultural Networks and Cultural Dialogue in Europe*, ed. P. Innocenti (Farnham and Burlington: Ashgate, 2014).
78. Anderson, '"Alternative Discourse"', 450–60.
79. Katherine E. Fleming, 'Greece in Chains: Philhellenism to the Rescue of a Damsel in Distress', in *Women and the Colonial Gaze*, eds Tamara L. Hunt and Micheline R. Lessard (Basingstoke and New York: Palgrave Macmillan, 2002); Efterpi Mitsi and Amy Muse, 'Some Thoughts on the Trails and Travails of Hellenism and Orientalism: An Interview with Gonda Van Steen', *Synthesis* (Special Issue: 'Hellenism Unbound', eds Efterpi Mitsi and Amy Muse) 5 (2013), accessed October 4, 2017, http://synthesis.enl.uoa.gr/hellenism-unbound-5-2013/interview-5-efterpi-mitsi-and-amy-muse.html; Gonda van Steen, *Liberating Hellenism from the Ottoman Empire: Comte de Marcellus and the Last of the Classics* (New York: Palgrave Macmillan, 2010).
80. Cohen, 'Managing and Interpreting Greece's Ottoman Heritage'; Alexandra Yerolympos, *Urban Transformations in the Balkans (1820– 1920): Aspects of Balkan Town Planning and the Remaking of Thessaloniki* (Thessaloniki: University Studio Press, 1996); Yiorgos Koumaridis, 'Urban Transformation and De-Ottomanisation in Greece', *East Central Europe* 33.1–2 (2006): 213–41; Mark Mazower, *Salonica: City of Ghosts* (London: Harper Perennial, 2004).
81. Fowden, 'Parthenon Mosque', n.pag; Tunalı, 'Another Kind of Hellenism?'.
82. *One Day of a Turkish Merchant's Family in Athens in 1759*, accessed November 11, 2021 http://nisafi.blogspot.co.uk/2011/10/one-day-of-turkish-merchants-family-in_31.html.
83. Leslie G. Kaplan, '"Writing Down the Country": Travelers and the Emergence of the Archaeological Gaze', in *Archaeology in Situ: Sites, Archaeology, and Communities in Greece*, eds Anna Stroulia and Susan Buck Sutton (Plymouth: Lexington Books, 2010); 75–108; see also Vassilios Varouhakis, 'L'archéologie enrage: Archaeology & National Identity under the Cretan State (1898– 1913)' (Ph.D. diss., University of Southampton, 2015).
84. John Ma, 'City as Memory', in *Oxford Handbook of Hellenic Culture*, eds George Boys-Stones, Barbara Graziosi, and Phiroze Vasunia (Oxford: Oxford University Press, 2009), 254.
85. Laurajane Smith, *The Uses of Heritage* (London and New York: Routledge, 2006); Laurajane Smith and Natsuko Akagawa, 'Introduction', in *Intangible Heritage*, ed. Laurajane Smith and Natsuko Akagawa (Abingdon and New York: Routledge, 2009), 1–10; Mirjam Brusius, 'The Middle East Heritage Debate Is Becoming Worryingly Colonial', *The Conversation*, April 25, 2016, accessed October 4, 2017, https://theconversation.com/the-middle-east-heritage-debate-is-becoming-worryingly-colonial-57679.

5

Spoils for the New Pyrrhus: Alternative Claims to Antiquity in Ottoman Greece

Emily Neumeier

In the winter of 1812, the Danish antiquarian Peter Brøndsted was busy wrapping up several months of excavation in the Peloponnese. At this point, the region was still a territory of the Ottoman Empire – the Battle of Navarino, which put an effective end to Ottoman rule in the Morea, would only take place several years later in 1827. This being the early days of archaeology, Brøndsted's excavation team did not have any kind of institutional affiliation or support from a museum or academic society. Rather, they could best be described as a motley group of gentleman scholars and diplomatic officers who had all made their way from Western Europe to Ottoman lands, searching for the material traces of classical antiquity. Brought together through their mutual mission to locate, document and, ideally, extricate Roman and Greek sculpture, the members of this 'little company of adventurers'[1] had pooled their resources in order to carry out the first major expedition to the Temple of Apollo Epicurius at Bassae, a monument from the fifth century BCE that even today impresses the visitor with its state of preservation, as well as its dramatic setting perched high up in the remote mountains of the Western Peloponnese [Figure 5.1].

Once the excavations were complete, Brøndsted began preparations to return home to Denmark. However, he resolved that before leaving the shores of the Morea he should first pay a visit to the great Ottoman governor to the north, the notorious Ali Pasha. In a later account of his travels, Brøndsted explained that his curiosity was piqued by a man whose numerous exploits were 'one of the principal themes of the popular songs, which we often heard in almost all of the provinces […] from Taygetus to Olympus and the Acroceraunian mountains as far as Carystos in Euboea'.[2] Ali Pasha's reputation was so far-reaching that one of Brøndsted's colleagues at the excavations, Otto von Stackelberg, recorded one of these popular songs in the final publication of the expedition's results [Figure 5.2]. Stackelberg notes in this volume that the workers from the local village would sing the tune while they laboured to uncover the stones from the site.[3] The lyrics of the folk ballad, which affirm Ali Pasha's status as a veritable popular icon during his own time, appear in Stackelberg's text alongside lithograph plates of the ground plans and sculptural friezes from the temple – images that have today come to define Enlightenment Europe's 'rediscovery' of ancient Greece [Figure 5.3]. The excavators were clearly aware that, as they busied themselves unearthing monumental warriors locked in eternal combat, they were also standing in the midst of a modern myth-maker.

Figure 5.1: The Temple of Apollo Epicurius at Bassae, detail from plate included in Otto von Stackelberg's *Der Apollotempel zu Bassae* (Rome: 1826), Plate 2. American School of Classical Studies, Gennadius Library.

Ali Pasha as Antiquarian

In the early nineteenth century, precisely at the moment when the British Museum welcomed the arrival of Lord Elgin's marbles (as well as the frieze from the Temple of Apollo at Bassae), local Ottoman administrators were also emerging as major players in the search for antiquity. Tepedelenli Ali Pasha, who along with his three sons served as the governor (*mutasarrıf*) of multiple Ottoman sub-provinces, maintained firm control over what is now northern Greece and southern Albania for almost forty years (1784–1820) [Figure 5.4 and Figure 5.5].[4] Ali Pasha can be considered as part of a new class of Ottoman provincial power-holders who were significant because they boasted local roots and were capable of amassing a level of economic wealth and political influence previously impossible for those outside of the imperial court.[5] Ali Pasha was also a prolific builder, invested in branding the local landscape with his architectural interventions – whether through his palace complexes or numerous defensive fortifications.[6] The vizier proved to be equally capable of mobilizing classical antiquity for his own aggrandizement. Stationed in his de facto capital in Ioannina, Ali Pasha found himself in the middle of what has been memorably described as a 'scramble

Spoils for the New Pyrrhus: Alternative Claims to Antiquity in Ottoman Greece

Figure 5.2: The lyrics and music of a Greek folk song about Ali Pasha, recorded in *Der Apollotempel zu Bassae* (Rome: 1826), 117. American School of Classical Studies, Gennadius Library.

Figure 5.3: A rendering of one of the reliefs from the frieze of the Temple of Apollo Epicurius from *Der Apollotempel zu Bassae* (Rome: 1826), Plate 4. American School of Classical Studies, Gennadius Library.

for the past',[7] and he in turn routinely appropriated the forms and figures of antiquity to secure his own political legitimacy in the region, developing a diverse range of strategies for inscribing these claims onto both urban and regional spaces.

The following pages will chart Ali Pasha's multiple engagements with antiquity, and discuss how this distinct tradition of antiquarianism overlapped and interacted with other competing narratives over common sites and objects of interpretation. The chapter will focus

Figure 5.4: 'Ali Tebelen, Pacha de Janina', detail from plate in Louis Dupré's *Voyage à Athènes et à Constantinople* (Paris: Dondey Dupré, 1825), Plate 7. American School of Classical Studies, Gennadius Library.

on three specific cases where the vizier staged encounters with the past. First, it will examine Ali Pasha's archaeological ventures at the ancient Roman site of Nikopolis (for which the governor brought Peter Brøndsted into his service) and reflect on how these activities were tied to Ali Pasha's large-scale development of the nearby port city of Preveza. Second, it will demonstrate how Ali Pasha made explicit claims about his own direct descent from King Pyrrhus, the great Hellenistic ruler of Epirus, most notably in a Greek inscription that the governor commissioned to be placed above the city gates in Ioannina. This claim was

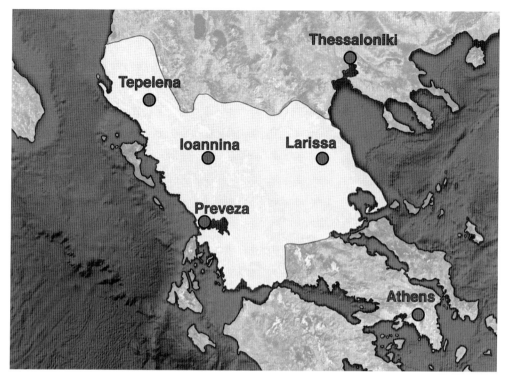

Figure 5.5: Map showing the approximate territory governed by Ali Pasha and his sons after 1812. The base image for the map was adapted from Google Earth. Emily Neumeier.

not isolated to public texts, however, but also found purchase in contemporary folk songs celebrating the life of the governor, lending crucial insights into local – both Muslim and Christian alike – perceptions of historical heritage. Last, the chapter will focus on another dramatic attempt by Ali Pasha to place himself within the long line of great classical heroes in the history of Epirus through the construction of his own commemorative palace on the site of the ancient Monument of Augustus in Nikopolis. With this act, the governor sought to establish a direct link between the Battle of Actium and Ali Pasha's own routing of Napoleon's troops amid the ruins of the ancient city.

In all of these examples, Ali Pasha's engagements with the past foreground the importance of locality. In other words, the success of these interventions depends entirely upon the specificity of the sites in which they are staged, from the walls of Ioannina to the bricks of Nikopolis. This approach stands in stark contrast to that of the vizier's European contemporaries as well as that of the central Ottoman administration. Although Western Europeans travelling in the region frequently remarked upon matters of ancient geography in their accounts,[8] their ultimate goal at that point was to discover and extract the choicest selection of carved marbles to fill their museums back home. As material evidence of the artistic and moral genius of classical antiquity (which, in the European world-view, served as the foundation of western civilization), these sculptures were perceived to be more at home in the galleries of the imperial museum rather than at their sites of origin. While diverging from this more universal-colonialist perception of the past,[9] Ali Pasha's method for embedding his own legacy into the landscape, which relied on re-establishing conscious links with (local) ancient rulers, also took a long view of history that transcended the political reality of the Ottoman state. In other words, this emphasis on cultivating spaces of local memory did not contribute to a broader vision of empire – which, however 'flexible',[10] worked to consolidate far-flung territories under a single political order.[11] Interestingly, the claims to global sovereignty made by Sultan Mehmed II and Süleyman I, who both famously styled themselves as the new Alexander and Caesar of Rome,[12] eventually gave way in the eighteenth century to another kind of localism in the capital, with royal mosques in the 'Ottoman baroque' style looking specifically to nearby Byzantine monuments.[13]

To delve further into the interplay between these alternative approaches to antiquity, let us return for a moment to Brøndsted, who, after leaving the Morea, eventually found Ali Pasha residing at his palace in the port city of Preveza. In conversation about nearby ruins, Ali Pasha voiced his astonishment at how the 'Franks, at the extremity of the world', were so 'well acquainted with [his] countries, and [his] cities'.[14] In his later account, Brøndsted reports the vizier's comment with a degree of smugness, mentioning in an aside that he had become accustomed to locals expressing their amazement at his knowledge of the region – 'a thing which often happens to us with the Turks'.[15] Yet, in what Brøndsted assumes to be a transparent expression of Ali Pasha's admiration, it is also possible to hear an edge of criticism as well. By emphasizing how far the Dane had trekked to visit his territory, Ali Pasha insinuates his confusion about why a Western European would spend a great deal of time learning the history of a country that is not his own, and then leave behind all the security of his friends and family to seek out old ruins. The governor equally may have wondered if Brøndsted's country was devoid of monumental remains of antiquity, and thus lesser in some way.

Ali Pasha's combined fascination and incredulity about the 'Franks' who came from 'the extremity of the world' highlights the complexity of the various cross-cultural encounters and exchanges that were taking place as a result of the 'opening' of Greece to the West. The zenith of Ali Pasha's career in the early nineteenth century coincided with an increased flow of Western European travellers into the regions largely under his control. The Napoleonic Wars had effectively closed Italy to individuals on their 'Grand Tour' and spurred them to seek new regions to explore. Once deterred by the difficulties of travelling within Ottoman lands, these groups (of primarily wealthy and well-educated men of privilege) began to find their way to Greece and Albania. At the same time, there was also a growing interest in the classical past among local Christian elites at the court in Ioannina, proponents of the so-called 'Greek Enlightenment'.[16] With many of these elites having travelled abroad in their youth and educated in intellectual centres such as Venice and Vienna, they had brought back with them the conviction that a well-rounded individual should be versed in the texts of ancient authors. While participating in a Europe-wide phenomenon, these elites were also aware that they were in some way specially positioned to receive these texts as they hailed from lands within the geographic domains of ancient Greece and Rome. Thus, while Ali Pasha may not have fully appreciated the personal motivations of an antiquarian like Brøndsted, he still understood that change was in the air, and that he could utilize knowledge gleaned from these western travellers to promote himself to the cultural milieu in his own region.

Additionally, the view of Ali Pasha as engaged in the exploration of antiquity upsets the common scholarly and popular perception that, within the Ottoman Empire, Muslim officials were at this time ambivalent at best to the traces of the classical past that had begun to attract the attention of European archaeologists and Greek revolutionaries. In a book chapter tracing how Ottoman perceptions of antiquity changed throughout the nineteenth century, Edhem Eldem describes the early phase of Ottoman attitudes toward archaeology as one of 'general indifference, resulting in an almost systematic compliance with western demands'.[17] Drawing on two case studies – one in Istanbul, the other in Athens – in which Lord Elgin interacted with authorities to secure permission to remove ancient sculptures from Ottoman lands, Eldem demonstrates that the elites in Istanbul freely accommodated such requests. In a fascinating document, an Ottoman imperial decree allows that 'stones of this kind, decorated with figures, are not held in consideration among Muslims, but are appreciated by the Frankish states',[18] thus using religion to rationalize what was essentially a diplomatic and commercial transaction. We must make a distinction, however, between the highest levels of decision-making at the Ottoman Porte and what was going on in the provinces at Ali Pasha's court. While the vizier was equally open to working with European visitors to locate sculpture found in his territory,[19] Ali Pasha – an Albanian Muslim – also endeavoured to position himself as the rightful heir to the region's ancient past through its sites, stories and stones.

Excavating Nikopolis and Building Preveza Anew

Ali Pasha arguably first became aware of the potential of digging for ancient sculpture by following the activities of his son, Veli Pasha, who, while serving as governor of the Morea (1807–12), became involved in archaeological excavations at Mycenae, Argos, and even Bassae.[20] Ali Pasha would get his own chance to search for old stones when Brøndsted finally made his way to Preveza. During their first audience, the vizier invited Brøndsted to join a short 'scientific excursion'[21] that he was organizing to some ruins located just outside the city. These ruins were in fact the remains of Nikopolis, the ancient Roman city founded by Octavian (the later Augustus) in commemoration of his naval victory over Marc Antony and Cleopatra at the Battle of Actium [Figure 5.6]. The significance of Nikopolis as a historical site must have intrigued Brøndsted but, after almost seven years of constant

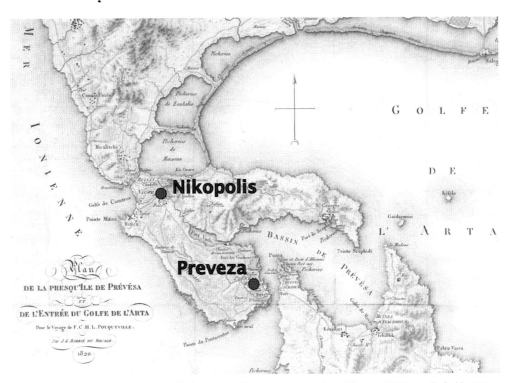

Figure 5.6: Map showing the location of Nikopolis in relation to Preveza, adapted from an 1820 map drafted by J. D. Barbié du Bocage. Adapted by the author, 2016. Actia Nikopolis Foundation, Preveza, IAN 0209.

travel, he preferred to depart immediately and press on for home. Despite these demurrals, Ali Pasha proved to be quite persuasive on the matter, and in the end Brøndsted reluctantly agreed to the proposal.

Several days later, the archaeologist found himself practically being frog-marched out to the site with the pasha, who rode in his richly adorned carriage accompanied by 100 guards. Once among the extensive ruins of the ancient city, Ali Pasha made himself comfortable in the small house of a farmer that had been refitted for the occasion with cushions and long *nargileh* pipes. After settling in, the governor asked Brøndsted first to relate everything that he knew about the ancient city. Once Brøndsted had finished rehearsing the history of Nikopolis, Ali Pasha nodded and replied that 'he had already been acquainted with every thing [Brøndsted] had just stated; and had merely questioned [him] on the subject, to compare [his] account with that which an Englishman had given [Ali Pasha], some time before'.[22]

With that, the governor invited Brøndsted to take a walk with him among the ruins so that the antiquarian could 'show him something handsome'.[23] Stopping at the ancient hippodrome, a ruin that even today holds a commanding presence on the site, Ali Pasha assured Brøndsted that he would soon have the inner space of the stadium smoothed so that his Albanian soldiers could practice their races and military exercises, 'as in former days'.[24] After an examination of the city's theatre and imperial palace complex, Ali Pasha reminded the young antiquarian of the ultimate purpose of their outing: archaeological excavations. Brøndsted insisted that any digging in Nikopolis would not produce any satisfactory results in terms of discovering ancient sculptures, as the city was known to have been plundered already by Constantine, but nevertheless offered to show the governor a temple within the old walls of the city that might yield some architectural fragments, if excavated carefully. Ali Pasha agreed, and they set off to summon the local workers.

As the twenty-odd men laboured to clear away the earth under two niches on the longer side of the temple, Brøndsted remarked to Ali Pasha that they were wasting their time because the workers, armed with only shovels and axes, did not have the suitable equipment for proper digging. Having just completed his own search for sculpture at Bassae, Brøndsted knew that, in order to move large blocks of stone, the local labourers would need iron levers and ropes to clear away debris and locate the marble sculptures they all so eagerly sought. Ali Pasha immediately ordered his headmen to bring all the tools from Preveza the following day and construct a shed to hold the equipment as well as 'the things we [were] going to find'.[25] After a few hours of work, the team had not found any statues, but had extracted three fine marble slabs, probably part of the temple's ancient pavement, which Ali Pasha had placed 'with the greatest care upon a sort of rolling/sedan-chair (chaise roulante) and covered with straw, to be conveyed to Prevesa'.[26] At the end of the work day, Ali Pasha rose from his perch where he had been observing the labourers, paid the villagers for their trouble, and alighted to his carriage to return to his palace in Preveza, with his ancient 'spoils' in tow.

Any discussion of Ali Pasha's archaeological activities inevitably turns to the problem of spolia. A term that first appeared in the fifteenth century to define goods or property seized by violent force, 'spolia' was adopted by art historians in the early twentieth century to describe the specific phenomenon of architectural sculpture or building materials being used outside of the context of their original creation.[27] Despite the wide currency that the theme of spolia is now enjoying as a theoretical tool – especially in concert with postmodern concerns like appropriation and assemblage – the question of architectural reuse continues to arise, especially within the context of the post-classical Mediterranean. This is to account for the fact that, well before the advent of modern concepts such as archaeological preservation and cultural heritage, which advocate for the total conservation of sites deemed to be of historic value, the primary way that medieval and early modern societies encountered the remains of classical antiquity was through the despoiling of ruins. The impetus behind this spoliation process ranged from the practical need for construction materials to demands of religion and aesthetics that went beyond simple pragmatism.

It is therefore not terribly surprising that several of the buildings commissioned by Ali Pasha – particularly palaces, mosques and city walls – incorporate stone blocks and sculptures taken from nearby ancient sites. This is most true in Preveza, where most of the buildings constructed by the vizier utilize spolia from the nearby ruins of Nikopolis.

There are some cases when excavations at Nikopolis yielded choice pieces of sculpture that the pasha could display in his palaces; the traveller Thomas Hughes remarked: 'Since our departure from Epirus I understand that [Ali Pasha's] excavators have discovered a very fine bust of Trajan which now decorates one of the principal rooms in the Prevesan seraglio.'[28] Yet, it can also be said that Ali Pasha's masons also used Nikopolis as a large open-air storeroom for building materials, ferrying blocks of stone to Preveza by the cartload. Because Nikopolis was a common stop on the itinerary of Western European travellers, we have several additional first-hand accounts of this despoliation process. Hughes further reported that in the acropolis of the ancient city,

> there is one spot, where the agents of the pasha had been making excavations, upon which some superb temple must once have stood: the numerous marble shafts and pieces of entablature that are discovered, are all carried off to be worked up in his forts and *serai* at Prevesa.[29]

We need not entirely rely on western travellers to document Ali Pasha's spoliation practices; an order in Greek from the governor's representative in Preveza requests that the headman of a nearby village send men to operate the large carts that will 'carry stones from Ai Petros for the works in Preveza,'[30] Agios Petros being the contemporary name for Nikopolis.

Meanwhile, the end results of this mass spoliation effort can still be observed today in the walls of Preveza itself. Several of the buildings or infrastructure projects commissioned by Ali Pasha in the city clearly bear architectural fragments brought from Nikopolis, to the point that modern archaeologists are often able to identify the specific ancient monument from which certain stones were taken. For example, the entire perimeter of the sea walls of the Pantocrator fortress, completed in 1815, includes in its lowest courses large slabs of masonry that stand in stark contrast with the smaller, rougher-cut limestone blocks that make up the upper registers of the wall. Besides this variegation in the overall appearance of the structure, the other clear indication that building materials were reused and not freshly quarried is the irregular shape of individual pieces, with blocks being cut down and fitted together in a kind of jigsaw pattern to make up a uniform height in the building courses. Although this recutting of blocks makes it more difficult to determine from where, exactly, in Nikopolis workers were sourcing their stone, clues were left behind. On the northwest façade of the Pantocrator's seawall, archaeologists have noted two slabs that have had deep channels carved into them, most likely for the conveyance of water, which correspond to other blocks found at the Roman bath-*nymphaeum* complex during twentieth-century excavations at Nikopolis [Figure 5.7].[31] In his diary from his travels with Lord Byron, John Hobhouse wrote that he saw at Preveza

> within the walls of the palace, which is also a kind of fort, [...] the masons cutting up antiques from Nicopolis for the building of some paltry house – but yet the Turks seem aware of the value of these curiosities.[32]

Figure 5.7: View of the northwestern sea wall of the Pantocrator fortress in Preveza, showing the spoliated blocks from Nikopolis reused in the lower courses of masonry, especially the two blocks from the Roman *nymphaeum* that can be seen in the bottom right corner. Emily Neumeier.

This quip cuts to the heart of scholarly discussions about spolia, which essentially strive to understand the extent to which we can ascribe meaning to the reuse of building materials. With the recycling of building materials being ubiquitous in all periods throughout the Mediterranean, even in the classical era, it seems far-fetched to interpret every instance of reuse as an index to ideological victory. Yet even efforts to reduce reuse to strict terms of economic pragmatism ring hollow when considered from the perspective of emerging methodologies such as energetics. There is no doubt that one of the primary reasons Ali Pasha's buildings in Preveza are composed of ancient material is simply because of the geographic proximity of Nikopolis. Even if we understand the widespread spoliation of this site as a practical measure, however, there is still something to be said about the clear preference for ancient materials when they are available, perhaps for reasons of aesthetics as well as economic expediency. The wholesale transport of several tons of large building blocks over a distance of about 7 kilometres remains a significant investment of time and money in the reconstruction of Preveza. In the surrounding region, there was certainly a long-standing tradition of incorporating classical materials into the fabric of notable monuments – one only has to look at the creative use of ancient columns to support the dome of the thirteenth-century Church of the Parigoritissa in nearby Arta. Yet Ali Pasha's spoliation of Nikopolis was on a scale of a different order, a scale that was not even possible in previous centuries, as the international borders determined by the Treaty of Passarowitz in 1718 blocked the Venetians from accessing the ancient site.[33] Western European travellers claimed that Nikopolis was brought to its final state of ruin not over centuries, but in a matter of decades at the hands of Ali Pasha:

> Within these last twenty years [the site] has suffered greater dilapidation than it probably had done for many preceding ages, since the fortifications and other extensive works at Prevesa owe in great measure their existence to the demolition of Nicopolis.[34]

In the city's archaeology museum, there is today an inscription written in Ottoman Turkish that celebrates the governor's building programme at Preveza. The first two lines read: 'So worthy of praise, abundant Preveza / Which Vizir Ali Pasa Tepedelenli built anew.'[35] This final phrase, 'built anew' (*müceddeden bina etti*), although quite conventional as far as Ottoman epigraphy goes, suggests themes of regeneration and rebirth. In the days of Ali Pasha, one city gave its life so another could be reborn.

The Imitator of Pyrrhus

Ali Pasha also sought to forge explicit connections between himself and heroes of the ancient past through the commissioning of public inscriptions and poetic works, which frequently refer to Ali Pasha as the new Pyrrhus. A great Hellenistic-era general and statesman, Pyrrhus (318–272 BCE) consolidated a number of tribal regions in ancient Epirus and brought them under the 'Epirote Alliance' [Figure 5.8].[36] This king frequently challenged and bested the early leaders of Rome, but at the considerable cost of his own men, which is why he is best remembered today with the phrase 'a Pyrrhic victory'. Perhaps the most notable example of Ali Pasha invoking the name of this local ancient ruler is a Greek inscription that once appeared over one of the entrances to the old walled city of Ioannina [Figure 5.9]. This marble plaque, virtually unknown to the wider scholarship on Ottoman epigraphy, is today on display at the city's Byzantine Museum. It commemorates the completion of Ali Pasha's renovation and reconstruction of Ioannina's walls in 1815 – a major infrastructure project that employed over a thousand labourers and masons.[37] The text itself consists of twenty lines of demotic Greek verse, organized into ten rhyming couplets, or *distich*s, with the second line of each couplet set off by an indentation on the left. Although the top left corner of the inscription has now been lost, obscuring our

Figure 5.8: Ancient Roman portrait bust of Pyrrhus, originally found at Pompeii, now at the Naples National Archaeological Museum. Emily Neumeier.

ability to comprehend the meaning of the first six lines in their entirety, it is nevertheless clear that this text not only records Ali Pasha's building efforts, but also situates this action within an imagined longer history of Ioannina's walls. The fragmentary text makes it difficult to discern the first six lines, but what remains indicates that the inscription begins with the initial construction of the city in ancient times, and then goes on to highlight the ineptitude of later rulers when the fortification walls inevitably required maintenance and repair:

Figure 5.9: Greek inscription commemorating Ali Pasha's reconstruction of the walls of Ioannina (1815). Tatiana Steriadi, 'Oi epigrafes tou kastrou', in *To Kastro ton Ioanninon*, ed. Barbara Papadopoulou (Ioannina: 8th Ephorate of Byzantine Antiquities, 2009), 114.

(7) In order to renew and rise up
(8) […] to recover the walls again
(9) As the former bishops pled
(10) And always asked for renovation
(11) And though when many centuries passed
(12) And with them many rulers and sovereigns
(13) None could take up the burden
(14) And prove themselves as a benefactor to this country
(15) And despite all the many years that passed,
(16) Failed to lay down a single stone

Having thus justified the urgent need for a restoration – and modernization – of the city walls, the text continues:

(17) Until the most powerful Ali Pasha the vizier of Epirus
(18) The renowned descendant of Pyrrhus the marvellous

(19) As another wondrous flame he brings this [city] back to life
(20) And restores it as beautiful as ever. (21) 1815[38]

    This inscription proposes a teleological view on the succession of rulers and civilizations that have ruled over the region, as Ali Pasha is presented as the necessary antidote to centuries of neglect, or decline. The claim that Ali Pasha – a self-identified Muslim and ostensibly an Ottoman official – is the best thing that has happened to Ioannina since antiquity stands as a fascinating counter-position to the conceit of the Ottoman Turk enslaving the oppressed Hellas that was being touted exactly around the same time by Greek revolutionaries and philhellenes alike. What we see here is a complex assertion of regional identity that cannot be accommodated by our current understanding of the emergence of nationalism in the Balkans.

    In the inscription, Ali Pasha and Pyrrhus are connected via their analogous legacies as strongmen rulers in the region, united by their duty to serve a shared homeland, which can be translated here as 'country' (*patrida*, Line 14), or 'fatherland'. The text even goes further to assert a clear genealogical kinship between the two heroes of Epirus; that is, along with his Ottoman administrative title (*veziris*, Line 17), Ali Pasha is designated as the progeny, 'the descendant' (*apogonos*, Line 18), of Pyrrhus. Ali Pasha's connection with Pyrrhus is further reinforced with the description of the vizier as 'another wondrous flame' (Line 19). The word used for 'flame' is not the common '*fotia*', which also appears in this inscription on Line 2,[39] but the rarer term '*pir*', creating a sophisticated pun on the name of Pyrhhus (*Pirou*), which occurs at the end of the line just above. Thus, Ali Pasha is another flame, another Pyrhhus, who, through his cleansing abilities, tears down the older city fabric only to construct it again.

    Even though this inscription was originally displayed prominently on the city walls as a public text, the esoteric style of the language would arguably have made it accessible only to a select educated elite in Ioannina. Despite the fact that the letter-forms themselves very much follow palaeographic standards found in contemporaneous ecclesiastical inscriptions throughout the region,[40] the nature of the text – a poem of rhyming couplets – seems to be unprecedented in the corpus of epigraphic material from Byzantine and Ottoman-era Epirus. Based on what we know about epigraphy and how it worked in pre-modern societies, however, we can imagine that the general content of such texts could be widely accessible to a largely illiterate population by means of oral transmission. Yet the question still lingers whether or not this reference to Ali Pasha and his connection to Pyrrhus is a one-off, and restricted to the sphere of a knowledgeable few in the vizier's court circle.

    We find evidence for a popular tradition that celebrates Ali Pasha and his connections with antiquity in the form of local Greek folk songs. Due to the more fluid nature of oral tradition, it is often difficult to determine when a particular song was first composed and gained popularity. An important exception to this caveat is the 'Ballad of Ali Pasha' ('Fillada tou Alipasa'), published by the French Hellenist Émile Legrand, which chronicles Ali Pasha's dramatic last stand and mourns his ultimate execution at the hands of the sultan's men.[41]

Although Legrand published this song in 1886, he relates in his preface to the text that he first transcribed the poem in Athens in 1875, as dictated by an old Epirote named Jean (Ioannis) Pagounis, who had been a baker in Ioannina and remembered the song from his youth, which could easily place this song shortly after Ali Pasha's death in 1822. This man was apparently illiterate and could recite the some 650-line poem by heart 'without hesitation'.[42] The sympathetic tone of the poem itself and the opening invocation that Ali Pasha's soul find God's mercy [*rahmet*] – a conventional Islamic prayer for the dead – indicates that the original composer was a Muslim originating from the Epirus region. This attribution serves as a clear reminder that the genre of Greek folk songs cannot be assumed to be the singular domain of Christians living in the Ottoman Balkans, but rather reflects a local tradition shared by multiple confessions living side by side.

As can be expected, the slain vizier is hailed in the opening lines of the 'Ballad of Ali Pasha' in evocative terms:

(5) The renowned Ali Pasha, the hero of Epirus,
(6) The awesome and terrible, the imitator of Pyrrhus.[43]

It is significant that at the very beginning of this epic poem, Ali Pasha is first and foremost designated as a formidable warrior from the region of Epirus, comparable to the ancient king Pyrrhus. The author never invokes Ali Pasha's official Ottoman titulature, but rather, if anything, describes the governor in terms oppositional to the imperial government. The specific word used here to describe Ali Pasha's relationship with Pyrrhus – '*o mimitis*', translated here as 'imitator' – again raises themes of regeneration and genealogy. As the '*mimitis*' (literally, 'the one who performs mimesis') of Pyrrhus, Ali Pasha is presented as the contemporary embodiment of the foregone hero of Epirus.

The linguistic sophistication of the Greek verse found in the public inscription points to an author well-educated in more advanced literary circles, who inevitably must be among the Greek-speaking intellectuals in Ali Pasha's court. It is a well-established fact that Ioannina – in many ways oriented more to the cultural and economic Adriatic zone than the capital in Istanbul – was a prominent centre for the Greek Enlightenment at the turn of the eighteenth century, boasting a number of Greek schools in operation during the tenure of the governor. We can understand this inscription, therefore, as a unique product of Ali Pasha's domains as well as his power base and court. Meanwhile, it is equally important to note that these references to antiquity, and more specifically King Pyrrhus, also extended beyond these more elite groups and pervaded popular song.

Victorious Triumph, From Augustus to Ali Pasha

The region of Epirus was full of ancient heroes ripe for appropriation. Back in Nikopolis, Ali Pasha constructed a palace to mark the place where he had routed Napoleon in a great battle.

The precise location of this site is significant because it seems that Ali Pasha's villa-cum-memorial was intentionally situated directly above the spot where, almost two millennia before the vizier's time, the ancient Roman emperor Augustus had built his own monument to commemorate his triumph at the Battle of Actium. As mentioned above, the entire city of Nikopolis was founded by Augustus to celebrate his victory over Antony and Cleopatra in a great naval battle that took place off the shores of Actium in 31 BCE. Several years after the conflict, on the northern side of this new city, the emperor ordered that a large monumental complex be built to serve as an official victory memorial [Figure 5.10 and Figure 5.11]. This particular site – the Tropaion – was significant in that this was the location where Augustus had established his own camp to watch the battle take place below.[44]

By Ali Pasha's time, Nikopolis, including the Actium monument, had fallen into complete ruin, abandoned around the ninth century and eclipsed in the early modern period by Preveza. In 1798, however, the ancient city again became the site of an important military incursion. Upon the collapse of the Venetian Republic, Napoleon's forces entered and occupied the formerly Venetian-controlled areas on the Greek mainland, including Preveza. As a result of this action, war broke out between the French and the Ottoman Empire; this was Ali Pasha's opportunity to invade Preveza, which had thus far been off-limits to the vizier's control. The ruins of Nikopolis stand on the main road between Preveza and Ioannina and, in order to reach the port at Preveza, the vizier's troops were forced to face the French redoubts and trenches thrown up around the ancient site [Figure 5.12]. On October 23, 1798, thousands of Ali Pasha's soldiers succeeded in overwhelming the combined French and insurgent Greek forces.[45]

In order to commemorate this victory, Ali Pasha would later arrange to have a villa erected on the hill north of the city, where he had set up his own tent to watch the defeat of Napoleon's soldiers below. Most significantly, although this structure no longer stands, it seems that it was erected directly on top of the ancient Actium monument.

It is clear that in the early modern period, the people living in this region were fully aware that the ruins that were visible on the surface at Nikopolis indicated the presence of a large ancient city – the seventeenth-century Ottoman traveller Evliya Çelebi, for example, related hyperbolically that 'nowhere, in no places, has a fortified city been built on such a scale', and that a Roman emperor had once brought a thousand ships to the place, betraying perhaps some kind of sustained local memory of the Battle of Actium.[46] Yet, it remains highly unlikely that Ali Pasha knew specifically about the Monument to Augustus when he first planned his offensive against the French. Recent research in the French military archives indicates that the French forces staged their defensive line in anticipation that Ali Pasha's troops would descend into the plain from the top of the hill at Michalitsi, which at the time was along the main land route from Preveza to Ioannina.[47] The knowledge that Michalitsi also served as the site of the Augustan Tropaion seems to have come only after the battle with the French took place.

Thus, shortly after the Battle of Nikopolis, what had been a practical strategic decision became an opportunity for drawing a connection between Ali Pasha's victory against

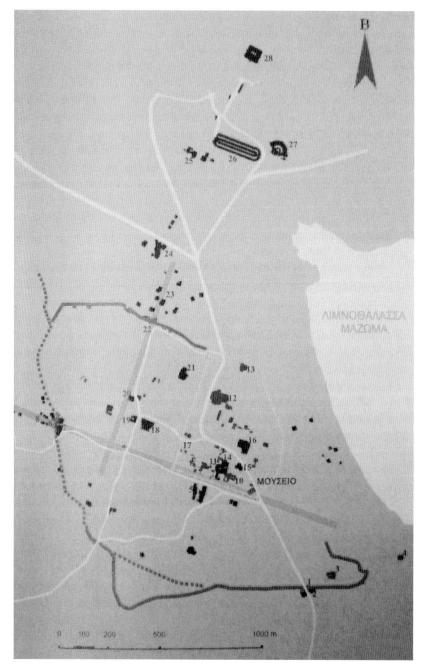

Figure 5.10: Map of ancient Nikopolis; the Monument of Augustus is north of the city, no. 28. Konstantinos Zachos.

Figure 5.11: Artist's reconstruction of the Monument of Augustus when it was first built. Konstantinos Zachos.

Napoleon and the triumph of Augustus at Actium, arguably one of the most famous military battles in ancient Rome. Ali Pasha mentioned to Brøndsted that he had already learned about the ancient history of Nikopolis from another English traveller, and this is most likely a reference to William Martin Leake, who visited the site in 1805.[48] Contemporary archaeologists credit Leake with the modern discovery of the Augustan monument.[49] By reading ancient authors such as Strabo and Suetonius, Leake identified the hill north of the city as the most probable site for the Actium memorial. It is plausible that, once Leake had explained the significance of this particular site to Ali Pasha, some six years after the Battle of Nikopolis, the governor arranged to have his own construction mark the place where two ambitious young leaders, separated by almost two millennia, had observed their fate unfold in the land and sea below.

By the time the traveller Thomas Hughes visited Nikopolis in 1813, Ali Pasha had already built his villa on top of the hill. In his own account, Hughes reported that 'behind the theatre, upon one of the highest peaks of the northern range of hills, stands a small serai belonging to the vizir'. He then confirmed that this palace had been:

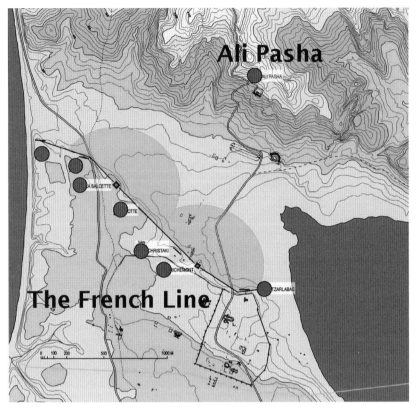

Figure 5.12: Map showing the positions of the French troops and Ali Pasha's camp in the 1798 Battle of Nikopolis. Adapted from a map by James Curlin.

Built upon the spot where [Ali Pasha] fixed his tent to observe the battle of Nicopolis, when his eldest son Mouchtar Pasha routed the French and Prevesans at the head of his Albanian cavalry. The same spot is assigned by many intelligent travellers to the tent of Augustus before the battle of Actium: there he built an [open-air] edifice to Apollo.[50]

From an archaeological perspective, it is entirely probable that the palace would have stood directly above the ancient site, as the foundations of the Actium memorial were cut into the very side of the hill, and once covered over with earth, would have created a convenient, flat platform upon which Ali Pasha could build. Unfortunately, no trace of the palace survives – recent excavations and ethnographic research has revealed that this site was looted during World War II, when Italian soldiers had locals smash stone blocks in order to construct guard-houses.[51]

It is possible, however, to catch a rare glimpse of this palace in a watercolour sketch by William Haygarth, with the house of Ali Pasha standing sentinel over the ancient city [Figure 5.13].[52]

Figure 5.13: William Haygarth's sketch of the site of Nikopolis (1810). American School of Classical Studies, Gennadius Library.

We also gain yet another perspective of this place from the land registers located in the State Ottoman Archives in Istanbul, which note that this structure was at the centre of the thriving agricultural holdings that Ali Pasha acquired upon his conquest of the area. Amid the ruins of Augustus's city of victory, the fields had come alive again with farmsteads yielding an abundance of produce for the surrounding region and the newly acquired port of Preveza.

In a register of Ali Pasha's landed properties prepared upon his execution in 1822, this residence is recorded under the entry for the 'Michalitsi farmstead' as a residence with an orchard.[53] Although Hughes rather generously refers to the structure at the top of the hill as a 'serai', the Ottoman register indicates that it was modest in size, having only one building (*'bir bab konak'*), as opposed to Ali Pasha's large palatial complexes at Ioannina or Preveza. No matter its size, this villa and its placement on the hill served as both a beacon of sorts for a centralized agro-economic regime, as well as a *lieux de memoire* that reminded visitors of Ali Pasha and Augustus and their profound connection across time – a coincidence so uncanny, it could only be explained by the force of destiny.

Conclusion: Confronting World Heritage

The assertion that Islamic societies possess an intrinsic aversion toward ancient civilizations which, for example, has been most recently rehearsed in contemporary news coverage of ISIS, finds deep roots in earlier narratives about Europe's discovery of ancient Greece and the birth of classical archaeology. Despite recent scholarly interventions, the view that the Ottomans were ambivalent to the ruins of antiquity acquired in their lands persists and is echoed in contemporary conflicts over the restitution of cultural artefacts between nation states. In 1812, precisely when Ali Pasha and Brøndsted visited Nikopolis, the final shipment of the Parthenon sculptures acquired by Lord Elgin arrived in London, ultimately headed to the galleries of the British Museum, where they can still be seen today. Indeed, the Elgin marbles remain a lightning rod in debates about cultural patrimony and the relevance of the encyclopaedic museum in the postmodern age. On their website, the Trustees of the British Museum contend that 'the Museum is a unique resource for the world', and that 'the Parthenon Sculptures are a vital element in this interconnected world collection. They are a part of the world's shared heritage and transcend political boundaries'.[54]

Many scholars have already noted that contemporary invocations of the primacy of world heritage are, potentially, simply coded ways of reaffirming a much older conviction that western powers are the most worthy stewards of antiquity, drawn in all of its forms from throughout the globe.[55] What the case study of Ali Pasha presents is an alternative view on antiquity, one that is not based on ethnicity, language or creed, but rather on place, a common locality. Throughout the centuries, Epirus continued to maintain a strong sense of regionalism, culminating in both a cultural and geographic insularity that made it notoriously difficult to control for a number of empires – from the Romans to the Byzantines and then the Ottomans. In many ways, Ali Pasha *was* the new Pyrrhus, successfully uniting a number of disparate tribes and micro-regions under a coherent political order. His view on antiquity could thus even be considered as an alternative proto-nationalist identity in the Balkans, an experiment that never got off the ground after Ali Pasha's death.

This investigation of Ali Pasha and his relationship with the ancient past has been inspired by a recent movement in Ottoman studies, wherein scholars interrogate the notion that classical and Near Eastern archaeology was a European invention imposed on a latent Ottoman population. Such academic interventions, primarily focusing on the late nineteenth century, still must ultimately grapple with the Ottoman intellectual elites in Istanbul and their palpable anxiety about 'catching up' with Western European nations. What is so fascinating about Ali Pasha's interest in antiquities, almost a century earlier in the early 1800s, is the complete absence of this anxiety, and in fact his sense of ownership and entitlement to the material located within the territory that he administered. In regards to the classical past, Ali Pasha exemplifies an Ottoman official that was fully in control of exploiting the political, monetary and cultural capital that could be gained by forging his own connections with local ancient heroes, embodied in material fragments, and embedded in the earth itself.

Acknowledgements

My thanks to Renata Holod, Devin Byker, Rachel Schneider Vlachos, Zoe Griffith and Michael Polczynski for offering their comments on earlier versions of this chapter. The material presented here is the result of several research trips conducted with the support of the US Department of Education and the University of Pennsylvania.

Notes

1. Frederick Cooper, *The Temple of Apollo Bassitas, Vol. 1: The Architecture* (Princeton: American School of Classical Studies at Athens, 1992), 13.
2. Peter Oluf Brøndsted, *Interviews with Ali Pacha of Joanina*, ed. Jacob Isager (Athens: Danish Institute at Athens, 1999), 35.
3. Otto von Stackelberg, *Der Apollotempel zu Bassae in Arcadien und die daselbst ausgegrabenen Bildwerke* (Rome: 1826), 117–18.
4. The bibliography on Ali Pasha is vast. Perhaps the best place to start is Katherine Fleming, *The Muslim Bonaparte: Diplomacy and Orientalism in Ali Pasha's Greece* (Princeton: Princeton University Press, 1999); and Dennis Skiotis, 'From Bandit to Pasha: First Steps in the Rise to Power of Ali of Tepelen, 1750–1784', *International Journal of Middle East Studies* 2–3 (July, 1971): 219–44.
5. Bruce McGowan, 'The Age of the *Ayans*, 1699–1812', in *An Economic and Social History of the Ottoman Empire, 1300–1914*, eds Halil Inalcık and Donald Quataert (Cambridge: Cambridge University Press, 1994), 667–68; Karen Barkey, *Empire of Difference: The Ottomans in Comparative Perspective* (Cambridge: Cambridge University Press, 2008), 244–52. Also, see Ali Yaycıoğlu, *Partners of the Empire: The Crisis of the Ottoman Order in the Age of Revolutions* (Redwood City: Stanford University Press, 2016).
6. I have completed a Ph.D. thesis on the topic of Ali Pasha as a patron of architecture. Emily Neumeier, 'The Architectural Transformation of the Ottoman Provinces under Tepedelenli Ali Pasha (1788–1822)' (Ph.D. diss., University of Pennsylvania, 2016).
7. *Scramble for the Past: A Story of Archaeology in the Ottoman Empire, 1753–1914*, eds Zainab Bahrani, Zeynep Çelik and Edhem Eldem, (Istanbul: SALT, 2011).
8. See especially William Martin Leake, *Travels in Northern Greece*, 4 vols (London: J. Rodwell, 1835) and John Cam Hobhouse, *A Journey through Albania […] during the Years 1809 and 1810*, 2 vols (Philadelphia: M. Carey, 1817).
9. Bruce Trigger, 'Alternative Archaeologies: Nationalist, Colonialist, Imperialist', *Man* 19.3 (1984): 360–61.
10. Gábor Ágoston, 'A Flexible Empire: Authority and Its Limits on the Ottoman Frontier', *International Journal of Turkish Studies* 9.2 (2003): 15–31.
11. For examples of local architectural patronage that does participate in a process of 'Ottomanizing' the provinces, see Irene Bierman, 'Franchising Ottoman Istanbul: The Case of Ottoman Crete', in *7 Centuries of Ottoman Architecture: 'A Supra-National Heritage'*, eds

Nur Akin, Afife Batur and Selçuk Batur (Istanbul: YEM, 2001), 199–204; and Heghnar Watenpaugh, *The Image of an Ottoman City: Imperial Architecture and Urban Experience in Aleppo in the 16th and 17th Centuries* (Leiden: Brill, 2004).

12. Gülrü Necipoğlu, *Architecture, Ceremonial, and Power: The Topkapi Palace in the Fifteenth and Sixteenth Centuries* (Cambridge, MA: MIT Press, 1991), 249; and Gülrü Necipoğlu, 'Süleyman the Magnificent and the Representation of Power in the Context of Ottoman-Hapsburg-Papal Rivalry', *The Art Bulletin* 71.3 (1989), 411.
13. Ünver Rüstem, 'Architecture for a New Age: Imperial Ottoman Mosques in Eighteenth-Century Istanbul' (Ph.D. diss., Harvard University, 2013), 281–87.
14. Brøndsted, *Interviews*, 70.
15. Ibid., 70.
16. Paschalis Kitromilides, *Enlightenment and Revolution: The Making of Modern Greece* (Cambridge, MA: Harvard University Press, 2013), 43, 302.
17. Edhem Eldem, 'From Blissful Indifference to Anguished Concern: Ottoman Perceptions of Antiquities, 1799–1869', in *Scramble For the Past: A Story of Archaeology in the Ottoman Empire, 1753–1914*, eds Zainab Bahrani, Zeynep Çelik and Edhem Eldem (Istanbul: SALT, 2011), 282.
18. Ibid., 293.
19. Ali Pasha was reported to have said to Brøndsted: 'My son wrote to me of the marbles found in the Morea; I myself, also have old stones in this country […], and if you have a mind to excavate some part in Albania, I will furnish you with as many people as you wish for nothing; – but it is to be understood that I will have my share of the marbles, and precious things that we find.' Brøndsted, *Interviews*, 64.
20. I explore Veli Pasha's excavations in the Morea in 'Rivalling Elgin: Ottoman Governors and Archaeological Agency in the Morea', in *Antiquarianisms: Contact, Conflict, and Comparison*, eds Benjamin Anderson and Felipe Rojas (Oxford: Oxbow Books, 2017), 132–158.
21. Brøndsted, *Interviews*, 68.
22. Ibid., 70.
23. Ibid., 70.
24. Ibid., 71.
25. Ibid., 73.
26. Ibid., 74.
27. Dale Kinney, 'The Concept of Spolia', in *A Companion to Medieval Art: Romanesque and Gothic in Northern Europe*, ed. Conrad Rudolph (Oxford: Blackwell, 2006), 240.
28. Thomas Smart Hughes, *Travels in Sicily, Greece and Albania*, vol. 1 (London: J. Mawman, 1820), 416.
29. Ibid., 416.
30. Letter from Tahir Abazi to Ali Aga Koutsi, April 1, 1818, Preveza, in *Archeio Ali Pasa*, eds Vasilis Panagiotopoulos, Dimitris Dimitropoulos and Panagiotis Michailaris, vol. 3 (Athens: Institute for Neohellenic Research, 2007), 84–86.
31. Athina Konstantaki, 'I poli tis Prevezas kai I Nikopoli apo ta teli tou 11ou eos tis arches tou 20ou ai.', in *Preveza B*, eds Nikos Karabelas and Michael Stork, vol. 1 (Preveza: University of Ioannina, Muncipality of Preveza and Actia Nicopolis Foundation, 2010), 10.

32. John Hobhouse, *Diary: Greece and Albania*, ed. Peter Cochran (1809), 49, accessed April 30, 2016, https://petercochran.files.wordpress. com/2009/12/04-greece2.pdf.
33. See James Curlin and Nikos Karabelas, 'Adi 31 Agosto 1797: A Dispute in the Venetian-Ottoman Border of Preveza', in *Proceedings of the 10th National Cartographic Conference (Ioannina 2008)* (Thessaloniki: 2010), 122–23.
34. Hughes, *Travels in Sicily*, 422.
35. The English translation is my own. My sincere thanks to Nikos Karabelas, who brought this inscription to my attention and made photographs of the object available to me. Georgios Liakopoulos is preparing a forthcoming study that will include a full treatment of this inscription.
36. N. G. L. Hammond, *Epirus: The Geography, the Ancient Remains, the History and the Topography of Epirus* (Oxford: Clarendon Press, 1967), 568–69; Plutarch, *Lives, Volume IX: Demetrius and Antony, Pyrrhus and Gaius Marius*, Loeb Classical Library, trans. Bernadotte Perrin (Cambridge, MA: Harvard University Press, 1920), 357–59.
37. Register of masons working at the 'Kastro' of Ioannina, September 19, 1801. *Archeio Ali Pasa*, eds Panagiotopoulos, Dimitropoulos and Michailaris, vol. 1, 184–87.
38. (1) […]Ο(ΣΤ) ΝΕΟΝ ΤΗΣ ΔΙΒΙΑΣ (2) […] ΕΣΟΝ ΤΗΣ ΦΩΤΙΑΣ (3) […] ΒΟΗΘΕΙΑΝ ΖΗΤΟΥΣΕ (4) […] ΠΟΤΕ ΔΕΝ ΗΜΠΟΡΟΥ(Σ)Ε (5) […] ΟΣΑ ΤΟΥ ΗΤΑΝ ΧΡΕΙΑ (6) […] ΤΟΥΤΟΥ ΠΑΡΕΥΘΥΣ Ν' ΑΝΑΨΗ ΤΗΝ ΦΟΤΙΑ (7) ΠΟΥ ΔΙΑ Ν' ΑΝΑΙΩΘΗ ΕΤΙ ΝΑ ΑΝΑΖΗΣΗ (8) ΤΑ […] ΩΜΕΝ(Α) ΤΕΙΧΗ ΤΟΥ ΠΑΛΙΝ ΝΑ ΑΝΑΚΤΗΣΗ (9) ΟΠΩΣ ΕΤ […] ΠΡΩΗΝ ΔΕΣΠΟΤΑΣ ΑΥΤΟΝ ΕΠΡΟΣΚΥΝΟΥΣΑΝ (10) ΚΑΙ ΔΙΑ ΑΝΑΚΑΙΝΙΣΜΟΝ ΠΑΝΤΑ ΠΑΡΑΚΑΛΟΥΣΑΝ (11) ΚΑΙ ΜΟΝΟΝ ΠΟΥ ΑΠΕΡΑΣΑΝ ΔΙΑΦΟΡΟΙ ΑΙΩΝΕΣ (12) ΚΑΙ ΚΑΘΕΞΗΣ ΠΟΛΛΟΤΑΤΟΙ ΥΠΑΤΟΙ Κ' ΗΓΕΜΩΝΕΣ (13) ΚΑΝΕΝΑΣ ΔΕΝ ΗΜΠΟΡΕΣΕ ΝΑ ΛΑΒΗ ΤΗΝ ΦΡΟΝΤΙΔΑ (14) ΚΑΙ ΕΥΕΡΓΕΤΗΣ ΝΑ ΔΕΙΧΘΕΙ ΕΙΣ ΤΑΥΤΗΝ ΤΗΝ ΠΑΤΡΙΔΑ (15) ΟΥΤΕ ΕΙΣ ΤΗΝ ΠΑΡΕΛΕΥΣΙΝ ΤΟΣΟΥΤΩΝ ΠΟΛΛΩΝ ΧΡΟΝΩΝ (16) ΗΜΠΟΡΕΣΑΝ ΝΑ ΒΑΛΛΩΣΙ ΚΑΝΕΝΑ ΛΙΘΟΝ ΜΟΝΟΝ (17) Ο ΚΡΑΤΙΣΤΟΣ Δ(Ε) ΑΛΗ ΠΑΣΙΑΣ ΒΕΖΥΡΗΣ ΤΗΣ ΗΠΕΙΡΟΥ (18) ΠΕΡΙΦΙΜΟΣ ΑΠΟΓΟΝΟΣ ΤΟΥ ΘΑΥΜΑΣΙΟΥ ΠΥΡΟΥ (19) ΩΣ ΑΛΛΟ ΠΥΡ ΘΑΥΜΑ[ΣΤ]ΟΝ ΤΟΥΤΟ ΤΟ ΑΝΑΣΤΑΙΝΕΙ (20) ΚΑΙ ΠΛΕΟΝ ΩΡΑΙΟΤΕΡΟΝ ΤΟ ΑΠΟΚΑΤΑΣΤΑΙΝΕΙ (21) ΑΩΙΕ The English translation is my own. A transcription of this text has been published in Christos I. Soulis, 'Tourkikai Epigrafai Ioanninon', *Ipeirotika Chronika* 8 (1933), (92–93); Tatiana Steriadi, 'Oi epigrafes tou kastrou', in *To Kastro ton Ioanninon*, ed. Barbara Papadopoulou (Ioannina: 8th Ephorate of Byzantine Antiquities, 2009), 116–17.
39. See note 38.
40. See, for example, the foundation inscriptions from the Church of Agios Nikolaos in Vasiliki (11 km north of Trikala), dated 1818, or from the church dedicated to the Theotokos in Roupsia (north of Ioannina), dated 1814.
41. Émile Legrand, *Complainte d'Ali de Tébélen, Pacha de Janina: Poème historique en dialecte épirote* (Paris: Imprimerie nationale, 1886).
42. Ibid., 8.
43. Ibid., 13.
44. Konstantinos Zachos, 'The *Tropaeum* of the Sea-Battle of Actium at Nikopolis: Interim Report', *Journal of Roman Archaeology* 16 (2003): 65.

45. James Curlin, '"Remember the Moment when Previsa Fell": The 1798 Battle of Nicopolis and Preveza', in *Preveza B*, eds Nikos Karabelas and Michael Stork, vol. 1 (Preveza: University of Ioannina, Muncipality of Preveza and Actia Nicopolis Foundation, 2010), 269.
46. Spiros Ergolavos, *Evliya Tselebi, Taksidi stin Ipeiro: Ena apokaliptiko dokoumento tou 17ou aiona* (Ioannina: Ekdoseis Ipeiros, 1995), 36.
47. Curlin, '"Remember the Moment when Previsa Fell"', 270.
48. Leake, *Travels in Northern Greece*, 180.
49. Zachos, 'The *Tropaeum* of the Sea-Battle of Actium at Nikopolis', 66.
50. Hughes, *Travels in Sicily*, 420.
51. Konstantinos Zachos, 'Excavations at the Actian Tropaeum at Nikopolis', in *Foundation and Destruction: Nikopolis and Northwestern Greece*, ed. Jacob Isager (Aarhus: Aarhus University, 2001), 29.
52. Nikos Karabelas, 'O Anglos theologos Thomas S. Hughes stin Preveza kai ti Nikopoli', *Prevezanika Chronika* 41–42 (2005): note 129.
53. Başbakanlık Osmanlı Arşivi Istanbul, MAD d.9767 (Shawwal 29, 1241 AH/June 6, 1826 CE), 17.
54. 'The Parthenon Sculptures: The Position of the Trustees of the British Museum', *The British Museum*, accessed March 23, 2015, http://www.brit-ishmuseum.org/about_us/news_and_press/statements/parthenon_sculp-tures/trustees_statement.aspx.
55. David Lowenthal, *The Heritage Crusade and the Spoils of History* (Cambridge: Cambridge University Press, 1998), especially 240–44; Immanuel Wallerstein, *European Universalism: The Rhetoric of Power* (New York: The New Press, 2006); Sophia Labadi, *UNESCO, Cultural Heritage, and Outstanding Universal Value* (Lanham, MD: AltaMira Press, 2013), 15.

6

Claiming the Classical Past: Ottoman Archaeology at Lagina

Amanda Herring

Lagina, home to the Hellenistic Sanctuary of Hekate, is one of only a few sites in Anatolia where neither the excavations nor the remains have fallen into the control of foreign archaeologists. Instead, Lagina has been excavated only by Ottoman and Turkish teams, and all of the objects found there have remained in Turkey. Lagina and the Temple of Hekate, which was abandoned in late antiquity, re-emerged into the public consciousness in the nineteenth century. While the first investigations of Lagina were undertaken by European travellers in search of remnants of the classical past, no archaeological campaigns took place there until Osman Hamdi (1842–1910), the director of the Imperial Museum in Istanbul, conducted excavations in 1891 and 1892.[1] Over the course of two seasons, Osman Hamdi and his team uncovered the remains of the Temple of Hekate and transported the building's sculpture to Istanbul for display in the Imperial Museum.

Osman Hamdi's excavations at Lagina took place at a time when the ways in which Ottoman society viewed the classical past and leveraged this past politically were changing. As part of a broader program of reform and modernization in the Ottoman Empire, the state and a number of its citizens, including Osman Hamdi, turned their attention to the ancient societies whose ruins lay within their borders, and engaged with the classical past through the collection of ancient objects and the practice of archaeology.[2]

In Europe, the reverence of the ancient past was already well-established and played a role in the construction of national identities. Through the study of classical language, culture, and art, western Europeans formed ideologies that highlighted connections between their own societies and those of the ancients. To support these claims, Europeans actively collected antiquities, many of which were obtained through archaeological investigations conducted at sites outside their own nations' borders, overlaying archaeology with imperialist implications.[3]

Given that many European-sponsored archaeological investigations took place in Ottoman territories, Ottoman engagement with archaeology was necessarily influenced by and responded to the European model. Yet this chapter argues that Osman Hamdi's work at Lagina did not simply mimic European practices, but moved beyond them and established a template for future Ottoman archaeological excavations. While Osman Hamdi had previously undertaken campaigns on behalf of the Ottoman state at Nemrud Dağı in southeast Anatolia and Sidon in Lebanon, both consisted of only a single round of excavation. By contrast, the Lagina campaign was designed as a long-term scientific expedition that involved collaboration with French archaeologists and maintaining Ottoman control over

Figure 6.1: Current state of the Sanctuary of Hekate at Lagina. Amanda Herring.

the archaeological process and its finds while cementing political alliances. In addition, while the plan was abandoned before completion, the work at Lagina was intended to culminate in the full-scale reconstruction of the Temple of Hekate at the Imperial Museum in Istanbul, a project unmatched by any European museum at the time. The scope of the Lagina campaign set it apart from previous Ottoman archaeological endeavours, indicating that the ancient past was now an important part of Ottoman cultural patrimony.

The Rediscovery of Lagina

Lagina, today part of the Turkish province of Muğla, was in the ancient period part of Karia, a region incorporated into the Greek world during the Hellenistic period. Attached to the city of Stratonikeia, Lagina was home to the only monumental temple dedicated to Hekate, the chthonic goddess of crossroads, magic, and liminality [Figure 6.1]. During its construction in the late second century BCE, only the sanctuary was located at Lagina, and the only people who lived on the site were the temple staff and their families. Stratonikeia lay ten kilometres to the southeast.[4]

The Temple of Hekate was lavish in its construction. Made entirely of marble, it was on the cutting edge of contemporary architectural design with its large pseudo-dipteral plan and its use of the Corinthian order. It was heavily decorated with sculpture, including, notably, a sculpted frieze depicting Karian myths and scenes from the life of Hekate wrapping around the exterior of the building in the entablature.[5] While it was constructed primarily to serve the needs of the local population, a description of the temple in the work of the Roman writer Strabo (c.64 BCE–c.23 CE) indicates that the temple was known internationally for the beauty of its construction, and that it attracted visitors from the wider classical world wishing to worship Hekate at her most important sacred site.[6] After operating for approximately 500 years, the temple fell into disuse and was eventually abandoned in late antiquity. While recent archaeological campaigns have found remains of a few Byzantine buildings on the site, it appears that with the closure of the temple, Lagina lost the prominence it once held and played host to only small settlements over the following centuries.[7]

Lagina regained some measure of international renown only in the nineteenth century when European interest in the ancient past reached an apex.[8] As movements such as philhellenism became a significant intellectual and political force in European societies, Europeans constructed ideologies that claimed themselves as the true inheritors of the classical tradition.[9] The possession of antiquities became a method for Europeans to reinforce such perceived connections to the ancients, and knowledge of ancient cultures became a key tenet in the formation of European national identities, especially in England, France, and Germany.[10] Europeans travelled first to Italy, and then further east to territories under Ottoman control, to record the remains of the ancient past and to acquire objects for their national museums.[11] It was during this period that some of the most famous, and largest, monuments entered national collections, including the Parthenon Marbles in the British Museum, the pediments from Aegina in the Glyptothek in Munich, and the Venus de Milo in the Louvre.[12]

However, laws that restricted foreign excavations and the export of antiquities were soon passed in both Greece and Italy. The Italian states created legislation as early as 1820; in Greece, one of the first acts of the state after it won independence from the Ottoman Empire was to outlaw the exportation of antiquities in 1827.[13] Such laws forced Europeans in search of antiquities to look further east to the Ottoman lands, where similar legislation had not yet been passed. The nineteenth century saw an antiquities race, as Europeans battled against each other to acquire objects from Ottoman territories for their national collections. These archaeological campaigns were constructed on imperialist models that emphasized European superiority. Europeans believed that removing antiquities from sites in Ottoman territories was entirely justified since, as the rightful inheritors of classical civilization, they had a greater appreciation and understanding of the objects than their Ottoman counterparts.[14]

It was these motivations that led to the first modern explorations of Lagina. The Temple of Hekate was known from ancient textual sources, but not firmly identified with any ruins until the middle of the nineteenth century. Interest was slower to build at Lagina than at many other classical sites in Anatolia due to its remote location off the main roads and far from any modern city or major archaeological site. While Stratonikeia, or Eskihisar as it had come to be known, was still inhabited, it was a poor and isolated village. Few travellers, either Ottoman or European, had reason to visit the town, leaving the ruins of Lagina undisturbed.

The first European to mention Lagina in print was Richard Pococke, an English clergyman and scholar who travelled eastward in the late 1730s and early 1740s, and later published a comprehensive account of his journey. His book, while providing a number of valuable observations about ancient ruins, is mainly a travelogue, not a scholarly study. Pococke first went to Eskihisar, which he identified as Stratonikeia thanks to its still-visible ancient ruins. After he left Eskihisar, he broke his journey in a village that the locals called Lakena, which he associated, correctly, with ancient Lagina. He described a castle on a hill outside the village but did not make any mention of the Temple of Hekate.[15] His account indicates that Lagina, while rarely visited, was in the consciousness of Europeans in the eighteenth century.

The site does not show up in literature again until Richard Chandler's 1775 account of his tour through Anatolia. Chandler, along with Nicholas Revett, an architect, and William Pars, a painter, was sent to Anatolia by the Society of Dilettanti between 1764 and 1766 to undertake a survey of the classical ruins of Ionia, later published in two volumes as *Ionian Antiquities* and *Travels in Asia Minor*.[16] While Chandler mentions the Temple of Hekate in *Travels in Asia Minor*, he does not describe the ruins of the temple, stating only that it was near Eskihisar and famous in antiquity.[17] Chandler's works, though written with a more scholarly agenda than Pococke's travel journals, shed no new light on the state of the ruins at Lagina. The site appears again in 1850 in the German classicist Ludwig Ross's work *Kleinasien und Deutschland*. He mentions a visit to both Lagina and Stratonikeia and discusses the ancient descriptions of the Temple of Hekate, but does not seem interested in further exploration of the site, adding no new information.[18]

It was not until 1863, when Charles Newton published his book *A History of Discoveries at Halicarnassus, Cnidus, and Branchidae*, that Lagina received more than a passing mention among the European community. Newton, an archaeologist and the first Keeper of Greek and Roman Antiquities at the British Museum, visited Lagina in 1856. He had been sent by the museum to the region primarily to find and uncover the remnants of the Mausoleum at Halikarnassos (modern Bodrum), but he also undertook a series of side trips to archaeological sites in the area.[19] Newton's published account of the Temple of Hekate was informed both by his exploration of Lagina and by the 1857 visit by Robert Murdoch Smith, an engineer who assisted Newton in his excavations.[20] Using his and Smith's data, including a set of photographs they took of the temple's frieze, Newton was able to put together an extensive report on the Temple of Hekate [Figure 6.2]. In the text, he created a precisely measured architectural plan and described in detail the architectural remains of the temple, including nine sculpted frieze blocks. He also translated a number of inscriptions he found on the site, examining what they revealed about the political and religious context of the temple.[21] His text provided the first modern images of Lagina, including a print of the sanctuary's only standing architectural element, the doorjamb of the propylon. [Figure 6.3]

Claiming the Classical Past: Ottoman Archaeology at Lagina

Figure 6.2: Images of two frieze blocks from the Temple of Hekate at Lagina from C. T. Newton and R. P. Pullan, *A History of Discoveries at Halicarnassus, Cnidus and Branchidae* (London: Day and Son, 1863), Plate LXXX. Getty Research Institute, Los Angeles (84–B749).

Figure 6.3: Image of ruins of the Propylon in the Sanctuary of Hekate at Lagina from C. T. Newton and R. P. Pullan, *A History of Discoveries at Halicarnassus, Cnidus and Branchidae* (London: Day and Son, 1863), Plate LXXVIII. Getty Research Institute, Los Angeles (84–B749).

The scientific nature of Newton's text is in sharp contrast to previous accounts of Lagina. Neither Newton nor Smith undertook any excavation at Lagina, but they explored all the visible ruins thoroughly, in some cases hiring a local crew to move stone pieces in order to catalogue them. It appears that Newton removed a single object from Lagina, a sculpted arm that came from the temple's frieze, now housed in the British Museum. He did not have a permit to remove objects, and it is probable that the arm was lying on the ground and that Newton pocketed it as a souvenir.[22] Newton's account represents the first time that Lagina was examined through an archaeological lens, rather than that of a curious traveller or dilettante, and represents a turning point in the history of archaeological exploration at the site.

By the 1880s, thanks to Newton's work, Lagina became a more common destination for classical scholars as they began to travel further afield in Anatolia in search of new sites for excavations and for new sources of antiquities. In 1881, two Austrians, Otto Benndorf and George Niemann, explored Lagina, discovering six previously unknown frieze blocks and inscribed sections of the temple walls. The Austrians were anxious to catch up with their opponents in the antiquities race, whose collections far surpassed their own. They therefore decided to fund the expedition of Benndorf and Niemann to determine the suitability of Gölbaşı (Trysa) in Lycia, the ruins of which had been described in print, but not yet excavated, as a possible location for an Austrian campaign. After spending a month at Gölbaşı the team stopped by Lagina and determined that it was another candidate for Austrian excavation. The next year, they secured a firman that allowed them to dig at both Gölbaşı and Lagina and to keep one third of the finds. However, the team began work at Gölbaşı and, due to Austrian satisfaction with the finds from this dig, never returned to Lagina.[23]

French scholars also visited Lagina in the 1880s, including Amédée Hauvette-Besnault and Marcel Dubois in 1880 and Charles Diehl and Georges Cousin in 1885. Both teams visited Lagina as part of larger tours of Asia Minor and published accounts of the inscriptions they found at the site.[24] Their articles raised both public and academic interest in Lagina, especially among French scholars, as indicated by the appearance of notices of their work in most of the important archaeological and classical journals of the day.

Notably, their articles attracted the attention of Joseph Chamonard and Philippe Legrand, scholars associated with the École française d'Athènes. In May 1891, during explorations at Lagina, they discovered thirteen new blocks of the frieze and took numerous photographs of the site and its sculpture. Chamonard, on his return to France, presented a lecture on Lagina at a meeting of the Académie des Inscriptions et Belles-Lettres on August 28, 1891. Lagina was a main topic at the meeting, and Chamonard's report received wide coverage not only in archaeological journals, but also in French-language newspapers published in France and Istanbul.[25] Chamonard was building a case to secure French governmental support to conduct excavations at Lagina, and the wide press coverage shows that the proposal enjoyed significant public interest.

Archaeology and Identity in the Ottoman Empire

As interest in Lagina grew among European archaeologists, attitudes towards archaeology and the classical past began to change in the Ottoman Empire. Beginning in the second half of the nineteenth century, Ottoman authorities curtailed foreign excavations and the resultant large-scale exportation of antiquities.[26] These efforts were part of a larger program of reform, modernization, and westernization, notably during the Tanzimat period between 1839 and 1876. The reforms included not only the reorganization of governmental agencies and the importation of technology such as railroads and the telegraph, but also new laws regarding antiquities and archaeological excavations.[27]

As part of these reforms, in 1839, the government issued the Imperial Edict of Gülhane, which promoted a new national identity known as Ottomanism. The edict established that all Ottoman citizens, regardless of ethnicity or religion, were equal before the law. It was intended to help keep the empire together by pushing its citizens to think of themselves as Ottoman, rather than as members of a specific ethnic or religious group.[28] The concept was more firmly incorporated into Ottoman self-image with the 1869 Nationality Law, which for the first time defined Ottoman citizenship and nationality in secular terms, without reference to religion.[29]

Connections with the ancient, and in particular the classical, past were purposefully included in formulations of this modernized Ottoman state and its associated identity.[30] In contrast to European characterizations of the Ottomans as a backwards people whose decline was highlighted by the decayed state of the classical ruins in their midst, modern Ottoman constructs placed the ancient remnants firmly within a common cultural heritage. All previous inhabitants of Ottoman lands, not just the Muslim forbears, were appropriated for the new national identity.[31] As part of this process of identity creation, Ottoman rulers began in 1846 to collect and house antiquities in a European-style assemblage that consciously included the Greco-Roman past within the narrative of national history. In 1869, Istanbul issued an edict restricting foreign excavations and declared that antiquities from around the empire be collected and brought to the capital.[32] The Imperial Museum was created to house the incoming objects.[33] This newfound interest in systematic antiquities collection mimicked the archaeological imperialist programs of the west, whereby objects were collected from a variety of cultures and placed under the roof of a single museum.[34]

Two additional laws were passed in 1874 and 1884 that strengthened Ottoman claims to antiquities by further regulating the archaeological process and the activities of foreign excavators within the empire. The 1884 legislation extended state ownership over all antiquities found within the empire in addition to making it illegal to export them.[35]

Osman Hamdi Bey

Osman Hamdi, director of the Imperial Museum between 1881 and 1910, played a central role in the creation and implementation of the antiquities laws.[36] Osman Hamdi was born in 1842 into a prominent and politically well-connected family.[37] His father sent him to Paris in 1860 to study law, but Osman Hamdi became interested in art instead, and studied painting under Gustav Boulanger and Jean-Léon Gérôme at the École des Beaux-Arts. While he was never able to support himself through his artwork, Osman Hamdi continued to paint throughout his life.[38]

In 1868, his father recalled him to Istanbul. Despite Osman Hamdi's objections, he returned with his French wife and two daughters and was given a position as Director of Political Affairs in the retinue of Ahmet Midhat Pasha, the governor of Baghdad.[39] Osman Hamdi's time with Midhat Pasha marked the beginning of his long career in Ottoman bureaucracy, which culminated in his tenure as the director of the Imperial Museum. Osman Hamdi was the first Ottoman citizen to hold the post. Before he took office, the position was held by Philip Anton Dethier, a German classicist. When Dethier died in 1881, the Ottomans asked the German consulate to help them find a suitable replacement. During the course of negotiations, however, the museum broke off talks and decided to hire Osman Hamdi. With his appointment, the Ottoman administration indicated that they were no longer willing to accept European domination in the cultural field. The appointment marked a clear move towards the appropriation of antiquity as cultural and national currency and announced the Ottomans as active players in archaeology and collecting.[40]

Under Osman Hamdi's leadership, the museum expanded its display space, took a more active role in collecting artefacts, oversaw foreign excavations and exportation, and conducted its own archaeological campaigns at Nemrud Dağı, Sidon, and Lagina. It became the centre of the archaeological world in the Ottoman Empire. Osman Hamdi and his staff decided which foreign teams were allowed to dig on Ottoman soil, and after 1884, which objects could be exported.[41] His personal involvement in the excavations at Lagina in the 1890s assured that the site and its remains would gain a place in Ottoman archaeological history.

Osman Hamdi's approach to antiquities was influenced by his political beliefs, first formed during his time in Paris and then working under Midhat Pasha in Baghdad. Midhat Pasha, a strong believer in the future of an Ottoman Empire as a modern, European-style polity, was one of the key reformers of the Tanzimat and the main writer of the first written Ottoman constitution.[42] Later, Osman Hamdi was also associated with the Young Turks, a group of revolutionaries who opposed the sultanate of Abdülhamid II (r.1876–1909) and who were, like their predecessor Midhat Pasha, western-leaning.[43]

As a proponent of nationalism, Osman Hamdi could not ignore the importance of classicism in the formation of European identities. He fought to keep ancient artefacts within the Ottoman Empire because of their role as political, cultural, and national indicators. Antiquities and the museum that housed them were an integral part of the formation of a modern Ottoman nation.[44] He adopted a mind-set that valued antiquity but modified it so that the Ottoman Empire had a greater right to the objects desired by Europeans.

Ottoman Archaeology at Lagina

Osman Hamdi displayed this approach in his work at Lagina. The increasing attention that the Temple of Hekate was receiving in European circles after Joseph Chamonard's August 1891 lecture on the site prompted Osman Hamdi to take immediate action. Osman Hamdi began work at Lagina in October 1891, effectively circumventing any French claims to the site.[45]

His campaigns at Lagina developed upon a pattern he had established in his previous archaeological excavations at Nemrud Dağı and Sidon. As would be the case at Lagina, Osman Hamdi's work at Nemrud Dağı – the location of the funeral monument of Antiochos I, a Hellenistic king of Commagene – was prompted by the interest of foreign archaeologists. In 1883, the Royal Prussian Academy of Sciences commissioned Otto Puchstein and Carl Humann to undertake an investigation of Nemrud Dağı. Osman Hamdi, supported by the Ottoman government, organized his own expedition to the site, accompanied by Osgan Efendi, a sculptor and teacher from the School of Fine Arts in Istanbul. While both teams examined the site in the spring of that year, it was Osman Hamdi who first notified the press, highlighting that an Ottoman team had made a great archaeological discovery. Osman Hamdi also published his findings.[46] While the immense size of the monument and its statues made it impossible for Osman Hamdi to transport the antiquities back to Istanbul, he claimed the site for the Ottomans through his publications and press releases. Four years later, Osman Hamdi worked for two months in the spring of 1887 excavating an ancient necropolis at Sidon in Lebanon. A local villager, Mehmet Efendi, had discovered the cemetery by chance when digging foundations for a new building. Osman Hamdi immediately went to Sidon to establish Ottoman claims to the finds and oversee the excavations. Uncovered at the site and subsequently sent to Istanbul were twenty-six sarcophagi, including the Alexander Sarcophagus.[47] The discovery drew international attention, and the sarcophagi became the centrepiece of the Imperial Museum collection, requiring the construction of a new building to house them.[48] It was a triumph for Osman Hamdi, and justified Ottoman involvement in archaeology.

The campaigns at Nemrud Dağı and Sidon established important precedents for Osman Hamdi's excavations at Lagina. At each site, instead of allowing foreign excavations, Osman Hamdi stepped in quickly, oversaw the excavations personally, and sent all of the important finds to Istanbul. He followed models established by European excavators, using the same archaeological methods, excavating in an area controlled by the state but far from the centre of the empire, and subsequently removing the antiquities found at the site to the imperial capital.

It was at Lagina that this process reached its height, at a moment when – due to the enactment of the antiquities laws, the success of Osman Hamdi's previous excavations, and the opening of the new Imperial Museum buildings – the importance of classical remains was cemented in Ottoman cultural policies. The work at Lagina, in contrast to Osman Hamdi's previous projects, was designed as a long-term campaign. Osman Hamdi excavated at Lagina for two seasons and planned for work to continue for multiple years until illness forced him to abandon activity at the site. His work there went beyond the previous model of a short archaeological dig followed by the quick expropriation of important finds. Instead, excavations at Lagina established a new template of Ottoman archaeology, with scientific excavations that emphasized the process of archaeology as well as its finds.[49] In addition, Osman Hamdi's campaigns were intended to culminate with the reconstruction of the Lagina temple in Istanbul. With this reconstruction Osman Hamdi did not merely emulate European archaeological endeavours; he surpassed them.[50]

An Ottoman team led by Osman Hamdi dug at Lagina between October 17 and 31, 1891.[51] They uncovered ten frieze blocks, bringing the known total up to 34. All of the extant blocks were moved to a temporary shelter in a nearby village. Osman Hamdi wished to immediately move the blocks to the Imperial Museum but was unable to do so for logistical reasons: the roads out of Lagina were simply not in good enough repair to transport the frieze. Instead, he ordered repair work on the road to the nearest port so that the blocks could be moved the next year.[52]

Osman Hamdi returned to Lagina on September 30, 1892, and continued excavations until October 20. A few more sections of the frieze, along with a number of inscriptions and architectural remnants, were uncovered. Work was called to a halt due to an outbreak of fever, which affected a number of the crew, including Osman Hamdi. It was decided to postpone further excavation work until the next year.[53] The uncovered frieze blocks were boxed up and shipped over the now repaired roads to Istanbul.

After leading the Ottoman team alone during the 1891 season, Osman Hamdi was accompanied in the 1892 season by French archaeologist Joseph Chamonard. In a widely publicized agreement, Osman Hamdi had arranged for Chamonard's assistance in a series of negotiations with Théophile Homolle, the director of the École française d'Athènes. They agreed that while all finds from the dig would remain in Ottoman hands, the French would receive publication rights.[54] As numerous journals and newspapers reported, a letter from Osman Hamdi inviting Chamonard was read by Homolle at a meeting of the Académie des Inscriptions et Belles-Lettres on September 2, 1892.[55]

That Osman Hamdi requested French participation and ceded publication rights speaks directly to the Ottoman agenda in archaeology in the late nineteenth century. As museum director, Osman Hamdi had to constantly balance his goal of amassing artefacts with the need to maintain cordial relations with western archaeological schools operating within the Ottoman Empire. Trouble with the foreign archaeological schools could complicate or even damage Ottoman political relations with European states. By inviting the French to participate in the excavations at Lagina, Osman Hamdi smoothed over any earlier French claims to the site that his project had undermined.[56] As it was Chamonard who had been pushing the hardest to undertake French excavations at Lagina, his participation in the Ottoman-led excavations was effective in silencing any French opposition, while keeping all the antiquities in Ottoman hands.

Letters exchanged between Osman Hamdi and Homolle in 1891 and 1892 attest that both were deeply invested in the Lagina venture.[57] In highly complimentary language, the two negotiated and reviewed the French-Ottoman partnership. One letter from Homolle dated

November 19, 1892, responds to Osman Hamdi's disappointment that an architect had not accompanied Chamonard to the Lagina during the 1892 season.[58] Homolle writes that it was not an indication of the French School's lack of investment in the Lagina project, but rather a misunderstanding, and assures Osman Hamdi that an architect would be provided in the following season. Throughout the letters, both Homolle and Osman Hamdi emphasize their hope for a continued relationship beyond their work at Lagina, and that the success of their international cooperation will function as model for future endeavours.

As the excavations at Lagina show, Osman Hamdi envisioned archaeology in the empire as a collaboration between Europeans and Ottomans.[59] Yet it was a collaboration in which Ottomans held significantly more power as the leading actors in these projects. Since the Ottomans maintained ownership of the most important product of archaeology, the artefacts themselves, it was acceptable that the Ottomans ceded publication rights. Osman Hamdi promoted this as a viable approach beyond Lagina in his publication in 1892 of *Une nécropole royale à Sidon*, a catalogue of the finds from the excavation.[60] Osman Hamdi co-authored this text with the French archaeologist, Théodore Reinach, establishing a collaborative relationship with a division of finds and publication rights.

For Osman Hamdi, deriving the full value from the collaborative arrangement at Lagina required that the public was aware of the Ottoman involvement in the excavations. Public recognition, particularly European recognition, legitimized Ottoman involvement in this formerly European-only activity and cemented the importance of antiquity in the formation of Ottoman identity.[61] Between 1891 and 1894, the Lagina excavations and Osman Hamdi's involvement were frequent news items in European and American archaeological journals and in European-language newspapers published in Istanbul, such as the English- and French-language *The Oriental Advertiser-Le Moniteur Oriental*.[62] In 1891, only Osman Hamdi's departure for Izmir with the museum's director of excavations, Bedri Bey, is mentioned.[63] It is clear that Osman Hamdi's first campaign at Lagina was organized hastily and that he was unsure of what he would find at the site.

By contrast, in fall 1892, notices relating to Lagina appeared regularly in the press. In all of these, Osman Hamdi's involvement is treated as being equal in importance to the antiquities themselves. The readers are kept updated on his journeys to and from the site, as well as descriptions of the sculpture and other antiquities found. The massive scale of the work necessary to crate and transport of all of these finds from Lagina to Istanbul, including the construction of the new road, was especially well-documented.[64] Many of the news reports are based on letters and telegrams from Osman Hamdi himself, highlighting that he saw publicity as an integral part of his job as director. European audiences were clearly interested in the results of the Lagina excavations, recognizing them as a significant and important endeavour as well as accepting the central role of Osman Hamdi and the Ottoman government in the field of archaeology. To properly record the excavations for posterity, a series of photographs was taken at Lagina during the 1892 season. These photographs highlight what Osman Hamdi saw as the most important aspects of the dig: the collaboration between the Ottomans and the French and the historical and artistic

Claiming the Classical Past: Ottoman Archaeology at Lagina

Figure 6.4: Photograph of workers excavating the Propylon at Lagina in 1892. Istanbul Archaeological Museums Archive.

significance of the finds. Most of the photographs depict the excavation process itself, with men in Ottoman dress labouring to move stone blocks or clear away dirt. They are set against the picturesque background of the site, notably the doorway of the sanctuary's propylon that was the site's most recognizable feature since a print of it was published in Newton's 1863 text [Figure 6.4]. Notable among the photographs is an image of Osman Hamdi and his French collaborators. The four men are carefully posed against a background of tumbled stone blocks and column drums [Figure 6.5]. Osman Hamdi stands in the centre of the photograph in a khaki suit and fez. Chamonard can be identified as the figure on the left of Osman Hamdi perched on a column drum in a suit and flat cap. The photographs provide a compelling visual representation of how the directorate of the excavation was organized, and how Osman Hamdi wanted the rest of the scholarly community to view the archaeological campaigns. Osman Hamdi, depicted prominently in the centre of the photograph, was the leader of the expedition. The French archaeologists who worked at the site were recognized as valuable members of the directorate, but they occupied secondary positions.

Figure 6.5: Photograph of Osman Hamdi Bey, Joseph Chamonard, and other members of the archaeological team at Lagina in September 1892. Istanbul Archaeological Museums Archive.

Other surviving photographs showing the removal of the frieze blocks from the Temple of Hekate shed additional light on the Ottoman excavations. In one, the blocks are lined up, with the sculpted figures facing out towards the viewer as workmen, overseen by Osman Hamdi, prepare the blocks for transportation [Figure 6.6]. Another photograph shows the blocks being carried safely away from the site in ox-carts, showcasing Osman Hamdi's capabilities as a responsible guardian of the past [Figure 6.7]. By focusing on the process of preparing and transporting the sculptural elements of the temple, these photographs highlight a tactical goal of Osman Hamdi's excavations, to recover remnants

Figure 6.6: Photograph of Osman Hamdi Bey overseeing workers prepare the frieze blocks from the Temple of Hekate at Lagina for transportation in 1892. Istanbul Archaeological Museums Archive.

of the classical past that would look impressive when placed on display in the Imperial Museum.

In 1892, Osman Hamdi devised a plan that all of the surviving architectural elements of the temple would be uncovered and shipped to the Imperial Museum during the next season. He planned to reconstruct the entire Temple of Hekate and its architectural sculpture at a site next to the museum and dedicate the new building to Karian art and archaeology. To oversee the construction, he hired Joseph-Albert Tournaire, a French architect who had won the Rome Prize in 1888 and had worked for the French at Delphi.[65] The imagining of such an ambitious and prominent project highlights the importance that Osman Hamdi attached to the Lagina excavations and its finds. An 1893 profile of Osman Hamdi published in the American magazine *The Century* reported that he believed that the Lagina frieze was more significant artistically and historically than even the Sidon sarcophagi, which were commonly viewed as the most important objects in the museum's collection.[66] The reconstruction of the Temple of Hekate and its sculpture would therefore provide the museum with a centrepiece that would compete with or even surpass the antiquities displays in European museums, while a specifically

Figure 6.7: Photograph of the frieze blocks from the Temple of Hekate at Lagina leaving the site on ox-carts in 1892. Istanbul Archaeological Museums Archive.

Karian museum would be a new and unique institution. The reconstruction project also underscores that Osman Hamdi had plans to continue excavations at Lagina, and perhaps even at other sites in Karia. Such future excavations would have been necessary to find all of the elements needed for the reconstruction and to fill the museum with impressive antiquities.

However, Osman Hamdi was still recovering from the illness he contracted at Lagina and was unable to return to the site in 1893. Plans were made to continue the excavations at Lagina in partnership with Chamonard and the French team but with Halil Edhem substituting as director.[67] Halil Edhem, Osman Hamdi's brother and associate at the Imperial Museum, had taken over the directorship of the museum while Osman Hamdi was in Europe, making him the logical choice as successor at Lagina.[68] In the absence of Osman Hamdi's leadership, however, the plans for excavation, along with the proposed reconstruction of the temple, were soon abandoned.[69]

Conclusion

After Osman Hamdi abandoned excavations at Lagina, the site fell into disrepair and received only sporadic attention until the late twentieth century. Halil Edhem, along with the German scholars Theodor Wiegand and Hubert Knackfuss, visited Lagina in 1902. They produced an accurate plan of the Temple of Hekate, but they did not conduct any further excavations.[70]

In the twentieth century, two major archaeological campaigns took place at Lagina. Both of these were conducted by Turkish teams. Between 1967 and 1971, Dr Yusuf Boysal of Ankara University conducted limited excavations at Lagina as part of a wider campaign that examined a number of sites in the area.[71] It was not until 1993 that full excavations at Lagina, led by Professor Ahmet Tırpan of Selçuk University, were resumed. The excavators, who have worked at Lagina almost every year since then, have re-examined and cleared much of the Hekate sanctuary, including not only the temple, the focus of Osman Hamdi's early efforts, but other structures on the site. In contrast to Osman Hamdi's plan to export the entirety of the Temple of Hekate back to Istanbul, all of the finds from these excavations have either remained at the site or been transferred into local museums.[72]

The frieze blocks that Osman Hamdi painstakingly packed and transported to Istanbul were placed on display in the Imperial Museum, and have remained in the museum's holdings since that period. Today, they share a gallery with blocks from the sculpted frieze of the Temple of Artemis at Magnesia on the Meander. The Magnesia sculptures are fitting companions to the Lagina frieze; not only do they represent the only other major example of Hellenistic architectural sculpture in the museum, but due to the efforts of Osman Hamdi, they entered the collections just a few years earlier than the Lagina sculptures. Both French and German archaeologists had attempted to purchase the frieze blocks, which had been found at Magnesia in 1887, but Osman Hamdi stepped in and claimed them for the Ottomans.[73]

The two friezes from Lagina and Magnesia are currently displayed side by side. Each frieze is organized into a rectangle mimicking the four sides of the building it originally decorated and is placed approximately ten feet above the viewer's head to approximate its original location in the entablature of the building. While Osman Hamdi's hopes of a complete reconstruction of the Temple of Hekate never came to pass, this installation echoes his original vision, giving museum visitors some sense of the sculpture's original architectural framework and impact.

The display of the Lagina frieze is a legacy of Osman Hamdi's excavations. His efforts not only secured the Lagina sculpture for the Ottoman state, but also signalled a change in how archaeology and the collection of antiquities were viewed in the empire. It is the large scope of Osman Hamdi's vision for the excavations at Lagina and the display of the resultant finds that set this dig apart from his previous campaigns at Nemrud Dağı and Sidon. While that vision never achieved its full promise, it provided a template for future excavations. The personal involvement of Osman Hamdi at Lagina, and his decision to allow the French to participate, delivered clear messages to the international scholarly community. The presence of the director of the Imperial Museum indicated that the dig was being conducted on behalf of the state, highlighting archaeology as a governmental priority. In addition, all of the finds stayed within Ottoman borders, and plans were made in the proposed reconstruction of the temple to make these finds an attraction for both scholars and tourists. Through the

Lagina excavations, the Ottomans indicated both their ownership over physical remains of the past and their control over the process of archaeology. At the same time, Osman Hamdi's politically motivated decision to include the French in a collaborative archaeological process elevated the campaign to an undertaking of international significance. The dig at Lagina was a statement that the Ottomans had done more than enter the antiquities race; they were now controlling it.

Notes

1. The only publication produced by a member of Osman Hamdi's excavations is Joseph Chamonard, 'Les sculptures de la frise du temple d'Hecate à Lagina', *Bulletin de correspondance hellénique* 19 (1895): 235–62.
2. For archaeology in the Ottoman Empire, see Alev Koçak, *The Ottoman Empire and Archaeological Excavations: Ottoman Policy from 1840–1906, Foreign Archaeologists, and the Formation of the Ottoman Museum* (Istanbul: Isis Press, 2011); Zeynep Çelik, *About Antiquities: Politics of Archaeology in the Ottoman Empire* (Austin: University of Texas Press, 2016); Zainab Bahrani, Zeynep Çelik, and Edhem Eldem, eds, *Scramble for the Past: a Story of Archaeology in the Ottoman Empire, 1753–1914* (Istanbul: SALT, 2011). For a look at archaeology in Turkey, see Scott Redford and Nina Ergin, eds, *Perceptions of the Past in the Turkish Republic: Classical and Byzantine Periods* (Leuven: Peeters, 2010).
3. For nineteenth-century archaeology, see Stephen L. Dyson, *In Pursuit of Ancient Pasts: A History of Classical Archaeology in the Nineteenth and Twentieth Centuries* (New Haven, CT: Yale University Press, 2006); Margarita Díaz-Andreu, *A World History of Nineteenth-Century Archaeology. Nationalism, Colonialism, and the Past* (Oxford: Oxford University Press, 2007).
4. For Karia, see Simon Hornblower, *Mausolus* (Oxford: Clarendon Press, 1982); Ronald T. Marchese, *The Historical Archaeology of Northern Caria* (Oxford: BAR, 1989); Jeremy LaBuff, *Polis Expansion and Elite Power in Hellenistic Karia* (Lanham, MD: Lexington Books, 2016). For Stratonikeia and Lagina, see Mehmet Çetin Şahin, *The Political and Religious Structure in the Territory of Stratonikeia in Caria* (Ankara: Safak Matbaası, 1976); Pierre Debord, 'Essai sur la géographie historique de la région de Stratonicée', *Mélanges Pierre Lévêque* 8 (1994): 107–121.
5. For the Temple of Hekate, see Peter Baumeister, *Der Fries des Hekateions von Lagina* (Istanbul: Ege Yayınları, 2007); Riet van Bremen, 'The Inscribed Documents on the Temple of Hekate at Lagina and the Date and Meaning of the Temple Frieze', in *Hellenistic Karia*, eds Riet van Bremen and Jan-Mathiue Carbon (Paris: De Boccard, 2010), 483–503; Ahmet Tırpan, Zeliha Gider, and Aytekin Büyüközer, 'The Temple of Hekate at Lagina', in *Dipteros und Pseudodipteros*, ed. Thekla Schulz (Istanbul: Ege Yayınları, 2012), 181–202.
6. Strabo, *Geography*, 14.2.25 (London: George Bell & Sons, 1903).

7. Ahmet A. Tırpan and Bilal Söğüt, 'Lagina, Börükçü. Belentepe ve Mengefe 2008 Yılı Çalışmaları', *Kazı Sonuçları Toplantısı* 31.3 (2009): 507–10; Vincenzo Ruggieri, *La Caria bizantina: topografia, archeologia ed arte* (Soveria Mannelli: Rubbettino, 2005), 100–04.
8. See notably the work of Johann Joachim Winckelmann and the poetry of the English Romantics: Johann Joachim Winckelmann, *History of the Art of Antiquity*, trans. Harry Francis Mallgrave (Los Angeles: Getty Research Institute, 2006); Damian Valdez, *German Philhellenism: The Pathos of the Historical Imagination from Winckelmann to Goethe* (New York: Palgrave Macmillan, 2014); Katherine Harloe, *Winckelmann and the Invention of Antiquity. History and Aesthetics in the Age of Altertumswissenschaft* (Oxford: Oxford University Press, 2013); David Roessel, *In Byron's Shadow: Modern Greece in the English and American Imagination* (Oxford: Oxford University Press, 2002); David Ferris, *Silent Urns: Romanticism, Hellenism, Modernity* (Stanford: Stanford University Press, 2000).
9. For philhellenism and classicism, see Suzanne Marchand, *Down from Olympus: Archaeology and Philhellenism in Germany, 1750–1970* (Princeton: Princeton University Press, 1996); Gábor Klaniczay, Michael Werner, and Ottó Gecser, eds, *Multiple Antiquities, Multiple Modernities: Ancient Histories in Nineteenth Century European Cultures* (Frankfurt: Campus Verlag, 2011); Francis Haskell, *Taste and the Antique: The Lure of Classical Sculpture, 1500–1900* (New Haven: Yale University Press, 1981).
10. Philip L. Kohl, 'Nationalism and Archaeology: On the Construction of Nations and the Reconstructions of the Remote Past', *Annual Review of Anthropology* 27 (1998): 223–46; Philip L. Kohl and Clare Fawcett, eds, *Nationalism, Politics, and the Practice of Archaeology* (Cambridge: Cambridge University Press, 1995); Bruce G. Trigger, 'Alternative Archaeologies: Nationalist, Colonialist, Imperialist', *Man* 19.3 (1984): 355–70.
11. The most influential books by European travellers include: James Stuart and Nicholas Revett, *The Antiquities of Athens* (London: John Haberkorn, 1762); Julien-David Le Roy, *Les ruines des plus beaux monuments de la Grèce* (Paris: Guerin and Delatour, 1758); Charles Texier, *Description de l'Asie Mineure* (Paris: Firmin Didot Frères, 1839–49). For relevant discussion, see David Constantine, *Early Greek Travellers and the Hellenic Ideal* (Cambridge: Cambridge University Press, 1984), Richard Stoneman, *Land of Lost Gods: The Search for Classical Greece* (London: Hutchinson, 1987); David Constantine, *In the Footsteps of the Gods* (London: Tauris Parke, 2011).
12. Ian Morris, ed., *Classical Greece: Ancient Histories and Modern Archaeologies* (Cambridge: Cambridge University Press, 1994); Michael Shanks, *Classical Archaeology of Greece: Experiences of the Discipline* (London: Routledge, 1996).
13. Díaz-Andreu, *World History*, 103. For the Greek War of Independence, see William St. Clair, *The Greece Might Still be Free: The Philhellenes in the War of Independence* (Cambridge: Open Book Publishers, 2008).
14. Sir William Martin Leake, who travelled through Greece and Anatolia for the British government, summarized the European position: 'To the traveller who delights in tracing vestiges of Grecian art and civilization amidst modern barbarism and desolation […] there is no country that affords so fertile a field of discovery as Asia Minor'. Sir William Leake, *Journal of a Tour in Asia Minor* (London: John Murray, 1824), iii.

15. Richard Pococke, *A Description of the East and Some other Countries,* vol. 2, part 2 (London: John Pinkerton, 1743–45), 63–66; Anita Damiani, *Enlightened Observers: British Travellers to the Near East 1715–1850* (Beirut: the American University, 1979), 70–104.
16. Richard Chandler, Nicolas Revett, and William Pars, *Ionian Antiquities* (London: T. Spilsbury and W. Haskell, 1769); Richard Chandler, *Travels in Asia Minor* (Oxford: Clarendon Press, 1775); Constantine, *Early Greek Travellers,* 188–209.
17. Chandler, *Travels in Asia Minor,* 192–195.
18. Ludwig Ross, *Kleinasien und Deutschland* (Halle: C.E.M. Pfeffer, 1850), 90–91, 103–04.
19. Ian Jenkins, *Archaeologists and Aesthetes in the Sculpture Galleries of the British Museum 1800–1939* (London: British Museum Press, 1992), 168–95.
20. William Kirk Dickson, *The Life of Sir Major-General Robert Murdoch Smith* (Edinburgh: William Blackwood and Sons, 1901), 72–81.
21. Charles T. Newton and Richard P. Pullan, *A History of Discoveries at Halicarnassus, Cnidus and Branchidae* (London: Day and Son. 1863), 554–72, 789–803.
22. Accession number: 1857,1220.452. Correspondence with Peter Higgs confirmed that piece came from Lagina and was placed in the museum's collections by Newton.
23. Otto Benndorf, *Vorläufiger Bericht über zwei oesterreichische archaeologische Expeditionen nach Kleinasien* (Vienna: Carl Gerold's Sohn, 1883), 13–19, 26; Otto Benndorf and George Niemann, *Reisen in Lykien und Karien* (Vienna: Carl Gerold's Sohn, 1884), 152–55; Stoneman, *Land of Lost Gods,* 294–95.
24. Amédée Hauvette-Besnault and Marcel Dubois, 'Inscriptions de Carie', *Bulletin de correspondance hellénique* 5 (1881): 179–94; Charles Diehl and Georges Cousin, 'Inscriptions de Lagina', *Bulletin de correspondance hellénique* 11 (1887): 5–39; Georges Radet, *L'histoire et l'oeuvre de l'École française d'Athènes* (Paris: A. Fontemoing, 1901), 364.
25. 'Académie des Inscriptions et Belles-Lettres', *Journal des débats politiques et littéraires,* August 30, 1891; 'Académie des Inscriptions et Belles-Lettres', *Journal officiel de la République Française,* August 30, 1891, 4289; 'L'École Française d'Athènes', *The Oriental Advertiser-Le Moniteur Oriental,* September 2, 1891, 3; 'Institut de correspondence hellénique', *Bulletin de correspondence hellénique* 15 (1891): 640; Théophile Homolle, 'La campagne d'été des membres de l'École française d'Athènes', *Comptes rendus des séances de l'Académie des Inscriptions et Belles-Lettres* 35.4 (1891): 272; Théodore Reinach, 'Bulletin épigraphique', *Revue des Études Grecques* 4 (1891): 334; A. L. Frothingham, Jr., 'Archaeological News', *American Journal of Archaeology and of the History of the Fine Arts* 7.4 (1891): 510–11; Charles Diehl, 'Bulletin archéologique', *Revue des Études Grecques* 5.17 (1892): 130; Salomon Reinach, 'Chronique d'Orient', *Revue Archéologique* 3.19 (1892): 119.
26. For Ottoman governmental attitudes towards antiquities, see Zeynep Çelik, 'Defining Empire's Patrimony: Late Ottoman Perceptions of Antiquities', in *Scramble for the Past,* eds Bahrani, Çelik, and Eldem, 443–77; Edhem Eldem, 'From Blissful Ignorance to Anguished Concern: Ottoman Perceptions of Antiquities, 1799–1869', in *Scramble for the Past,* eds Bahrani, Çelik, and Eldem, 281–329.
27. Roderic Davison, 'Nationalism as an Ottoman Problem and the Ottoman Response', in *Nationalism in a Non-National State: The Dissolution of the Ottoman Empire,* eds William W. Haddad and William Ochsenwald (Columbus: Ohio State University Press, 1977), 78–88;

Fatma Müge Göçek, *Rise of the Bourgeoisie, Demise of Empire: Ottoman Westernization and Social Change* (Oxford: Oxford University Press, 1996); Selim Deringil, *The Well-Protected Domains: Ideology and the Legitimation of Power in the Ottoman Empire, 1876–1909* (London: I.B. Tauris, 1998); Doğan Gürpınar, *Ottoman/ Turkish Visions of the Nation, 1860–1950* (Houndsmills: Palgrave Macmillan, 2013), 164–90.

28. Davison, 'Nationalism as an Ottoman Problem', 39–40, 47.
29. Ussama Makdisi, 'Ottoman Orientalism', *The American Historical Review* 3 (2002): 768–78.
30. Wendy M. K. Shaw, *Possessors and Possessed: Museums, Archaeology and the Visualization of History in the Late Ottoman Empire* (Berkeley: University of California Press, 2003), 65–70.
31. For the role antiquities played in Ottoman definitions of patrimony and modernity, see Çelik, 'Defining Empire's Patrimony', 446–47, 470; Çelik, *About Antiquities*, 95–133; Makdisi, 'Ottoman Orientalism', 783–85; Ussama Makdisi, 'Rethinking Ottoman Imperialism: Modernity, Violence, and the Cultural Logic of Ottoman Reform', in *The Empire in the City: Arab Provincial Cities in the Late Ottoman Empire*, eds Jens Hanssen, Thomas Philipp, and Stefan Weber (Würzburg: Ergon, 2002): 41–48; Benjamin Anderson, '"An Alternative Discourse": Local Interpretations of Antiquities in the Ottoman Empire', *Journal of Field Archaeology* 40.4 (2015): 450–60; Fredrik Thomasson, 'Justifying and Criticizing the Removals of Antiquities in Ottoman Lands: Tracking the Sigeion Inscription', *International Journal of Cultural Property* 17 (2010): 493–517.
32. Shaw, *Possessors and Possessed*, 31–32, 46–82; Eldem, 'From Blissful Ignorance to Anguished Concern', 312–21.
33. Shaw, *Possessors and Possessed*, 83–88.
34. Ibid., 65–70, 149–71; Çelik, 'Defining Empire's Patrimony', especially 458–60.
35. For the antiquities laws, their implementation, and the reaction of foreign excavators, see Shaw, *Possessors and Possessed*, 89–97, 108–24; Koçak, *Ottoman Empire and Archaeological Excavations*, 83–93; Izabella Donkow, 'The Ephesus Excavations 1863–1874 in Light of the Ottoman Legislation on Antiquities', *Anatolian Studies* 54 (2004): 109–17.
36. Mustafa Cezar, *Sanatta Batı'ya Açılış ve Osman Hamdi*, 1st ed. (Istanbul: Türkiye İş Bankası, 1971); Edhem Eldem, 'An Ottoman Archaeologist Caught Between Two Worlds. Osman Hamdi Bey (1842–1910)', in *Archaeology, Anthropology and Heritage in the Balkans and Anatolia*, ed. David Shankland (Istanbul: Isis Press, 2004), 121–49; Edhem Eldem, *Osman Hamdi Bey Sözlüğü* (Istanbul: Kültür ve Turizm Bakanlığı, 2010); Renata Holod and Robert G. Ousterhout, eds, *Osman Hamdi Bey and the Americans* (Istanbul: Pera Museum, 2011); Zeynep Rona, ed., *Osman Hamdi Bey ve Dönemi Sempozyumu 17–18 Aralık 1992* (Istanbul: Tarih Vakfı Yurt Yayınları, 1993).
37. Salomon Reinach, 'Hamdi Bey', *Revue archéologique* 15 (1910): 408–09.
38. For Osman Hamdi's education and painting, see: Wendy M. K. Shaw, 'The Paintings of Osman Hamdi and the Subversion of Orientalist Vision', in *Essays in Honour of Aptullah Kuran*, eds Çiğdem Kafescioğlu and Lucienne Thys-Şenocak (Istanbul: Yapı Kredi Yayınları, 1999), 423–34; Zeynep Çelik, 'Colonialism, Orientalism, and the Canon', *The Art Bulletin* 78.2 (2003): 202–05; Wendy M. K. Shaw, *Ottoman Painting: Reflections of Western Art from the Ottoman Empire to the Turkish Republic* (London: I. B. Tauris, 2011), 41–78; Ahmet Ersoy, 'Osman Hamdi Bey and the Historiophile Mood', in *The Poetics and Politics of*

Place: Ottoman Istanbul and British Orientalism, eds Zeynep Inankur, Reina Lewis, and Mary Roberts (Istanbul: Pera Museum, 2011), 131–41; Edhem Eldem, 'Making Sense of Osman Hamdi Bey and His Paintings', *Muqarnas* 29 (2012): 339–83.

39. Eldem, 'Ottoman Archaeologist', 126; Shaw, *Possessors and Possessed*, 98.
40. Shaw, *Possessors and Possessed*, 88–97.
41. Ibid., 157–58.
42. Robert Deveraux, *The First Constitutional Period: A Study of the Midhat Constitution and Parliament* (Baltimore, MA: The Johns Hopkins Press, 1962). For a discussion of Osman Hamdi's time with Midhat, see Eldem, 'Ottoman Archaeologist', 126; Edhem Eldem, *Un Ottoman en Orient. Osman Hamdi Bey en Irak (1869–1871)* (Paris: Actes Sud, 2010).
43. In his obituary, Reinach describes him as 'le plus parisien des Ottomans, le plus ottoman des Parisiens', as well as calling him a *midhatiste* and stating that Osman Hamdi once referred to himself as the 'Jeunes Turcs, dont je suis le plus vieux'. See Reinach, 'Hamdi Bey', 407 and 411–12; Eldem, *Ottoman Archaeologist*, 121–49. For the Young Turk movement, see M. Şükrü Hanioğlu, *The Young Turks in Opposition* (Oxford: Oxford University Press, 1995); Stefano Taglia, *Intellectuals and Reform in the Ottoman Empire: the Young Turks on the Challenges of Modernity* (London: Routledge, 2015).
44. For museums' role in the formation of national identity, see Peter Aronsson and Gabriella Elgenius, eds, *National Museums and Nation-Building in Europe 1750–2010: Mobilization and Legitimacy, Continuity and Change* (London: Routledge, 2015; Nick Prior, *Museums and Modernity: Art Galleries and the Making of Modern Culture* (Oxford: Berg, 2002). For museums in the Ottoman Empire, see Shaw, *Possessors and Possessed*, especially 19–29; Wendy M. K. Shaw, 'From Mausoleum to Museum: Resurrecting Antiquity for Modernity', in *Scramble for the Past*, eds Bahrani, Çelik, and Eldem, 423–40; Ayşe H. Köksal, 'National Art Museums and the 'Modernization' of Turkey', in *National Museums: New Studies from Around the World*, ed. Simon J. Knell (London: Routledge, 2011), 163–79.
45. Chamonard, 'Les sculptures', 235–62; Baumeister, *Der Fries des Hekateions*, 3–10.
46. Osman Hamdi Bey and Osgan Efendi, *Le Tumulus de Nemroud-Dagh: voyage: description, inscriptions avec plans et photographies* (Istanbul: Imp. F. Loeffler, 1883); Edhem Eldem, *Le voyage à Nemrud Dağı d'Osman Hamdi Bey et Osgan Efendi* (Paris: De Boccard, 2010); Herman A. G. Brijder, 'A Survey of Previous Explorations and Archaeological Activities on Nemrud Dağı and in other Commagenian Sanctuaries and Sites. The Sites Revisited and Reviewed', in *Nemrud Dağı*, ed. Herman A. G. Brijder (Berlin: De Gruyter, 2014), 184–96.
47. [Osman] Hamdy [Hamdi] Bey, 'Mémoire sur une nécropole royale: découverte a Saïda', *Revue archéologique* 10 (1887): 138–50; Henri Metzger, *La correspondance passive d'Osman Hamdi Bey* (Paris: Boccard, 1990), 11–23.
48. The discoveries at Sidon were widely covered in archaeological journals and newspapers. See A. L. Frothingham, Jr., 'Archaeological News', *The American Journal of Archaeology and the History of the Fine Arts* 3.3/4 (1887): 431–32; 'Antiquities at Stamboul: If It Is Not Alexander's Tomb, Whose Tomb Is It?', *New York Tribune*, April 22, 1888, 12; Ferdinand Delaunay, 'Académie des Inscriptions et Belles-Lettres', *Journal official de la République française*, July 20, 1887, 3369–70; Ph. Berger and G. Maspero, 'Le sarcophage de Tabnith roi de Sidon', *Revue archéologique* 10 (1887): 1–10.

49. Osman Hamdi's work at Lagina met the requirements for scientific archaeological excavations in the nineteenth century, including a well-documented excavation process and publication of the finds. Letters exchanged between Théophile Homolle, the director of the École Française d'Athènes, and Osman Hamdi consistently refer to the campaign at Lagina and/or its participants as scientific. See Metzger, *Correspondance passive*, 46–48. For scientific archaeology in nineteenth-century Europe, see Marchand, *Down from Olympus*, 97–103.
50. The full-scale reconstruction of an ancient monument was unparalleled in any European museum at the time. In Berlin, the reconstructed Pergamon Altar went on display in 1901, while the reconstructed Babylonian Ishtar Gate opened 1928. In London, the Nereid Monument from Xanthos was first displayed as part of a reconstructed façade in the mid-twentieth century. See Can Bilsel, *Antiquity on Display: Regimes of the Authentic in Berlin's Pergamon Museum* (Oxford: Oxford University Press, 2012), 117–24, 177–83; Jenkins, *Archaeologists and Aesthetes*, 143–53.
51. Gustave Mendel, *Catalogue des sculptures grecques, romaines et byzantines*, vol. 1 (Istanbul: Musée Impérial, 1912), 429; Metzger, *Correspondance passive*, 45.
52. Mendel states that the frieze blocks were housed in the village of Ileïneh. This is most likely a transliteration of the settlement known as Leyne, which is today called Turgut. Mendel, *Catalogue*, 430; Frothingham, 'Archaeological News 1891', 151.
53. Mendel, *Catalogue*, 430.
54. Published in Chamonard, 'Les sculptures', 235–237. While Chamonard's article indicates that a comprehensive publication of the Temple of Hekate was in the works, this never appeared. Chamonard's article did heighten interest in Lagina. See Henri Lechat, 'Bulletin archéologique', *Revue des études grecques* 9.34 (1896): 279; Pierre Paris, 'Bulletin archéologique de la religion grecque, décembre 1894', *Revue de l'histoire des religions* 33 (1896): 63.
55. 'Les académies', *Le Matin*, September 3, 1892, 'Académie des Inscriptions', *Le Temps*, September 4, 1892; Julien Havet, 'Bulletin mensuel de l'Académie des Inscriptions', *Revue archéologique* 3.20 (1892): 371; François de Caussade, 'Sociétés Savantes', *L'Ami des monuments et des arts parisiens et français* 6 (1892): 249; Alexandre Bertrand, 'Mémoire de Lechat sur le sculpteur Endoios', *Comptes rendus des séances de l'Académie des Inscriptions et Belles-Lettres* 36.5 (1892): 305; 'Académie des Inscriptions et Belles-Lettres', *Journal des débats politiques et littéraires*, June 3, 1892; 'Académie des Inscriptions et Belles-Lettres', *Journal officiel de la République française*, September 6, 1892, 4458; 'Notes of the Month (Foreign)', *The Antiquary* 27 (1893): 143.
56. That the French felt a proprietary claim over Lagina is seen in French-language journals and newspapers highlighting Chamonard and Legrand's role (see citations in n. 55). Homolle, 'Rapport verbal', 349 states explicitly that the French were associated with the excavations because Osman Hamdi recognized their rights based on their prior discoveries.
57. Metzger, *Correspondance passive*, 46–48. 58. Ibid., 46–47.
58. Archaeological campaigns sponsored by the Imperial Museum after 1892 show the influence of the Lagina excavations. The majority of these excavations, including those at Tralles, Alabanda, Kültepe, Kedesh, and Yortan, saw collaboration between European and Ottoman

archaeologists, a scientific archaeological process, the export of finds to the museum, and scholarly publications. For a list all of the archaeological excavations sponsored by the Ottoman government between 1884 and 1906, see Koçak, *Ottoman Empire and Archaeological Excavations*, 102–19.

59. Osman Hamdy [Hamdi] Bey and Théodore Reinach, *Une nécropole royale à Sidon: fouilles de Hamdy Bey* (Paris: Leroux, 1892).
60. As Osman Hamdi was primarily concerned that European audiences and members of the archaeological community were cognizant of his activities, I have focused here on English, French, and German sources. Many of these European-language sources would have been accessible to the Ottoman elite, many of whom knew at least one European language, most commonly French. For the use of French in the late Ottoman Empire, see Göçek, *Rise of the Bourgeoisie*, 119–33. Çelik highlights that most Imperial Museum publications were in French and argues that the museum targeted foreign visitors and the Ottoman elite. Çelik, *About Antiquities*, 65–97
61. Théodore Reinach, 'Inscriptions d'Asie-Mineure', *Revue des études grecques*
62. (1892): 412; 'Lettre de Grèce', *Journal des débats politiques et littéraires*, June 11, 1893, 2; Salomon Reinach, 'Chronique d'Orient', *Revue archéologique* 3.21 (1893): 96; Salomon Reinach, 'Chronique d'Orient', *Revue archéologique* 3.22 (1893): 351; Théophile Homolle, 'Institut de Correspondance hellénique', *Bulletin de correspondence hellénique* 17 (1893): 184; John P. Peters, 'An Art Impetus in Turkey', *The Century Illustrated Monthly Magazine* 45.4 (1893): 550–58; Sabine Méa, 'Le Musée de Constantinople et son conservateur', *Le Rappel*, August 15, 1894; Eduard Hula and Emil Szántó, *Bericht über eine Reise in Karien* (Vienna: In Commission bei F. Tempsky, 1894), 36.
63. In 'Chronique', *The Oriental Advertiser-Le Moniteur Oriental*, October 9, 1891, 3.
64. 'Les Fouilles de Lagina', *The Oriental Advertiser-Le Moniteur Oriental*, September 12, 1892, 3; 'Chronique', *The Oriental Advertiser-Le Moniteur Oriental*, September 22, 1892, 3; 'Les Fouilles de Lagina', *The Oriental Advertiser-Le Moniteur Oriental*, September 23, 1892, 3; 'Archaeology', *The Oriental Advertiser-Le Moniteur Oriental*, October 12, 1892, 2; 'Chronique', *The Oriental Advertiser-Le Moniteur Oriental*, October 29, 1892, 3; 'Archaeology', *The Oriental Advertiser-Le Moniteur Oriental*, October 31, 1892, 2, 3; 'Archaeology', *The Oriental Advertiser-Le Moniteur Oriental*, November 3, 1892, 2; 'Archaeology', *The Oriental Advertiser-Le Moniteur Oriental*, November 10, 1892, 2, 3; 'Les fouilles en Grèce', *The Oriental Advertiser-Le Moniteur Moniteur Oriental*, June 16, 1893, 3.
65. News items in French archaeological journals published in 1893 and 1894 name Tournaire as the architect engaged by Osman Hamdi. Mendel names the architect as Pontremoli. This is likely Emmanuel Pontremoli, who worked at a number of sites in Anatolia. Metzger follows Mendel's identification, but I have followed the likely more accurate accounts contemporary to the excavations. See Théophile Homolle, 'Rapport verbal fait à l'Académie sur les travaux de l'École française d'Athènes pendant le printemps et l'été de 1893', *Comptes rendus des séances de l'Académie des Inscriptions et Belles-Lettres* 37.5 (1893): 349; Georges Perrot, 'Rapport de la Commission des Écoles d'Athènes et de Rome sur les travaux de ces deux Écoles pendant les années 1892–1893', *Comptes rendus des séances de l'Académie des Inscriptions et Belles-Lettres* 38.1 (1894): 71; Vital Cuinet, *La Turquie d'Asie: Géographie*

administrative, statistique, descriptive et raisonnée de chaque province de l'Asie Mineure, vol. 3 (Paris: Ernest Leroux, 1894), 661–62; Mendel, *Catalogue des sculptures*, 430; Metzger, *Correspondance passive,* 45.

66. Peters, 'Art Impetus', 558.
67. Homolle, 'Rapport verbal', 349; Perrot, 'Rapport', 71.
68. Osman Hamdi's trip to Europe in 1893 included diplomatic visits and a stay in Switzerland for health reasons. See 'Chronique', *The Oriental Advertiser-Le Moniteur Oriental*, August 7, 1893, 3; 'Chronique', *The Oriental Advertiser-Le Moniteur Oriental*, August 22, 1893, 3; 'Chronique', *The Oriental Advertiser-Le Moniteur Oriental*, September 19, 1893, 3; 'Hamdi Bey in Paris', *The Oriental Advertiser-Le Moniteur Oriental*, September 21, 1893, 2.
69. Perrot, 'Rapport de la Commission', 71; Metzger, *Correspondance passive*, 45–48.
70. Mendel, *Catalogue des sculptures*, 430; Edhem-Bey, 'Fouilles d'Alabanda', 443–59.
71. Yusuf Boysal, 'A Report on the 1969 Turgut Excavations', *Anadolu* 12 (1970): 81–93.
72. Yearly excavation reports from Lagina are published in *Kazı Sonuçları Toplantısı*.
73. Alain Davesne, *La frise du temple d'Artémis à Magnésie. Catalogue des fragments du Musée du Louvre* (Paris: A.D.P.F., 1982), 10–11.

Part 3

Imagining Antiquity in Modernity

7

Destruction as Layered Event: Twentieth Century Ruins in the Great Mosque of Gaza

Eli Osheroff and Dotan Halevy

After the ancient city of Palmyra-Tadmur was recaptured from ISIS in March 2016, several newspapers ran articles featuring 'before and after' pictures of the historical site aiming to demonstrate the destruction performed by ISIS militants.[1] Ironically, however, tracing that destruction through the juxtaposed images proved rather difficult. The observer was ostensibly given the awkward task of recognizing ruins of ruins; in other words, to differentiate the destruction made by ISIS from that carried out eons ago – the ruination of what was already in 'ruins'. Indeed, it could be argued that the ruins left by ISIS in Tadmur consisted of two different elements denoted by the same term. The first of these is 'ruins' as noble, romantic, archeological remains from previous cultures that have been beautified by the winds of time. The second is that of the horrendous rubble caused by some recent act of destruction. The first type of ruins is characteristic of heritage sites and national parks, the other of war zones and abandoned industrial areas. The case of ISIS in Tadmur, however, indicates how contrived this distinction might be by showing the ways in which one type of ruins can easily turn into the other. It is not just that today's ruins of war might one day become heritage sites, but that today's heritage sites can also turn into ruins of war. Ruins can be both noble and terrible, and interpreting them one way or another in fact testifies to a power struggle. This dual nature of ruins becomes clearer when we consider the shared origin of both types: the destructive event itself. The purpose of this chapter is to expose the links between these ruins of antiquity and ruins of modernity to show that acts of destruction should be understood far beyond their immediate circumstances. We argue that destruction should be thought of as layered event, it has a 'before' and an 'after' that transcends the local space and instantaneous time in which it occurs. A broader perspective on events of destruction exposes hidden layers that tie together contemporary constructions with archeological remnants, violence of war with artistic creation, and intellectual debates with vandalism.

The destruction of antiquities by ISIS attracted a considerable amount of attention, often, as many have noted, even more than the destruction of actual lives in the Middle East.[2] The intense coverage of this subject in light of the struggle against ISIS brings to mind another recent round of such cultural atrocities – the annihilation of the Buddhas of Bamiyan in Afghanistan by the Taliban regime in 2001. That act gave birth to one of the most compelling and influential writings on the subject of intentional destruction, an essay by Finbarr Barry Flood.[3] By analyzing cases of historical Islamic iconoclasm as well as the Bamiyan case, Flood demonstrated that the phenomenon of iconoclasm in Islamic history unfolded by means of varied practices and manifestations, exhibiting a diversity that cannot be ascribed to a monolithic theological imperative. Flood described the destruction of the Bamiyan Buddhas as a form of insurgency against the cultural sensitivities of the Western powers – the very entities that for years made Afghanistan their imperialist playground, protecting and documenting Afghan 'heritage' while excluding living Afghans from similar protection. In Flood's words, 'it is imperative to recognize that those events have a logic rooted not in the fictions of an eternal or recurring medievalism but in the realities of global modernity'.[4]

Flood's purpose in writing this essay was novel. He depicted his work as critical of the idea, then prevalent in both scholarly work and popular media, of a 'cultural pathology known as Islamic iconoclasm', which situated the Bamiyan destruction 'within a long, culturally determined, and unchanging tradition of violent iconoclastic acts'.[5] Yet, while it is true that ideas about the essential characteristics of Islam are still widespread, it does seem that something has changed in the last fifteen years. Scholars and journalists alike seem to look today at the ISIS phenomenon and antiquities destruction as more than 'an extreme interpretation of the faith', and frequently claim that these 'should be seen in a political context'.[6] Scholars studying ISIS link western hegemony and political crisis in the Middle East with the rise of eschatological tendencies and violent religious interpretation of Holy Scriptures – of which iconoclasm is a part.[7] In other words, if once Orientalist tendencies were to locate the causes of such acts in some intrinsic cultural core, the interpretive leaning of political Islam has now turned more dynamic and contextualized. It is as if ISIS's radical distortion of Islam is helping to hammer the last nails in the coffin of essentialist perceptions of Islam, at least in academic discourse.[8] While 'Orientalist' explanations about the 'nature' or 'core' of religion are rarer in current academic discourse, they nonetheless appear to have remained widespread in media, popular culture, politics, and policy making.

We build upon these important developments in research in the following analysis and maintain that the individual case of antiquities destruction can lead us even further. It is not only the meaning of ruins, we argue, that is fought over here, but also, and more essentially, the meaning of what generates these ruins – that is, the destructive event. To better demonstrate this idea, let us consider seriously ISIS's own explanation of their acts. As elaborated in an article for their mouthpiece *Dabiq*, by smashing ancient idols ISIS was not fighting against classical idolatry but rather against western culture's usage of these vestiges of the pre-Islamic period to implant distinct identities in the hearts of Muslims and nurture modern 'idols' like nationalism and democracy.[9] In ISIS's worldview and interpretation of Muslim tradition, the ancient civilizations represented by these archeological relics were demolished by God as a punishment for impiety in pre-Islamic times. Their ruinous state of being randomly scattered upon and underneath the ground, therefore, reflected the role God designated for them as warning signs for future generations. By unearthing and collecting these remnants and branding them as objects of historical heritage, western culture directly subverts their divine destiny and transforms them from taboo to totem. ISIS intentionally challenges the western notion of 'ruins' as admirable voices from the past and asserts the other meaning of 'ruins'– the remains of a demolished civilization. It is, in other words, the destruction itself and not that which was destroyed that makes these antiquities significant. By their own violent destruction of these relics, ISIS is trying to return the element of 'ruinous' back to the ruins. What is striking in these arguments is not just their complexity, but also the marginal importance assigned to a strict adherence to the religious law of banning anthropomorphic art in comparison to more abstract notions of past and history. While in popular media (western or other) these acts are usually depicted as stemming from a sort of extreme religiosity, the actual explanation in official ISIS propaganda touches on a historical-intellectual debate. In the group's perception, destruction of antiquities is rooted in former acts of destruction as part of a recrudescent, perhaps circular, historical trend.

This chapter follows these insights and suggests broadening the debate around other historical cases of destruction as well.[10] Expanding these discussions beyond concepts of religious zeal and 'radicalization' will show how destructive processes are always part of larger cultural and political narratives. Acts of destruction, we argue, involve conflicting and mutable interpretations, which necessitates subtle consideration of the destroyers' motivations, goals, and understanding of history. To show how this argument is valid in historical cases outside Islamist discourse, we analyze contextual interpretations of the destruction that took place in the Great Mosque of Gaza (al-Jami' al-'Umari al-Kabir) in the twentieth century. By examining how different contemporary observers depicted the mosque itself, its ruins, and its historical relics we wish to tease out the links between smoking ruins of war and aesthetic ruins of an imagined past, and consequently to point to the iterative nature of destruction. We focus on two particular examples in relation to this site. The story of the toppling of the mosque during the First World War will first reflect how in the aftermath of large-scale destruction, debris of war are shifted to be an artistic and literary display. Secondly, the debate over a Jewish candelabrum engraving on one of the mosque's pillars and its defacement will hint at the motivation preceding acts of destruction, which may turn historical relics into relics of violence.

British Aestheticization of Ruins in the Aftermath of Destruction

British artillery damaged much of the Great Mosque of Gaza on May 1, 1917. This event occurred several days after the second failed attempt to take the city from its Ottoman defenders and a few months before it was eventually conquered in late October of the same year. Throughout this period of trench warfare, both armies shelled one another's positions heavily. In the process, the town of Gaza, which had become an Ottoman military stronghold in the preceding months, was partially destroyed. None of the faceless buildings leveled by the British Howitzers were considered worthy of recording in internal military memos. It is therefore interesting to find that the destruction of the Great Mosque of Gaza elicited discontent, shame, and even fear among British officers. This section discusses the varied interpretations of this destruction and shows that even the seemingly obvious consequences of shelling a building can be historically and ethically contextualized in various ways, depending on the observer.

The Middle East Brigade of the British Royal Flying Corps was the first to mention the incident in its daily intelligence report: 'On May 1, a [munitions] dump in the neighborhood of the large Mosque in Gaza was shelled by siege battery and five direct hits were obtained, a large explosion followed, this unfortunately resulted in considerable damage to the mosque'[11] [Figure 7.1]. The message soon reached the headquarters of the Egyptian Expeditionary Force (EEF), infuriating the commander-in-chief, General Archibald Murray. Murray hastily dispatched a message to Lieutenant-General Chetwode, who had ordered the shelling of the mosque. Marking his displeasure, Murray argued that the orders that 'distinctively prohibited the destruction of this mosque' were clearly known to all division commanders and that such 'ill-advised' operations might result in the 'most undesirable consequences'.[12] Chetwode replied to the accusations two days later. He accepted full responsibility for overseeing and approving the artillery plan but argued that the destruction was amply justified. He explained that 'the protection of the lives of my men is always one of peculiar urgency […] It was well known to the whole force that the Minaret of Gaza was the only O.P. [observation point] […] it had already been responsible for loss of life'.[13] Indeed, it seems that for Chetwode, as a commander in the front, nothing was dissociated from the space-time boundaries of the battle. From the EEF headquarters camp a few miles back, things looked different: the battleground had a past and a future, and thus the broader dimensions of destruction overshadowed its tactical necessity.

The British military command generally avoided damaging religious symbols out of concern that it might stir up latent pan-Islamic solidarity among Muslims, especially those under British rule in India. Such a development could have played into the hands of the Germans, who tried vigorously to provoke an Islamic holy war against the British Empire.[14] This risk was rooted, in this case, in the fact that the mosque was one of the most ancient religious symbols of Greater Syria. According to the Muslim tradition it was originally built by the second Caliph 'Umar ibn al-Khattab (r.634–44), for whom it was also named, following the Arab conquest of Palestine in the seventh century. It was rebuilt by the crusading forces as a basilica in 1149 and restored as a mosque under the Mamluks in several building campaigns, the final of which occurred in 1340.[15] At that time, the structure was widened and a tall hexagonal minaret added. Another round of renovations by the Ottomans during the 1870s made the mosque one of the most magnificent in the area on the eve of the First World War [Figure 7.2]. Aside from its architectural splendor, one of the mosque's rooms hosted a library that contained hundreds of religious manuscripts and books dating back to the thirteenth century.[16] Alongside the libraries of al-Aqsa Mosque in Jerusalem and al-Jazzar Mosque in Acre, the Gaza library was the finest in Palestine.[17] The destruction of such a religious and historic institution was therefore 'distinctively prohibited'.[18]

The fear of a boomerang effect caused by wartime destruction was not limited to the Islamic context, however. It reflected a notion that crossed and connected the varied geopolitical theatres of the Great War. When the Palestine campaign was launched in early

Destruction as Layered Event: Twentieth Century Ruins in the Great Mosque of Gaza

Figure 7.1: The Great Mosque of Gaza after its bombardment in 1917. Library of Congress prints and photographs division.

1917, the political ramifications of architectural atrocities were already well ingrained in the consciousness of high-ranking military officers. On the western front, in France and Belgium, the British regularly accused the German 'Huns' of deliberate destruction of architectural monuments. Photos and drawings of the battle zones' maimed cathedral halls or toppled church spires were used to tarnish the enemy's image as an ignorant

Figure 7.2: The Great Mosque of Gaza in the last quarter of the nineteenth century. Library of Congress prints and photographs division.

philistine.[19] Wellington House, the British propaganda bureau, disseminated these images worldwide in different formats. One of the best known was *The Western Front* journal, wherein drawings by the first 'official artist' of the British army, Muirhead Bone, were featured in colour.[20]

Two of Bone's famous drawings, appearing on the covers of the first and second issues of *The Western Front*, published in 1916, are instructive for our case. Both portrayed the renowned 'The Leaning Virgin of Albert', a damaged statue of the Virgin Mary on the tower of the Albert town basilica located on the Somme front in northern France. During the battles, the statue was hit by artillery but remained hanging from the top of the tower. 'The Leaning Virgin' became associated with a myth that the side that eventually toppled the statue would be the one to lose the war. Far beyond a mere superstition that circulated among ill-fated soldiers on the war's deadliest front, this myth reflected a primeval dread of being the destroyer. As Julia Hell has shown in other wars, here as well the destructive power of the modern battlefield conjured up references to Scipio Africanus, the Roman conqueror of Carthage, who wept at the sight of his enemy's city perishing in flames.[21] The moment of glorious victory had allowed Scipio to see beyond the Roman-Punic war theatre and to grasp that the destruction he was inflicting on a rival empire heralded the inevitable destruction of his own empire. The eternal ruin, the monument that no longer fears being eradicated, encompasses the memory of what was lost and at the same time reminds the beholder that destruction one inflicts sows the seeds of the destruction one will suffer. The seemingly moral condemnation of the destruction of the Gaza mosque should thus be seen within the larger framework of an imperial existential fear of the disastrous repercussions of such an act.

From Carthage back to Gaza, and from the Roman to the British Empire, the toppled mosque was now a problem urgently to be addressed. Murray, the Commander of the EEF, notified the High Commissioner to Egypt, Reginald Wingate, and asked how the incident should be publicly presented. In his reply, Wingate said of such cases that 'least said soonest mended', and advised no press releases unless the Arab newspapers or public referred to the matter. However, he advised Murray to state in any future official communiqués 'that a Turkish ammunition dump in or near the mosque at Gaza had exploded, damaging the structure'.[22] These instructions illustrate how the British reframed their destructive act. As we have seen, the Royal Air Corps first reported that the mosque was damaged by shelling aimed at a neighboring dump. Chetwode, however, claimed that artillery deliberately targeted the minaret, and finally Wingate ordered a statement that a Turkish ammunition dump had exploded, without mentioning how this had occurred.

The question remains, what really happened to the mosque on May 1, 1917? Testimony recorded in a journal of a British soldier who watched this event from his trench helps resolve the deliberate opacity of official accounts:

> Wherever one went, one felt that the Turkish eyes from the top of the minaret were watching every movement we made. The minaret would have to go – and go it did. The gunners saw to that! Judging too from a severe explosion one afternoon, a goodly part of the Turkish ammunition stored within the mosque must have gone too![23]

This witness statement shows how the different explanations for targeting the mosque coalesced. The aim was to take down the minaret, and the subsequent explosions of Turkish ammunition were a welcome, albeit unplanned, result. Hence, Wingate chose not to stick to the real course of events but cleverly switched the cause and effect. It worked. An official military report published in the Egyptian press a few days later took up his narrative and was cited two weeks later in Mecca in the Arab weekly *al-Qibla*.[24] Wingate's move was now complete; from then on, in most war narratives from Gaza, both British and Arab, the Turkish ammunition dump was mentioned as both the original target of the British shelling and the reason for the collapse of the mosque.[25] The British avoided the moral onus of

Figure 7.3: The Leaning Virgin of Albert drawn by James McBey, 1917. The Cleveland Museum of Art.

deliberately shelling the building by shifting the blame to the Ottomans, who had made it an ammunitions depot.

It was not only the high-ranking officers, however, who were busy re-contextualizing this destruction. The auxiliary arm of wartime art also worked to further lessen British responsibility for the fate of the mosque. When the city was completely occupied by British troops in the beginning of November 1917, the official artist adjunct to EEF, James McBey, made two paintings of the toppled mosque. McBey had joined the forces just a few months earlier upon request from General Murray, who wanted his campaign in Sinai and the one envisioned in Palestine to be artistically documented, as had been done on the western front. McBey was thus provided with issues of the *Western Front* as a model and asked to produce similar images for purposes of art and propaganda. But it seems that McBey could also do without these examples. Earlier in the war, McBey visited the Somme to paint and even made his own version of 'The Leaning Virgin of Albert' [Figure 7.3].[26] However, unlike the dark, glum atmosphere of his paintings from Europe, his Middle Eastern compositions were light and joyous. Whereas in 'The Leaning Virgin', strict lines and sharp angles express the terrifying concreteness of the recent destruction, the vague, watercolour pyramid that represents the destroyed mosque in Gaza seems like some topographical remnant, a natural part of the surrounding landscape [Figure 7.4]. In McBey's personal journal, no

Destruction as Layered Event: Twentieth Century Ruins in the Great Mosque of Gaza

Figure 7.4: James McBey, 'The Minaret, Gaza', 1917. Imperial War Museums, London.

differentiation can be detected between his references to 'ruins' that he was drawing as post-battle rubble and those denoting historical sites. Indeed, it seems like he treated both objects rather similarly.[27] As a Europe-trained etcher who earned vast recognition partially due to his drawings of Moroccan *kasbah*s (old, fortified cities), McBey was inspired by the longstanding orientalist artistic tradition that saw ruins in the Orient as an integral element of the scenery. For the case of the Gazan mosque, he took this approach a step further by applying orientalist aesthetics to fresh ruins of a recent conflagration.[28] He transformed the ruins of the Great Mosque from dreary to picturesque, blurring the effect of destruction and absolving the destroyers of blame.

Comprehending Arab Ruins from the Abandoned Encampment to the Razed Islamic City

Were the British fears of Muslim-religious rage justified? For at least one prominent Muslim figure in Gaza, this destruction was more than just an offense to his religion. Following rumors about the destruction of the city, 'Uthman Mustafa al-Tabba', who was the mosque's manuscripts curator before the war and at the time a refugee in Ramla, decided to try to salvage what he could of his beloved mosque library. By the time he got there, his hometown was a wreck. Aside from the damage done to the prominent sanctuaries and public buildings by the British shelling, he discovered that further devastation was inflicted on almost every house by the new town-dwellers – the Ottoman soldiers. From using timber disassembled from the roofs of houses to revet their dugouts, to pillowcases that were stuffed with sand as a means of fortification, the soldiers consumed any useable material they could find. Occasional sacking of property left behind by the evacuated civilians became a common practice during the months of skirmishes.

In his monumental encyclopedic work on the history of Gaza, al-Tabba' reflected on the experience of watching his town, mosque, and library turn into the debris of war. What he described, however, took the reader far beyond Gaza of the time. For al-Tabba' – a devout and learned Muslim – the destruction of sites and sights of the city conjured images of devastation tied to Qur'anic verses, Muslim history, and classical Arabic poetry.[29] Only a brief passage from his testimony can be cited here, yet it is reflective of his overall message. Halfway into his chapter on Gaza during the Great War, the following verses are woven into the text:

> Stand in front of Gaza and weep over her quarters,
>   Lament the ruins of her mosque leaning on its lofty pillars
> miscreants have razed her with annihilating fire sent by their myriad shells and missiles
> the Turks have razed all her interiors obliterated her life with bare hands
> this animated city has become forlorn as though she were never inhabited by men[30]

Presumably in these lines al-Tabba' is merely inviting his listeners (or readers) to mourn his devastated town. Yet, phrasing his stanzas with a specific jargon, he also transcends the time and space of World War I Gaza to situate himself within a lineage of poets who throughout Arab history have stood and wept at the sight of desolated ruins. The most renowned of these is probably the sixth century poet Imru' al-Qays, who in his first *qasida* appealed to his listeners in a similar manner: 'Stay – Let us weep at the remembrance of our beloved, at the sight of the station where her tent was raised'.[31] Using this scene as the typological opening of the classical poetic tradition, Arab poets throughout the generations have re-experienced the grief of discovering abandoned ruins where only yesterday stood the encampment of their beloved.[32] As Arab poetry evolved, the beloved damsel and the remnants of her encampment also took on metaphorical meanings to create subgenres of poetry. Here, al-Tabba' was inspired by elegies (*marathi*) composed for cities that were destroyed by rivals of Islam.[33] Muslim poets used this genre, for instance, to mourn the devastated city of Basra after the Zanj rebellion (868–83), the city of Qayrawan destroyed by the Banu Hilal and Banu Sulaym (1057), and of course the cities of al-Andalus, which fell from Muslim control over the course of the Reconquista (718–1492).[34] Al-Tabbaʿ thus understood the fate of Gaza in the context of the plunder of these symbolic Islamic cities. When he elaborates on the Ottoman soldiers in Gaza, this idea become more prominent:

> They broke and even uprooted the mosques' *minbar*s and scattered the Qur'an books and other manuscripts. They looted books from the houses of Gaza's scholars and notables, took what they took from them, and sold the others for insignificant prices… I saw pages of Qur'an and *tafsir*, books of *hadith* and other religious volumes lying on the side of the road and others dumped in the garbage. I recalled the fall of al-Andalus, the disaster inflicted by the Mongols and their criminal acts […][35]

Al-Tabbaʿ's concern for the fate of books links the fall of his town and the loss of its library to the acts of the Mongols, i.e., the destruction of Baghdad in 1258. Muslim chroniclers who depicted this decisive event in Islamic history were preoccupied with the fate of the books held in the ʿAbbasid 'House of Wisdom'. Ibn Taghribirdi (*d*.1470) described, for instance, that 'the books [of Baghdad] that held all of the world's sciences and knowledge were burned down […] the Mongols mixed them with water and clay to build bridges instead of using bricks'.[36] Since he was probably familiar with this or similar depictions, al-Tabbaʿ situated his own town in the same context.

But Gaza is no mere replica of Baghdad. Al-Tabbaʿ's placement of Muslim Ottoman soldiers in the shoes of the infidel Mongols makes these two events also historically contingent. Surely thinking beyond religious demarcations, al-Tabbaʿ vehemently accuses the people who ostensibly were the Muslim protectors of Gaza of causing the havoc in the city. This paradox enables us to penetrate more deeply into the cultural background of al-Tabbaʿ. For him, the fall of Gaza is not an isolated event but a result of the 'Turks' disgraceful operations, despicable behavior, faulty plans, unstable policies and corruption'.[37] Clearly, this echoes perceptions emblematic of his generation of Arab thinkers, who were influenced by the two main intellectual trends of the late nineteenth-century Middle East: the Arabic cultural renaissance (*al-Nahda*), and Islamic modernism. For both of these intellectual traditions, the fall of Baghdad was iconic as a seminal moment of historical rupture: the final blow to an age of prolific Arabic and Islamic creativity.[38] Indeed, Islamic modernists frequently accused the Turkic dynasties of the Islamic world, before and after the Mongols, of causing Islamic thought to stagnate and Islamic culture to decline.[39] These ideas must have been at the forefront of al-Tabbaʿ's thoughts as he witnessed the ravaging of his city by 'Turkish' Ottoman soldiers. Centuries-old narratives of standing in front of the ruins of the abandoned encampment and historical Islamic cities shaped his observation of the destruction of his hometown of Gaza. Far beyond a local event, the ruins of the Great Mosque encapsulated the ruins of his own Arabo-Islamic culture and history.

Origins of Destruction

Our second story of destruction in the Great Mosque of Gaza requires us to leap sixty years forward in time. It begins with a frustrated Israeli tour guide named Issahar Goldart who in the 1970s occasionally visited the Great Mosque of Gaza. On a tour in February 1978, he was upset to find that a precious remnant of Jewish history was gone: a small engraving of a candelabrum incised on one of the mosque's pillars had been erased.'It was corrupted by evildoers' Goldart later stated.[40] In what follows, we wish to suggest a way of understanding this act of destruction and the context in which it took place. As we argued in the previous section, acts of destruction may have roots in places hidden from sight. In this case, we need to go back in time to British Mandate Palestine in 1943, and to a book published the same year.

The History of Gaza was written by 'Arif al-'Arif, a prominent Palestinian historian and district officer of Gaza from 1939 to 1943. The book provides a wide-ranging chronological history of the city from the ancient to modern era. Adhering to a genre of history writing that was common at the time, it was comprehensive and included chapters such as 'Gaza and the Canaanites', 'Gaza and the Philistines', 'Gaza and the Jews', and so forth. Specific chapters were devoted to the mosques of Gaza and to the modern-day city. The book's trajectory mirrored and reconfirmed the Palestinian historical narrative during the British Mandate period.[41] For example, in the ancient section, the Canaanites are depicted as the indigenous Arab inhabitants of the land and the Israelites are considered to be newly arrived colonizers.[42] However, al-'Arif added his own spice to the stew, making it a little more genuine. He included non-Arabic characters in the text, mainly in English and Hebrew – two of seven languages in which he was proficient [Figure 7.5].[43] This was not merely a manifestation of his talent for languages, but also a reflection of the multiethnic cultural tolerance with which he was acquainted as a subject of the late Ottoman Empire.[44] A graduate of Istanbul University, a journalist, a translator, and an officer in the Ottoman army, al-'Arif was a man of letters of the late Ottoman world. Although his book was written many years after this world had collapsed, its multilingual style preserved some of that cosmopolitan spirit. The extensive use of Hebrew in the book is a case in point. Consistent with its Palestinian orientation, the book presents the perspective that the Jews were almost never able to conquer Gaza during ancient times and actually thrived under Muslim rule.[45] The claim that Jews enjoyed a golden age under Arab-Muslim aegis was not unique to al-'Arif, but he was perhaps the first Palestinian intellectual to develop it into a cohesive narrative. To bolster his argument, al-'Arif quoted extensively from Jewish sources, both ancient and modern. One intriguing source was *The Land of Israel Handbook*, a bestseller by the Jewish-Zionist traveler Ze'ev Vilnay. It was published in 1941, only two years before al-'Arif's *The History of Gaza*.[46] It is our suggestion that al-'Arif uses Jewish sources in his book in order to engage in an implicit controversy with Zionist claims to the land. When al-'Arif points to Jewish historical presence in Gaza – as Vilnay does – he claims something very different from Zionist scholars. While for Zionist

Destruction as Layered Event: Twentieth Century Ruins in the Great Mosque of Gaza

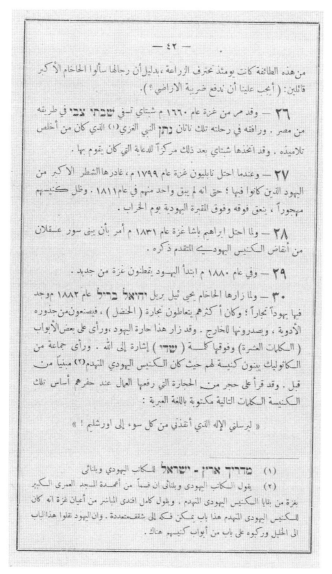

Figure 7.5: Hebrew script in al-'Arif's *The History of Gaza*. 'Arif al-'Arif, *Tarikh Ghazza [The History of Gaza]* (Jerusalem: Matba'at Dar al-Aytam al-Islamiyya, 1943), 42–43.

historians Jewish remnants were often times a justification for claiming Jewish modern sovereignty over Palestine, al-'Arif utilizes the same findings to hint for the opposite, that Jews may prosper under Arab or Muslim rule if only they would forsake their colonial ambitions for political hegemony.

Strikingly, it was inside the Great Mosque of Gaza – renovated during the 1920s – where al-'Arif seemed to identify the embodiment of this shared Jewish-Muslim history. The passage of the book that discusses the Great Mosque includes a sketch of an engraving of a Jewish candelabrum incised on one of the mosque's pillars. A *shofar* (horn), *etrog* (citron), a *lulav* (ceremonial palm frond) encircled by a leaf wreath, and the name Hanania Bar Ya'acov in Hebrew and Greek are easily recognized on its sides [Figure 7.6]. Al-'Arif states briefly that the pillar might have been a remnant of a synagogue brought to Gaza by sea that was then repurposed as spolia in a Byzantine church that predated the seventh-century Mosque.[47] The significance of the relief's origin notwithstanding, it is the origins of this explanation given by al-'Arif that is of more importance for us here.

The first scholar to scientifically document the engraving was the noted archaeologist and orientalist Charles Clermont-Ganneau during his expedition to Palestine in 1873–74. Clermont-Ganneau assumed that the pillar was originally part of the ruins of a Jewish synagogue in Caesarea, sent by Empress Eudoxia in the beginning of the fifth century when she built a basilica in her name in Gaza.[48] In his book, Clermont-Ganneau describes how he had to rope together several ladders placed on the slippery carpets of the mosque to get high enough to sketch the engraving for his survey. It was a frightening experience: 'a single false step and I should very likely have been thrown down and dashed on the ground'; he ultimately produced a copy of the *bas-relief* he deemed satisfactory.[49] After first appearing in Clermont-Ganneau's book, where it was used to suggest the unoriginality of Islamic architecture [Figure 7.7], the sketch found its way into Vilnay's handbook, where it was used to reinforce his argument for an enduring connection of the Jews to the land [Figure 7.8].[50] Thus, al-'Arif was the third author to use this 'objective' remnant to support a tacit political argument. In al-'Arif's case, just as the Hebrew characters could exist within an Arabic book, Jews too could have a share in the history of Palestine if they agreed to forsake their Zionist ambitions.

Contesting Jewish History in the Great Mosque of Gaza

A fierce scholarly attack soon began against al-'Arif's work, triggered by his claims of the Jewish archaeological findings in the city. In 1943, less than a year after *The History of Gaza* was published, the Gazan literary figure Hilmi Abu Sha'ban (1911–1978) published a booklet with a similar title, *The History of Gaza: Criticism and Interpretation*. As its title implied, this text was designed to refute the totality of al-'Arif's claims, reflecting the social, cultural, and political tensions that existed within Arab-Palestinian society. Al-'Arif was a high-ranking officer in the British Mandate regime, whereas Abu Sha'ban was a dissident who had spent time in prison during the Great Arab Revolt (1936–1939) against the British.[51] Al-'Arif was a well-off Jerusalemite while Abu Sha'ban came from a poor family in peripheral Gaza. Above all, however, al-'Arif was a 'man of yesterday', a creation of an ethnically and religiously inclusive Ottoman society where Zionism had been merely a latent threat, whereas Abu

Figure 7.6: The candelabrum sketch in al-'Arif's *The History of Gaza*. 'Arif al-'Arif, *Tarikh Ghazza [The History of Gaza]* (Jerusalem: Matba'at Dar al-Aytam al-Islamiyya, 1943), 333.

Sha'ban grew up under the less cosmopolitan era of the British Mandate, experiencing daily the escalating struggle against Zionism.[52]

Of the many ways this generational conflict manifested in Abu Sha'ban's work, one is essential here: Abu Sha'ban undertook a fundamental criticism of al-'Arif's approach to

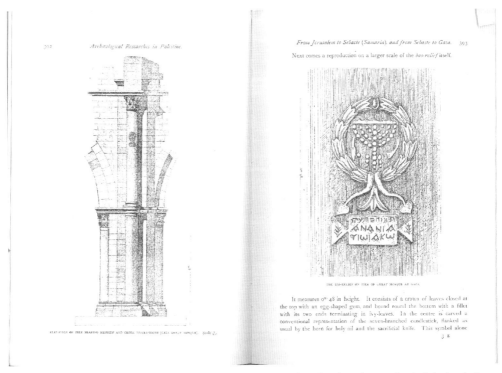

Figure 7.7: The candelabrum first documented in Clermont-Ganneau's *Archaeological Researches in Palestine during the Years 1873–1874*. Charles Clermont-Ganneau, *Archaeological Researches in Palestine during the Years 1873–1874* (Jerusalem: Raritas, 1971), 392–93.

history, especially the Jewish history of Palestine. In the sub-chapter 'Illustrations and Pictures', Abu Shaʻban writes that 'three of the pictures that were published by the author raise doubts, as they have one intention, to prove that Jews settled in Gaza […] and to create historical rights for them […]. All of this in a book written by an Arab-Muslim […]'.[53] After criticizing al-ʻArif for giving too much attention to the history of Jews in Gaza, Abu Shaʻban takes a close look at the candelabrum relief and the Hebrew writing beneath it but gives it a radically different interpretation than his counterpart. In his view, the candelabrum is not an exclusively Jewish symbol, but rather a Roman icon that could never have been brought to Gaza from al-ʻArif's 'alleged Jewish synagogue' (*al-kanis al-yahudi al-mazʻum*).[54] In the same manner, the Hebrew letters of Hanania Bar Yaʻakov, he believed, were not necessarily written by a Jew. In Abu Shaʻban's words: 'it is mentioned in the Encyclopedia Britannica […] that Hebrew letters were used in the writings of [different] languages, among them Greek […] writing in Hebrew does not necessarily implicate a Jewish origin […]'.[55]

For several reasons it might be tempting at this stage to explain this refutation as a form of religious extremism. The book, for example, opens with a line from the Qur'an (2:286)

Destruction as Layered Event: Twentieth Century Ruins in the Great Mosque of Gaza

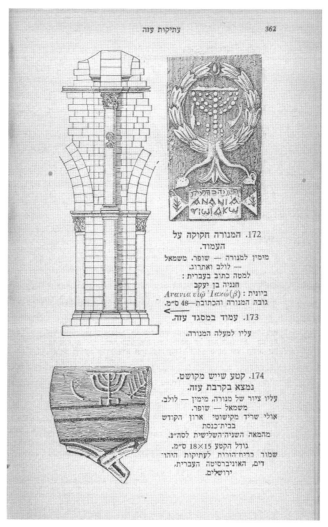

Figure 7.8: The candelabrum sketch in Vilnay's *Handbook for Eretz Israel*. Ze'ev Vilnay, *Madrikh Eretz Israel [Handbook for Eretz Israel]* (Jerusalem: Tur, 1941), 362.

asking for help to overcome the infidels. In addition, and as noted above, Abu Sha'ban criticizes al-'Arif for not writing in line with contemporary nationalistic Arab-Muslim beliefs. Furthermore, Abu Sha'ban operated within a cultural context that was influenced by Egyptian Islamic reform movements. In writing this criticism he enjoyed the support of prominent religious figures such as the aforementioned al-Tabba', who himself harshly criticized al-'Arif.[56] However, if we read Abu Sha'ban's argument carefully, we see that there is no evidence of any religious claim *per-se*; that is, of any claim based on Islamic jurisprudence, customs, or theological discourse. Even the appearance of ritual pagan symbols in the mosque does not seem to make any difference. Abu Sha'ban operates almost exclusively within the boundaries of national discourse such that Jewish history is negated on a purely national (rather than religious) basis. His claim is based upon one of the most hotly debated political issues of the time, the question of Jewish historical rights in Palestine. Thus, the logic went, if Hebrew was written by a Greek, then Hanania Bar Ya'akov was not Jewish, a fact that would weaken or negate Zionism's claims in Gaza. The Hebrew language, a candelabrum, and other non-Muslim ritual symbols in and of themselves did not create the problem, but in order to live with them peacefully their meaning had to be radically altered, from Jewish symbols to Greek ones. Abu Sha'ban knew that, in this time of national struggle, accepting the fact that this pillar originated in a shattered Jewish sanctuary would mean accepting a future shattering of his own people. This discourse reveals a split in the emerging Palestinian national thought that can best be interpreted as the divergence between the older, Ottoman-Arab elite and the younger Arab nationalists who grew up under western colonization, rather than a schism between extremist Islam (Gaza) and moderate or secular national Arabism (Jerusalem). Not much is known about al-'Arif's response, since most of his personal diaries are not available to the public. However, we do know that in his next study, published in 1947, his approach to Jewish history was completely different. In a book dedicated to al-Haram al-Sharif, *The History of the Sacred Jerusalemite Compound* he makes almost no mention of the history and remains of the Jewish temple that was previously located on the site of the Dome of the Rock.[57] Here, al-'Arif adapted his works to the newer, more exclusive version of Arab nationalism. In so doing, not only the Jewish history of Palestine, but also its cosmopolitan Ottoman past, was erased from his record.

We can now fast-forward roughly three decades to better situate the story of our Israeli tour guide, discovering in 1978 that the candelabrum engraving had been defaced. Luckily for him, he was at least left with a decent picture of the precious remnant he had managed to take three years earlier in 1975. Naïve as this simple act may sound, it was the setting of this photographic act that connects the historical debate about the candelabrum previously presented with its later destruction. Goldart indicated that he took this picture in the dead of night with the assistance of two military jeeps. These were there to illuminate the candelabrum with their headlights and probably also to secure the area for this nighttime visitor.[58] At the time, the Gaza Strip had been under Israeli military rule for almost a decade and had, since 1970, undergone a counterinsurgency that resulted in the deaths of dozens and the demolition of thousands of houses.[59] The same military power responsible for this violence facilitated the archaeological fascination of Israeli travelers and enthusiasts such as Goldart. Guided by pre-1948 travel handbooks like the aforementioned one by Vilnay, and adventurously documenting ancient remnants, as had Clermont-Ganneau in the nineteenth century, Israelis 'returned' to Gaza in the 1970s to seek traces of the city's Jewish past. In 1978, when the engraving was defaced, this sought-after Jewish legacy in Gaza was revived by the active construction of Israeli settlements. The documentation of heritage in the headlights of army vehicles – but also in the shadow of martial law – makes the link between archaeology and colonialism particularly clear. Archaeological research and colonial endeavors have a shared history, and the Israeli case is not an exceptional one.[60] Wrong as he was in his historical interpretation of the relief, Abu Sha'ban was right in terms of his political foresight. The act of defacing was no mere act of evil, as Goldart put it, but rather a tragic form of resistance.[61] Flood reminds us not to overlook the 'coexistence between the Buddhas and the Muslim population that marveled at them over a millennium before they were obliterated by the Taliban'.[62] In a similar manner, the Palestinians of Gaza lived peacefully for centuries with the Jewish symbol on the mosque pillars until the occupation of the site in the 1967 war and the military regime and colonization process that followed. Its removal between 1975 and 1978, probably by Palestinians, can be contextualized as an implicit demand to end the military occupation. Unlike the case of ISIS in the Middle East and the Taliban in Bamiyan, this was a modest, quiet, minor act, not a globally performed extravaganza of rage. We will probably never know who defaced the candelabrum, but whether it was an act of simple vandalism or a planned act to keep Israeli tourists and army alike outside the mosque, it represented an act of insurgency in the face of external hegemony.

Conclusion

In a short video released after ISIS militants raided the archeological museum in Mosul, a religiously attired and groomed figure talks to the camera against a background of mutilated statues. Unlike in ISIS's more official and westward-aimed magazine *Dabiq*, this figure explains the destroyers' rationale in terms of a desire to follow the example of the Prophet Muhammad in his war against *shirk*, or paganism. 'The Prophet, may prayer and peace be upon him,' he states, 'removed the idols and burned them with his noble hand upon conquering holy Mecca', thus drawing a clear connection between the destruction in the Mosul museum and historical Islamic iconoclasm.[63] By narrating the story of the Great Mosque in Gaza, we have tried to situate ISIS's modern destruction of antiquities in the context of a much broader discussion about historical memory in the Middle East. The contours and nuances of that discussion undermine simplistic, theologically-based explanations for ISIS's behavior, such as 'following the prophet' or 'fighting *shirk*' by pointing to concrete and discursive historically-grounded struggles over the identity of antiquities and their preservation in the modern Middle East. One aspect highlighted here is the enormous influence western hegemony exerted, and still exerts, over the shaping of the definition of the Middle East's cultural heritage, including through carrying out or provoking acts that ruin it. Considering heritage destruction as one possible means of insurgency against this hegemony does not excuse this phenomenon, but rather offers nuanced and complex explanations for it.

It is well known that interpretation of ruins and antiquities serves as an arena for political struggle. This chapter has taken this notion forward by demonstrating how the mechanism that provoked the creation of these ruins – that is, the destructive act – is also politically contested. Adding the meaning of destruction to this equation suggests that it is not only the history of the ruins as past relics that is disputed, but more importantly, what meaning these relics carry as ruins. ISIS's understanding of antiquities as proof of the failure of past civilization challenges the romantic notion of their existence exactly because such notions obscure the fact that these antiquities were once indeed ruined. This western romanticization, we have shown, was the method employed by James McBey's portrayal of the bombed mosque in order to efface British responsibility for its destruction. Although aiming his arrows towards the 'Turks', 'Uthman al-Tabba' takes the opposite approach and limns the ruins he sees while accepting destruction as a recurring historical event. Al-'Arif and Hilmi Abu Sha'ban delve into a similar discussion when interpreting the relic within the Great Mosque. Al-'Arif's liberal upbringing and late-Ottoman perceptions made him see the Jewish candelabrum engraving as part and parcel of Gaza's cultural landscape. For Abu Sha'ban, however, the here-and-now implication of such liberal understanding of antiquities could not have been valid.

That said, destruction and relics are not only the subject of these debates but are also themselves the means through which the debate takes place. ISIS chooses to destroy the destroyed in order to enhance its claim over the past, and so, too, did the demolisher of the candelabrum engraving in the Great Mosque in Gaza. The struggle over the signification of ruins thus brings about more destruction and more ruins in perpetual motion. In a short story aptly titled 'The Circular Ruins', Jorge Luís Borges depicts this dynamic masterfully. 'For what had happened many centuries before was repeating itself,' he writes, 'The ruins of the sanctuary of the god of Fire was destroyed by fire.'[64] This chapter has thus suggested understanding destruction not as an isolated historical event but as a lens through which history can be read. As we have tried to demonstrate in the case of the Great Mosque of Gaza, historicizing a site by its destructions may challenge the ostensible causality and ramifications of such events and expose the hidden and contested meanings that lead to them.

Making the category of destruction as the medium of historical analysis thus allows a different sort of contemplation on the question of heritage and preservation. The motive fundamentally is not to lament what is lost, but rather to investigate under what circumstances such loss is possible, and preventable. Creating a safe environment for peoples and their heritage without creating new ruins that will take centuries to become 'beautiful' again requires interpreting these histories of destructions, putting them in context, and preventing both the acts and interpretations of modern-day zealots from taking the leading role in the play.

Acknowledgments

Eli Osheroff wishes to express his gratitude to Abigail Jacobson and Liat Kozma, the supervisors of his MA thesis, upon which part of this paper is based. He also thanks several sponsors who supported the process of writing: the Chaim Herzog Center for Middle East Studies and Diplomacy of Ben Gurion University of the Negev; the Tami Steinmetz Center for Peace Research at Tel Aviv University; the Cherrick Center for the Study of Zionism, the Yishuv and the State of Israel in the Hebrew University; the Yad Izhak Ben Zvi, Yad Ora Foundation; and the Francis Gunter Foundation.

Dotan Halevy wishes to thank Ami Ayalon, Yoav Alon, Nurit Tsafrir, Meir Bar-Asher, and Iyas Nasser for their insightful comments on previous versions of this chapter.

Notes

1. See for instance: 'Ancient Sites Survived Islamic State Occupation', *Wall Street Journal*, March 29, 2016, accessed August 29, 2016, http://www.wsj. com/articles/syrias-palmyra-can-be-repaired-in-five-years-1459176051.
2. Thanassis Cambanis, 'Why ISIS' Destruction of Antiquities Hurts So Much', *The Boston Globe*, March 10, 2016, accessed September 1, 2016, https://www.bostonglobe.com/ideas/2015/03/10/why-isis-destruction-antiquities-hurt-much/vtoaEhENkSH5ZFpzfrYbVJ/story.html.
3. Finbarr Barry Flood, 'Between Cult and Culture: Bamiyan, Islamic Iconoclasm, and the Museum', *The Art Bulletin* 84 (2002): 641–59.
4. Ibid., 654.
5. Ibid., 641.
6. 'Destroying History's Treasures', *The Economist*, March 7, 2015, accessed August 29, 2016, http://www.economist.com/news/middle-east-and-africa/21645749-jihadists-are-attacking-more-regions-people-destroying-historys. See also Ken Chitwood, 'The Streak of Doubt that Underlies ISIS' Destructive Acts of Religious Fervor', *The Conversation,* August 31, 2015, accessed September 1, 2016, https://theconversation. com/the-streak-of-doubt-that-underlies-isis-destructive-acts-of-religious-fervor-46703.
7. William McCants, *The ISIS Apocalypse* (New York: St. Martin Press, 2015); see, for example, McCants' discussion on the connection between the U.S. invasion of Iraq, the turbulence of the Arab spring, and the rise of eschatological and apocalyptic perceptions in the Arab world, 99–118, 145–47; see also Yoram Schweitzer and Omer Einav, eds, *The Islamic State: How Viable Is It?* (Tel Aviv: Institute for National Security Studies, 2016); especially the essays by Kobi Michael, Ofir Winter, Meir Litvak and Yoram Schweitzer, 15–54.
8. The July 2017 issue of *International Journal of Islamic Architecture* upon which this volume expands showcases the new and innovative academic approaches towards the relationships between Muslim societies and archeological heritage. See specifically the introductory essay here as well as: Stephennie Mulder, 'Imagining Localities of Antiquity in Islamic Societies', *International Journal of Islamic Architecture* 6.2 (2017): 229–54.
9. 'Erasing the Legacy of a Ruined Nation', *Dabiq* 8 (March 2015): 22–24. In this regard, and for a different interpretation of ISIS's religious motivation, see the essay in this volume by Miroslav Melčák and Ondřej Beránek, 'ISIS's Destruction of Mosul's Historical Monuments: Between Media Spectacle and Religious Doctrine', also published in *International Journal of Islamic Architecture* 6.2 (2017): 389–415.

10. For such entanglement of mirroring destruction projects in the case of Palmyra itself see: Mulder, Introduction to this volume and 'Imagining Localities', 229–37.
11. 'Resume of Operations Middle East Brigade R.F.C for Week Ending May 3, 1917', AIR 1/2286/209/75/24, British National Archives.
12. 'Arthur Linden-Bell to Philip Chetwode', May 3, 1917, PWC/1/3/5, Imperial War Museum Archives, London.
13. 'Philip Chetwode to Arthur Linden-Bell', no date, PWC/1/3/5, Imperial War Museum Archives.
14. Tilman Ludke, *Jihad Made in Germany: Ottoman and German Propaganda and Intelligence Operations in the First World War* (Berlin: Lit Verlag, 2006), especially 62–70, and 115–25; Eugene Rogan, *The Fall of the Ottomans: The Great War in the Middle East,* (New York: Basic Books, 2015), 46–48.
15. For a more detailed account on the history of the mosque up to the Mamluk period see Denys Pringle, *The Churches of the Crusaders Kingdom of Jerusalem* (Cambridge: Cambridge University Press, 1993), vol. 1, 208–16.
16. 'Uthman Mustafa al-Tabba', *Ithaf al-a'izza fi ta'rikh Ghazza* (Gaza: Maktabat al-Yaziji, 1999), vol. 2, 119.
17. Salim 'Arafat al-Mubyyid wa Muhammad Khaled Kalab, *Maktabat al-jami' al-'Umari bi-madinat Ghazza* (Amman: Awruqa lil-Dirasat wa-lil-Nashar, 2013), 9.
18. 'Arthur Linden-Bell to Philip Chetwode', Imperial War Museum Archives.
19. Nicola Lambourne, 'Production versus Destruction: Art, World War I and Art History', *Art History* 22 (1999): 356.
20. *The Western Front: Drawings* (London: Authority of War Office from the Offices of Country Life, 1916).
21. Julia Hell, 'Imperial Ruin Gazers, or Why Did Scipio Weep?' in *Ruins of Modernity*, eds Julia Hell and Andreas Schonle (Durham, NC: Duke University Press, 2010), 169–70.
22. 'Reginald Wingate to Archibald Murray', May 3, 1917, FO141/773, British National Archives.
23. John More, *With Allenby's Crusaders* (London: Heath Cranton, 1923), 29.
24. 'Maydan Filastin', *al-Qibla,* May 22, 1917.
25. See for instance H.S. Gullat, *The Australian Imperial Force in Sinai and Palestine* (Sydney: Angus and Rogerstone, 1922), 429.
26. James McBey, 'Albert', in *Etchings and Dry Points of James McBey 1883–1959,* eds Martin Hardie and Charles Carter (San Francisco: Alan Wofsy Fine Arts, 1997), 179.
27. McBey Diary 1916–1918, Aberdeen Art Gallery Library Collections. We wish to thank the Gallery curators Liz Louis and Jason Finch for providing access to this precious document.
28. James McBey, *The Minaret, Gaza,* ink and watercolour on paper, 1917, Imperial War Museum (London), art.IWM ART 1678.
29. al-Tabba', *Ithaf al-a'izza,* vol.1, 315–18.
30. Ibid., 317.
31. Gabriel Levin, 'On the Hanging Odes of Arabia', *Parnassus: Poetry in Review* (2006): 6–27.
32. Ibid.

33. Charles Pellat, 'Marthiya" *Encyclopeadia of Islam 2,* http://referenceworks.brillonline.com/entries/encyclopaedia-of-islam-2/marthiya-COM_0691?s.num=0&s.f.s2_parent=s.f.book.encyclopaedia-of-islam-2&s.q=Marthiya, accessed August 29, 2016.
34. Ibid.
35. al-Tabbaʿ, *Ithaf al-aʿizza,* 315.
36. Jamal al-Din ibn Taghibirdi, *al-Nujum al-zahira fi muluk Misr wa ʿl-Qahira* (Cairo: Dar al-Kutub, 1929), vol. 7, 51.
37. al-Tabbaʿ, *Ithaf al-aʿizza,* 318.
38. Reuven Snir, *Baghdad: City of Verse* (Cambridge: Harvard University Press, 2013), 28–29; Shireen T. Hunter, 'Introduction', in *Reformist Voices of Islam: Mediating Islam and Modernity,* ed. Shireen T. Hunter (New York: Armonk, 2009), 6.
39. Ulrich W. Haarmann, 'Ideology and History, Identity and Alterity: The Arab Image of the Turk from the Abbasids to Modern Egypt', *International Journal of Middle East Studies* 20.2 (1988): 186–7, Sylvia G. Haim, 'Introduction', in *Arab Nationalism: An Anthology,* ed., Sylvia G. Haim (Berkeley: University of California Press, 1962), 23–25.
40. Issachar Goldart, 'Menorah, Shofar ve-Lulav ba-Misgad be-ʿAzzah', in *The Logic in the Madness: Zeev Galili's Blog,* last modified July 28, 2009, accessed April 29, 2016, http://www.zeevgalili.com/2009/07/5109.
41. Yoni Furas, 'In Need of a New Story: Writing, Learning and Teaching History in Mandatory Palestine' (Ph.D. diss., University of Oxford, 2015), 182–86.
42. ʿArif al-ʿArif, *Tarikh Ghazza* (Jerusalem: Matbaʿat Dar al-Aytam al-Islamiyya, 1943), 13–15.
43. ʿArif al-ʿArif, *Mujaz siratihi kitabihi wa-muʾalafatihi 1892–1963* (Jerusalem: Matbaʿat al-Maʿarif, 1964), 8.
44. Michelle U. Campos, *Ottoman Brothers: Muslims, Christians, and Jews in Early Twentieth Century Palestine* (Stanford: Stanford University Press, 2011), 1–2.
45. al-ʿArif, *Tarikh Ghazza,* 40–44.
46. Zeʾev Vilnay, *Madrikh Eretz Israel* (Jerusalem: Tur, 1941).
47. al-ʿArif, *Tarikh Ghazza,* 332–33.
48. Charles Clermont-Ganneau, *Archaeological Researches in Palestine during the Years 1873–1874* (Jerusalem: Raritas, 1971), 396.
49. Ibid., 390–391.
50. Vilnay, *Madrikh,* 261.
51. Salim ʿArafat al-Mubyyid, *Hilmi Musbah Abu Shaʿban: al-adib al-shaʿir wa ʿl-sahafi al-thaʾir* (Gaza: independent publishing, 2004), 13.
52. Campos, *Ottoman Brothers,* 1–19.
53. Hilmi Abu Shʿaban, *Tarikh Ghazza: naqd wa-tahlil* (Jerusalem: Matbaʿat Beit al-Maqdis, 1943), 39.
54. Ibid., 44–49.
55. Ibid., 51.
56. Ibid., 10–11.
57. ʿArif al-ʿArif, *Tarikh al-Haram al-Qudsi* (Jerusalem: Matbaʿat Dar al-Aytam al-Islamiyya, 1943).
58. Goldart, 'Menorah'.
59. Jean-Pierre Filiu, *Gaza: A History* (London: Hurst and Company, 2014), 140–45.

60. For a concise account of the history of archaeology in the holy land in the nineteenth century see Neil Asher Silberman, *Digging for God and Country: Exploration, Archeology, and the Secret Struggle for the Holy Land, 1799–1917* (New York: A.A. Knopf, 1982). On the specific Zionist case in the twentieth century see Nadia Abu El-Haj, *Facts on the Ground: Archaeological Practice and Territorial Self-Fashioning in Israeli Society* (Chicago and London: The University of Chicago Press, 2001).
61. Goldart, 'Menorah'.
62. Flood, 'Between Cult and Culture', 654.
63. 'Islamic State Destroys Statues in Mosul,' last modified February 26, 2016, https://www.youtube.com/watch?v=ZFIo0gM0BWo, accessed August 30, 2016.
64. Jorge Luis Borges, 'The Circular Ruins' (trans. James E. Irby) in *Labyrinths; Selected Stories & Other Writings,* eds Donald A. Yates and James E. Irby (New York: New Directions, 1962), 61.

8

In Situ: The Contraindications of World Heritage

Wendy M. K. Shaw

The Contraindications of World Heritage

Public representations of world heritage preservation-related issues have recently proliferated. In June 2015, the Bamiyan Buddhas reappeared in the sandstone niches that had sheltered them until their 2001 destruction under the Taliban. Holograms have advantages over stone: new technologies enable the Buddhas to shine forth, by night or day, anywhere in the world.[1] In February 2016, in the interest of preventing future cataclysms, the United Nations formalized a training centre for the 'Blue Helmets of Culture' to protect 'the world's cultural patrimony'.[2] For three days in April 2016, a 6-metre marble scale model of the arch of Palmyra, enabled by increasingly accurate digital reproductive technologies, graced London's Trafalgar Square in an act of supposed defiance against an internationally unrecognized authoritarian Islamist regime that roots its ideology in an eclectic selection of theological precedents.[3]

In the meantime, on the same planet, an unprecedented number of internally and globally displaced people struggle for survival.[4] Many originate from the same regions as the monuments under threat. As their numbers increase, countries with access to the extensive resources of the European Union build ever-higher physical and discursive fences, turning forced migrants away as many drown at sea or wither in inhumane refugee camps. Instead of maintaining the human dignity of those fleeing from war, we focus on monument preservation. Yet is the declaration of concern over a globalized heritage equivalent to the protection of local cultures? What should we do when we recognize that the world does not respond to crisis by pooling its resources to protect lives, living standards, or historical sites? Do current debates about preservation suggest an exchange rate between human lives and the patrimony of the dead? Seemingly incognizant of powerful professional critiques of the Eurocentric, universalist modernism implicit in the concept of 'world heritage', these public expressions suggest that the rhetoric of outrage against heritage destruction may be no less ideologically founded than the performance of destruction that they decry.[5]

The destructive and restitutional practices embedded in the histories of four diverse case studies – the modern town of Tadmur (beside Palmyra, Syria); the modern Geyre (over Aphrodisias, Turkey); the modern Wadi Halfa (near Abu Simbel, Egypt and Sudan); and Bamiyan (Afghanistan) – exemplify the local cultural costs of site preservation under the rubric of world heritage.[6] In popular (and often scholarly) accounts, heritage preservation appears simply as a shining knight battling the dark forces of destruction. Yet far from purely constructive, sites we think of as authentically historical are often reconstructions built over destroyed habitation of local communities. This makes them highly contested political symbols, enabling their destruction to serve as propaganda. Ethical preservation only becomes possible when its local costs and long-term implications are recognized, and when the meanings invested in sites by local populations are respected. The past can only retain value for the future if it does not come at the cost of the living present.

Are Ruins Ancient?

London's scale model of the Palmyrene Triumphal Arch serves as metonym for the complex erasure of cultures embodied not only by the recent history of the site, but also by the modern processes of its memorialization. In mid-May 2015, ISIS gained control of over half of Syria as it captured the town of Tadmur, about 500 metres from Palmyra, from the control of the Syrian Army. Approximately 15,000 of 25,000 residents fled into the surrounding desert. Recording its inhumane conditions in video footage released (along with its prisoners) on May 28, ISIS forces dynamited the infamous Tadmur Prison on May 30, planting ISIS's flag in the broken head of the destroyed bust of President al-Assad at its entrance. Reportedly on the same day, ISIS laid improvised explosive devices (IEDs) around the ruins of Palmyra, which had been recognized as a UNESCO World Heritage Site in 1980. ISIS also distributed footage of bulldozers and power drills crushing original and reconstructed figural statuary on the site and in its museum. On June 22, ISIS released video of the destruction of two contemporary shrines nearby: the tomb of Mohammad ibn 'Ali, believed to be a descendant of Imam 'Ali, revered by local Shi'ites, 5 kilometres north of Palmyra; and the tomb of the sixteenth-century Sufi sage Nizar Abu Bahaeddin, revered by local Sunnis, located in an oasis 500 metres from Palmyra. On July 4, ISIS staged a mass execution in the city's ancient amphitheatre. On August 18, they executed the respected archaeologist Khaled al-As'ad and hung his body in the main square of the site. Dramatic mushroom-cloud footage of the destruction of the Temple of Baalshamin was released on August 23; the Temple of Bel was similarly destroyed on August 30; and the monumental arch was destroyed in October. On March 27, 2016 the Syrian Arab Army, manned largely by Russian and Afghan soldiers, retook the site, with publicity footage of soldiers and vehicles symbolically milling about on the ruins, which had become all the more famous through their destruction. The May 5 concert of European classical music in the amphitheatre performed the presumed universalism of western culture, which enables the contemporary site of Tadmur to become appropriated as western though affiliation with Palmyrene heritage.[7] Through western media coverage, the conquest and reconquest of an uninhabited city preserved for touristic use served as an apt symbol for the classic orientalist battle between essentialized positions of a 'barbaric' Islam against a 'civilized' West.[8]

ISIS carefully crafted its display of targeted destruction in Tadmur/Palmyra as a sophisticated exposition of its ideology. The initial destruction of the prison was a potent symbol and defied the decades of violent political repression under the authoritarian regimes of Syria and Iraq, which had been upheld under the Ba'athist promise of a renaissance of Arab identity. Under both regimes, identification with archaeological sites served as a means of defining a cohesive national identity through affiliation with ancient civilizations as symbolic of the diverse religious, ethnic and linguistic populations that coexisted throughout the region until the modern era.[9] International recognition of ancient civilizations considered as 'world heritage' served as a means of broadening the framework of 'western heritage' initiated through Hegelian historiography, without challenging its implicit hierarchies of civilization progressing ever westward. The overlap of local with global historiographic ideology provided tacit support for these regimes as symbolically partaking in a rhetorically egalitarian global order.[10] Similarly, regime policies of the mid-twentieth century that had regulated top-down, state-approved expressions of Islam relegated Islamic discourse to marginalized, impoverished and disenfranchised fringes, and these proved fertile ground for the acceptance of reductive, militant and vehemently anti-western interpretations of Islam. In this context, the persistence of local shrines signified a diversity of Islam disallowed under recent Islamist regimes.[11] Thus, the destruction of both Palmyra and the shrines by ISIS, as well as the theatrical executions, collectively indicated a taking control of history hardly different from the processes of reinscription that have been underway for centuries.

How old is Palmyra? Although today it is generally described as a Roman city of the second century ad, the reassembly of its ruins is modern. Until the eighteenth century, Palmyra was remembered as part of the literary mythology of Zenobia.[12] This shifted in 1697 through the travel writings of a group of Englishmen who travelled from Aleppo to Palmyra in 1678 and 1691. Over the following three centuries, a series of images brought back by European travellers created the ancient site of Palmyra in the European imaginary. Just a year later, in 1692, the Dutch Consul in Aleppo, Coenraet Calckberner, commissioned the artist who had accompanied the travellers, G. Hofsted van Essen, to paint the ruins.[13] In the resulting painting, now in the Allard Pierson Museum, Amsterdam, colourful little red and blue men play hide-and-seek between stones, some collapsed in heaps, others erect as pins in a cushion. In the foreground stands the European ambassador, a document unfurled in his right hand, left hand confidently at his waist, as his oriental companions mill about him like planets about the sun, a small hired posse with modern rifles and exotic tobacco pipes at the ready. The distant landscape, particularly the fortress on a high hill on the horizon, matches the medieval fortress of today, but the artist's imagination adds a fantastic acropolis on the far left and some pyramids behind a massive hulk of a ruin on the far left. The image displays a site in absolute ruins, a playground for the adventurous traveller.

Six years later, Cornelis de Bruijn included an illustration inspired by van Essen's painting in his *Reizen van Cornelis de Bruyn* of 1698 [Figure 8.1]. In depicting Palmyra, he denigrated the contemporary Arab name for the site, Tadmur, as a mere alias. Perhaps because he did not actually visit the site, he did not feel obliged to include any oriental

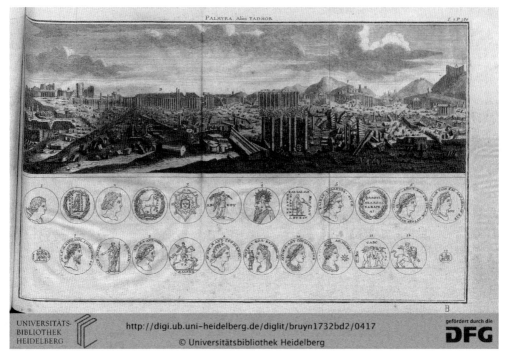

Figure 8.1: 'Palmyra alias Tadmur (1698)', in Cornelius le Bruyn. *Voyages de Corneille le Bruyn au Levant: C'est-à-dire, dans les principaux endroits de l'Asie Mineure, dans les isles de Chio, Rhodes, Chypre, &c.; de même que dans les plus considérables villes d'Egypte, Syrie, & Terre Sainte…*, vol. 2 (Delft: Henri de Kroonevelt, 1700), 380a. Heidelberg University Library.

companions in fancy dress, but instead simply portrays two lone Europeans on horseback surveying a wasteland.

Advised of the wonders of the site through the circulation of this popular image, the British travellers James Dawkins and Robert Wood, along with their hired Italian draughtsman Giovanni Battista Borra, arrived at Tadmur in 1751. Borra depicted the ruins as never before: no disorder mars the scene; no distant hills distract from the splendour of antiquity; scattered columns have grown into walls; landscaped shrubs replace the detritus of ages; minute travellers, led by orientals, explore comfortably on horseback as the draughts-man takes in the conveniently labelled scenery [Figure 8.2]. In Borra's painting, Hofsted's eclectic exotic fantasies of acropolis and pyramids have been replaced by the neoclassical fantasy of the Enlightenment, where monumentality has not yet given way to romance.

A few decades later, Gavin Hamilton reimagines the visit by shifting the focus from the site itself to its apparent discovery: background to foreground, landscape to portrait, scientific to sensual [Figure 8.3]. Gone are the sharp lines and sharp focus of Borra's rigid vistas and architectural plans. Instead, clear perspectival lines draw the gaze towards

In Situ: The Contraindications of World Heritage

Figure 8.2: *The Ruins of Palmyra*, in Robert Wood and James Dawkins, *Les ruines de Palmyre, autrement dite Tedmor, au désert* (London: A. Millar, 1753), pl. 43. Heidelberg University Library.

Figure 8.3: Gavin Hamilton, *James Dawkins and Robert Wood Discovering the Ruins of Palmyra* (1758), oil on canvas, 310 × 389 cm. National Galleries of Scotland.

the gateway to the past, discovered by heroes in the foreground whose classicizing imagination clads them in togas. The European travellers leave the orientals who frame them in the shadows of the present as they bask in the aura of the past. Like the orientals in the earlier images, these characters are local guides with apparently no more relationship to the ruins than the visitors. Like the Europeans, they are mere interlopers from the present treading through the rubble of the past, but unlike their European contemporaries, they are unable to travel through time through the magical medium of literary classicism.

What, then, was Tadmur? The name itself is ancient, from Semitic roots, appearing in the second millennium BCE, long before the Romans renamed the city 'Palmyra' by reference to the palm trees that grew in the oasis of the Efqa Spring sometime in the first century BCE. The location first appears in Ottoman documents in 1724, when the inhabitants of the ruins between Tadmur and Raqqa received information about their new habitations in Aleppo, where they presumably were moved.[14] Although it is not clear why this relocation took place, Ottoman officials may have been responding to a new European interest in Palmyra by transferring locals. What is clear is that there were people living in the ruins of Tadmur, and they probably had not just moved there. In fact, habitation had been consistent enough since the ancient period that the Roman name never superseded the name of the town. Some visitors recognized the overlap between the modern name and that of the Biblical site: for example, the missionary William Wright, who visited Palmyra in 1872.[15] Yet despite the town's apparently uninterrupted occupation, in every European illustration the inhabitants of this town are invisible. As in Hamilton's painting, they fade into the background because they lack the illumination of classicism and because they are rendered imperceptible by the act of naming: by the selective appellation of the town as Palmyra in English through a preference for Roman and Christian sources over local names. As Thomas Love Peacock intoned in his 1806 poem 'Palmyra':

> No sound of man the solitude pervades,
> Where shattered forms of ancient monarchs lie… No form is near, no steps intrude,
> To break the melancholy reign Of silence and of solitude.[16]

If, for westerners, the locals of Palmyra were invisible because they were oriental, for urban Ottomans they were invisible because of class, frequently measured through literacy. In his novel *al-Huyam fi-jinan al-Sham* ('Passion in Syrian Gardens'), serialized in newspapers in Beirut in 1876, Salim al-Bustani combined the modern, bourgeois western practices of reading and the mixing of the sexes with the modern means of knowing about the region through its histories. In the novel, he recounts the tale of European visitors drawn to greater Syria through books. Connecting with a local bourgeois Beiruti, their shared interest in the past leads them to visit Tadmur together. Soon after their arrival they are captured by a Bedouin tribe, and are later rescued by a woman who can translate between the local Bedouin language and French. She explains, '[T]he travellers have come to our country to look upon it, because in it are ancient ruins that clarify the histories that they read.'¹⁷

The narration establishes a distinction between the bourgeois who identifies with the region temporally, as narrated history grafted onto space, and local Bedouin populations who identify with it spatially. Yet the actual inhabitants, the Bedouin, are not equipped to know what they see. The earliest photograph of a presumably local figure at the site, by the late nineteenth-century local Beiruti photographic outfit Maison Bonfils, reveals a boy, his penury underscored by rough, bare feet and rags, sleeping on the ruins in an unlikely and thereby symbolic pose, as if a metaphor for a relationship simultaneously of comfort and blindness, and a projection of the European reverie associated with the site onto the native who is too naive to appreciate civilization from an appropriate distance [Figure 8.4].

For the site to embody history, its true identity had to come from a text written about it elsewhere. Jacques Derrida suggests that 'writing is that forgetting of the self, that

Figure 8.4: Maison Bonfils, *Palmyra, Sculpture of a Capital, Syria* (c.1867–1899) albumen print. Library of Congress, Washington, DC, LOT 13550, no. 286.

exteriorisation, the contrary of the interiorising of memory, of the *Erinnerung* that opens the history of the spirit'.[18] The Enlightenment classicism inherent to the colonial understanding of the Levantine landscape depends on a transformation of internalized memory into an exteriorization, which enables experience to be written into a Hegelian model of history and established within a narrative of western civilization. History depends on this displacement from the silent presence of history in the landscape to the inscription of those who imagine it from afar. In an era when Ottoman modernization required the settlement and hegemonic normalization of nomadic populations, such discourse divested locals of their land, as interlopers in a narration of space through history in which they were not equipped to partake.[19]

Like oil and water, two overlapping spaces discursively separate: Palmyra, an ancient site embalmed in a European imagination that divested it of habitation; and Tadmur, a site that persisted between, among, and perhaps even despite the ruins, transgressing their temporality with a supposed profound disinterest in history. Despite the absence of locals in European depictions, the habitation of the region had been continual, and its residents had also produced histories of their own. Palmyra had served as an important centre in antiquity because it offered an oasis, and this oasis continued to inform its use as an important stop along the East–West trade route before, during, and after the Umayyad caliphate in the early eighth century.

> Archaeologists have shown that the famous temple of Bel which is laid out north/south was used as an Umayyad mosque after having served as a church. Considering the size of the temple of Bel complex, the importance of Palmyra/Tadmur to trade and the probable size of the permanent population involved in producing agricultural products and serving the needs of traders and travellers, the mosque must have been a congregational rather than private or court mosque.[20]

So what was the town of Palmyra/Tadmur before its redemption as a site of civilizational heritage? The settlement consisted of a village intricately woven into ancient ruins. Archaeologist Gertrude Bell's 1900 description underscores how the modern town intertwined with historical spaces:

> It is a mass of columns, ranged into long avenues, grouped into temples, lying broken on the sand or pointing one long solitary finger to Heaven. Beyond them is the immense Temple of Baal; *the modern town is built inside it* and its rows of columns rise out of a mass of mud roofs. And beyond, all is the desert […] It looks like the white skeleton of a town, standing knee deep in the blown sand. We rode down to one of the two springs to which it owes its existence […] I had tea and received all the worthies of the town – the Mudir is an old Turk who talks much less Arabic than I do – and when I had sent them away happy I walked out and down the Street of Columns into the Temple of the Sun – the town, I should say, for it is nearly all included within its enormous outer walls. A few

Figure 8.5: American Colony, Jerusalem, *Palmyra (Tadmor): Native Village among Ruins of Temple of the Sun* (c.1900–1920), stereograph, 5 × 7 in. Library of Congress, Washington, DC, LC-M32-770.

suburbs extend outside and lots of gardens with fruit trees and date palms in them, but the wind is so strong that the fruit mostly blows off before it has time to ripen.[21]

Early photographs taken from a slight elevation by the American Colony in Jerusalem reveal the selective choice of viewing position in earlier paintings [Figure 8.5]. They show low-lying mudbrick houses that adopt the ruins as a protective shell, like a hermit crab in a found habitation. Their inhabitants owned the site not, like Dawkins and Wood, through an illuminated portal opened across the dark fabric of time through the magic curtain of history, but simply by living there [Figure 8.6].

Unlike in the paintings, where male European travellers depict themselves in the company of native male guides, the anonymous photographers of Tadmur reveal a city inhabited and maintained by women. At first glance, this continues the venerable tradition of Eugene Delacroix's *The Women of Algiers in their Harem* (1834), a celebration of colonialism through the exposure of native women to the European gaze.[22] Yet here we see a different exposure: not that of the (imaginary) lazy concubine awaiting her master

Figure 8.6: American Colony, Jerusalem, *Palmyra (Tadmor): Street of Village in Temple of the Sun* (*c.*1900–1920), glass, dry plate negative. Library of Congress, Washington, DC, LC-M32-771.

so much as of the hardworking villager. Plastering their walls, smiling quizzically at the camera – perhaps the first they have seen – the women fail to function as objects for an orientalizing gaze [Figure 8.7]. Rather, they expose a condition of the native woman, nearly a hundred years ago, mistress of her domain and outside of dominant western narratives of the eastern/Muslim woman as a victim of her servile status beside men. Such photographs capture the women of the village before modern ideologies disenfranchised them under the guise of saving them from a present renamed as tradition. In this process, the position from which they can articulate their own experiences becomes disavowed, and they become the subaltern class of a homogenized, national female identity.[23]

In 1929, when these photographs were taken, Henri Arnold Seyrig, the newly appointed General Director of Antiquities in Syria and Lebanon (under French Mandate), arranged for the relocation of the villagers to a new site outside of the town [Figure 8.8]. It would appear that the work of the women was in vain, since the village inside the ruins was destroyed to make way for the extensive archaeological excavations and reconstruction of the ruins of the ancient site, which became renowned as the antique city of Palmyra. The new town, adjacent

Figure 8.7: American Colony, Jerusalem, *Palmyra* (1929), nitrate negative. Library of Congress, Washington, DC, LC-M33-80520-x.

to the area now designated as a World Heritage Site, offers new roads and gardens with modern two-story houses supposedly designed based on vernacular architecture. In the American colony photograph, a few ruined columns lie scattered at our feet as we stand in the site of the ruins; our backs to the site we (represented in the gaze of the photographer that stands in for the French colonial administrator who enables the work of the archaeologist) now master, surveying the peace offering before us.

In this new space, the female villager becomes the subaltern of the archaeological site as men take on the new dominant forms of labour enabled by archaeology: first as day labourer

Figure 8.8: American Colony, Jerusalem, *Palmyra: The New Village: Substituting the Old Village Formerly in Temple Courts* (c.1929), glass, dry plate negative. Library of Congress, Washington, DC, LC-M32-3749.

for the digging and then as tourist guide. As the modern town becomes a service space for the resurrected Roman city, its original name subsumed to a footnote, its citizens become parts of a global, capitalist economy depending less on agricultural labour than on a monetary economy tied to cities and, increasingly, to international travel. As Gayatri Spivak points out, such a figure

> is actually engaged in consolidating the Self of Europe by obliging the native to cathect the space of the Other on his home ground [...] He is wording *their own world*, which is far from an uninscribed earth, anew, by obliging *them* to domesticate the alien as Master.[24]

As in the early drawings of Palmyra that excluded locals in favour of an abstracted 'oriental' guide, the local-transformed-into-tourist-guide loses his tactile relationship with a space that becomes transposed into a historical narrative, which distances that space from him and at the same time, brings it closer for the European visitor.

When the Russian artist and traveller Alexander Evgenevich Yakovlev visited the site in 1933 as part of the Trans-Asian Expedition organized by the French automobile company

Figure 8.9: Alexander Yakovlev, *Palmyra* (1933), oil on canvas, 100 × 252 cm. MacDougal Auctions.

Citroen, he painted six works recording the ruins of Palmyra [Figure 8.9]. In his diaries, he wrote,

> in the sad lifelessness of evening in the desert, where a thin, dark curtain of sand obscures the vivid colours of sunset [there appeared before him an] extraordinary vision – the colossal skeleton of a dead city stretched across several kilometres […] the view was revealed through a valley of death, a valley where dozens of towers were built to preserve hundreds and thousands of corpses.[25]

Yet unlike the earlier painterly visions of Palmyra, his painting includes a few picturesque women who add colour and movement to the scene as they gather water from this valley of death, presumably from the wells of their old town, perhaps near the Sufi shrine destroyed in 2015.

Ara Güler captures a similar moment at the village of Geyre, on the site of ancient Aphrodisias, in 1958, before its excavation and transformation into a touristic destination [Figure 8.10].[26] Official renditions of the history of the village, offered by its chief excavator Kenan Erim, suggest that it was relatively new, established as a result of new migrations in the eighteenth century – coinciding with the modern habitation of Tadmur.[27] Was this a change in habitation, perhaps due to the movement of populations? Or a shift in Ottoman record keeping? Settlements emerge at particular locations for geographical reasons, for example, access to water sources, which do not often change suddenly. Were these modern habitations? Or was the discourse of modernity a means of establishing a distinction between ancient and modern eras of habitation, so that the former could be safely resurrected at the cost of the latter, the interloper, the squatter on land always already owned by history?

At Geyre, ancient columns have been resurrected, but the resurrection comes at the cost to those whose relationship with the ruins was, like in Tadmur, not aestheticizing

Figure 8.10: Ara Güler, *Geyre Village* (1958), black and white photograph. Magnum Photos, GUA1964003W00001.

nor historicizing, as in a museum, but pragmatic. Güler's photographs reveal ancient architectural elements embedded in everyday life. Column capitals support the unequal lengths of the wooden columns on the interior and exterior of the small mosque portico [Figure 8.11]. The villagers look away from the columns, toward the elaborate vernacular wall painting of a village mosque. Above their heads, we cannot quite see if a roundel to the left of the *mihrab* is a calligraphic panel of the name of the Prophet Muhammad, adjacent to what looks like a hand of Fatima hanging down under some kind of tree of life. We cannot quite see paintings of palm trees, tropes for Mecca, flanking the top of the *mihrab*. The carefully wrought vernacular architecture is out of focus because what we see is profoundly different from what the villagers see: the columns in the foreground that hold the building up. To sit on a ruin, incorporate it into a house or use it as part of a mosque is a mode of appropriation no less valid than to hang it on the wall as part of a private collection or to place it in a museum. It simply represents a system of value distinct from that based on remoteness built through the ideology of historicity.

But does this historicity represent the absolute value of the site? Any tourist or scholar enjoying a respite from the urban cacophony of modernity, who has wandered through a quiet landscape cluttered with ruins in the hot, dry sun of an Anatolian summer, listening to crickets chirp and smelling the dried grasses, might consider that the pleasure of the

In Situ: The Contraindications of World Heritage

Figure 8.11: Ara Güler, *Mosque in the Village of Geyre* (1958), black and white photograph. Magnum Photos, GUA 1964003W00017.

experience may have more to do with our own remoteness from nature and from a moment of intimacy with nature, than with the historicity of the ruins themselves. Guides may justify our pleasure as moral, protestant labour through the posts and lintels of history, but in the end, tall columns function as sublime frames for lone clouds in a blue sky. Instruction about history reforms our gaze away from its pleasures into discourses of civilization and ownership of the past. Preserved archaeological sites and museums symbolize the egalitarianism of republican values through a performance of the State, safeguarding treasures for the people who constitute it. Yet this performance not only reforms a nationalized paradigm of identity for a local population, it also constructs a gauge of historicity that informs the fungible value of antiquities in a market vaster than the collection of any museum.[28]

The preference for the history of ruins over the legacy of habitation produces a rupture in the temporality of the site. While ruins may have been carved in antiquity, they have been resurrected as part of modernity. Their resurrection favours the imagination of long-dead cultures over contemporary cultures that have preserved intangible heritage with no clear single source of origin. The resurrection of ruins comes at the cost of the destruction of the living aspect of the very heritage that ruins are supposed to represent. How old are ruins? It is a tricky question.

How Old Is World Heritage?

The definition of world heritage is intimately linked to the politics of favouring ancient civilizations over local, often minority, populations, and the purported progress of modernist economic development over traditional local economies. This is nowhere more evident than at the town of Wadi Halfa and the touristic heritage site of the Nubian Monuments, most famously, Abu Simbel.

There, between unprecedented rescue archaeology and accompanied by the forced evacuation of approximately 100,000 Nubians from the rising waters of the Nile caused by the construction of the Aswan High Dam, the concept of world heritage was born.[29]

Conquered by Egypt in stages after 1821 and governed separately as of 1899 as a British colony following the 1882 British occupation of Egypt, the Republic of Sudan finalized its independence from Egypt in 1956, after a transitional period following the declaration of the Egyptian Republic as independent from Britain in 1953. Yet the Nile River and the apportioning of its waters continued to tie the young nation-states together.[30] As Egypt overthrew the British-backed monarchy, its leadership believed that the country could only compete with the power established by Iraq (through the Baghdad pact of 1955) with resources to be enabled by the construction of a larger dam than that built under the British in 1898–1902 in Aswan (at the first cataract of the Nile River). Although the dam was initially funded by the United States, Egypt's increasing closeness with Communist regimes led to a withdrawal of funds, with the Soviet Union ultimately providing funding for the dam project in 1958. Egypt would benefit from the construction of the dam through hydroelectric energy for industrialization; control over agricultural production through control over annual floods; and tourism enabled by a regularized river. The damage would take place in Sudan, in the historic home of the Nubian people. Although an alternative plan was proposed that would have spread out the water rather than collecting it at the third cataract, it was rejected under a change of the Sudanese government in 1956.

The initial damming of the river had already led to extensive regional change, with the new lake destroying habitation 60 km to the west at Wadi as-Sabua and reaching as far as Wadi al-Halfa in the south.[31] During the subsequent first Nubian migration of the Kenuzi people, villagers from Wadi as-Sabua had been forced to move several times to higher ground. The absence of fertile farming land ultimately led them to cities. However, at Wadi al-Halfa the arrival of water encouraged the town's growth. Established as a port for Nile steamers from Aswan, the town developed in the 1860s under Khedive Ismail Pasha in his effort to incorporate the region into greater Egypt; the town developed further under British rule, with the inclusion of a directorate (including a garden with English roses) and a hotel. Both Ismail Pasha and King Farouk built mosques in the town, one without and one with a minaret, but each strengthening Cairo's symbolic power in the south. Although a railway from Cairo initially had been attempted under Ismail in 1874, the British use of the port against the Mahdist resistance at the end of the century led to the establishment of a railway to Khartoum in 1899. Around the same time, the city gained importance as a prison for some leaders of the rebellion.[32]

These multiple shifts of governance in a short period of time led to a diverse population, including Greek traders and northern Egyptians, two of whom – Hassan Orabi and Ahmed Batul – were credited with developing an anonymous local masonry practice through the development of dramatic decorative design for the traditional mudbrick courtyard houses of the region, which became larger through the availability of cast-off iron railroad tracks.[33] The recent growth of the town – up to 11,600 (and 34,000 in the district) in 1956, when the pre-evacuation census was taken – was often used as evidence for the lack of historicity, and thereby lack of importance, of the site in comparison with the antiquities preserved through the international mobilization of funds under the aegis of UNESCO.[34] The decision to relocate local populations was taken in 1959. Extensive demonstrations in Wadi Halfa and Khartoum University in October 1960 were silenced with martial law. At the time of resettlement, in 1963, most villagers moved either north to Cairo or south to Khartoum, with less than half choosing to stay in the replacement villages. Movement of archaeological sites took place between 1963 and 1973, with reconstruction beginning in 1977.[35] Not only were many undocumented prehistoric and Nubian archaeological sites drowned, but the dispersal of the indigenous Nubian populations in the region endangered their language and destroyed vernacular architecture and other indigenous practices particular to Nubian village communities.

The political context of the subsequent UNESCO-led international rescue campaign to preserve what they now termed 'world heritage' suggests that the interests of the many states funding the effort reflected the soft diplomacy of the Cold War, such that the greater Soviet investment for the Suez Canal and the Aswan Dam was symbolically met through the rescue of heritage. Responding to archaeologists' objections regarding the loss of Pharaonic and Greco-Roman sites to flooding, an extensive campaign was launched to support the rescue of what would be dubbed the 'Nubian Monuments' when they were added to the UNESCO World Heritage Sites List in 1979. These not only included the largest and most famous monument, Abu Simbel, but also the Temple of Dakka and the Temple of Maharraqa, moved to the same outdoor archaeological park now known as the 'Wadi es-Sebua Temple Complex

Area', as well as those temples given to foreign museums.[36] The regularization of the Nile enabled millions of tourists to visit the new archaeological park, but the effect on Nubians has largely been subsumed into national narratives of modernization in both Egypt and Sudan.

Friedrich W. Hinkel's 1978 *Auszug aus Nubien* ('Exile from Nubia') embodies this narrative of modernization. Beginning with images of idyllic rural Nubia – villagers tending animals by a river; women milling grain or baking bread; men slaughtering goats or making pots under thatched straw awnings; children squatting in the courtyard of a mudbrick house; locals using gasoline canisters to carry water; the smiling face of a local man juxtaposed with a closeup of a braying camel – he records native life for posterity. This gives way to an overview of the Pharaonic heritage of the region, with brief mention of prehistoric rock carvings that he associates more directly with the Nubians (presumably since native populations are more primitive, or because the Nubians are not Egyptian).[37] This in turn gives way to excavations in which locals work on site, recovering 'their' ancient heritage as a prelude to their dislocation. Scenes of the walking human exodus alternate with those showing preparations for the engineering marvel of relocating Abu Simbel. Villagers nervously gaze upon a model of their new housing: a square modern village similar in bare spirit to the new Tadmur constructed next to Palmyra [Figure 8.12]. They receive payment for their loss, although translating date palms into fungible wealth proves tricky.[38] The section Hinkel reserves for the heritage of the Nubians quickly shifts from a brief description of New Wadi Halfa – where only 3,000 citizens decided to stay – to the city of Khartoum, lying far to the south. Through the subsequent celebration of the modern institutions of the colonial city – the universities promising education to villagers and women and, above all, the museums that will preserve national heritage – Hinkel's work describes the transformation of a culture marked by living economic, social, and cultural practices and relationships, into one defined through the symbolism of heritage tied locally to the nation, and ultimately to world heritage. During the same period, extensive anthropological surveys, funded by the Ford Foundation, were conducted to preserve Nubian heritage. These would take place through the period of relocation.[39] Decisions made by the state were legitimated as an element in the inevitable march of modernity: 'the force-majeure sacrifice for the mother land'.[40] Life was embalmed in knowledge.

As ancient settlements in remote provinces become lucrative nexuses of tourism, museums become symbolic stages upon which to deconstruct local and build national identity around the symbolic ownership of antiquities.[41] While UNESCO went to great pains to ensure that both the new nation-states involved, Egypt and Sudan, should have a say in what would later be termed 'rescue archaeology', the people most affected by the move had no nation that could represent their interests.

Who Are the Barbarians?

On April 19, 2016, as the then-London Mayor Boris Johnson unveiled the scale model of Palmyra's Triumphal Arch, he intoned, 'we stand in solidarity with the Syrian people who

In Situ: The Contraindications of World Heritage

Figure 8.12: 'The model of their new village interests them all'. Nubian villagers looking at a model of New Wadi Halfa c.1963, in Friedrich M. Hinkel, *Auszug aus Nubien* (Berlin: Akademie Verlag, 1978), 57. Friedrich M. Hinkel.

are here in a spirit of defiance. Defiance of the barbarians who destroyed the original of this arch as they destroyed so many other monuments and relics'.[42] As much as ISIS's iconoclastic performances recall the destruction of the Buddhas of Bamiyan destroyed by the Taliban, Johnson's demagogic use of the word 'barbarian' recalled the United Nations' response to the Taliban's 'barbaric' edict of destruction of the statues.[43] But what is more barbaric, to destroy a dead civilization or to kill living people?

Built into the cliff-face in Bamiyan – an historic node on the Silk Road located in a basin of the Hindu Kush mountain range of Afghanistan – the small (sixth-century) eastern and large (seventh-century) western Buddha sculptures, destroyed by the Taliban in March 2001, signify a long-standing legacy of cross-cultural interaction. Constructed as part of extensive, ornately painted Buddhist cave temple complexes, they served a Buddhist community that survived the earliest period of Islamic rule – marked by the conquest of Kabul by the Ghaznavids in 970 – after which time Islam became the dominant regional religion. In 1218, the geographer Yaqut al-Hamawi praised their grandeur. His identification of the larger statue as *Surkhbud* (the red) and the smaller as *Khinkbud* (the white) suggests that by the thirteenth century their identity may have been incorporated into suffix '*bud*' (idol) with no direct association with Buddhist religious practice.[44] During the Mongol invasions of 1220, the region was decimated in revenge for the death of Genghis Khan's son. According to legend, the Hazara people who populate the valley in recent memory are descendants of the Mongols.

Despite a degree of damage to the Buddhas over the centuries, their sheer size has made them impossible or not worth the trouble to destroy. Records of damage to the site under Islamic rule rely on the reports of the military-backed British travellers, who first brought the statues to the attention of westerners in the nineteenth century. In 1824, William Moorcroft and George Trebeck cited the Mughal ruler Aurangzeb as having shorn off their faces before having taken the throne. Likewise, in 1831 Alexander Burnes, the first European traveller to draw the site, attributed damage to the statues' arms and legs to cannons fired at them because of the 'religious zeal' of Nadir Shah (r.1736–47). According to analysis undertaken in the 1970s and 1980s, the faces were probably absent in the originals, with the sheer surfaces completed through the insertion of wooden masks.[45] The expectation of 'complete' statues and the desire to blame Muslim rulers for desecration underscores the ideological presumptions about the propriety of entire sculptures; the propensity of supposedly iconoclastic Muslims to desecrate the figures; and the precarious identification of Aurangzeb and Nadir Shah as guilty of having destroyed the statues. Nonetheless, accusations of pre-modern destruction by Islamic rulers, which do not seem to have any independent verification, persist uncritically in discussions today.

These and subsequent European authors indicate dissatisfaction with the identification of local populations of the Buddhas as male and female, alternately identified as Key-Umursh and his consort, Adam and Eve, or Silsal and Shahmama. By 1922, when the Délégation Archéologique Française en Afghanistan – created under the protection of King Amanullah Khan – carried out an archaeological survey with photographic documentation of the statues under André Godard, the statues had already been identified as Buddhas.[46] The site became popular with travellers to exotic regions, including the same 1933 Citroen Trans-Asian Expedition that had stopped in Palmyra.

Unlike Palmyra, identified with western civilization since its re-emergence as a material site in the seventeenth century, Bamiyan remained comparatively obscure until after the statues' destruction. One indicator of this relative global importance is their inclusion on the World Heritage Sites List. While the site of Palmyra became included on the List as of its initial application to UNESCO in 1980, the decision about whether to include the Buddhas of Bamiyan at the time of its initial application in 1995 was deferred; due to war and unstable governance, they were only included on the List in 2003, after they had gained world renown as a result of their destruction.[47]

The empty niches of the Bamiyan Buddhas have served as far more potent ideological icons than their original occupants had since the heyday of Buddhism in Bamiyan. The West eagerly used the destruction as a sign of radical Islamic difference from the West through a primitive and violent iconoclasm, despite level-headed objections that the statues had remained peacefully in place under Muslim hegemony for over a millennium.[48] Indeed, even the leader of the Taliban, Mullah Omar, issued a decree in 1999 that the Bamiyan Buddhas should not be destroyed because they could be an important source of income for future tourism.[49]

The Taliban destroyed the statues not because of a return to pure Islamic iconoclasm so much as through a very contemporary understanding of media and propaganda enabled through the display of staged destruction disseminated through the relatively new global medium of the Internet. The horror of the western media and of secular Muslim elites fed into a narrative in which the West emerged as idolaters of historical objects. Thus Rahmatullah Hashemi, the Taliban ambassador-at-large, responded to global outrage at the destruction of the Bamiyan Buddhas by claiming that nations willing to pay to preserve statues were hypocritical if they were not equally willing to save a million Afghans facing starvation – a rationale likely to function as effective propaganda among many impoverished people throughout the region.[50] The February 26, 2001 document ordering the destruction states that 'these statues were and remain shrines for unbelievers. These unbelievers continue to worship and respect them.'[51] When UNESCO emissaries pointed out that Buddhists no longer lived in the valley, and thus the statues were not worshipped, the Taliban responded that if Buddhists had still been there they would have respected their rites. Far from a contradiction, the Taliban seemed to implicate the UN emissaries and all that they represented, as the worshippers whose idols were being destroyed. Why else might they hold these statues in higher regard than the human lives lost to famine? Likewise, as western tourists flock to a 'temple complex area' deep in the Nubian desert, one might wonder what is being worshipped. As the Taliban has benefited from the propaganda of their anti-western display of destruction couched in neo-Islamic rhetoric, so too has ISIS, which has hidden its lucrative trade in antiquities behind a façade of iconoclastic destruction. The Taliban benefitted in the years following the destruction of the Buddhas by allowing for the removal of 80 per cent of the murals that had been recorded in the Buddhist temple caves of Bamiyan as of 1995.[52] As Lynn Meskell points out, discourse concerning the Bamiyan Buddhas has been deeply embedded within a 'rhetoric of rescue' justifying American intervention in Afghanistan.[53]

Although global discourses have, since 2001, framed the loss as one of 'world heritage', it ought to be difficult to mourn for sites that no one ever knew existed. If the beneficiaries of the destruction were the Taliban, those harmed were not their western enemies so much as the Hazara people who had maintained the primary military resistance. Driven from their homes in the late 1990s, many had returned to the valley and found shelter in the hundreds of caves surrounding the Buddhas. Arrested and forced to lay the dynamite that not only destroyed the statues but also their own shelters in 2001, the remaining and resettled local population began to be evicted from the caves in 2003, when the basin, now empty of the Buddhas, was declared a World Heritage Site.[54] The community has become yet another displaced subaltern local minority, victim of the substitution of global humanitarian concern with concern for world heritage.

Ruins and the Displaced Promise of Eternal Life

By erasing the labour of removing local populations, uncovering buried sites, and reconstructing the past, the rubric of 'world heritage' erases the legacies of 'the local' embedded in diverse places. Having lost the function of *memento mori* ascribed to them in the romantic imagination of the eighteenth century, ruins now appear as signs of miraculously uninterrupted survival since time immemorial. Instead of remembering our shared human mortality, we use ruins as objects of focus for a promise of eternal life. Just as countries mourn over the genocides of the twentieth century while building fences against the refugees of the twenty-first, public outcry over heritage destruction becomes a marker of our civilized sensibilities and distracts us from fully considering our collective failure in the humanitarian protection of living people. Under such conditions, it can no longer surprise us that authoritarian regimes use artefact annihilation as propaganda through which to question a false trade-off between the protection of objects or the protection of human life.

Media reports concerning heritage destruction often frame the sites as authentic and unmediated survivors from ancient times, giving almost no weight to the habitation and reconstruction that has produced layered systems of value at the sites.[55] As it has developed since the 1970s, the concept of world heritage has become a means of transforming lived local culture into nodes of pilgrimage for the global tourism industry. The subordination of direct humanitarian protection to the procedures of documentation afforded by the concept of 'world heritage' underscores a postcolonial order not of national liberations, but of a globalized culture in which human cultural diversity becomes streamlined into a single, hegemonic form. In cases where industrial growth threatens local minority populations, international concern for antiquities stands in lieu of concern for devastated populations – such as in Abu Simbel in the past, but also more recently, for example: Hasankeyf, Turkey, where a local village was flooded to make way for a dam; the rescue excavation of Mes Aynak, Afghanistan, threatened by a Chinese coppermining corporation; or, in China, the thousands of archaeological sites and villages inundated under the Three Gorges Dam. The recovery of antiquities and the documentation of anthropology, to the extent that they occur, become expressions of humanitarian preservation. However, the very concept of 'recovery anthropology' that documents the planned obliteration of a living culture suggests a scientific legitimation of regional depopulation, which may be no less detrimental than the historical ethnic cleansing enforced through the destruction of ancient sites.

The solution is not simply to desist in our drive toward preservation and to let sleeping stones lie, but to memorialize sites in the complexity of their resurrection. As professionals working in fields related to preservation, we must foster the public recognition that the rhetoric of ownership can often be no less polemic than the performance of destruction that it decries. Discussions of the relationships between modernity and antiquity must take place not only at the highest echelons of academic writing and public policy, but also in introductory courses, museum exhibits and documentaries. The amnesia of representing sites as transparent windows to or miraculous survivors of our appropriated past plants the ideological seeds for the propagandistic efficacy of heritage cleansing. It is only when we publicly acknowledge the complexities of ownership embedded in the material resurrection of the past that we will be able to realistically weigh whether our desire for scientific knowledge or our pleasure in tourism ethically recompenses the erasure of living cultures that has also accrued as a result of the preservation of sites of world heritage. In the face of the climate cost of travel and the cataclysms of war, it may be high time to reduce the valorization of the tourist as the globalized, value-free owner of universalized history. Ruins belong to the nineteenth century; tourism to the twentieth. Instead of reproducing the simulacral ideal of the authentic physical site, virtual and reproductive technologies of the twenty-first century can enable us to recreate the past while cherishing the present, and to magnify rather than hide the complicated and uneven stitches between the two.

Acknowledgements

Thanks to the editors of this volume for their intelligence, diligence and patience during the review process.

Notes

1. Edward Delman, 'Afghanistan's Buddhas Rise Again', *The Atlantic*, June 10, 2015.
2. Hannah McGivern, 'Italy's Blue Helmets of Culture are on standby for UNESCO', *The Art Newspaper*, March 1, 2016, accessed March 16, 2017, http://theartnewspaper.com/news/news/italy-s-blue-helmets-of-culture-are-on-standby-forunesco/.
3. Although often labelled as fundamentalist, the so-called 'Islamic State' (IS/ISIS) roots its ideology in modern reinterpretations of Islam, leading to my use of the term 'neo-Islamic'. See Khaled M. Abou El Fadl, *The Great Theft: Wrestling Islam from the Extremists* (New York: HarperCollins, 2013). Regarding the reproduced Palmyrene Triumphal Arch in London, see Mark Brown, 'Palmyra's Arch of Triumph Recreated in Trafalgar Square', *The Guardian*, April 19, 2016, https://www.theguardian.com/ culture/2016/apr/19/palmyras-triumphal-arch-recreated-in-trafalgar-square.

4. 'Worldwide Displacement Hits All-Time High as War and Persecution Increase', June 18, 2015, accessed March 16, 2017, http://www.unhcr. org/558193896.html.
5. Ralph Slatyer, 'How the World Heritage Convention Works', *Ambio* 12.3–4 (1983): 140–45; Sophia Labadi, 'Representations of the Nation and Cultural Diversity in Discourses on World Heritage', *Journal of Social Archaeology* 7.2 (2007): 147–70.
6. Such a list of case studies could include far more sites, with varying local, national, and global sensitivity. These sites have been selected largely due to the clarity of visual information documenting the discourses surrounding their authenticity and as examples of some of the complexities that arise when consideration of the past does not meet the nuance of contemporary local identities and politics.
7. Allison Cuneo, Susan Penacho and LeeAnn Barnes Gordon, 'Special Report: Update on the Situation in Syria', September 3, 2015, accessed March 16, 2017, http://www.asor-syrianheritage.org/special-report-update-on-the-situation-inpalmyra/; 'A Russian Orchestra Plays Bach and Prokofiev in the Ruins of Palmyra', *The Economist*, May 6, 2016.
8. Mirjam Brusius, 'The Middle East Heritage Debate Is Becoming Worryingly Colonial', *The Conversation*, April 25, 2016, http://theconversation.com/the-middle-east-heritage-debate-is-becoming-worryingly-colonial-57679.
9. James F. Goode, *Negotiating for the Past: Archaeology, Nationalism and Diplomacy in the Middle East, 1919–1941* (Austin: University of Texas Press, 2007); see also, Ömür Harmanşah, 'ISIS, Heritage, and the Spectacles of Destruction in the Global Media', *Near Eastern Archaeology* 78.3 (2015): 170–77.
10. Michael L. Galaty and Charles Watkinson, *Archaeology under Dictatorship* (New York: Springer, 2004).
11. Abou El Fadl, *Great Theft*, 35–41.
12. Wendy Shaw, 'Preserving Preservation', in *Tales from the Crypt: Museum Storage and Meaning*, eds Mirjam Brusius and Kavita Singh (London: Routledge, 2017), 152–67.
13. Marinus Antony Wes, *Classics in Russia 1700–1855* (Leiden: E. J. Brill, 1992), 12; 'Gezicht op de ruïnes van Palmyra', accessed March 16, 2017, https://www.uvaerfgoed.nl/beeldbank/en/bijzonderecollecties/xview/? identifier=hdl:11245/3.1968;metadata=Palmyra.
14. Prime Minister's Archives of the Republic of Turkey, 'Tedmur ile Rakka arasında harabelerde sakin reayanın Haleb dahilinde iskanları hakkında emir isdarına dair tezkire', Hijri, 25/11/1136, 137:6837/C.DH.
15. William Wright, *An Account of Palmyra and Zenobia with Travel and Adventures in Bashan and the Desert* (London: Thomas Nelson and Sons, 1895), 191.
16. 'Palmyra', *Thomas Love Peacock*, accessed February 27, 2017, http://www. thomaslovepeacock.net/palmyra.html.
17. Elizabeth M. Holt, 'Narrative and the Reading Public in 1870s Beirut', *Journal of Arabic Literature* 40.1 (2009): 49–50.
18. Jacques Derrida, *Of Grammatology*, trans. Gayatri Spivak (Baltimore: John Hopkins University Press, 1997), 24.
19. Ussama Makdisi, 'Ottoman Orientalism', *The American Historical Review*, 107.3 (2002): 768–96.

20. Jere L. Bacharach, 'Marwanid Umayyad Building Activities: Speculations on Patronage', *Muqarnas* 13 (1996): 27–44 (31).
21. Letter, dated May 20, 1900 (emphasis added), http://www.gerty.ncl.ac.uk/ letter_details.php?letter_id=1192/.
22. Zeynep Çelik, *Urban Forms and Colonial Confrontations: Algiers under French Rule* (Berkeley: University of California Press, 1997), 190–192.
23. Gayatri Spivak, 'Can the Subaltern Speak?', *A Critique of Postcolonial Reason: Toward a History of the Vanishing Present* (Cambridge, MA: Harvard University Press, 1999), 269–312.
24. Spivak, *A Critique of Postcolonial Reason*, 211 (original emphasis).
25. '50. Yakovlev, Alexander (1887–1938)', *MacDougall's Fine Art Auctions*, accessed March 16, 2017, http://www.macdougallauction.com/Indexx. asp?id=17228&lx=a.
26. 'Turkey: The Ruins of Aphrodisias, 1964', *Magnum Photos*, http://www. magnumphotos.com/C.aspx?VP3=SearchResult&STID=2S5RYDY7TLXD. The date on the *Magnum* website is incorrect, see Ara Güler, *Afrodesias Çığ lığ ı* (Istanbul: Yapı Kredi Yayınları, 2009).
27. Kenan Erim, 'de Aphrodisiade', *American Journal of Archaeology* 71.3 (July, 1967): 233–243.
28. Michael D. Danti, 'Ground-Based Observations of Cultural Heritage Incidents in Syria and Iraq', *Near Eastern Archaeology* 78.3 (2015): 132–141.
29. Various scholars identify the 'birth' of world heritage between the 1870s and the 1960s. This chapter situates its birth in the events leading up to its modern institutionalization with UNESCO's adoption of the World Heritage Convention in 1972. See Heike C. Alberts and Helen D. Hazen, 'Maintaining Authenticity and Integrity at Cultural World Heritage Sites', *Geographical Review* 100.1 (2010): 56–73; Melanie Hall, ed., *Towards World Heritage: The International Origins of the Preservation Movement* (London: Routledge, 2011); John Merryman, 'Two Ways of Thinking About Cultural Property', *American Journal of International Law* 80.4 (1986): 831–53.
30. Terje Tvedt, *The River Nile in the Age of the British: Political Ecology and the Quest for Economic Power* (London: I.B. Tauris, 2004), 282.
31. Photographs of ancient sites lost during the dam project are available at https://oi.uchicago.edu/sites/oi.uchicago.edu/files/uploads/shared/docs/ oimp24.pdf, accessed March 13, 2017.
32. Hassan Dafalla, *The Nubian Exodus* (London: C. Hurst & Co, 1974), 38.
33. Dafalla, *Nubian Exodus*, 12; Marian Wenzel, *House Decoration in Nubia* (Toronto: University of Toronto Press, 1979); Louis Werner, 'The Decorated Houses of Nubia', *ARAMCO World* 57.4 (2006), accessed March 16, 2017, http://archive.aramcoworld.com/issue/200604/the.decorated.houses.of.nubia.htm.
34. D. J. Shaw, 'Resettlement from the Nile in Sudan', *Middle East Journal* 21.4 (1967): 462–87; Fekri A. Hassan, 'The Aswan High Dam and the International Rescue Nubia Campaign', *The African Archaeological Review* 24.3–4 (2007): 73–94.
35. whc.unesco.org/document/6878, accessed March 16, 2017.
36. Fekri A. Hassan, 'The Aswan High Dam'.
37. Friedrich W. Hinkel, *Auszug aus Nubien* (Berlin: Akademie Verlag, 1978).
38. Dafalla, *Nubian Exodus*, 77–78.

39. Lilli Zabrana, 'Abandoned Nubian Villages in Upper Egypt: Material Culture Reviewed by Social Anthropological Field Studies', in *Egyptian & Egyptological Documents, Archives Libraries* 4 (2013–14): 197–209.
40. Dafalla, *Nubian Exodus*, xiv.
41. See also, Yorke Rowan and Uzi Baram, eds, *Marketing Heritage: Archaeology and the Consumption of the Past* (Walnut Creek, CA: Alta Mira Press, 2004).
42. Brown, 'Palmyra's Arch of Triumph', *The Guardian*.
43. 'General Assembly "Appalled" by Edict on Destruction of Afghan Shrines; Strongly Urges Taliban to Halt Implementation', press release, General Assembly, 9 March, 2001, accessed March 16, 2017, http://www.un.org/ press/en/2001/ga9858.doc.htm.
44. Catharina Blänsdorf, Stephanie Pfeffer and Edmund Melzl, 'The Polychromy of the Giant Buddha Statues in Bamiyan', in Deborah Klimburg-Salter, ed., *The Kingdom of Bamiyan. Buddhist Art and Culture of the Hindu Kush* (Naples and Rome: Instituto Universitario Oriantale and Instituto Italiano per il Medio ed Estremo Oriente, 1989), 237.
45. R. Sengupta, 'Restoration of the Bamiyan Buddhas', in Deborah Klimburg-Salter, ed., *The Kingdom of Bamiyan. Buddhist Art and Culture of the Hindu Kush* (Naples and Rome: Instituto Universitario Oriantale and Instituto Italiano per il Medio ed Estremo Oriente, 1989), 205–220.
46. Catherina Blänsdorf and Michael Petzet, 'Description, History, and State of Conservation before the Destruction in 2001', in Michael Petzet, ed., *The Giant Buddhas of Bamiyan: Safeguarding the Remains* (Paris: ICOMOS, 2009), 17–35, accessed March 1, 2017, http://www.icomos.de/pdf/ ICOMOS_Publikation_Bamiyan.pdf.
47. Barbara T. Hoffman, *Art and Cultural Heritage: Law, Policy and Practice* (Cambridge: Cambridge University Press, 2006): 33. This discrepancy results from war and instability in Afghanistan since 1979.
48. Finbarr Barry Flood, 'Between Cult and Culture: Bamiyan, Islamic Iconoclasm, and the Museum', *The Art Bulletin* 84.4 (2002): 641–59.
49. Luke Harding, 'How the Buddha Got His Wounds', *The Guardian*, March 3, 2001, accessed March 16, 2017, http://web.archive.org/web/20060228113747/ http://www.guardian.co.uk/Archive/Article/0,4273,4145138,00.html.
50. Barbara Crossette, 'Taliban Explains Buddha Demolition', *New York Times*, March 19, 2001, http://www.nytimes.com/2001/03/19/world/taliban-explains-buddha-demolition.html.
51. Flood, 'Between Cult and Culture', 655.
52. Christian Manhart, 'The Destruction of the Buddha Statues in March 2001 and the First UNESCO Activities', in Petzet (2009), 37–40.
53. See also Lynn Meskell, 'Conflict Heritage and Expert Failure', in Sophia Labadi and Colin Long, eds, *Heritage and Globalisation* (London: Routledge, 2010), 192–201.
54. 'Bamiyan's Ancient Cave Dwellings Shelter Homeless Afghans', *Dawn*, July 28, 2015, http://www.dawn.com/news/1196891.
55. Christina Cameron, 'From Warsaw to Mostar: The World Heritage Committee and Authenticity', *APT Bulletin*, 39.2–3 (2008): 19–24.

Part 4

Imagining Antiquity in the Contemporary World

9

The Masjid al-Haram: Balancing Tradition and Renewal at the Heart of Islam

Muhsin Lutfi Martens

The Masjid al-Haram in Mecca al-Mukarramah, the spiritual abode of Islam and the Muslim world, is a complex of holy sites and built spaces. Throughout the history of Islam, dynasties and rulers have taken it upon themselves to extend, modernize, and embellish the mosque and its surroundings. Each successive building scheme was a consequence both of ever-increasing numbers of worshippers from around the world and a response to natural and man-made damage. The expansion scheme initiated in 2007 was by far the largest building project to date and revived many longstanding questions about the need to balance 'tradition' with 'modernity' at the religious epicentre of the Muslim world. As the discussion around these types of projects tends to be polarized, it is suggested by this chapter that the current polemical discourse fails to examine the wider contextual history of the site, including its built history prior to the modern era. As such this chapter attempts to re-evaluate some aspects of the mosque's history of destruction and reformation, including that of the Ka'ba, firmly within the context of its historic development. Drawing on various historical sources, it examines the responses by early Muslim chroniclers and historians to different cycles of destruction and rebuilding, as well as compares these accounts to contemporary Muslim responses to modern building programs. Particular attention is given to the expansion of the mosque's courtyard and the removal – and subsequent relocation – of the Ottoman arcade designed by the celebrated architect Mimar Sinan (d.1588). By examining cycles of building and destruction at the mosque, it is suggested that a more complex picture emerges than what is immediately apparent from the media reports on redevelopment work at the sacred complex.[1]

Sinan's arcade

In 1558 the Ottoman Sultan Suleyman, 'Kanuni' ('The Magnificent') (r.1520–66) sent the court architect Mimar Sinan to Mecca to prepare plans for an eventual renovation and extension of the Masjid al-Haram. After completion, Sinan returned to Istanbul and submitted his design to Mehmet Aga[2] (1540–1617), who subsequently travelled to Mecca to oversee the work. New bulbous domes and marble support columns replaced the earlier flat wooden roof of the mosque arcade, and the *mataf* (the area of the courtyard immediately around the Ka'ba) was completely repaved. The elevated ground facing the Ka'ba was at that point surrounded on all four sides by a monumental gabled, colonnaded portico, which was

Figure 9.1: Sinan's Masjid al-Haram arcade is sandwiched between the *mataf* and the twentieth-century arcade seen here in the foreground. This photograph was taken before its removal in 2015. Muhsin Lutfi Martens.

lavishly decorated, both inside and out, with carved coloured marbles. True to Ottoman construction techniques, many of the columns and capitals were in fact taken from earlier periods of antiquity [Figure 9.1]. As a finishing touch, the renowned Ottoman painter Abdullah Lutfi was commissioned to decorate the interior of the arcade's domes with 'gold motifs and calligraphic compositions' [Figure 9.2].[3]

Later, in 1629, a flash flood engulfed the entire Haram, undermining the foundations of the Ka'ba and sweeping away part of the *Hijr* wall, a low semicircular barrier, set apart from, but considered integral to, the structure of the Ka'ba. What remained of the Ka'ba was then levelled and the structure needed to be entirely rebuilt. The building that stands in the midst of the Haram today is, in effect, from the 1629 rebuild.[4] Such was the quality and functionality of the Ottoman workmanship that it was not until much later – in the middle of the twentieth century – that another renovation and expansion was deemed necessary. Beginning in 1955, King Abdulaziz (r.1932–53) commissioned the first of many extensions to the mosque during the modern (i.e., post-Ottoman) Saudi era. As part of these

Figure 9.2: A conservator inspecting some of the whitewashed paintings (attributed to Abdullah Lutfi?) at the Masjid al-Haram. Muhsin Lutfi Martens.

renovations, the Mas'a gallery connecting al-Safa' and al-Marwah was extended to reach the mosque. At the same time a two-story extension was built around Sinan's arcade using reinforced concrete arches clad in carved marble and artificial stone. The extension also linked the arcade to the street via eleven gates. Shortly thereafter, King Fahd (r.1982–2005) approved another major extension consisting of a new wing and an outdoor prayer area on the southeast side of the mosque. This redevelopment was not limited to the mosque but extended across the city of Mecca. In order to make way for new buildings, important sites dating from the early centuries of Islam were demolished, as were Ottoman-era houses and forts, ancient wells, and graveyards. Strikingly, the Islamic Heritage Research Foundation estimates that more than 98 per cent of the Kingdom's historical and religious sites have been lost since the 1980s.[5]

Despite numerous flash floods, demolitions, the extensive modern building campaigns, and the terrorist siege of the Haram in 1979,[6] Sinan's centuries-old arcade remained at least partly intact. The arcade's domed porticos, with their dozens of carved marble

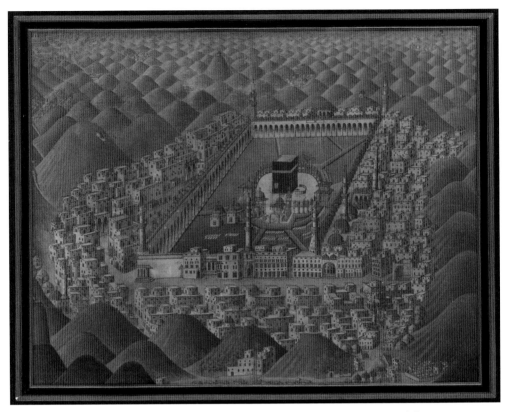

Figure 9.3: This eighteenth-century Ottoman painting shows a topographical view of the Masjid al-Haram in Mecca before the Saudi extension. Sinan's portico can be seen surrounding the courtyard. Uppsala University Library.

columns – some of which date back to the earliest centuries of Islam – both architecturally and aesthetically frame the Ka'ba. They have become synonymous with the great mosque itself. For example, as Charlotte Maury indicates, many of the references and documents related to Mecca in the Islamic world – Hajj certificates, prayer books, manuscripts dealing with the pilgrimage, and, after the seventeenth century, even the walls of mosques and private houses from Egypt to Bosnia – feature the domed porticos of the arcade as a central aspect of the holy site.[7] Through the dissemination of such images [Figure 9.3], the Ottoman arcade has become in the minds of people around the world an indelible part of their mental picture of the Haram, seemingly inseparable from the Ka'ba itself. Incidentally, Abdullah Lutfi, the artist responsible for decorating the inside of Sinan's domes, was largely responsible for creating this image and his depictions of the Haram would go on to influence a generation of artists after him; his paintings were copied by contemporaries and later artists until the nineteenth century. According to Ziauddin Sardar, almost all classic illustrations of the Haram seen in books of Islamic art and the Hajj are either Lutfi's painting or images inspired by it.[8]

It is not surprising, then, that the 2013 announcement of a proposed multi-billion-dollar expansion of the Haram and the removal of the arcade caused widespread dismay. Alarmed at the prospect of losing the last surviving Ottoman section of Islam's holiest site, the Turkish Foreign Affairs Ministry held continuous discussions with the Saudi authorities in hope of preserving the structure. According to Ihsan Özkes, a Turkish Islamic cleric, 'The issues about Mecca should not be left entirely up to Saudi Arabia. Saudis should take into consideration the sensitivities of the Muslim world over the portico issue.'[9] However, Muslim governments elsewhere, mindful of the urgent need for expansion in order to accommodate the growing number of pilgrims wanting to perform Hajj, remained largely silent on the issue.[10] Concern for pilgrims' safety and wellbeing may well have outweighed considerations for historical preservation of the sacred mosque. However, for those working in the heritage sector, the potential loss of the Ottoman arcade came to represent the latest clash in a longstanding dispute between those who have dedicated themselves to the preservation of Mecca's architectural heritage and those in enthusiastic pursuit of redevelopment and modernization.

While the Turkish government understands the need to expand the Haram, it nevertheless criticises the building developers for, in its view, wantonly disregarding the archaeological, historical, and cultural heritage of the mosque.[11] There is also internal concern within Saudi Arabia. Speaking more generally, Dr Irfan al-Alawi, a Saudi national and Executive Director of the Islamic Heritage Research Foundation, warned that the destruction of heritage in Mecca amounts to 'cultural vandalism'.[12] Others, such as Dr Hatoon al-Fassi, a native Meccan and history professor at King Saud University in Riyadh, accuse the Saudi Bin Laden construction conglomerate, which is overseeing the rebuilding of the mosque, of seeking to 'turn Mecca into Las Vegas'.[13] In short, both al-Alawi and al-Fassi are concerned that in their drive for profit, the developers are completely disregarding the built heritage of Mecca. Proponents of the 2013 redevelopment project responded to such criticism by citing the urgent need to expand the Haram for the ever-growing number of pilgrims that come to Saudi Arabia, which is forecast to reach 17 million annually by 2025.[14]

Quoting Prince Khaled al-Faisal, an official spokesperson for the redevelopment project, the Arab News reported that 'of all the countries that have ruled Mecca, Saudi Arabia has undertaken the greatest reforms in the city. The expansion projects are conducted in a modern and sophisticated manner.'[15] From the perspective of Meccan authorities, the changes are entirely necessary. There is validity to their argument that the increasing number of pilgrims necessitates redevelopment to allow for a safer environment: more than 2000 people have been killed due to mass stampedes caused by overcrowding in the last few decades. For those pilgrims who, like the author, witnessed the aftermath of the fatal stampede in Arafat during the 2015 Hajj, which killed more than 700 people, the urgent need for new development is clear.

Extending the Haram

While many aspects of such rampant redevelopment in Mecca may seem to be a modern phenomenon, it is not altogether unprecedented, and issues related to the relative destruction and appropriation of its sacred heritage, land, and property have long been divisive factors in the history of Islam's holiest city. The first-ever extension of the Masjid al-Haram came early in the Islamic period, as the Prophet Muhammad's (PBUH) unification of Arabia prompted huge crowds to descend upon the mosque during the Hajj season. Following the accession of Caliph 'Umar Ibn al-Khattab, the need to create a larger space justified continual extensions to the holy mosque. Commenting on this first extension, the biographer and geographer Yaqut al-Hamawi (1179–1229) wrote in his *Mu'jam al-Buldan* (5/146):

> The first one to build a wall around the Ka'bah was 'Umar ibn al-Khattab (may Allah be pleased with him); there was no wall around it during the time of the Prophet (peace and blessings of Allah be upon him) or Abu Bakr. [The wall was built] because people were building their houses too close to the Ka'bah and making the space around it too small for people. 'Umar said: 'The Ka'bah is the House of Allah, and a house needs a courtyard. You have encroached on its space, it has not encroached on yours.' So he bought those houses, demolished them and added that space to the space around the Ka'bah. He also destroyed the houses of people in the vicinity of the Ka'bah who had refused to sell, and kept the money aside for them until they came and took it later on. He built a wall around the mosque, lower than the height of a man, and lamps were placed on it.[16]

Yaqut's account is interesting for two reasons: firstly, the refusal of some inhabitants of Mecca to sell their homes despite the reputable status of the caliph and the religious objective of his project; and secondly, the precedent that is set for later rulers in dealing with opposition to the mosque's building expansion.[17] According to the art historian Muhammad Alami, Caliph 'Umar simply acted on his belief that destroying buildings around the Haram constituted a *rasion d'etat*. In other words, 'Umar understood that in order to extend the Masjid al-Haram, it was necessary to demolish houses in Mecca.[18] Following the death of 'Umar, 'Uthman, the third caliph, was forced to expand the Masjid al-Haram again due to an increase in the Muslim population of the Levant. The historian and religious jurist al-Tabari (839–923 CE) reports that 'Uthman attempted to buy the houses around the mosque that were to be destroyed in order to expand the Haram. However, al-Tabari writes:

> Some people refused to sell (their houses); nonetheless he destroyed them, and he put the money in the *bayt al-mal*. As these people (whose houses he had destroyed against their will) denounced him, he put them in jail. He then told them: 'don't you know what made you so insolent toward me? It is my gentleness that made you so insolent. 'Umar has done the same, and you did not dare denounce him!'[19]

It is interesting to observe the legality again evoked in al-Tabari's account, used to justify the caliph's concern with the appropriation of land for the extension of the mosque. Moreover, it is also significant to note the parallels with the modern era, in that the acquisition represented a palpable concern in relation to the implications of destroying and redeveloping built heritage.

It is possible that people resisted the original wave of destruction of buildings around the Haram because they feared it would erase memories of the Prophet and his family from the urban fabric of the city. This rationale seems to hold up in view of the outcry that met the Umayyads when they attempted to demolish and rebuild the Masjid al-Nabawi (the Prophet's Mosque in Medina), including the adjoining rooms belonging to the Prophet's wives. The historian Yaqubi provides an account:

> When he (the governor of Medina) was destroying the rooms, Qubayb Ibn ʿAbd Allah Ibn al-Zubayr went to him and […] said: how in the name of God can you, oh ʿUmar, efface one of the verses of the Qurʾan? Don't you know that God says: 'those who call you from behind the rooms.'[20]

This quotation references a Qurʾanic verse which speaks specifically to the rooms the Umayyads were destroying.[21] The historian al-Tabari confirmed the destruction, quoting a mason who claimed to have seen the message from al-Walid to destroy the Prophet's mosque and his wives' rooms, further adding:

> For they (the people) will not oppose you (in destroying houses). And if someone refuses, ask some respected men to make a just appraisal of the house you need, and destroy it. Then give them the money. Be aware that you are not acting without precedent, for you have that of ʿUmar and ʿUthman.[22]

Again, Yaqubi and al-Tabari make mention of the legal precedent set down by ʿUmar and ʿUthman to justify the destruction of property around the sacred sites. However, of particular significance in Yaqubi's account of the event is that Ibn al-Zubayr objects on the basis that they would be destroying a physical connection to the life and times of the Prophet Muhammad, something that was given special mention in the Qurʾan. It indicates that the inhabitants of Mecca and Medina considered the preservation of architectural heritage associated with the Prophet Muhammad paramount to the expansion of the site. Indeed, as evidenced in the twelfth-century chronicles of Ibn Jubayr, Muslim leaders saw it fit to preserve and augment historic sites linked to the life of the Prophet Muhammad. 'All of Mecca is filled with venerable memories', exclaimed Ibn Jubayr, and rare was the pilgrim who did not take the opportunity to visit those places.[23] During his time in Mecca, Ibn Jubayr visited various sites and tombs connected to the life and times of the Prophet, reporting that 'people make pious visits there, make their ritual prayers and weep, since it was the place where the Prophet seated himself'.[24] For those who adhere to Wahhabism, the strain of

Islam that came to dominate the Hijaz in the early twentieth century, such visits to shrines, tombs, or religiohistorical sites were considered as akin to worshipping something other than God: a grave sin. Thus, the twin forces of Wahhabi doctrine and urban development have destroyed all the physical remnants of the Prophet's life that figure prominently in Ibn Jubayr's account of his visit to Mecca.

From its inception in the eighteenth century, Wahhabism has vigorously attacked any potential object or site that could be misconstrued as a source of idolatry. As such, the iconoclasts who supported the destruction of Mimar Sinan's arcade were intensely aware that it was important to those like al-Alawi, who believe that 'many of these columns signified certain areas of the mosque where the Prophet sat and prayed'.[25] For instance, since Ottoman times, it has been orally reported that one of the columns incorporated into the arcade indicates the area where the Prophet Muhammad left Mecca on his miraculous night journey (*Isrāʾ wal Miʿraj*) to Jerusalem.[26] The historical record is therefore being deleted, according to al-Alawi, and 'a new Muslim would never have a clue (about where he sat) because there's nothing marking these locations now'.[27]

Therefore, whilst such destruction of Mecca's built heritage is evidently carried out for the practical purposes of safety and capacity, it may also have political and ideological motives, such as the desire to stamp a national identity on the sanctuary. For example, al-Alawi also suggests a nationalistic agenda for such destruction, stating in an interview with CNN that:

> [The] authorities were inclined not to value aspects of Mecca's heritage that dated from before Saudi control over the city – such as the portico, going back centuries to Ottoman sovereignty over the city – because that evidence of a pre-Saudi Mecca undermined the kingdom's important position in the Islamic world as guardians of the city.[28]

Regardless of the validity of such an argument, it would be naïve to think the Meccan authorities were not aware of the implicit 'identity politics' presented by the Ottoman arcade. Indeed, as al-Alami points out:

> It was mainly for these reasons, according to al-Jahiz, that the ʿAbbasids destroyed the Umayyad palaces. It was for this same reason that Ibn Khaldun called the mosque at Damascus '*Bulat al-Walid*', meaning that the building showed little suitability as a mosque, and was more explicitly designed to advertise al-Walid's power and wealth.[29]

Almost since the beginning of Islam, conflicts over political power have been transferred to building projects centred on Mecca, with newly victorious factions often undoing the architectural work of the group they just ousted or adding their own to cement their authority. In 692, Abdallah ibn al-Zubair, the grandson of the first caliph, Abu Bakr, drove out the ruling Umayyads, who subsequently bombarded Mecca with catapults from outside the city. The desecration of the Masjid al-Haram, including the Kaʿba, in the midst of the fighting provided the pretext for the victorious ibn al-Zubair to knock down and rebuild the Ka'ba according to earlier foundations established by the Prophet Ibrahim. The exterior was made more accessible by the addition of two doors set at ground level, and two windows were added to the structure. However, history records that the Meccan nobles were, at least initially, opposed to rebuilding the sanctuary, in particular Abdallah ibn 'Abbas, who said, 'Leave it in the state that Allah's Messenger approved of, for I am afraid that there may come after you people who will keep knocking it down and rebuilding it until people lose respect for it. Rather you should repair it.'[30] Later, ibn 'Abbas' words of warning were vindicated when Umayyad armies retook the city in 692 and Caliph 'Abd al-Malik ibn Marwan systematically eradicated all traces of ibn al-Zubair's dedication to the holy precinct, before proceeding to refurbish the mosque with all the 'embellishment befitting imperial glory',[31] covering every surface in the sanctuary, including the porticoes, in gold and silver slabs.[32] For Sardar, author of *Mecca: The Sacred City*, 'they rebuilt Mecca to flaunt their earthly power'.[33] The Abbasids later repeated the process of rebuilding when they deposed the Umayyads, stamping their own identity onto Mecca, particularly during the reign of al-Mansur (714–75). He built new extensions on the northern and western sides, almost doubling the capacity of the mosque; added seven new gates and marble pillars to the portico; and decorated the interior with mosaics and Quranic calligraphy. Later, al-Mansur's son, Caliph al-Mahdi (r.775–85), continued the work by adding two new arcades around the Ka'ba as well as five new gateways. Special marble columns were imported from Egypt and Syria for this work, many of which were reused in Sinan's arcade approximately 800 years later.

The Relocation of Sinan's Arcade

Since there are multiple angles from which to interpret the history of expansion work carried out at the Masjid al-Haram in Mecca, the question of whether its redevelopment has always been entirely motivated, and justified, in terms of better preparing the sacred site for the increasing influx of pilgrims will no doubt continue to be debated. It has been shown that throughout the holy city's history, each successive ruling dynasty has rebuilt or reconstructed areas of the mosque and its environs, stamping its own particular identity and presence on the sanctuary. The situation is not very different today, except perhaps in the speed and extent of destruction.

This chapter has intentionally avoided taking sides on this debate as its aim has been to provide a broader and more balanced perspective than has been presented elsewhere by narrating some of the recurrent themes and issues that have underlined the various demolition and building campaigns carried out at the site over the past 1600 years. It has attempted to reframe the debate in relation to a broader historical context, thereby showing how the development of Mecca's built environment and ensuing social and cultural losses have always been criticised by some, while others have welcomed them as signs of progress and enhancement of the safety of pilgrims. Those that have been most vehement in their criticism are perhaps guilty of not fully appreciating the enormous and delicate nature of the challenges that have faced the custodians of the mosque. Today the challenges are unprecedented, with more people flocking to perform Hajj than at any other time in Islam's history, and the response to the increased overcrowding requires a more robust approach on a much larger scale. Moreover, today, as in the past, there are also those that are guilty of the idealization and romanticization of the holy city's history. However, as this chapter has tried to show, a reading of the past sometimes raises uncomfortable truths since, as al-Alami has stated, the 'expropriation of land for the building of religious architectural structures has a history of its own, a history that was first implemented against the interests of Muslim private individuals'.[34] Seen from a historical viewpoint, questions relating to the destruction of Mecca's heritage have clearly always been a complex and highly emotive issue even during the reign of the so-called 'Rightly Guided Caliphs'. It is hard to today believe that 'Uthman, the third caliph and one of the Prophet's closest companions, was denounced by the inhabitants of Mecca for his expropriation of land despite his important religious credentials and the religious aims of his expansion project. Reflecting on the history of Mecca's long cycle of demolition and rebuilding, in some respects the situation today is not very different from those times, making present-day criticisms seem less remarkable.

Unbeknownst to many critics of the 2013 redevelopment project, the Turkish and Saudi governments mutually agreed to reintegrate the Ottoman arcade into the new expanded courtyard in the Masjid al-Haram with the aim of preserving it for posterity.[35] While this agreement was made in 2013, it was not implemented until 2015. Consequently, the Turkish-owned Gürsoy Grup, a specialist conservation company, was appointed to carefully document, dismantle, restore, and reinstall the Ottoman-era porticoes within the new courtyard. While much of the porticoes' fabric – including the columns, cladding stones, and calligraphic cartouches – that had been removed and stored offsite in Arafat was re-incorporated, the actual brick and stucco Ottoman domes could unfortunately not be saved due to the impracticalities of moving such huge brick and stucco structures. Just prior to the demolition of these domes, conservators were brought in to photograph and take material samples from some of the paintings on the underside of the domes [Figure 9.4].

As a result of the reinstallation of Mimar Sinan's arcade further away from the Ka'ba, up to 30,000 worshippers can now perform *tawaf* (circumambulation) per hour, which is an increase of over 20,000 people per hour than was possible before the 2013 renovation. In total, the *tawaf* area can now accommodate 105,000 worshippers every hour. This reintegration of the Ottoman-era architecture in the Masjid al-Haram is emblematic of a number of conservation and archaeological projects currently underway in Saudi Arabia that indicate a newfound sensitivity to the preservation of Islamic and pre-Islamic heritage in the Kingdom. Some of these conservation projects include the site management of Mada'in Saleh, the massive archaeological site of Al-'Ula in the Medina region, and the conservation and redevelopment of the Jeddah historic area (placed on the UNESCO's

The Masjid al-Haram: Balancing Tradition and Renewal at the Heart of Islam

Figure 9.4: The Ottoman domes of Sinan's arcade at the Masjid al-Haram during their demolition. Muhsin Lutfi Martens.

World Heritage list in 2014). The reintegration of Sinan's portico, largely unreported in the western media, can thus be viewed as representative of a greater maturity and effort towards striking a balance between remembering the past and providing for the future in the heart of the Islamic world.

Notes

1. Koca Mi'mar Sinan Aga (1490–1588) was the chief architect and engineer for the Ottoman sultans Suleyman the Magnificent, Selim II, and Murad III. 'Mimar' is the Turkish term for architect.
2. Mehmet Aga is known to have built the Istanbul's Sultan Ahmet Mosque, popularly known as the Blue Mosque. He became the chief imperial architect in October 1606 and was among a few Ottoman artists to be honoured by a full biography during his lifetime.
3. Esin Emel, *Mecca the Blessed, Madina the Radiant* (New York: Crowne Publishers, 1963), 180.

4. Francis E. Peters, *Mecca: A Literary History of the Muslim Holy Land* (Princeton, NJ: Princeton University Press, 1994), 289.
5. Carla Power, 'Saudi Arabia Bulldozes Over its Heritage', *Time Magazine*, November 14, 2014, accessed October 29, 2019, https://time.com/3584585/ saudi-arabia-bulldozes-over-its-heritage/.
6. A terrorist attack on the mosque took place on November 20, 1979.
7. Charlotte Maury, 'Depictions of the Haramayn on Ottoman tiles; Content and Context', in *The Hajj: Collected Essays*, ed. Venetia Porter and Liana Saif (London: The British Museum, 2013), 143.
8. Ziauddin Sardar, *Mecca: The Sacred City* (Bloomsbury: London, 2014), 194.
9. Anon., 'Saudis use Hajj Quotas as Political Leverage', *Dunya Times*, July 27, 2013, accessed February 25, 2016, http://en.dunyatimes.com/article/saudis-use-hajj-quotas-as-political-leverage-88549.html.
10. Sardar, *Mecca*, 347.
11. Loring M. Danforth, *Crossing the Kingdom: Portraits of Saudi Arabia* (Oakland, CA: University of California Press, 2016), 110.
12. Tim Hume and Samya Ayish, 'Mecca Redevelopment Sparks Heritage Concerns', CNN, February 7, 2013, accessed February 7, 2016, http://www. edition.cnn.com/2013/02/07/world/meast/saudi-heritage-destruction-mecca/.
13. Sarra Grira, 'The Bin Laden Conglomerate "Wants to Turn Mecca into Las Vegas"', France 24, November 29, 2012, accessed November 29, 2012, http:// observers.france24.com/en/20121129-bin-laden-group-mecca-construction.
14. Anon., 'KSA likely to see 30 million religious tourists by 2025', *Arab News*, August 23, 2016, accessed October 3, 2018, http://www.arabnews.com/ saudi-arabia/news/814841.
15. Anon., 'Heritage "Not Hit by Mecca Expansion"', *Arab News*, April 21, 2013, accessed March 1, 2016, http://www.arabnews.com/news/448862.
16. Yaqut Al-Hamawi, *Muʿjam al-Buldan*, ed, F. Wüstenfeld, 6 vols, (Leipzig, 1955), 1866–73. See also Yaqut al-Hamawi, *Muʿjam al-Buldan*, 5 vols (Beirut: DarSadir lil Tibaʿah wa-al-Nashr; Dar Bayrut lil-Tibaʿah wa al-Nashr, 1955).
17. The decision to demolish these houses was probably not taken lightly, especially considering ʿUmar's famous refusal to pray in the Jerusalem church on the basis that he did not want his people to take advantage of this act to justify demolishing the church to make way for a mosque. Therefore caliph ʿUmar clearly did not conceive of any inconsistency as a discriminatory act in destroying Muslim homes.
18. Mohammad H. Alami, *Art and Architecture in the Islamic Tradition: Aesthetics, Politics and Desire in Early Islam* (New York: I.B Taurus, 2011), 177.
19. Ibid., 34.
20. Yaqubi, *Tarikh al-Yaʾqubi*, vol. 2 (Beirut: Dar Sadir lil Tibaʿah wa-al-Nashr, 1992), 284.
21. Here, Ibn al-Zubayr is referring to *Surat al-Hujurat* verse 4 in the Holy Qurʾan.
22. Yaqubi, *Tarikh*, vol.3, 676. Translation from Alami, *Art and Architecture*, 259.
23. Translation from Peters, *Mecca*, 131.
24. Ibid.

25. Jerome Taylor, 'The Photos Saudi Arabia Doesn't Want Seen – and Proof Islam's Most Holy Relics are being Demolished in Mecca', *The Independent*, March 15, 2013, accessed March 20, 2016, http://www.independent.co.uk/news/world/middle-east/the-photos-saudi-arabia-doesnt-want-seen-and-proof-islams-most-holy-relics-are-being-demolished-in-8536968.html.
26. The author learned from workmen at the Haram that when this column and its base were excavated in 2015, a deep aroma permeated the air. Some offered the explanation that 'the column carried the memory of the Messenger of Allah'. However, a more mundane explanation could be the widespread practice of pouring and rubbing the column with sweet perfumes by generations of pilgrims to the holy site. As a result, when the column was excavated the aroma was released into the air. The author can corroborate that there was indeed a strong aroma coming from the column base which had been underground for decades.
27. Taylor, 'The Photos Saudi Arabia Doesn't Want Seen'.
28. Hume and Ayish, 'Mecca Redevelopment Sparks Heritage Concerns'.
29. Alami, *Art and Architecture*, 184.
30. Nasiruddin Al-Khattab, *The History of Mecca*, trans. Nasiruddin al-Khat-tab (Riyadh: Darussalam Publishers, 2002), 37. Ibn al-Zubayr justification for bringing the door down to ground level was based on the Hadith Al-Bukhari (1583) reported where Aisha asked the Prophet: 'Why is its door high up? He said: Your people did that so that they could admit whomever they wished and keep out whomever they wished.' In another Hadith, the Prophet also said: 'Were it not that your people are still so close to the time of *Kufr* (disbelief), I would have knocked the Ka'ba down and rebuilt it with two doors, a door through which the people could enter and a door through which they could exit.' Nasiruddin, *The History of Mecca*, 37.
31. Sardar, *Mecca*, 87.
32. The more pious citizens of Mecca were scandalized by the behaviour of the Umayyad leaders. However, according to Emel Esin 'the majority, while disliking the excesses of the Umayyads, nonetheless did their best to avoid stirring up additional dissention that might further weaken the Islamic state in the already troubled world [...] to them, it more than ever symbolized man's struggle against the worldly temptations that surrounded it'. Esin, *Mecca*, 136.
33. Sardar, *Mecca*, 87.
34. Alami, *Art and Architecture*, 175.
35. Zehra Atasoy, 'Kabe' nin revakları Türk firmaya emanet', *Arkitera*, March 4, 2013, accessed March 15, 2019, http://www.arkitera.com/haber/12451/ kabe-nin-revaklari-turk-firmaya-emanet3. While the agreement to reintegrate the Ottoman arcade was made in 2013, and not implemented until 2015, from conversations the author had with colleagues at the Haram, it was unclear whether this agreement would be honoured or undertaken as per the original specifications. Critics of the Haram's expansion in Europe and North America were actually unaware that this agreement was even made. For example, in 2014, Sardar wrote: 'There are spectacular plans to further redevelop the sacred mosque so that it can accommodate up to 5 million worshippers. With a casual disregard for history, the Saudis are rebuilding the Ottoman-era section of the Haram, the oldest surviving of the sacred

mosque. The interior, and exquisite beauty, with intricately carved marble columns, built by a succession of Ottoman sultans – Sultan Suleyman, Sultan Salim I, Sultan Murad III, and Sultan Murad IV – from 1553 to 1619, will give way to a series of multi-storey prayer halls, eighty meters high. The columns, which are adorned with calligraphy of the names of the Prophet's companions, will be demolished. Indeed the whole of the sacred Mosque will be bulldozed.' Sardar, *Mecca*, 346–47.

10

ISIS's Destruction of Mosul's Historical Monuments: Between Media Spectacle and Religious Doctrine[1]

Miroslav Melčák and Ondřej Beránek

The attacks on archaeological artefacts and historical monuments directed by ISIS are often considered to be modern revivals of the phenomenon of iconoclasm. This interpretation – espoused widely in the media as well as in scholarly circles – has recently become the object of criticism. Ömür Harmanşah, after analysing propagandistic material produced by ISIS, argues that the group's behaviour toward heritage sites should be viewed not as traditional iconoclasm but as a form of Latour's 'iconoclash': a highly effective method of producing powerful visual imagery with the intention of disseminating it through visual media and social networks in order to shock the audience.[2] Indeed, Harmanşah extends his argument to assert that heritage is, in fact, being destroyed for the express *purpose* of producing this shocking visual imagery. In this respect, iconoclasm loses its traditional meaning and exists, as he puts it, 'only as a historical reference, a rhetoric'.[3] Here, we will argue that while Harmanşah's analysis is well founded, it is only applicable in relation to a limited portion of the heritage destroyed by ISIS. It aptly captures the theatrically staged destruction of, for example, the Assyrian artefacts in Mosul Museum; the reliefs in Ashurnasirpal II's palace in Nimrud; and the Christian symbols found on Mosul's Christian architecture. It cannot, however, fully explain the rationale behind the destruction of a whole range of modest, rather insignificant architectural monuments for which ISIS has never publicly claimed responsibility in their propaganda material and that were, in some cases, not even reported by local people.

Here, we argue that iconoclasm, and specifically the iconoclasm inherent in the Islamic religious doctrine of *taswiyat al-qubur*,[4] should not be considered merely as a pretext for destruction but rather as one possible genuine rationale behind ISIS's destructive behaviour. Based on the opinions of both some medieval and modern, mostly Salafi, authorities, the doctrine of *taswiyat al-qubur* disapproves of the building of any constructions above graves in order to prevent them from turning into objects of worship. This religious prohibition appears to be the main factor influencing ISIS's behaviour toward architectural landmarks in the city of Mosul, which we have chosen as the subject of our case study. As will be shown below, in Mosul, approximately 86 per cent of all identified destroyed monuments were funerary (tombs, shrines, cemeteries) or related structures (mosques attached to tombs and shrines). In this chapter, we are not arguing that iconoclasm is exclusive to Islam, nor are we claiming that ISIS's behaviour is motivated solely by religious interpretive frameworks. Other factors are naturally at play (political motivation, intimidation of both the local and international audience, mafia-like objectives, among others) and these tend to differ between the various locations where the group or its affiliates are active.[5] Ultimately, the terroristic rationale is omnipresent in ISIS's activities, which are aimed at weakening the enemy, subjugating the population and utterly discrediting all opposing entities. However, we wish to explore the notion that religious interpretation also plays a role in these events.

Instead of relying on contradictory media reports, which have often proven to be inaccurate with regard to the Christian monuments as well as many Islamic religious sites, the main source for the data comes from satellite imagery showing the actual scale of destruction. The analysis covers the period between June 2014 and the end of August 2015, when the most recently analysed picture was taken. Through satellite imagery, we have only been able to verify the destruction of monuments that have been seriously damaged or have been completely razed to the ground. As for partial destructions (for example, the plundering of interiors or the elimination of Christian religious symbols), these were often taken into account only on the basis of media reports. In these cases, though highly probable, the information is largely unverified. We are aware that our analysis is limited by our observation of only the first fifteen months of ISIS's rule in the city of Mosul. This is, however, a sufficiently representative sample for our examination of the religious motivations of ISIS's destructive behaviour.

Typology of the Destroyed Monuments of Mosul

The destruction of architectural monuments began shortly after ISIS seized control of the town on June 10, 2014. Only ten days later, the first monument, the tomb of the famous Mosul historian Ibn al-Athir was bulldozed. Later in the same month, the Mosque of Shaykh Fathi met the same fate. This modest prelude foreshadowed the course of events to come in subsequent months. The contradictory media reports from this period mean that it is often difficult to assess the exact dates of the destruction of the monuments; however, we can deduce that it happened in several waves: July 2014, 11 monuments; September 2014, 4 monuments; December–January 2014–15, 3 monuments; February 2015, 3 monuments; March 2015, 4 monuments. Other destructive episodes that have been detected via the satellite images were either not reported in the media at all, or cannot be linked with any reported destructions with certainty (14 monuments). In summary, by the end of August 2015, when the last satellite image was analysed, the total number of destroyed monuments in the city of Mosul had reached 41. Of these, we have been able to identify 34 monuments; the identity of the other 7 monuments remains unknown.[6]

The identified monuments can be divided into six typological groups: mosques of the prophets; mosques and shrines of the family of the Prophet Muhammad; mosques of eminent, often venerated people native to, or associated with the town; individual tombs of Mosul residents; Christian monuments; and cemeteries (both Islamic and Christian).

Mosques of the Prophets

The first group, comprising five mosques of the prophets Yunus, Jirjis, Khidr, Daniyal and Shith, gave Mosul the honourific epithet *madinat al-anbiya'* (the City of the Prophets), by which the town is known to this day. Four mosques were built on the sites of the prophets' alleged tombs. The exception is the twelfth-century Mosque of the Prophet Khidr, whose alleged tomb was never physically marked by any funerary structure and, since the Ottoman period, it has been believed that he is interred in the mosque between the *mihrab* and *minbar*.[7] The oldest of the mosques was that of the Prophet Yunus (Jonah) in the ruined field of ancient Nineveh (today a part of eastern Mosul), a location associated with him since pre-Islamic times. The tomb was reportedly found by Jalal al-Din Ibrahim al-Khatni in 1365 during the construction of a congregational mosque. At around the same time, the Mosque of the Prophet Jirjis (George) was built by Timur in *c*.1393–94 on the site of a modest shrine containing the tomb of that prophet (mentioned for the first time in 1175–76). The mosques of both the Prophet Daniyal (Daniel) and the Prophet Shith (Seth) were monuments of much later origin. The Jalili governor, Ahmad Basha ibn Sulayman Basha, established the Mosque of the Prophet Shith in 1815–16 by transforming a small, seventeenth-century mosque adjacent to the tomb [Figure 10.1]. As for the Prophet Daniyal (Daniel), he seems to have the shortest history in Mosul, since his tomb was 'discovered' only during the first half of the nineteenth century after a local resident had a dream that he had seen Daniyal's tomb while attending the mosque of Ma'ruf ibn Ibrahim al-Sulayman.[8]

Mosques and Shrines of Prophet Muhammad's Family

The second group of monuments represents a collection of fourteen shrines of the members of the Prophet Muhammad's family (*ahl al-bayt*). In most cases, these were either attached later or incorporated into mosque compounds bearing the same name.[9] Largely, this unique segment of Mosul architecture is the product of the political and religious ambitions of one of its earlier rulers, Badr al-Din Lu'lu' (*d*.1259). This Shi'i Armenian *mamluk* served as Atabeg (provincial governor) subordinated to the last Zengid rulers, and replaced them as an independent ruler in 1233. One of the features of the transition of power was that Badr al-Din sought to suppress the historical memory of the Zengids' supremacy. This was carried out, among other actions, through the closure of the Sunni, often Zengid-funded, madrasas and their transformation into shrines for the members of the family of the Prophet Muhammad, who trace their lineage through the Prophet's daughter, Fatima, and her husband, 'Ali ibn Abi Talib.[10]

In four cases, we know the identity of the transformed buildings. The Shrine of Imam 'Abd al-Rahman (the son of either Hasan or Husayn ibn 'Ali – both identifications being open to question) was the result of the transformation of the al-'Izziyya Madrasa built by the Zengid ruler, 'Izz al-Din Mas'ud ibn Qutb al-Din Mawdud (*d*.1193). The Shrine of 'Ali al-Asghar, the grandson of 'Ali, was originally the al-Nizamiyya Madrasa founded by the Seljuq vizier,

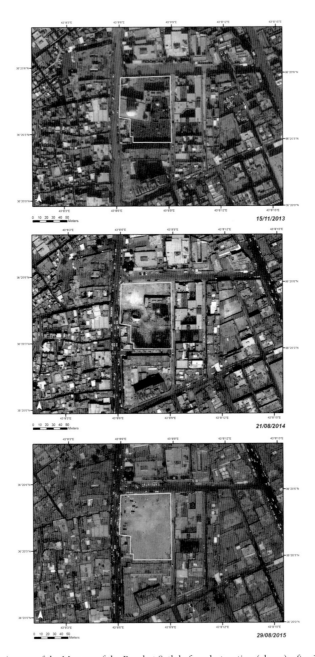

Figure 10.1: Satellite images of the Mosque of the Prophet Seth before destruction (above), after implosion (middle) and after razing (below). WorldView-2 and WorldView-3 © 2015 DigitalGlobe, Inc., distributed by European Space Imaging GmbH/ARCDATA PRAHA, s.r.o. (processed by Lenka Starková).

Nizam al-Mulk (*d*.1092). The Shrine of Imam Muhsin (grandson of 'Ali), which was part of the destroyed mosque bearing the same name, was once a component of the al-Nuriyya Madrasa of the Zengid ruler, Nur al-Din Arslan Shah ibn 'Izz al-Din Mas'ud (*d*.1210). The Shrine of Yahya ibn al-Qasim, the great-grandson of 'Ali, was, at its foundation, attached to the al-Badriyya Madrasa, which was established by Badr al-Din Lu'lu' before 1218, when he served as the Atabeg of the Zengid rulers [Figure 10.2].[11]

In one case, that of the Shrine-Mosque of Imam al-Bahir (the great-grandson of Husayn ibn 'Ali), the shrine was built on the site of a former madrasa, the original identity of which is unknown. In the case of the Shrines of Shah Zanan (the wife of Husayn ibn 'Ali) and 'Awn al-Din ibn al-Hasan (the grandson of 'Ali), the madrasa-origin of the buildings is presumed [Figure 10.3]. Another three buildings: the Shrine of Imam 'Ali al-Hadi (allegedly the grandson of the 8th Twelver Imam 'Ali al-Rida); the Shrine of Uways al-Qarani (the companion of 'Ali), attached to the mosque of the same name in the seventeenth century; and the Shrine-Mosque of Imam Ibrahim (the great-grandson of the 4th Twelver Imam 'Ali Zayn al-'Abidin) were also ascribed to Badr al-Din Lu'lu'. However, these were, most probably, 'stolen-identity' tombs, i.e., sites originally belonging to other people.

Apart from Badr al-Din's foundations, there are an additional four shrines of unknown origin that have been subject to destruction: the Shrine of Zayd ibn 'Ali (allegedly the great-grandson of the 4th Twelver Imam 'Ali Zayn al-'Abidin); the Shrine of Hamid wa Mahmud (the descendants of 'Ali); the Shrine of al-Sitt Nafisa (the great-granddaughter of Hasan ibn 'Ali); and the Shrine-Mosque of al-'Abbas (allegedly the son of 'Ali).

The great majority of the shrines (interchangeably referred to as *mazar*, *mashhad* or *maqam*),[12] probably originated long after the death of the people with whom they are associated, which implies that these may not be their actual tombs. In the context of Mosul, they could possibly be described as 'symbolic tombs' or commemorative structures. Still, it is obvious that they were perceived as funerary monuments, as is evident, for example, from a discourse on the identity of the entombed people, where centuries-long established identifications of some shrines with famous members of the Prophet's family have been substituted for historically and geographically 'more likely' candidates.[13] As will be seen below, small cemeteries placed adjacent to some shrines also emphasized their funerary character.

Mosque-Tombs of Eminent Mosul Residents

The third group of destroyed monuments comprises mosques associated with residents of Mosul from different historical periods. With only one exception (the Mosque of al-Ridwani),[14] all of these mosques demonstrably contained a tomb.[15] Four of them were built on, or next to, the earlier tomb of a significant person: the Mosque of Qadib al-Ban (next to the tomb of Qadib al-Ban al-Mawsili, *d*.1177–78); the Mosque of Hamu al-Qadu (above the tomb of 'Ala' al-Din, allegedly a descendant of the Sufi shaykh, 'Abd al-Qadir al-Jilani, *d*.1166); the Mosque of Shaykh Fathi (next to the tomb of the Mosul ascetic from the eighth

Figure 10.2: Ernst Herzfeld, Shrine of Yahya ibn al-Qasim. Friedrich Sarre and Ernst Herzfeld, *Archäologische Reise im Euphrat-und Tigris-Gebiet, Band III* (Berlin: Dietrich Reimer/Ernst Vohsen, 1911), Tafel CI.

Figure 10.3: Ernst Herzfeld, Shrine of 'Awn al-Din ibn al-Hasan. Friedrich Sarre and Ernst Herzfeld, *Archäologische Reise im Euphrat-und Tigris-Gebiet, Band III* (Berlin: Dietrich Reimer/Ernst Vohsen, 1911), Tafel IC.

or ninth century); and the Mosque of 'Ajil al-Yawar (above the tomb of a twentieth-century shaykh of the Shammar tribe and the grandfather of Ghazi al-Yawar, the first provisional president of Iraq after Saddam Hussein). Another two mosques incorporated the tombs of their founders, i.e., the Mosque of Abu al-'Ala' and the Mosque of al-Abariqi (both from the Ottoman period).[16] In one case, a sponsor of the mosque's renovation was interred in the mosque courtyard (the Hammam al-Saray Mosque).

Individual Tombs of Mosul Residents

Of the individual tombs in Mosul, the nineteenth-century Tomb of Shaykh al-Shatt (originally a Sufi shrine in the courtyard of the mosque bearing the same name); the Tomb of Ibn al-Athir (the famous historian [*d*.1233]); and the Tomb of Shaykh Lolan (died in the 1960s), have fallen prey to destruction. The same fate has affected the tomb (referred to as *mashhad*) of 'Isa Dadah, another descendant of 'Abd al-Qadir al-Jilani.

Christian Monuments

As for the destruction of Christian monuments in 2014–2015, this has also frequently been cited in the media. The satellite imagery, however, has revealed only one case of total destruction: the al-Tahra Syriac Orthodox Church [Figure 10.4]. Another Christian monument, the Monastery of Mar Kurkis (St George), was only partially destroyed on the western façade.[17] It seems that in the case of Mar Kurkis, the objective was to eliminate the monumental cross decorating the wall, while the remainder of the exterior of the monastery complex appears to be still intact. Reports on the destruction of other Christian monuments are too contradictory to assess their veracity. Though satellite imagery indicates that they are still standing, based on evidence from other areas under ISIS control we are inclined to believe the veracity of the prevailing reports indicating that many, if not all of them, have been plundered from within, desecrated, and that some of them were set on fire.[18] It is worth mentioning that among the propaganda photos that document the destruction of Christian monuments, only staged photographs of ISIS members destroying Christian symbols (crosses, bells, icons, holy statues) and graves have been shown.[19] Images of the total destruction of Christian architecture are absent. What have frequently appeared in the media are pictures of destroyed Christian monuments from elsewhere in the Middle East.[20]

Cemeteries

Another category of destroyed sites in Mosul is cemeteries. Satellite imagery has revealed the destruction of four small Islamic burial sites attached to the Shrines of 'Awn al-Din ibn

ISIS's Destruction of Mosul's Historical Monuments

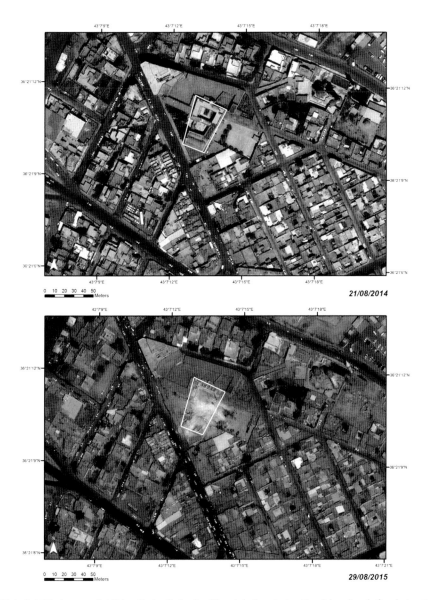

Figure 10.4: Satellite images of al-Tahra Syriac Orthodox Church before destruction (above) and after destruction (below). WorldView-2 and WorldView-3 © 2015 DigitalGlobe, Inc., distributed by European Space Imaging GmbH/ARCDATA PRAHA, s.r.o. (processed by Lenka Starková).

al-Hasan, Shah Zanan and 'Isa Dadah, and to the Mosque of Uways al-Qarani [Figure 10.5]. The destruction of additional Islamic burial grounds is suspected but awaits verification by means of satellite imagery.[21] Interestingly, ISIS has also turned its attention to Christian burial sites. The cemetery adjacent to the Monastery of St George has definitely been bulldozed (according to a picture provided by a local resident), as has the English Cemetery, which contained more than 300 graves of British, Australian, Canadian and Turkish soldiers who died during the two World Wars.[22]

Of the destroyed monuments that do not fit into any of the defined groups, there is one Shi'i monument (the Mosque and Husayniyya [Shi'i congregation hall] of Rawdat al-Wadi), in addition to the Ottoman madrasa of the 'Abdal Mosque. The destruction of artefacts in

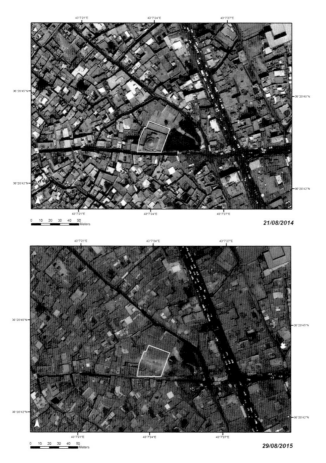

Figure 10.5: Satellite images of the Mosque of Uways al-Qarani and adjacent cemetery (east of the mosque) before destruction (above) and after destruction (below). WorldView-2 and WorldView-3 © 2015 DigitalGlobe, Inc., distributed by European Space Imaging GmbH/ARCDATA PRAHA, s.r.o. (processed by Lenka Starková).

Mosul Museum and statues of *lamassu* (an Assyrian protective deity) at the Nergal Gate of Nineveh must also be mentioned at this point.[23]

An analysis of the 36 identified destroyed monuments in Mosul (including the Mosques of al-Ridwani and al-Abariqi [see note 6]) reveals that the vast majority, comprising 31 of the 36 monuments (approx. 86 per cent), were tombs of actual people, symbolic tombs (referred to as shrines) of members of the family of the Prophet Muhammad, or mosques built on or next to tombs with which they were associated, usually bearing the name of the entombed person. Only three monuments have no funerary origin (a Shi'i mosque, a church and a monastery). In the case of two monuments, all information on the tombs within is missing.

ISIS's *Taswiyat al-Qubur* in the Context of Salafi Teachings

Destructive behaviour toward both Islamic and non-Islamic funerary architecture is a phenomenon that can be observed in many parts of the contemporary Islamic world. The perceived duty to level graves (*taswiyat al-qubur*) is inherent in the Salafi tradition and is often vigorously invoked by Saudi religious authorities.[24] These modern advocates of *taswiyat al-qubur* are motivated by their conviction that they act in the name of pure monotheism. According to their interpretation, graves, tombs and mosques containing a deceased person are to be levelled to the ground in order that they should not become places of worship. In this form of pure monotheism as envisioned by the Salafis, veneration of a human being, dead or alive, is a kind of *shirk* (polytheism) and, as such, is tantamount to idolatry. Even the fear of idolatry associated with graves (*fitnat al-qubur*) justifies, in Salafi opinion, their removal.[25] Salafi-influenced arguments for the destruction of statues and sculptures proceed from a similar logic.

An early benchmark for the fight against the practice of erecting sacred structures over graves was clearly established by the medieval theologian Ibn Taymiyya (d.1328). Ibn Taymiyya was mainly concerned with the possibility that the veneration of graves and their visitation might cause doctrinal impurity and lead to the convergence of monotheistic religions. Although Ibn Taymiyya's ideas were not widely embraced in the pre-modern era, his thought had an extensive influence on later Salafi movements. It was mainly Muhammad ibn 'Abd al-Wahhab (d.1792), the progenitor of the religious theology embraced as the foundational ideology of the Saudi state, who incorporated many of Ibn Taymiyya's ideas into his refutation of the cult of grave veneration. Yet the zeal at the beginning of the nineteenth century with which Ibn 'Abd al-Wahhab's later followers sought to destroy funerary sites across the Arabian Peninsula and in parts of Iraq, seems to have exceeded the zeal of both Ibn Taymiyya and Ibn 'Abd al-Wahhab.

In recent centuries, the legal justification adopted by Muhammad ibn 'Abd al-Wahhab in relation to the issue of graves has been elaborated, in particular, by the official Saudi religious establishment. The texts produced by the Saudi 'ulama' have since been appropriated by various radical movements, which have converted the guidelines into practice. The harsh stance against certain traditional Muslim pious activities (most notably *ziyara*, the visitation of graves), which had always constituted an important part of Islamic religious practice, has been supported to a large extent by the workings of the Saudi Permanent Committee for Scholarly Research and Fatwas (*al-lajna al-da'ima li-l-buhuth al-'ilmiyya wa al-ifta'*), which is charged with providing rulings on a wide range of religious matters. The Committee has made a clear declaration regarding funerary architecture: 'Building over graves is a disagreeable heresy (*bid'a*) [...] and leads to polytheism (*shirk*). It is therefore incumbent upon the ruler of Muslims or his deputy to remove what is over graves and level them to the ground.'[26] Since its creation, the Committee has sought to serve Muslims far beyond Saudi Arabia and has helped to establish or influence contemporary networks of religious scholars all across the Islamic world, who have since played their part in formulating and disseminating a very strict viewpoint in relation to graves, tombs and shrines. The impact is clear in the rise of various radical Salafi organizations that have recently destroyed dozens of funerary monuments, including al-Qaeda in Yemen and various groups that have organized coordinated attacks against funeral sites in Libya, Algeria, Pakistan, Somalia and Mali.[27] ISIS does not seem to be an exception. With regard to funerary architecture, it has employed very similar rhetoric, using almost the same arguments, while referencing the same religious and ideological sources.

The obligation to destroy funerary sites has been stressed by the former leader of ISIS, Abu 'Umar al-Baghdadi (d.2010). When articulating the fundamentals of the Islamic State, he mentioned specifically 'the necessity to destroy and eradicate all manifestations of idolatry [*shirk*] and prohibit the means leading to it'. He particularized his statement by reference to the prophetic hadith (tradition) quoted in the *Sahih* of Imam Muslim (d.875) on the authority of Abu al-Hayyaj al-Asadi, which states: 'Do not leave a statue without destroying it, or a raised grave without leveling it.'[28] This hadith has been utilized by the proponents of *taswiyat al-qubur* as the central argument against erecting any constructions above graves since the very beginning of the religious discourse on the topic (originating as early as the seventh century). With regard to Mosul, the hadith was quoted immediately after the seizure of the town by ISIS and can be found in the thirteenth article of ISIS's 'Charter of the City', the *Wathiqat al-madina*. In the document, the hadith is used as the sole explanation of ISIS's stance in relation to idolatrous shrines and tombs.[29] Judging by ISIS-produced propaganda material, it is conceivable that ISIS felt obliged, at least to a certain extent, to explain their motivation for the destruction to the local people. This can be deduced from the content of widely circulated treatises, designed as e-leaflets, which explained the necessity of the destruction of the graves. The treatises were written in simple language and in a comprehensible style, obviously with the intention of being easily absorbed by common people. At least one of the leaflets was intended to be distributed 'shortly before or during the destruction of tombs'.[30] It consisted of an abbreviated version of one of the most authoritative writings on the prohibition of building on graves, composed by the Yemeni reformer Muhammad al-Shawkani (d.1839), who had been strongly influenced by Muhammad ibn 'Abd al-Wahhab. In the treatise, al-Shawkani claims that 'erecting graves, building domes over them and praying near them constitute a major innovation'.[31] Another, though anonymous, leaflet was explicitly intended for the people of Mosul, since it advocated for the necessity to destroy the tombs of the four Mosul prophets (Yunus, Jirjis, Shith and Daniyal), making reference to the opinions of several medieval authorities, as well as to the Sunna of the Prophet. In the leaflet, destruction of tombs is advocated within the broader intention of 'annihilating the sources of *shirk*' and 'removing them from the hearts of people', arguing that 'if given the opportunity […] [the people must] destroy the domes and buildings on graves and shrines'.[32] The destruction in Mosul was allegedly also approved by a fatwa issued by one of ISIS's religious leaders, Husam Naji al-Lami, who based his arguments on the Prophetic tradition.[33]

Conclusion

To conclude, this chapter will return to its initial objective and attempt to assess the extent to which ISIS has utilized its destructive activities in Mosul for propaganda purposes. The destruction of architectural heritage that occurred shortly after ISIS's seizure of the town was bountifully reported in the world media, as well as on different social media networks. This applied to the destructions of June and July 2014. Some of them were filmed, and short clips showing the destruction found their way into news articles throughout the world.[34] The destructions of June and July were also followed by the publication of two photographic reports produced by ISIS, summarizing the scale of the destructions (among other items, nine Mosul monuments were reported).[35] The reports were disseminated on a mass scale through news servers and the printed media. The presentation of the June and July waves of destruction can certainly be considered to be a part of ISIS's performative visualizations, intended to propagate an image of violence among both the inhabitants of the occupied city and the outer world. This, however, by no means applied to all detected acts of destruction. With a few exceptions (the destruction of the Mosque of Imam Muhsin and the suspected destruction of the Mosque of al-Abariqi,[36] as well as the staged devastation of Mosul Museum and Christian symbols on church architecture), the other destructive acts in Mosul were not utilized in ISIS's visual propaganda (photo series, journal publications, videos) at all. To the best of our knowledge, this state of affairs applies to 30 of all 41 destroyed monuments; in other words, approx. 73 per cent. The information was mainly reported by local people, who contacted the media operating in non-occupied parts of Iraq. Furthermore, nine of the destructive acts were only discovered by reference to satellite imagery analysis; we did not detect them in either the English or the Arabic media.[37] Such acts can certainly be considered as representing a strategy employed by ISIS as a means of intimidating the local people. Here, however, it should be recalled that in many less publicized cases, the destruction affected rather modest, less significant buildings, all of which contained a tomb.

The actual motivation behind ISIS members' behaviour is certainly very difficult to ascertain. We cannot deny the impact of the political context as well as the skilful manipulation of religious sentiments by ISIS leaders, whose aim is to control the ideological terrain. However, we have obtained clear empirical data that show that the majority of identified destroyed monuments in Mosul, amounting to at least 86 per cent, were either tombs or structures containing a tomb, and that of these, only a small portion were publicized by the organization. These findings lead us to the conclusion that the undeniable objective behind ISIS's destruction of monuments has been precisely what they claim it to be: the elimination of funerary-related architecture. Taking into account the justifications that ISIS has provided in an effort to explain their destructive actions to the people, referencing the opinions of both medieval and more recent religious authorities, we find it reasonable to describe their behaviour as being, at least partially, religiously motivated. In addition, the relatively limited reference to the destruction of monuments in Mosul in ISIS' propaganda material fails to support the notion that the destructions were mainly aimed at producing visual imagery.

List of Mosul Monuments Destroyed by ISIS from June 2014 to August 2015 (see Figure 10.6 for corresponding map locations)

(Authors' note: the information on the monuments is unevenly recorded. Categories below given as 'unknown' indicate that information is either unavailable to the authors or not known for certain.)

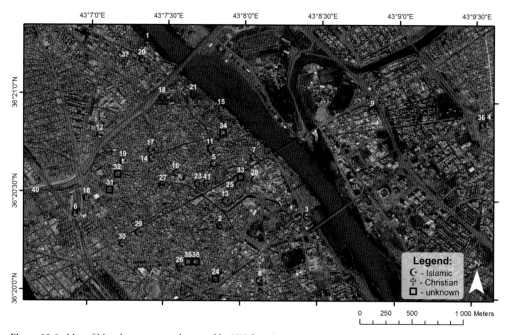

Figure 10.6: Map of Mosul monuments destroyed by ISIS from June 2014 to August 2015 (prepared by Karel Nováček). WorldView-2 © 2015 DigitalGlobe, Inc., distributed by European Space Imaging GmbH/ARCDATA PRAHA, s.r.o. (processed by Lenka Starková).

1. *Shrine of Imam Yahya ibn al-Qasim* Founder: Badr al-Din Lu'lu' (*d.*1259)

   Period: Atabeg
   Date of construction: 1239–40; originally adjacent to Madrasa al-Badriyya
   State: ruined

2. *Shrine of Imam 'Awn al-Din (known as Ibn al-Hasan)*

   Founder: Badr al-Din Lu'lu' (*d.*1259)
   Period: Atabeg
   Date of construction: 1248–49
   State: partly ruined

3. *Mosque of the Prophet Khidr (alternatively al-Jami' al-Ahmar, al-Jami' al-Mujahidi)*

   Founder: Mujahid al-Din Qaymaz
   Period: Atabeg
   Date of construction: 1179–80
   State: razed

4. *Mosque of the Prophet Yunus*

   Founder: the alleged tomb of the Prophet Yunus was found by Jalal al-Din Ibrahim al-Khatni during his reconstruction of the site as a congregational mosque (*jami'*) in 1365
   Period: the site has a long history since the Assyrian period
   State: razed

5. *Mosque of the Prophet Jirjis*

   Founder: the modest shrine of the prophet Jirjis was reconstructed as a *jami'* by Timur (*d.*1405)
   Period: Timurid
   Date of construction: 1175–76 is the first mention of the Shrine of Jirjis
   State: razed

6. *Mosque and Tomb of Qadib al-Ban al-Mawsılı*

   Founder: originally the house of Qadib al-Ban where he was buried in 1177–78
   Period: Ottoman (with Atabeg origin)
   Date of construction: the site was reconstructed in 1711 by Ahmad ibn Salih, and again in 1958
   State: ruined

7. *Mosque of Hamu al-Qadu*

   Founder: al-Hajj 'Abdallah Chalabi ibn Muhammad ibn 'Abd al-Qadir
   Period: Ottoman
   Date of construction: 1880–81; the mosque includes an earlier tomb of 'Ala' al-Din ibn 'Abd al-Qadir al-Jilani
   State: ruined

8. *Mosque of the Prophet Shith*

    Founder: Ahmad Basha ibn Sulayman Basha al-Jalili
    Period: Ottoman
    Date of construction: 1815–16 saw the reconstruction of a small mosque with the adjacent tomb as *jami'*
    State: razed

9. *Mosque and Husayniyya in the al-Faysaliyya Neighbourhood (Rawdat al-Wadi)*

    Founder: unknown
    Period: Modern
    Date of construction: 1960s
    State: razed

10. *Tomb of Ibn al-Athir (Qabr al-Bint), d.1233*

    Patron: recorded inscription witnessing the reconstruction of the tomb in 1888–89 by 'Abdallah ibn Hamu al-Qadu; the building covering the tomb was removed in 1938 during the construction of the Ibn al-Athir Street
    Period: in existence since the Atabeg era
    State: razed

11. *Mosque of Imam Ibrahim*

    Founder: al-Shaykh Ibrahim al-Muhrani al-Jarrahi
    Period: Atabeg
    Date of construction: mid twelfth century; only later reconstructed as the Shrine of Imam Ibrahim
    State: ruined

12. *Mosque and Tomb of Shaykh Fathi (building 1 and building 2)*

    Founder: unknown
    Period: the entombed person lived in the eighth or ninth century; the construction above the grave probably originated in the Zengid period; rebuilt in the Ottoman period and the late twentieth century
    State: two buildings of the complex razed, one still standing
    Date of construction: unknown
    State: razed

13. *Mosque of Abu al-'Ala'*

    Founder: Unknown
    Period: Ottoman
    Date of construction: unknown
    State: ruined

14. *Mosque and Shrine of the Prophet Daniyal*

    Founder: Ma'ruf ibn Ibrahim al-Sulayman (mosque); Inja Bayraqdar Muhammad Pasha (shrine)
    Period: Ottoman
    Date of construction: 1813–14
    State: ruined

15. *Tomb of Shaykh al-Shatt*

    Founder: originally a Sufi lodge (*takiyya*) built by Muhammad Efendi al-Afghani (called Shaykh al-Shatt) in the courtyard of the mosque bearing the same name
    Period: Ottoman (nineteenth century)
    Date of construction: unknown
    State: ruined

16. *Shrine of 'Ali al-Asghar (Ibn al-Hanafiyya)*

    Founder: Badr al-Din Lu'lu' (*d*.1259)
    Period: Atabeg; reconstruction of an earlier Seljuq building (Madrasa of Nizam al-Mulk, eleventh century)
    Date of construction: unknown
    State: ruined

17. *Mosque (and Shrine) of Uways al-Qarani with cemetery*

    Founder: al-Hajj Jum'a al-Hadithi (mosque)
    Period: Ottoman with earlier phases
    Date of construction: 1683–84 (mosque); the Shrine of Uways al-Qarani originating probably in the thirteenth century
    State: ruined

18. *Shrine of Imam 'Abd al-Rahman*

    Founder: Badr al-Din Lu'lu' (*d*.1259)
    Period: Atabeg; originally Madrasa al-'Izziyya of 'Izz al-Din Mas'ud ibn Qutb al-Din Mawdud (*d*.1193)
    Date of construction: unknown
    State: ruined

19. *Mosque and Shrine of Imam al-Bahir*
    Founder: Badr al-Din Lu'lu' (*d*.1259)
    Period: Atabeg (shrine); Ottoman (mosque)
    Date of construction: unknown
    State: ruined

20. *Mosque and Tomb of Imam Muhsin*

    Founder: Badr al-Din Lu'lu' (*d*.1259)
    Period: Atabeg; originally Madrasa al-Nuriyya of Nur al-Din Arslan Shah ibn

'Izz al-Din Mas'ud (*d*.1210)
Date of construction: unknown
State: ruined

21. *Shrine and Cemetery of 'Isa Dadah*

    Founder: unkown
    Period: Zengid; originally a *ribat* built by Sayf al-Din Ghazi (*d*.1149)
    Date of construction: unknown
    State: ruined

22. *Mosque of 'Ajil al-Yawar* *(not on the map)

    Founder: unknown
    Period: Modern
    Date of construction: 1943
    State: ruined
    *Location: South Mosul, al-Tayaran Neighbourhood

23. *Hammam al-Saray Mosque*

    Founder: unknown
    Period: the mosque probably originating in the Mongol period (reconstructed in the seventeenth century by al-Shaykh Yunus)
    Date of construction: unknown
    State: ruined

24. *Unknown structure*

    State: razed

25. *Shrine/Mosque of al-'Abbas*

    Founder: unknown
    Period: unknown origin; Ottoman; modern
    Date of construction: unknown
    State: ruined

26. *Shrine of Imam Zayd ibn 'Ali*

    Founder: unknown
    Period: Atabeg origin?
    Date of construction: unknown
    State: ruined

27. *Mosque/Shrine of Shah Zanan (called Umm al-Tis'a) and adjacent cemetery*

    Founder: ascribed to Badr al-Din Lu'lu' (*d*.1259)
    Period: Atabeg
    Date of construction: unknown
    State: cemetery ruined; likely the mosque as well (not clearly visible in the satellite image)

28. *Madrasa of the 'Abdal Mosque*

   Founder: al-Shaykh 'Abdal ibn Mustafa al-Shafi'i
   Period: Ottoman
   Date of construction: 1669–70
   State: razed

29. *Shrine of Imams Hamid wa Mahmud*

   Founder: unknown
   Period: unknown; Ottoman period reconstruction
   Date of construction: unknown
   State: razed

30. *Shrine of Imam 'Ali al-Hadi*

   Founder: Badr al-Din Lu'lu' (*d*.1259)?
   Period: Atabeg
   Date of construction: unknown
   State: ruined

31. *Unknown religious structure*

   State: ruined

32. *Unknown religious structure*

   State: ruined

33. *Unknown religious structure*

   State: razed

34. *Unknown religious structure*

   State: ruined

35. *Unknown religious structure*

   State: ruined

36. *Tomb of Shaykh Rashid Lolan*

   Founder: unknown
   Period: modern
   Date of construction: 1960s
   State: ruined

37. *al-Tahra Syriac Orthodox Church*

   Founder: unknown
   Period: unknown origin; Ottoman
   Date of construction: reconstructed in 1744–45
   State: ruined

38. *Unknown religious structure*

   State: ruined

39. *Mar Kurkis (St George) Monastery *(not on the map)*

   Founder: unknown
   Period: Ottoman with earlier origin
   Date of construction: in the nineteenth century on the site of an earlier church (attested to in the tenth century)
   State: The western façade of the church as well as the adjacent cemetery have been destroyed
   *Location: the northern periphery of Mosul, al-'Arabi neighbourhood

40. *English Cemetery*

   Founder: unknown
   Period: modern
   Date of construction: post-1915
   State: ruined

41. *Shrine of al-Sitt Nafisa*

   Founder: unknown
   Period: Atabeg
   Date of construction: unknown
   State: ruined

Acknowledgements

This chapter was prepared within the framework of grant project No. 14-16520S ('Death, Graves, and the Hereafter in Islam: Muslim Perceptions of the Last Things in the Middle Ages and Today'), funded by the Czech Science Foundation (GAČR). We are grateful to our colleagues, the archaeologists Karel Nováček (Palacký University Olomouc) and Lenka Starková (University of West Bohemia Plzeň), who prepared the data for the analysis.

Notes

1. This is a reprint of a paper resulting from research conducted in 2015–2016, and data may now be obsolete. For updates we refer readers to the webpage www.monumentsofmosul.com and Karel Nováček, Miroslav Melčák, Ondřej Beránek, and Lenka Starková, *Mosul after Islamic State: The Quest for Lost Architectural Heritage* (Palgrave Macmillan, 2021). The central argument of the research, however, remains unaltered.
2. Ömür Harmanşah, 'ISIS, Heritage, and the Spectacles of Destruction in the Global Media', *Near Eastern Archaeology* 78.3 (2015): 175–76.

3. Ibid., 176.
4. The term iconoclasm carries more than one meaning and is not, of course, an exact equivalent of *taswiyat al-qubur*. Originally, it referred to the destruction of religious icons, idols and images for both religious and political reasons. Its meaning, however, widened over the nineteenth century so that it can also be applied to venerated institutions or monuments that are regarded by an opposing group as fallacious or superstitious. In our usage, the term iconoclasm thus refers to 'the destruction of and/or suspicion against physical representations of the divine, the sacred, the transcendent' and can also be applied to the destruction of other objects besides icons, such as tombs or shrines. See Willem van Asselt, Paul van Geest, Daniela Müller and Theo Salemink, eds, *Iconoclasm and Iconoclash: Struggle for Religious Identity* (Leiden: Brill, 2007), 4. Cf. also 'Iconoclasm', *Oxford English Dictionary Online*, accessed December 31, 2016, https:// en.oxforddictionaries.com/definition/iconoclasm.
5. For example, according to recently published lists of destroyed monuments in the province of Nineveh, the main target of the destruction in the context of the whole province has probably been Shiʻi mosques and Husayniyyas. Within the province, the area of Sinjar, Bahzani and Baʻshiqa has lost predominantly Yezidi monuments, while the area of al-Hamdaniyya has lost many Christian monuments. The main objectives of the destruction thus seem to naturally depend on the religious composition of the given area. Dhunnun ibn Matta al-Mawsili, *al-Mawsil bayna ihtilalayn 2003–2014. Mudhakkirat muwatin ʻiraqi* (Baghdad: Dar Sutur, 2016), 173–92.
6. See Map [Figure 10.6] and List of Mosul Monuments Destroyed by ISIS from June 2014 to August 2015 at the end of this chapter. Of the seven unidentified monuments, two are, with high probability, the Mosque of al-Ridwani (a picture of the destroyed mosque has appeared on Facebook) and the Mosque of al-Abariqi (having appeared in an ISIS propaganda video – see endnote 36). These two mosques were taken into consideration in the calculations (the ratio of funerary-related monuments and the ratio of monuments having appeared in the propaganda material to the number of all identified destroyed monuments). The complete list of destroyed monuments in Mosul, created on the basis of the analysis of satellite imagery, is also available on the website *Monuments of Mosul in Danger*, accessed May 14, 2016, http://monumentsofmosul.com. The website contains an interactive map and shows images of the monuments before and after destruction. The content of the website is regularly updated.
7. Saʻid al-Diwahji, 'al-Jamiʻ al-mujahidi fi al-Mawsil', *Sumer* 11 (1955): 180.
8. The main reference sources utilized for the analysis of the destroyed monuments are: Ahmad ibn al-Khayyat, *Tarjamat al-awliya' fi al-Mawsil al-hadba'* (Mosul: Matbaʻat al-jumhuriya, 1966); Saʻid al-Diwahji, *Jawamiʻ al-Mawsil fi mukhtalif al-ʻusur* (Baghdad: Matbaʻat Shafiq, 1963); Niqula Suyufi, *Majmuʻ al-kitabat al-muharrara fi abniyat madinat al-Mawsil*, ed. Saʻid al-Diwahji (Baghdad: Matbaʻat Shafiq, 1956); Ahmad al-Sufi, *Khitat al-Mawsil* (Mosul: Matbaʻat al-ittihad al-jadid, 1953); Yasin al-ʻUmari, *Munyat al-udaba' fi tarikh al-Mawsil al-hadba'* (Mosul: Matbaʻat al-hadaf, 1955); Friedrich Sarre and Ernst Herzfeld, *Archäologische Reise im Euphrat und Tigris-Gebiet* (Berlin: Dietrich Reimer/Ernst Vohsen, 1920); J. M. Fiey, *Mossoul chrétienne* (Beyrouth: Imprimerie catholique, 1959).
9. A shrine attached to a mosque is referred to as a shrine-mosque.
10. For this reason, Badr al-Din's architectural patronage is often explained by his alleged adherence to Shiʻism, which might incline one to perceive his monuments as being

exclusively, or primarily Shi'i throughout time, which is evidently not the case. Even though we are not aware of any research that discusses the specific visitation patterns of Shi'i Muslims at the 'Alid shrines in modern Mosul, we have deduced from inquiries by Mosul residents that the shrines and the mosques attached to them were attended by the Sunni population predominantly, and should not be, at least in the context of recent tragic incidents in the town, perceived as Shi'i monuments. The shrines of the family of the Prophet Muhammad, which are venerated by both Sunnis and Shi'is, are historical places of shared religious culture, even though the academic literature more often emphasizes conflict over cooperation in this matter. For a more in-depth discussion on the subject, see Stephennie Mulder, *The Shrines of the 'Alids in Medieval Syria: Sunnis, Shi'is and the Architecture of Coexistence* (Edinburgh: Edinburgh University Press, 2014), e.g., 1–8.

11. Sa'id al-Diwahji, 'Madaris al-Mawsil fi al-'ahd al-atabaki', *Sumer* 13.2 (1957): 114.
12. Even though these terms are usually translated as one all-encompassing word, 'shrine', they are semantically different from each other. While *maqam* refers to the place of sojourn of the person it is associated with, the term *mazar* means a place of visitation (*ziyara*) often with the intention to get a blessing (*baraka*). *Mashhad*, on the other hand, designates a place of memorial. The application of the terms is rather vague and apparently does not correspond with any specific architectural forms. For more information see, for example, Stephennie Mulder, 'Shrines in the Central Islamic Lands', in *The Cambridge History of World Religious Architecture* (Cambridge: Cambridge University Press, forthcoming); Aliaa El Sandouby, 'The Ahl al-Bayt in Cairo and Damascus: The Dynamics of Making Shrines for the Family of the Prophet' (Ph.D. diss., University of California Los Angeles, 2008), 13–18.
13. In this respect, see, for example, the work of Isma'il al-Mawsili, *al-Athar wa al-mabani al-'arabiyya fi al-Mawsil 'ala daw' al-naqd al-hadith* (Amman: Dar Ghayda' li-l-nashr wa al-tawzi', 2012).
14. The destruction was confirmed by a photograph provided by a local resident (see also endnote 6).
15. In the case of the al-Ridwani Mosque, the information on the existence of a tomb is missing, which does not necessarily mean that the tomb was actually absent.
16. The location of the mosque of al-Abariqi has not been identified in the satellite images. It appeared in an ISIS propaganda video (although shown still standing; see endnote 36). Its destruction is highly probable.
17. This is attested to by a photograph provided by a local resident and viewed by the authors.
18. According to media reports, several churches and monasteries have been converted into mosques, storage centres or even ISIS quarters.
19. See, for example, pictures reproduced in 'Islamic State (ISIS) Vandalizes Churches in Iraq, Removing Crosses Atop Them, Destroying Statues and Icons', *Memri*, March 16, 2015, accessed April 13, 2016, http://www. memrijttm.org/islamic-state-isis-vandalizes-churches-in-iraq-removing-crosses-atop-them-destroying-statues-and-icons.html; Abdelhak Mamoun, 'ISIS Destroys Ancient Christian Cemeteries, Converts Church into a Military Office in Nineveh', *Iraqi News*, April 19, 2015, accessed May 5, 2016, http://www.iraqinews.com/features/isis-destroys-ancient-christian-cemeteries-converts-church-military-office-nineveh/.

20. Samuel Andrew Hardy, 'Pornographic Iconoclasm in Terrorist Propaganda: Islamic State Cinema and Audience Reactions', *EUNIC*, accessed April 23, 2016, http://washington-dc.eunic-online.eu/?q=content%2Fpornographic-iconoclasm-terrorist-propaganda-islamic-state-cinema-and-audience-reactions-0.
21. 'The War Against Idolatry: Extremists in Mosul Force Their Prisoners to Vandalize Graves', *Niqash*, December 17, 2015, accessed April 23, 2016, http://www.niqash.org/en/articles/security/5180/Extremists-in-Mosul-Force-Their-Prisoners-To-Vandalise-Graves.htm.
22. 'Mosul War Cemetery', *Commonwealth War Graves Commission*, accessed April 17, 2016, http://www.cwgc.org/find-a-cemetery/cemetery/6'9702/ Mosul%20War%20Cemetery.
23. For detailed analysis of this destruction, see Christopher Jones, 'Assessing the Damage at the Mosul Museum, Part 1: The Assyrian Artifacts', *Gates of Nineveh*, accessed June 20, 2016, https://gatesofnineveh.wordpress.com/2015/02/27/assessing-the-damage-at-the-mosul-museum-part-1-the-assyrian-artifacts/; Christopher Jones, 'Assessing the Damage at the Mosul Museum, Part 2: The Sculptures from Hatra', *Gates of Nineveh*, accessed June 20, 2016, https://gatesofnineveh.wordpress.com/2015/03/03/assessing-the-damage-at-the-mosul-museum-part-2-the-sculptures-from-hatra/. The destruction of the museum artefacts and the statues (bearing all the signs of a staged performance intended to shock the world audience) was not taken into consideration within the framework of this chapter, since it primarily analyses the destruction of Mosul architectural monuments. In the period succeeding the time span of the analysis, i.e. between September 2015 and June 2016 (when this chapter was being written), the global media 'only' reported on the destruction of the Mashki and Adad Gates and the Southwest Palace of Sennacherib in Nineveh (April–May 2016). See Michael D. Danti, Amr al-Azm, Allison Cuneo, Susan Penacho, Bijan Rouhani, Marina Gabriel, Kyra Kaercher, and Jamie O'Connell, *ASOR Cultural Heritage Initiatives (CHI): Planning for Safeguarding Heritage Sites in Syria and Iraq: Weekly Report 91–92 (April 27–May 10, 2016)*, 80–81, 93–4, accessed June 10, 2016, http://www.asor-syrianheritage.org/asor-cultural-heritage-initiatives-weekly-report-91-92-april-27-2016-may-10-2016/.
24. Salafism refers to the specific tendency within Islam that places particular emphasis on a return to the piety and principles of the prophet Muhammad and *ul-sulaf al-salih*, the pious predecessors, as the only true understanding of Islam. Although all Muslim scholars look to the first generations of Muslims as role models, the majority believe that the institutions and historical developments that scholars have accepted within their thinking and practice over the centuries also represent legitimate expressions of Islam. While some of the roots of Salafism may be found in medieval times, it is a fairly recent phenomenon that was, until the eighteenth century, only propagated by a tiny fringe of Muslims. For more, see, for example, Joas Wagemakers, 'Salafism', *Oxford Research Encyclopedia of Religion*, accessed November 5, 2016, http://religion.oxfordre.com/view/10.1093/acrefore/9780199340378.001.0001/acrefore-9780199340378-e-255?rskey=ntOZG8&result=14; or Henri Lauzière, *The Making of Salafism: Islamic Reform in the Twentieth Century* (New York: Columbia Univesity Press, 2016).
25. For more about this specific topic, see O. Beranek and P. Tupek, 'From Visiting Graves to Their Destruction: The Question of Ziyara through the Eyes of Salafis', *Crown Paper* 2, Brandeis University, July 2009. See also Marco Schöller, *The Living and the Dead in Islam: Studies in Arabic Epitaphs, vol. II, Epitaphs in Context* (Wiesbaden: Harrassowitz Verlag, 2004);

Thomas Leisten, 'Between Orthodoxy and Exegesis: Some Aspects of Attitudes in the Shari'a toward Funerary Architecture', *Muqarnas* 7 (1990): 12–22; or, more recently, James Noyes, *The Politics of Iconoclasm: Religion, Violence and the Culture of Image-Breaking in Christianity and Islam* (London: I.B. Tauris, 2013).

26. 'Abd al-'Aziz ibn Baz, Muhammad ibn al-'Uthaymin, 'Abdallah ibn Jibrin, and Salih ibn Fawzan al-Fawzan, *Al-Bida' wa al-muhdathat wa ma la asla lahu* (al-Riyad: Dar Ibn Jurayma, 1998), 294.
27. It is noteworthy, however, that historically funerary architecture was not only targeted from a radical religious position. Many sites were destroyed, for instance, during the Turkish secular Republicanism of the 1930s and 1940s or during the Soviet anti-religious campaigns of the 1920s and 1930s.
28. Abu 'Umar al-Baghdadi, 'Qul inni 'ala bayyina min rabbi', in *Majmu' tafrighat kalimat al-qada bi-Dawlat al-'Iraq al-islamiyya* (Nukhbat al-i'lam al-jihadi: Jumada al-ula, 1431 / May 2010), 14, accessed May 15, 2016, https://archive.org/download/Dwla_Nokhba/mjdawl.doc.
29. 'Wathiqat al-madina', accessed May 11, 2016, https://azelin.files.word-press.com/2014/06/islamic-state-of-iraq-and-al-shc481m-charter-of-the-city.pdf.
30. 'Namudhaj min al-matwiyat al-da'wiyya allati wuzzi'at fi wilayat Ninawa qubayla wa athna'a hadm al-adriha', accessed August 9, 2014, http://just-paste.it/sh_sodor.
31. Ibid.
32. 'Al-Qawl al-fasil fi mashru'iyyat hadm al-qubur al-maz'uma li-anbiya' Allah', accessed August 9, 2014, http://justpaste.it/QoulFasl.
33. 'Mufti Da'ish al-shar'i: Hadamna maraqid al-Mawsil istinadan li-hadith nabawi', *al-Ghad*, November 17, 2014, accessed May 13, 2016, http//:www. alghad.com/articles/836900.
34. Selected cases of the destruction also appeared in ISIS's English-language journal, *Dabiq*. See 'On the Destruction of Shirk in Wilayat Ninawa', *Dabiq* 2 (July 2014): 14–17; 'Da'wah and Hisbah in the Islamic State', *Dabiq* 3 (September 2014): 16–17 (which positions the destruction of shrines within their broader proselytization efforts). In Issue 13 on page 36, *Dabiq* argues that one of the reasons for pronouncing *takfir* (excommunication) against the Shi'i is that 'they are the sect most famous for grave-worship amongst all deviant sects. Much of the grave-worship that entered into the practice of 'Ahl us-Sunnah' (the Sunnis) originated from Rafd and the Rafidah (the Shi'is).' For the issues of *Dabiq*, see http://www.clarionproject.org (accessed may 11, 2016).
35. 'Taqrir 'an hadm al-adriha wa al-awthan fi wilayat Ninawa', accessed August 9, 2014, http://justpaste.it/atrah; 'Mulhaq taqrir hadm al-adriha fi madinat al-Mawsil', accessed August 9, 2014, http://justpaste.it/Adrah.
36. See ISIS's propaganda video (published in January–February 2015) on the legal validity of the destruction of tombs, entitled 'Izalat mazahir al-shirk – hadm al-adriha al-shirkiyya', accessed April 8, 2016, https://www.youtube. com/watch?v=EEhWzVBqX-c.
37. And vice versa, false media reports have also appeared on the destruction of monuments, which were, according to the satellite imagery, still standing.

11

The Radicalization of Heritage in Tunisia

Virginie Rey

On March 18, 2015, three gunmen disguised in military fatigues arrived at the Bardo district in Tunis. Once they were in front of the world-famous Bardo Museum, they opened fire on a busload of tourists and rushed inside, taking numerous hostages with them. The terror lasted for three hours before Tunisian special forces stormed the building and ended the siege. Twenty-four people were killed and fifty were wounded. Responsibility for the attacks was claimed by the Islamic State (ISIS) terrorist group, which had recently come to prominence for its bold and spectacle-fixated style of terror in Syria and Iraq. The attack made headlines around the world. The significance of the Bardo attack lay not only in the numbers killed, but also in the centrality of the museum site to Tunisian public life. Formerly the Beylical residence and locus of political power in Ottoman times, the Bardo complex was converted into a museum under French colonial rule. Following Tunisian independence, it was repurposed to house the national parliament and an adjoining military complex, with the museum remaining on site. Since the recent revolution, which began in late 2010, the Bardo compound has attained an additional significance as the site of a renewed spirit of democracy. Inside the parliamentary buildings, members of special committees charged with drafting the country's new constitution sat for countless hours during 2012 and 2013. Simultaneously, televised debates from the adjoining parliamentary chambers were broadcast across Tunisia to audiences witnessing, for the first time in their lifetimes, genuinely unmediated political debate. Meanwhile, on the street outside the entrance gate to the Bardo, protestors gathered spontaneously each day to press their demands in the new democratic space that had opened up in Tunisia.

With its internationally renowned collection of mosaics, the museum has always been a key site in the national imagination. In 2000, the Bardo was chosen to be part of a national heritage scheme financed by the World Bank. This led to the building's renovation starting in 2003, through which the museum acted as a renewed tourism beacon and site of a fruitful and friendly collaboration with France [Figure 11.1]. ISIS was well aware of the centrality of the museum in the national imagination when it chose to strike the Bardo last year. In an almost ironic choice of language, the group adopted a potent counter-discourse to the Enlightenment myth of the museum, describing the Bardo as a 'den of infidels and vice in Muslim Tunisia'.[1]

While it has been the most brutal and traumatic of all publicized events since the revolution, the Bardo attack is but one incident within a larger patrimonial crisis in Tunisia. Since the Jasmine Revolution, heritage, with its strong ties to identity and memory, has been at the

Figure 11.1: The Bardo Museum. Virginie Rey.

centre of significant political agitation. It has been used by various factions of civil society to express their difference from, support for or defiance toward the 'imagined community' promoted by the state through *patrimonialization*, by which I mean the transforming of sites, customs, or cultural traits into marketable heritage. Since the revolution, new sites and celebrations have been created to project an image of an emerging democratic Tunisia, while existing ones have seen their role changed. Others have been the target of violence and hijacking perpetrated by extremist religious groups who reject the very idea of 'western'-inspired Tunisian national heritage, or indeed of any heterodox religious history in the country, calling into question its connection to secularism and democratic ideals and its meaning for a true Muslim society.

In her book, *Uses of Heritage*, Laurajane Smith shows how patrimonial 'awareness' and practices are by no means bound to western values and understandings of heritage.[2] While different in nature from western modes, heritage preservation and valorization have existed in various forms outside Europe, including in Tunisia and the Arab world in general. The introduction of western-style patrimonial practices, however, coincided with the growing economic, political, and cultural penetration of the French and the British into the region during the nineteenth century, as well as an increasing interest in antiquity and archaeology more broadly around the world.[3] Attempts at cultural preservation were made by some Ottoman dignitaries,[4] but it was really under the French Protectorate (1881–1956) that a European-style 'patrimonial consciousness' was first shaped.[5] During this period, attention was predominantly given to the study and preservation of Roman antiquity, an historical epoch more readily associated with western grandeur and national ideals.[6] In the aftermath of colonialism, Tunisian elites placed greater emphasis on reorganizing the institutions inherited from the French. Yet colonial patrimonial practices were maintained nonetheless and reinforced through a politics of ultra-patrimonialization whereby a maximum of Tunisian sites, objects, and practices were constructed as national heritage.

In post-revolutionary Tunisia, attacks on cultural heritage sites have also led to further divisions between those remaining within a nationalist framework. Certain critical anthropologists and historians, for example, are resurrecting past debates regarding practices of state patrimonialization, trying to distance themselves from approaches they see as embodying a reductionist vision of Tunisian identity. We will see how others in the cultural field continue to defend official cultural identities and practices inherited from independence, arguing that the origins of recent 'heritage incidents' mostly lie in a lack of financial and administrative support from the government rather than issues of representation and interpretation.

Against the backdrop of this moment of turbulent challenges to the history of heritage development in Tunisia, this chapter explores the 'radicalization' of heritage since the revolution, focusing on four groups: the Amazighs (ethnolinguistic group indigenous to North Africa), the Jews, the Ibadis, and the Salafis. It concludes that after decolonization under Tunisia's first president Habib Bourguiba (1956–87) and following the excessive patrimonial policies of his successor Zine El Abidine Ben Ali (1987–2011), the heritage sector may soon encounter its most critical challenge yet: creating an inclusive and dynamic space for all communities.

Patrimonialization from the Fringe

Mohammed Bouazizi was a 26-year-old street vendor living in the central Tunisian town of Sidi Bouzid. On the morning of December 17, 2010, as he was preparing to sell fruit and vegetables at the town market, he saw his cart confiscated by a policewoman who had been humiliating him for months. He went to see the governor to protest this harassment, but the governor refused to receive him. Desperate, Bouazizi went to a local petrol station, bought a tank of petrol, poured it over his body, and lit himself on fire. Mohammad Bouazizi could not have known that his act of self-immolation would provoke an unprecedented political cataclysm in the country and beyond, resulting in Ben Ali's ouster on January 14, 2011, and spark a pro-democracy uprising across the Middle East that later came to be known as the

'Arab Spring'. It was not the first time that political self-immolation had occurred in Tunisia, but if Bouazizi's death had such a profound impact on public opinion – rallying thousands of Tunisians within hours – it was because this young man's story embodied the desperation of many Tunisians, especially those in central agrarian regions suffering from a precarious existence and abuse under an authoritarian system based on corruption and clientelism.

One of the consequences of the 'Jasmine Revolution' in Tunisia has been the dramatic re-emergence in the public sphere of particular social categories and strata whose voices had hitherto been silenced through repression or marginalization and whose identities had been absent from official narratives of nationhood supported by the state. Especially prominent has been the political assertion of marginalized cultural groups such as Tunisian Jews, the Amazigh and Afro-Tunisian communities.[7] Self-consciously Muslim groups have also come to the fore. The huge electoral success of the democratic Islamist Ennahda Party in October 2011 and the rise of more radical Salafi parties that, unlike Ennahda, do not support a compromise between religion and democracy, have called into question Tunisia's myth of secularism built by the preceding regimes, suggesting an urgent need for the country to recognize social identities that do not fit the inherited model of Tunisian modernity.

When Tunisian independence was achieved in 1956, the country's first president Habib Bourguiba espoused a politics based on developmentalism and modernization. Islam, while elevated as the official religion of Tunisia in the 1959 constitution, was mostly constructed in the imaginary of the state as a cultural element, and Islamic political movements were muzzled, especially from the 1980s onwards.[8] During Ben Ali's rule, these frames of reference were more or less maintained, but the construction of national historical time frames underwent a transformation. Historian Driss Abbassi explains that the beginning of Ben Ali's presidency marked a shift from what he calls a *histoire-mémoire immédiate* (immediate history-memory), focused on Bourguiba's personality and achievements, to a *histoire-mémoire de longue durée* (history-memory of the long duration), employing Braudel's term, a stratified vision of history building its way up from antiquity to the present day.[9] Under Ben Ali, Tunisian identity was no longer rooted in the present but in diverse spaces and times, giving way to a multidimensional identity whose various components were the Mediterranean, the Maghreb, the Arab world, and Islam, existing alongside one another.[10] Antiquity, which had been neglected during the Bourguiba era, was brought back to the fore of Tunisian history.[11] Abbassi argues that such a vision of identity not only allowed Ben Ali to promote Tunisia's ties with Europe and Tunisians living abroad but also, in a period inflected by the rise of religious fundamentalism, to continue the work of his predecessor Bourguiba in the construction of a secular Tunisia in which Islam and the medieval era were prevented from occupying the central axis of Tunisian history and memory.

This pre-Islamic/Mediterranean identity, with its strong connection to Europe, while aiming to be inclusive of all, did not appeal to everyone. Rached Ghannouchi, one of the founding members of the Ennahda Movement and its intellectual leader, was a fervent critic of both the Bourguiba and Ben Ali regimes in Tunisia. In an interview he gave with François Burgat in 1992, Ghannouchi explained that he considered Bourguiba's victory against the

French colonial power not as a victory for Arab/Islamic civilization in Tunisia but rather as one against it, which paradoxically upheld the same westernizing tendencies.[12] For those who lived according to Islamic principles, the process of westernization endorsed by Bourguiba and continued under Ben Ali was experienced as a kind of violence against their identity.[13]

Amazigh, Jewish, and Black African Tunisians (*Tunisiens Noirs*), likewise, felt that their identities and history were marginalized or suppressed during the Bourguiba/Ben Ali years. These minority groups have become increasingly politically active since the revolution, pushing for their grievances to be heard by the newly elected government. Some have organized themselves into political parties (more than a hundred parties have been legalized since the revolution). Others have taken their demands to the streets. Others again have created Facebook pages (e.g. 'Assurance de la Citoyenneté sans Discrimination de Couleur' and 'Témoignage pour Dénoncer la Discrimination de Couleur') or civil associations such as the Tunisian Association for Amazigh Culture (2011), the Tunisian Association of Support to Minorities Aqlyyat (2011), the Association de Défense des Droits des Noirs (2011), or the Coalition pour les femmes de Tunisie (2012).

Other central instruments used for the representation of identity in post-revolutionary Tunisia have been patrimonial practices and institutions. In the same way that the state has long used heritage to promote sanctioned national narratives, many minority movements in Tunisia have looked to heritage to propose their own counter-narratives. In this process, festivals and museums have acted as platforms to project 'cultural capital', in Bourdieusian terms, in the hope that it will later translate into social and political change. So was born in Tunis the Musée des Arts et Traditions du Judaïsme Tunisien in December 2012 under the patronage of Dar el-Dhekra (the House of Memory), an association fighting for the safeguarding and rehabilitation of Jewish heritage since 2011. The display of Jewish culture in museums is not entirely novel in Tunisia, having been a feature of representation practices during the Protectorate (at the Bardo) and continued after independence (in the creation of an ethnographic exhibition in the Musée d'Arts et Traditions Populaires of Djerba in 1970). In 2008, the Djerba museum was renovated and its section on Jewish culture was enlarged and enriched [Figure 11.2]. A display of Jewish jewellery was also created in 2006 at the Museum of Traditional Heritage of Moknine. If, in Tunis, the Musée des Arts et Traditions du Judaïsme largely draws on the same themes – artisanship, traditions, celebrations, etc. – used in state institutions, it does not, unlike public institutions such as the museum of Moknine, celebrate what Aomar Boum calls the 'memories of absence', a remembrance of a disappearing, sometimes lost, Jewish community in Tunisia. On the contrary, through the museum, Dar el-Dhekra is hoping to educate Tunisians about a hitherto marginalized segment of Tunisian heritage and to rehabilitate it. The president of Dar el-Dhekra explains that the association is strictly cultural. Ninety per cent of its members are non-Jewish Tunisians but consider this heritage as their own. While he claims that politics are not involved, the opening of the first museum entirely dedicated to Jewish culture in Tunisia is an obvious act of resistance against the dictates of cultural homogeneity promoted by the

Figure 11.2: Jewellery at the Museum of Traditional Heritage in Djerba. Virginie Rey.

state.[14] It has since prompted the Tunisian government, in partnership with civilians, to consider opening the first public museum of Judaism in Tunisia.[15]

The Festival for Amazigh Culture in Tamazret is yet another example of the politicization of heritage by a minority group. Created in 1992, the festival has been used since the revolution by members of various Amazigh groups, such as the Association for the Protection of Amazigh Heritage (est. 2002), as a platform to organize conferences aiming, among other things, to promote the importance of Amazigh culture and heritage and to encourage the state to protect, preserve, and maintain this heritage.[16] This image differs greatly from the safe and unchanging narrative propogated in similar state-sponsored events. The International Festival of the Sahara (or Festival of Douz) in Douz is one such example. Created in 1910 by the French as the Camel Festival, it took its current appellation under the presidency of Habib Bourguiba who turned the event into the best-known festival in Tunisia and a major international event in 1967. Orchestrated by six different national ministries, the festival proposes many attractions – camel and horse races, pottery making, hunting, poetry recitation, and music concerts – to international visitors and locals alike, while being broadcasted on national television. The Festival of Douz plays on the orientalist image of the roaming nomad. In a manner resembling the representation of Bedouins in Syria and the Gulf, Amazigh groups – commonly labelled Berbers in the mainstream discourse of tourism – are presented as the living carriers of an 'authentic' Arab culture based on honour, masculinity, and hospitality along the lines of that promoted by the state.[17] The Festival of Douz, like many other state-sponsored patrimonial sites and events in Tunisia, is rooted in what Barbara Kirshenblatt-Gimblett calls 'the insatiable and promiscuous human appetite for wonder'.[18] It works on a 'celebratory' and a 'remembrance' approach. It is a model that gathers civilians around a notion of a shared and indivisible 'heritage' while displacing, even concealing, issues related to change, conflict, and marginalization. In Tamazret, Amazigh ethnicity is celebrated as a living distinct ethnolinguistic culture that demands the right to exist outside the referents of Arabism and traditionalism in which it was maintained by the preceding governments.

The Two Faces of De-Patrimonialization

While the idea of heritage as a central element to 'construct civilization' has led some groups in Tunisia to use patrimonial institutions and events as canvases on which to recount their own story, conversely, it has prompted others to express their contempt by attacking heritage sites, public or private. Such has been the case of radicalized Salafi groups who see in the heritage industry evidence of Tunisia's corruption by western secular values. Examples include the desecration of several Jewish cemeteries as well as the Synagogue of Djerba (the Ghriba), where the Jewish Spring Festival, an important religious celebration that attracts many tourists and Jewish pilgrims, is held every year. The festival was twice the object of terrorist attacks, in 1985 and in 2002, causing the deaths of many locals and tourists.[19] In August 2012, Amazigh activists were also targeted and had to cancel a series of conferences due to a threat from Islamists who accused them of being collaborators with the West, 'serving a secular agenda hostile to the Islamic identity of Tunisia'.[20]

Less publicized than terrorist attacks on heritage, but equally important, have been attempts by Salafi groups to de-patrimonialize and reclaim religious sites, resulting in the occupation of local Ibadi mosques on the island of Djerba and in the town of Le Kef.[21] The most significant battle took place one day after Ben Ali's ouster, when Salafis took control of the Fadhloun Mosque, a popular tourism site in Midoun. They pushed the maintenance staff out and kept non-Muslims at bay [Figure 11.3]. Tourism signs were removed from the site and a petition was addressed to the Ministry for Religious Affairs demanding the space be reserved for religious purposes only. A new room for prayer and a protective tarpaulin were added to the site without any permission given by the Tunisian authorities.[22] The El Bessi Mosque in Oualagh, the Tajdidt Mosque in Fatou, the Tlakin Mosque in Ghizen, and the Moghzel Mosque in Béni Maaguel are other examples of patrimonialized mosques reclaimed by Salafi groups since the revolution.[23] These illegal reclamations have prompted

Figure 11.3: The Fadhloun Mosque in Djerba. Virginie Rey.

a strong indignation from professionals, yet in the face of the state's inability to intervene and the lack of funding for the heritage sector, they have been left with little means to resist. In a typical patrimonial response motivated by the urgency of disappearance, the Musée du Patrimoine Traditionnel of Djerba in Houmt Souk and the Zaouia Sidi Zitouni decided to host in 2015 'Mosquées de Djerba', an exhibition celebrating the architecture and the history of Djerbian mosques.[24]

The local population has also been involved in acts of resistance. Djerba has a long tradition of patrimonial activism in Tunisia. Following the excessive politics of tourism development pursued by the Bourguiba government in the late 1960s, a group formed by local activists and lovers of the island was created. The formation of this group led, in 1976, to the official launch of the Association pour la Sauvegarde de l'Ile de Djerba (ASSIDJE), a non-profit civil organization responsible for the promotion and the preservation of the environment, architecture, and traditions of the island.[25] Since its foundation, the ASSIDJE has been an active patrimonial partner for local governmental agencies, cataloguing monuments and promoting cultural tourism in Djerba. The protection and restoration of Ibadi mosques has featured significantly on the agenda of the association. Recently, members have been involved in the renovation of the El Bassi Mosque and the project to create, within its walls, a museum dedicated to the display of Ibadi architecture in Djerba.[26] In reaction to the Salafi hijacking of the mosques, the president of the ASSIDJE has incited local Ibadi communities to take a strong stance against Salafi interventions. Responding to his call, many have physically stood up – sometimes against their own sons – to defend what they consider intrinsic elements of their Islamic identity against what they see as the menace of 'obscurantism'.

The ASSIDJE explains that the lack of funding provided by the Institut National du Patrimoine (INP) – the umbrella organization responsible for preservation and research in the realm of heritage – to renovate and maintain the mosques, is the main factor responsible for their decline.[27] His disparaging view is shared by many professionals, especially in the museum sector. In the months following the revolution, the press was immediately galvanized to articulate the urgent situation of museums in Tunisia. Recurring concerns included the necessity to give museums a clear juridical status, to decentralize their management, to train and employ more staff, to invest in new technology, and to create a better relationship between museums and universities.[28] These debates are not new. During our interview, Habib Ben Younes explained that museums have always been marginalized within the cultural sector.[29] There is no official text to clearly define their status, functions, and objectives. In addition to this juridical lacuna, museums also suffer from a lack of autonomy, being financially and administratively dependent on the central government in Tunis. Another problem identified within the heritage sector comes from a lack of police intervention around heritage sites. After the 2002 attacks on the Ghriba, the island was placed under close protection. Since the revolution, police intervention has drastically diminished, if not ceased. But this is not all. Reporting on these events for dissident independent newspaper *Nawaat* in 2015, journalist Teycir Ben Naser has also revealed that following the Salafi interventions, new considerations relating to the preservation of these mosques have surfaced, paradoxically calling into question their very patrimonialization.[30] Among them is the idea that it is precisely because they have been turned into heritage, that they have been 'museumified', that mosques have deteriorated over time, making them an easy target for extremists. This is the opinion of anthropologist Walid Ben Omrane, who explained to Ben Naser that the current strategy of transforming mosques into museums will not prevent them from being hijacked.[31] The best remedy against deterioration and usurpation, instead, is to restore their initial purpose, that of active Ibadi religious sites.

The Anthropological Trap

Ben Omrane is not the only Tunisian anthropologist to point to issues surrounding patrimonialization. In 2009, Tunisian history professor Abdelhamid Larguèche saw the problem as twofold: visibility and representation.[32] 'Berber culture', for example, remains largely under-represented in the national imagery compared to Roman and Islamic heritage, Larguèche argues.[33] This issue has prompted him to describe it as a 'rejected form of heritage' in Tunisia, one that has remained the domain of French ethnographers, urbanists, and historians such as André Louis and Stanley Hallet, or Thomas Penchon, but one that is still waiting to be discovered by Tunisian researchers.[34]

Even more troubling, in his view, is the excessive governmental fabrication of heritage since the 1990s. As Myriam Bacha and Habib Saidi observes, the 'construction' of heritage was not a priority in the first decades following independence.[35] In this period focused on modernization and development, much emphasis was placed on celebrating the present and the future, two periods dominated by the figure of Bourguiba himself. Notwithstanding efforts on the part of the government to revisit its relationship with heritage in the 1970s, action for the development of a state-led patrimonial movement found its ultimate expression at the end of the next decade, following Ben Ali's ascension to power in the late 1980s. Under Ben Ali, Tunisia's march toward patrimonialization first materialized with institutional changes. Between 1988 and 1994, an armada of new organizations related to the preservation, the management, the popularization, and the survey of heritage were created directly inside the Ministry of Culture, now renamed the Ministry of Culture and Heritage Conservation: L'Agence National de Mise en Valeur du Patrimoine Archéologique et Historique (National Agency for the Promotion of Archaeological and Historical Heritage, or ANMVEP),[36] *La Cellule de Promotion des Sources, de la Mémoire et de l'Identité Nationale*[37] and *La Commission Nationale du Patrimoine*.[38] Government support of a 'patrimonial' approach to Tunisian heritage also became evident with the nomination of Abdelaziz Daoulatli as director of the *Institut National d'Archeologie et d'Art* (INAA) in 1991. Daoulatli had worked for several years as the director of the International Centre for the Study of the Restoration and Preservation of Cultural Property (ICCROM) in Tunisia. He was highly committed to a 'conservation' and 'preservation' rhetoric such as promoted by UNESCO and led the way to marked changes within the cultural sector, including museums. Under his leadership, the INAA was reformed and its name was transformed into *L'Instiut National du Patrimoine* (INP) in 1993. Its structure was modified into four sections: La Direction de la Programmation, de la Publication, de la Coopération et de la Formation; La Division de la Sauvegarde et des Monuments et des Sites (DSMS); La Division du Développement Muséographique (DDM); and La Division de l'Inventaire Général et de la Recherche (DIGR). Regional bodies were also created in Tunis, Sfax, Le Kef, Sousse, Kairouan, and Gafsa: respectively, the general inspection of the north-eastern region; the general inspection of the southern Sahel; the general inspection of the north-western region; the regional inspection of the Sahel; the general inspection of the western centre; and the general inspection of the south-western region. A year later, these institutional changes were also accompanied by legislative ones. In February 1994, the Code du Patrimoine (Heritage Code) was promulgated, officially designating any sites, rituals, and objects belonging to Tunisia's history as heritage.[39]

If in Tunisia patrimonialization touches any period of history and heritage form, Larguèche explains that it has had more profound and dangerous repercussions in the case of living minorities, resulting in their 'folklorization' and 'museumification'. In order to avoid such phenomena, Larguèche calls for a more responsible use of anthropology: 'If in the past, historians of the Maghreb region could do without anthropology, historians of today cannot ignore the complexity of patrimonialization at the risk of writing a history that is distant from [Tunisian] people and their expectations.'[40] But can this be achieved when anthropology is serving patrimonialization? For Tunisian professor Imed Melliti, the problem originates from the pariah status of ethnography in Tunisia and its recuperation by the heritage sector after independence.[41] In the period directly following Tunisian independence, ethnography was strongly associated with colonialism and banned from the inner sanctum of the social sciences, both in the Centre d'Études et de Recherches Économiques et Sociales and in academia. It was recuperated in the mid-1960s by a new institution created within the INAA to research, exhibit, and preserve vernacular culture, the Centre des Arts et Traditions Populaires (CATP). If researchers were excited about their new role, excitement was intertwined with a strange feeling of confusion. CATP researchers remained in many ways 'self-proclaimed' ethnographers. Unlike their colleagues in archaeology, they lacked direction and support from universities and research institutions.[42] This led to a rather confused approach to anthropology – combining multiple disciplines such as archaeology, human geography, history, sociology, and ethnology departing from. In principle, vernacular culture was praised as being an active, yet to be revived part of Tunisia's identity. In reality, the CATP's commitment to exhibiting and analysing anthropological change was almost non-existent in their research and museums that gave a very traditional outlook on vernacular culture.[43] This unidimensional vision of identity was not shared by all members of the CATP. Already in 1979, the late specialist on traditional costumes Fethia Skhiri was highly critical of this approach calling it, after Michel de Certeau, 'cadaveric'.[44]

Imed Melliti explained that the CATP's patrimonial approach to anthropology had devastating consequences for the discipline in Tunisia. Commenting on the quote from Mohammed Masmudi, ex-director of the CATP, he writes:

Such words that resound like a funerary sermon show the extent to which the 'folklorist' approach to culture and the museographic attitude of curators would largely dominate this ethnographic project actively promoted in Tunisia, almost as a way to clear one's conscience regarding traditional culture whose tangible manifestations were being swept away.[45]

And that approach, Melliti argues, has continued to permeate the work of the heritage sector despite new developments in the field of anthropology since the 1990s.[46] As Stéphanie Pouessel suggests, the 1990s in Tunisia marked the beginning of a clear reinvestment on the part of Tunisian intellectuals in the field of social anthropology.[47] This movement within the humanities led to a more encompassing vision of Tunisian history and memory, and the promotion of an idea that has burgeoned even more since the revolution: that of a *Tunisie plurielle*, a pluricultural Tunisia where a diversity of cultures coexist. Following the pioneering work of Jocelyn Dakhlia on communities in the south of Tunisia in 1990, new publications were produced on the history of minorities, marginality, and exclusion in Tunisia.[48] Pouessel argues that these studies were harbingers of resistance against the dominant Arab/Muslim vision of the Tunisian national identity defended by both the Bourguiba and the Ben Ali governments.

In the case of the Ibadi mosques of Djerba, clashes between reality and patrimonial fantasy are obvious. This is why for Ben Omrane protecting the mosques is less important than giving them back some 'legitimacy' through their reintegration into the social and religious fabric of the island.[49] If the local population of Djerba does not want the island to become an open-air museum or a lair for extremism, Ibadis need to reclaim their history, to claim their right as a community, Ben Omrane declares. This might require reconnecting with the core principles of the Ibadi faith. Indeed, in the Ibadi tradition, the state, though tolerated, is not recognized as a figure of authority. Power is retained by the community. In this unique organizational model, anthropologist Pierre-Philippe Rey sees the opportunity for a 'meeting point between those who wish to preserve Islamic heritage and those who want to rid this heritage from the oppressive forms it has taken'.[50] According to this model, the local community would be leading debates with the state, not the contrary. It would be in charge of finding solutions to preserve its own traditions. In the conclusion of his social exegesis of Ibadi traditions, Habib Gouja argues that it could be a solution to fight against the 'museumification' of heritage.[51] But can minorities in Tunisia escape the temptation of a patrimonial approach to culture when their identities are not fully recognized, if at all, by the state?

Je Suis Bardo

Following the Bardo attack on March 18, 2015, the response from the newly elected political elite was immediate. On March 29, the Tunisian government organized a silent anti-terrorist rally in Tunis. Following the model of the Parisian 'republican march' held two months earlier in the wake of the Paris *Charlie Hebdo* attacks, the event comprised two marches: a march for civil society and a march for political personalities and dignitaries, including Tunisian president Mohammed Beji Essebsi, French president François Hollande, Palestinian president Mahmoud Abbas, Algerian president Adelmalek Sellal, and the Italian politicians Matteo Renzi and Federica Mogherini. Hundreds of thousands of people joined the cortège, which walked the most important axes of the city centre of Tunis, finishing in front of the Bardo Museum itself where politicians gathered. The streets were garlanded with Tunisian flags and banners proclaiming 'Je suis Bardo' ('I am Bardo') 'Le monde est Bardo' ('The world is with Bardo'). In sometimes chaotic scenes, the visiting dignitaries laid floral wreaths at a plaque bearing the names of all who died. Army trumpeters played a lament for the victims. This rally and the slogans that accompanied it drew inspiration from the bloody events in Paris. Just as *Charlie Hebdo* galvanized international public opinion, so did the Bardo attacks in Tunisia. Arriving at the entrance to the museum alongside Hollande, Caid Essebsi said: 'Tunisians proved today they are not afraid of terrorism. When Tunisia is targeted, all Tunisians stand as one.'[52] He had promoted the march with television slots appealing for a large turnout to demonstrate 'national unity' in the face of terrorism. The moderate Islamist party Ennahda, which has one minister and three junior ministers in the coalition government, also endorsed the march. Behind the politicians, the Bardo Museum was cast as the standard-bearer of the revolutionary principles of democracy and freedom of speech represented by the revolution.

This status is quite ironic given that heritage sites like museums have often promoted a kind of republican unity, obscuring many facets of Tunisian culture that could not be corralled into a homogenous version of the national culture. Museums have often been timid in voicing plurality, diversity, multiculturalism, and issues of gender, presenting instead a homogenous, safe, and highly customary version of identity. This paradox echoes the fallout of the *Charlie Hebdo* attacks in France, where calls for national unity and defence of democracy in reality stamped out voices of dissent and disagreement. In his controversial essay, 'Qui est Charlie? Sociologie d'une crise religieuse', French anthropologist and historian Emmanuel Todd suggests that far from being a symbol of tolerance, the march that followed the *Charlie Hebdo* massacre on January 11, 2015 was rather a return to a new republican consensus in France that is intolerant of any other conception of national identity.[53]

Undeniably, the Jasmine Revolution has given new opportunities to marginalized groups to voice their existence in Tunisia. In the wake of this identity explosion, there was a brief opening for the heritage sector to shift from the monolithic outlook on culture it had hitherto upheld. Unfortunately, the violence of Salafi attacks has led to the reassertion of heritage as a symbol of democracy and republican values, suggesting it will not deviate from the demands of state-sponsored national consensus despite the calls of critical anthropologists. Because attacks on heritage are seen as attacks on democracy, and because democracy and republicanism are inalienably connected in the Tunisian mind, not only can terrorism not have any revolutionary effect on heritage, but, in a reversed movement, it might also annihilate any opening for discussion, rather pushing people to continue to maintain the existing patterns in a movement of 'protest' and 'resistance'.

Yet the revolution, if it is to be true to the principles of democratic free speech with which it was launched, needs to depart from this unifying instinct and take this moment to re-evaluate the position of culture in the country. This must be undertaken not only by addressing the financial and administrative lacunae of the heritage sector, but also the narrative it supports. If many efforts have already been made to create a bigger bond between local people and their culture, by making, for example, the museum a more engaging and visitor-friendly experience, and this in often difficult financial and administrative conditions, there is still a pressing need to create a public space that is genuinely open to all voices, even those that are difficult to hear and reconcile. In the context of religious and community revivalism, this must necessarily include Islamic versions of Tunisian identity, not to mention Jewish, Amazigh, and other marginalized voices that have struggled to find a place in the national landscape. To borrow Michel de Certeau's words, culture needs to be re-articulated *au pluriel*, and groups need to be taken as active political voices in the system, not as passive remnants of forgotten traditions.[54] In order to do this, curators, archaeologists, historians, and architects need to put themselves in the role of social anthropologists. This not only requires a critical stance toward culture, but also an openness to new trends, to new emergent forms of culture in the country, in order to reimagine the relationship of modernity to tradition, and above all to see Tunisian culture as a force in constant transition and development. The work of some heritage workers is already leaning in that direction.[55] The social upheavals that have shaken Tunisia since the revolution and the subsequent creation, reappropriation, and destruction of heritage suggest that it is time for Tunisia to depart from the republican trajectory, to open a new path that is capable of incorporating dissent and counter-narratives, and look at culture in the present.

Acknowledgements

I am indebted to the University of Melbourne, which financed my fieldwork research in Tunisia. Many thanks to Stephen Pascoe for offering helpful comments on earlier drafts of this chapter.

Notes

1. Bouazza Ben Bouazza and Paul Schemm, '20 Killed in Tunis Museum Attack, Including 17 Foreign Tourists', *Haaretz*, March 19, 2015, accessed January 10, 2016, http://www.hareetz.com/news/middle-east/1.647594?v= 87581259F7407E3BFEF864E5F257129F.
2. Laurajane Smith, *Uses of Heritage* (London: Routledge, 2006).
3. Christel Braae, 'The Early Museums and the Formation of their Public', in *Middle Eastern Cities, 1900–1950: Public Places and Public Spheres in Transformation*, eds N. Korsholm and J. Skovgaard-Petersen (Aahrus: Aahrus University Press, 2001), 112–32.
4. Houcine Jaidi, 'Kheireddine Pacha et son projet de musée archéologique à Tunis', *Pallas* 56 (2008): 93–117.
5. Myriam Bacha, *Patrimoine et monuments en Tunisie (1881–1920)* (Rennes: Presses Universitaires de Rennes, 2013).
6. Nabila Oulebsir, *Les usages du patrimoine: Monuments, musées et politique coloniale en Algérie (1830–1930)* (Paris: La Maison de Sciences de l'Homme, 2004); Edward Said, *Orientalism* (London: Routledge, 1978).
7. Xavier Torres de Janon, 'Challenging Tunisia's Homogenous Arabness: Post-Revolutionary Civil Society Activism for the "Invisible" Tunisian Amazigh', *Independent Study Project*

(ISP) Collection, paper 1939, accessed November 15, 2015, http;//digitalcollections.sit.edu/isp_collection/139; Safa Ben Said, 'Tunisia's Amazigh Identity: Deeply Embedded, Little Recognized', *Tunisia Alive*, March 18, 2014; Stéphanie Pouessel, *Noirs au Maghreb: enjeux des connections identitaires à l'Afrique* (Paris and Tunis: IRMC-Kathala, 2012); Lilia Blaise, 'Les noirs de Tunisie feront-ils leur révolution?', *SlateAfrique*, July 17, 2012, accessed March 20, 2016, https://m.slateafrique.com/91197/ les-noirs-de-tunisie-feront-ils-leur-revolution-recisme-esclavage/.

8. Political Islam in Tunisia started in the 1970s with the creation of movements such as Tabligh (1970) and Al-djam'a al-islamiyya (1972), but it was really in the 1980s that Islamism gained in popularity. See A. Allani, 'The Islamists in Tunisia between Confrontation and Participation: 1980-2009, *Journal of North African Studies* 14 (2009): 257–72. In 1981, hitherto a clandestine movement, Al-djam'a al-islamiyya legalized its status under the name Mouvement de la Tendance Islamique (MTI. Sometimes tolerated and invited to the table of negotiation, Islamist parties in Tunisia were more often condemned and repressed by the Bourguiba and Ben Ali governments that constructed the display of religious zeal as a menace to Tunisian democracy and progress. See Fabio Merone and Francesco Cavatorta, 'The Rise of Salafism and the Future of Democratisation', in *The Making of the Tunisian Revolution: Contexts, Architects, Prospects*, ed. Nuri Gana (Edinburgh: Edinburgh University Press, 2013), 254.
9. Driss Abassi, *Entre Bourguiba et Hannibal: identité tunisienne et histoire depuis l'Indépendance* (Paris: IREMAM/Karthala, 2005), 155–229.
10. Ibid.
11. This antiquity renaissance can be observed in other Arab states in the same period. On Syria and Iraq see Stéphane Valter, *La contruction nationale syrienne* (Paris: CNRS, 2001); Eric Davis, *Memories of State: Politics, History and Collective Identity in Modern Iraq* (Berkeley: University of California Press, 2005).
12. This interview was cited in Mohammad Fendri, 'Une histoire nationale controversée: la politique culturelle de la Tunisie face à un tournant décisif' (paper presented at the Eurolog Symposium, April 26–27, 2012, Tunis).
13. Ibid.
14. 'Trois questions à Jacob Lellouche, Président de l'Association Dar el Dhekra', *Le Mag*, May–June 2012, 26.
15. Habib Trabelsi, 'Pour un musée du patrimoine judaïque tunisien', *Kapitalis*, May 28, 2016, accessed April 2, 2017, http://kapitalis.com/tunisie/2016/05/28/pour-un-musee-du-patrimoine-judaique-tunisien/.
16. Lahcen Mawassi, 'Tunisia: Amazighs Face Islamist Harassment', *Eurasia-review*, September 1, 2012, accessed November 23, 2015, http://www.eura-siareview.com/01092012-tunisia-amazighs-face-islamist-harassment/.
17. On Bedouins in Syria, see Virginie Rey, *Le Festival des Steppes: opportunités et contradictions d'une manifestation culturelle en Tunisie* (MA diss., Université de Genève, 2006).
18. Barbara Kirshenblatt-Gimblett, *Destination Culture: Tourism, Museums, and Heritage* (Berkeley: Berkeley University Press, 1998), 150.

19. Dora Carpenter-Latiri, 'The Ghriba in the Island of Jerba (or Djerba) or the Reinvention of Shared Shrine as a Metonym for a Multicultural Tunisia', in *Sharing the Sacra: The Politics and the Pragmatics of Inter-Communal Relations around Holy Places*, ed. Glenn Bowman (London: Berghahn Books, 2012), 118–38.
20. Mawassi, 'Tunisia: Amazighs'.
21. Ibadism is a branch of Islam that emerged in Bassora in the second half of the seventh century. Today, Ibadi minorities are present in Oman, Algeria, Lybia, and Tunisia.
22. Carlo Perelli and Giovanni Sistu, 'Jasmine for Tourists: Heritage Policies in Tunisia', in *Contemporary Issues in Cultural Heritage Tourism*, eds D. Arnold, A. Benson and J. Kaminski (London: Routledge, 2014), 82; Naceur Bouabid, 'Les mosquées de Djerba: un patrimoine en péril', *Kapitalis*, April 16, 2015, accessed June 20, 2015, http://www.kapitalis.com/afkar-2/28864-les-mosquees-de-djerba-un-patrimoine-en-peril.html.
23. Guillemette Mansour, 'Djerba secrète', *Seabel Magazine* 3 (2014): 32.
24. The exhibition was the result of a study tour undertaken in Djerba in 1989 by architecture students of the Catholic University of America. It was first hosted by the Club Tahar in July 2014 and the Université Libre de Carthage in November that same year.
25. On tourism development During Bourguiba's tenure, see Habib Saidi, *Sortir du regard colonial: politiques du patrimoine et du tourisme en Tunisie depuis l'Indépendance* (Ph.D. diss., Université Laval, 2007), 169–71.
26. Naceur Bouabid, 'Un fait divers instaure la mosquée el-Bassi en un musée consacré à l'architecture des mosquées de Djerba', *Archi-Mag*, November 10, 2009, accessed November 15, 2015, http://www.archi-mag.com/actu_165.php.
27. Teycir Ben Naser, 'Des mosquées et des ruines: comment sauver le patrimoine Ibadi djerbien?', *Nawaat*, September 10, 2015, accessed November 20, 2015, nawaat.org/portail/2015/09/10/des-mosquees-et-des-ruines-comment-sauver-le-patrimoine-djerbien/.
28. Habib Ben Younes, 'Les musées en Tunisie: les enjeux', *La Presse de Tunisie*, March 5, 2011; Hela Hazgui, 'Patrimoine: les musées tunisiens, conférence de Habib Ben Younès à Art'Libris. Encore du pain sur la planche', *La Presse de Tunisie*, March 7, 2011; Houcine Jaidi, 'Quel avenir pour les musées tunisiens?', *La Presse de Tunisie*, May 18, 2011.
29. Interview with Habib Ben Younes, November 14, 2012.
30. Ben Naser, 'Des mosquées et des ruines'.
31. Ibid.
32. Abdelhamid Larguèche, 'L'histoire à l'épreuve du patrimoine', *L'Année du Maghreb* 4 (2008): 191–200.
33. Ibid.
34. See, for example, André Louis and Stanley Halley, 'Evolution d'un habitat: le monde "berbère" du sud tunisien', *Revue de l'Institut des Belles Lettres Arabes* (1979): 249–268; Thomas Penchon, 'La langue berbère en Tunisie et la scolarisation des enfants berbérophones', *Revue Tunisienne des Sciences Sociales* 5 (1968): 173–86.
35. With the exception of the Ribat (a small fortification) in Monastir, no site was added to the national heritage list between 1956 and 1985. Myriam Bacha, 'La construction patrimoniale tunisienne à travers la législation et le journal officiel, 1881–2003: de la complexité des

rapports entre le politique et le scientifique', *L'Année du Maghreb* 8 (2008): 108–09; Saidi, *Sortir du regard colonial*, 133–50.
36. Law 88-11 of February 25, 1988. The ANMVEP changed its name in 1997 to AMVPPC (Agence de Mise en Valeur du Patrimoine et de la Promotion Culturelle).
37. Decree 94–1639 of August 1,1994.
38. Decree 94–35 of February 24, 1994.
39. The code said, 'All vestiges inherited from past civilisations or generations, discovered or researched, on land or at sea, are considered archaeological, historical or traditional heritage, whether they be pieces of furniture, buildings, documents, manuscripts or else relating to the realms of arts, science, beliefs, traditions, everyday life, public or historical events and whose national or universal value has been proven'. Law 94–35 of February 24, 1994.
40. Largueche, 'L'histoire à l'épreuve du patrimoine', 199.
41. Imed Melliti, 'Une anthropologie indigène est-elle possible? Réflexions sur le statut de l'anthropologie en Tunisie', *Arabica* 53 (2006): 173–74.
42. Samira Gargouri-Sethom, 'Un centre d'arts et traditions populaires, pour-quoi?', *Cahiers des Arts et Traditions Populaires* 9 (1987): 142.
43. Virginie Rey, *Social Spaces of Mediation: Tunisian Ethnographic Museums (1881–2015)* (Ph.D. thesis, University of Melbourne, 2016).
44. Virginie Rey, 'Le PatrimoineVivant: Ethnographic Dilemma in Independent Tunisia', *Journal of North African Studies* (2017).
45. Melliti, 'Un anthropologie indigène est-elle possible?', 167.
46. Ibid.
47. Stéphanie Pouessel, 'D'ici et d'ailleurs: L'anthropologie en Tunisie', *Le Carnet de l'IRMC*, accessed June 20, 2014, http://irmc.hypotheses.org/1293.
48. Habib Kazdaghli, 'L'engagement des Juifs tunisiens dans l'anticolonialisme, 1919–1956', in *Histoire communautaire, histoire plurielle: la communauté juive de Tunisie*, eds A. Allagui and H. Kazdaghli (Tunis: Centre de publication, 2000), 217–37; Abdelhamid Largueche and Dalenda Largueche, *Marginales en terre d'Islam* (Paris: Cérès, 2000); Abdelhamid Largueche, *Les ombres de Tunis: pauvres, marginaux et minorités aux 18e et 19e siècles* (Paris: Arcantères, 2000).
49. Ben Naser, 'Des mosquées et des ruines'.
50. Pierre-Philippe Rey, 'Préface', in *Essai d'une lecture patrimoniale d'une source théologique ibadite*, ed. Habib Gouja (Paris: L'Harmattan, 2015), 28–29.
51. Habib Gouja, ed., *Essai d'une lecture patrimoniale d'une source théologique ibadite*, ed. Habib Gouja (Paris: L'Harmattan, 2015), 164.
52. https://www.theguardian.com/world/2015/mar/29/tunisian-french-presidents-unity-rally-tunis-museum-attack.
53. Emmanuel Todd, *Qui est Charlie? Sociologie d'une crise religieuse* (Paris: Seuil, 2015).
54. Michel de Certeau, *La Culture au Pluriel* (Paris: Union Générale d'Edition, 1974).
55. Virginie Rey, 'The Journey of an Tunisian Ethnographic Museum from Colonial to Post-Revolutionary (1936–2015)', *Anthropology of the Middle East* 12 (2015): 1–21.

12

Heritage Crusades: Saving the Past from the Commons

Ian B. Straughn

'There Is No Time to Waste'

A little over a decade ago, anthropologist Lila Abu-Lughod posed the provocative question 'Do Muslim women really need saving?' The article she penned took aim at various self-proclaimed feminist discourses that served the march to war in Afghanistan under the pretext of 'saving brown women from brown men'.[1] Without dismissing the very real trauma and oppression faced by the women of Afghanistan and elsewhere in the Muslim world and beyond, she questioned how war, complete with its bombings of villages (intentional or collateral) and destruction of infrastructure, could serve as an agent of positive change that might make life better for this particular category of humanity. Her intervention targeted the very logic of how efforts for the supposed liberation of one group can come at the destruction of the broader social fabric upon which that group depends. This chapter seeks to build upon such an exposition of the logics of care that entangle the Middle East in a set of moral imperatives. More specifically, I want to examine how ethical concerns over cultural heritage materialize evaluative discourses about the Middle East, including the varied claims for interventions to save that heritage from any number of (existential) threats. While much alarm has surfaced in the wake of tragedies such as destruction at the hands of ISIS or the systematic looting and damage to historical sites resulting from war and the collapse of state institutions in Iraq, Syria, Libya and elsewhere, this chapter proposes to draw attention to a series of other practices that have often become subsumed within the category of "threat" as part of the salvation discourse. Ultimately, I contend that, despite potentially good intentions, there has been a rush to condemn actors outside of the professional and state-sanctioned ranks of heritage management as ignorant iconoclasts, looters and thieves. Such blanket condemnation fails to consider certain vernacular forms of engagement with the past outside of a universalizing heritage discourse, engagements that demonstrate their own types of care, commitment and sense of the commons. Put more bluntly, how has the rhetoric of preservation and meaning-making, with its mission to save the past in the name of humanity writ large, positioned itself as morally superior? How has that heritage complex restricted local practices that do not necessarily frame themselves within such universal ethics and claims to salvation of a cosmopolitan shared heritage?

As an illustration of this salvation discourse, consider the voice of Mohamed Ibrahim – Egypt's Minister for Antiquities following the ousting of President Muhammad Morsi – who wrote in an op-ed for the *Washington Post* in October 2013:

> Egypt's future lies in its history [...] But thieves are raiding our archaeological sites [...] taking advantage of Egypt's security situation to loot our nation's economic future and steal from our children. Egyptians need the people and the government of the United States to support our efforts to combat the systematic and organized looting of our museums and archaeological sites. Imagine a world in which the stories of King Tut, Cleopatra, Ramesses and others were absent from the collective consciousness.

It concludes:

> It is our common duty, in Egypt and around the world, to defend our shared heritage. International institutions, governments, business, archaeologists and other experts must come together to explore how to help countries in need protect their treasures. The efforts of groups such as the International Coalition to Protect Egyptian Antiquities are appreciated – but much more aid is necessary. The youths of Egypt deserve more. There is no time to waste.[2]

Dr Ibrahim's editorial establishes a clear agenda and moral imperative as it outlines the threats to Egypt's valuable archaeological and cultural treasures and establishes the necessary response. For him, criminal actors are stealing from innocent youth and future generations, who desperately need the Egyptian state to re-establish security with the assistance of the United States (and others). What could be controversial about this? And if thieves are not enough, three months after he had made his appeal, 'terrorist' bombs in downtown Cairo severely damaged the recently renovated Islamic Art Museum in an attack on the security headquarters across the street. Whether to combat pure greed or Islamist ideological hostility or indifference, the argument offered by Ibrahim is for increased state control and international cooperation to rescue Egypt's heritage from is dark fate of destruction and indifference.

Is it so simple? What makes such acts of destruction necessarily condemnable? Is Muslim culture, writ large, marred by an iconoclastic impulse that requires outside intervention for it to be quelled and transformed? The image of the Muslim iconoclast, which has itself, by now, become iconic, is not far removed from these recent events in Cairo and elsewhere in the Middle East, particularly considering that at the moment of the writing of this chapter (Fall 2016), heritage rescue teams are descending on the ancient ruins of Palmyra in Syria to assess the damage caused by ISIS. The image of the barbaric iconoclast is part of a long-standing orientalist tradition of representing Islam. It serves as code for articulating the failure of Muslims, more broadly, to cultivate the material and visual sensibilities of secular modernity. The destruction of the Bamiyan Buddha statues at the hands of the Taliban has come to serve as the standard twenty-first-century reference point. That image of Afghans and of Islam (particularly when the latter is erroneously conceived of as an independent agentive force unconnected to Muslims themselves) that is so destructively opposed to a notion of a universally shared cultural heritage must endure, must expand to fill the negative space left by those once towering colossi. Despite the best efforts of scholars, such as Finbarr Barry Flood, to demonstrate that this was an act whose logic was 'rooted not in the fictions of an eternal recurring medievalism but in the realities of global modernity',[3] comments such as Dr Ibrahim's offer no room for such Islamic iconoclasm to be rehabilitated, let alone for those acts to signal a critique of western materialism, capitalism and (neo)-imperialism. Rather, its destructive traces must remain as a memorial that justifies the many other acts of destruction that were its supposed corrective. In the 'War on Terror', this process has engendered new logics and meanings that both bespeak and belie other forms of violence that must be confronted, eliminated and, when necessary, solicited and manufactured.

The fields of archaeology, museology and cultural heritage have played important roles in identifying the ways in which the past has been employed to support forms of social injustice, colonial dominance and a politics of exclusion.[4] These critiques, directed at both professionals in heritage-related fields and at other actors and institutions who lay claim to authoritative interpretations or control of the past, are grounded in a realization that not all pasts, or their material traces, can (or should) be preserved or known. As Barbara Mills has asked, would we even want to preserve and know everything about the past, given not only the practical impediments but also the difficulties that such knowledge would pose in the construction of compelling narratives?[5] Archaeologists often call attention to the fact that they are engaged in their own destructive process, that of excavation. We justify such loss, however, as a necessary practice in pursuit of knowledge about the past. For example, consider all that is lost in the metres-high back-dirt pile that emerged from excavations in the city centre of ancient Petra [Figure 12.1]. Mixed within this new archaeological *tell* are the traces of multiple excavations strewn with ceramic fragments and other artefacts that did not make the cut of individual excavators as they bagged the day's finds. That effort toward preservation has entailed what Ian Russel has termed a 'commanded forgetting'.[6] He has recently pushed archaeologists to confront this condition through an explicit ethics of forgetting, one that would, in his words, allow the field to 'find a way to love oblivion and decay'.[7]

Such moments of forgetting should alert us to the need to then pay attention to the possibility of constructive forces that come with acts of destruction and works of oblivion. In other words, if we are able to recognize that the act of destruction that characterizes archaeological excavation contains within it the constructive act of generating a past, we might then recognize that there can be other modes of seemingly destructive engagement that are situated within alternative ethical discourses about the role of material traces and memory in the pursuit of the past. My contention here is that before passing judgement on practices that fall outside the standard protocols of 'universal' preservation manuals and international legal mandates, there is a responsibility not only to examine and analyse the actors' explicit and implicit ethical claims, but also to consider how they appeal to certain authorities.

Figure 12.1: The immense back-dirt pile resulting from numerous modern archaeological excavations at Petra, Jordan, 2009. Ian Straughn.

'Islam Is Large'

An example, therefore, is in order. In 2005 it seemed that even the very birthplace of the Prophet Muhammad itself was threatened with destruction by an impending multibillion-dollar development project in the heart of Mecca [Figure 12.2]. The outcry from various Muslim intellectuals was not without foundation, given the track record of the Saudi authorities, who had removed, after some apparent excavations, the house of the Prophet's first wife Sayyida Khadija in order to expand the bathroom facilities of the sacred complex of the *Haram*.[8] In this case, it was Muslims tarring other Muslims with the image of the iconoclast. Dr Sami Angawi, a leading Saudi architect, scholar and activist for democratic reform in the KSA (Kingdom of Saudi Arabia), remarked to *The Independent* that 'Mecca should be the reflection of the multicultural Muslim world, not a concrete parking lot'.[9] This statement condemning the Saudi state's treatment of a shared Muslim patrimony is part of a long-standing debate about the iconicity of the material past and its political, economic and theological valence.

At stake in this debate was not solely a capitalist disregard for preserving the historic landscape of Mecca in order to champion the ultra-modern urban planning that has come to predominate in the petro-states of the Gulf. Instead, critics like Angawi pointed to this project as part of a long-standing pattern of Wahhabi efforts to cleanse the landscape of certain classes of religio-historical sites in order to prevent Muslims from engaging in acts that Wahhabi and other Salafi groups consider idolatrous. The present controversy over the Prophet's birthplace appears, on the surface, to be very much about the authority of the state to make certain kinds of claims over what is, and what is not, Islamic. Yet, among the most contentious aspects of this perceived assault on the Meccan landscape is its relationship to debates among Muslim scholars, debates that surfaced long before the emergence of the Saudi state or even the Wahhabi movement. At issue has been the permissibility and proper practice of *ziyara* – the visitation of sites, typically shrines and graves, but also inclusive of locales as diverse as natural features or the loci of important events, which are considered to possess a form of divine blessing (*baraka*) that can accrue to supplicants.[10] For opponents of such practices, any promise of *baraka* is outweighed by the danger that visitors might begin to ascribe divinity to the place itself (*shirk*). Such places, then, are considered dangerous and need to be eliminated from the landscape, or else strictly controlled, as is currently the case at the Prophet's tomb in Medina. Thus, in an effort to 'block the means (to evil)' (the juridical principle known in Arabic as *sadd al-dhara'i'*) by which the believer might commit a grave sin, measures should be taken to prevent the production of new places that might foster such practices. A salient example of this principle was the burial of the Saudi ruler King Fahd (d.2005) in a simple unmarked grave in a sprawling public cemetery.

Such a vision for a moral physical landscape has not been without its opponents. Josef Meri has documented the extensive arguments between Hanbali followers of Ibn Taymiyya, who sought to severely curtail practices such as visitations to saints' shrines (*ziyara*) and other devotional practices, and those, particularly Sufi thinkers and practitioners, who sanctioned them.[11] With such medieval religious heavyweights as Ibn Taymiyya on one side and al-Ghazali on the other, current debates about the heritage landscape are deeply rooted in the politico-religious fractures of the Muslim world along Salafi/Sufi and Sunni/Shi'i lines. The result is that such arguments have come to play out in spheres beyond that of the religious scholarly community. For example, the American master calligrapher Muhammad Zakariya has critiqued this puritanical vision of the heritage space as 'unable to accommodate the difficulty and complexity – the depth and texture – of (Islam) and, ultimately, of its essential meaning.'[12] He goes on to say, 'Islam is large. Muslims are not *mushriks* [those who ascribe partners to God; idolaters].'[13] This statement serves to rebuke broadly construed efforts to 'block the means' that strike many Muslims as infantilizing and insulting to their intelligence by challenging them as a form of iconoclastic materiality run amock. There is a suggestion here that such pre-emptive strikes against the commission of grave sins are potentially more harmful because of how they simultaneously disrupt what is also good and legitimate. These negative effects tend to outweigh any presumed protective intention. Ultimately, the fear is of stagnation, where creative impulses are treated as highly morally suspect in order to avoid innovation in social practice (*bid'a*), particularly within the Salafi tradition.

This highlights once again the counterintuitive aspects of iconoclasm. Its alignment with the forces of conservatism and antipathy to innovation would seem to suggest an affinity with preservation and heritage. Yet, it is precisely the opposite that has happened. Instead of striving to maintain the city as it was in the time of the Prophet, the once unadulterated heights of the Jabal Omar overlooking the haram complex continue to be filled in with triumphs of hyper-modern architecture [see Figure 12.2]. More generally, the physical face of Mecca has undergone far more profound and extensive transformations under the rule of the Saudi state and its Wahhabi doctrines than during any previous time in the city's history. This 'narrowing' of Islam, as critics of the Wahhabi movements conceive it, is not about a failure to embrace the technological modern. The call to recognize that "Islam is large" seeks to find room for an emic Islamic heritage movement that can embrace the material past and do so without labelling it as an unwelcome and deviant innovation. Anthropologists and

Figure 12.2: Beginning of construction of several new hotels towering over the Haram, Mecca, Saudi Arabia, early 2007. Meshal Obeidallah/Wikimedia Commons.

other social scientists have analysed these devotional practices, particularly as they relate to spaces revered for their sanctity and blessing, and have forcefully argued against claims that they fail the test of modernity.[14] Rather, they offer opportunities to challenge powerful state and religious authorities to debate the role of the material past within the Islamic tradition.

Such an argument has precedence among earlier Muslim scholars. Enter the voice of the tenth-century Muslim traveller to Egypt al-Mas'udi, describing his consternation at the destruction of Pharaonic ruins by contemporary Muslims who viewed them as idolatrous works of the despised Pharaoh. He writes to his future progeny, saying:

> Look, son, what the Pharaohs built and how it is being destroyed by these idiots. Nothing is more tragic and sad than the loss of what these ruins offer to those who would regard them and consider their lessons […] What sort of wisdom preaches that these ruins should be removed from the face of the Earth?[15]

For al-Mas'udi, the value of such localities of antiquity within the Islamic exegetical tradition is that they serve to strengthen the Qur'anic injunction to search out and contemplate the lessons (*'ibar*) that the Divine has left in the landscape for believers. It is an approach to the material past that neither replaces, nor removes, but reminds. This argument, however, is not for preservation as the default mode by which to engage with the past. Rather, its value *lies in its ruination*, what the archaeologist ascribes to taphonomic processes, both natural and artificial, but which al-Mas'udi, alternatively, has located within the will of the Divine. At another level, al-Mas'udi signals that such monuments are part of a commons, an emic notion of religio-cultural patrimony and one that should continue to be available to those who seek to engage with it. It is to that right of common access to the past that I will now turn.

Treasure Hunting and 'Commoning'

Well before al-Mas'udi's reproach to those defilers of the Giza Plateau, its monuments attracted a different sort of destructive attention. The pyramids, and other structures, offered a ready resource of cut stone blocks that would serve as building materials in numerous constructions in the expanding metropolis across the Nile, namely Cairo (the historical *Misr/Fustat/al-Qahira* urban complex). Surveys of Islamic-period constructions from the Tulunid, Fatimid and later dynasties have recorded the repurposing of material taken from Pharaonic- and classical-period monuments for city walls, mosques and other architectural projects.[16] Given the size of the materials and the logistical hurdles involved in their transport, this form of recycling was most probably orchestrated through official channels. Such reuse has an obvious economic explanation as a low-cost alternative to quarrying and mining new building materials. However, this functionalist reading does not necessarily foreclose the possibility of ideological motivations or symbolic associations with which such materials were aligned in order to control or neutralize the power of the past.[17] As Flood has demonstrated in his study of spolia reused from Coptic and Byzantine contexts in varied Muslim architectural settings, there are diverse motivations and potential re-ascriptions of meaning that can accompany such practices of reuse as part of public buildings.[18] In most cases, such spoliation practices were directed by ruling elites who had the necessary resources. At such a scale, it is unlikely to have become incorporated amongst the broader urban populace into widespread practices of what I will term 'commoning': the practice of asserting communal usufruct rights to certain material traces of the past. The same might not be true in the case of the practices of treasure hunting undertaken by the population of Egypt in the early centuries following the seventh-century Arab conquests. The widespread circulation of various manuals that promoted get-rich-quick schemes attests to another set of motivations and engagements with heritage.[19] Such manuals taught the hunter how to read subtle signs in the earth; summon the assistance of helpful (though potentially dangerous) *jinn* (spirits); and, most importantly, decipher ancient scripts and perform their magic. This was not simply a hobby; indeed, for many it served as a career, at which point state intervention and regulation were introduced. By the ninth century, under the Abbasid governor and de facto ruler of Egypt Ahmad ibn Tulun, the first treasure hunters' guild was established with its own official functionary, the *naqib al-mutalibin* (supervisor of treasure hunters).[20] These guilds are evidence of some of the earliest efforts by the state to assert its authority over the past and its antiquities, largely in response to their potential financial value.

Centuries later, concern about these practices would introduce a new regime of control following the emergence of the modern Egyptian Antiquities Service and the European archaeological establishment. At one point, the French Egyptologist Gaston Maspero would suggest that his Egyptian colleague Ahmad Kamal edit and publish one of the more well-known treasure hunting manuals in an effort to demystify such beliefs and quell some of the more destructive approaches to the monuments. The result was the production of both an Arabic edition and French translation of *Kitab al-durr al-maknuz wa al-sirr al-ma'zuz fi al-dala'il wa al-khabaya wa al-dafa'in wa al-kunuz* (The Book of the Treasured Pearl and the Concealed Secret with Regard to Indicators, Caches, Burials and Riches).[21] For Kamal, this work was in part meant to educate fellow Egyptians about the ruination of national monuments and to mark a turning point in how they might engage with their material past in the future, through the emerging fields of Egyptology and archaeology. As he states, 'les antiquités de l'Égypte auraient ainsi une chance de salut en plus' (the antiquities of Egypt would thus have a chance of future salvation).[22] Indeed, he saw potential in the knowledge produced by such manuals for the modern scholar who was willing to read between the lines. He demonstrated that it was possible to decipher some of the geographic and empirical data buried within the magic spells and discussions of *jinn* guarding entrances to chambers filled with fabulous wealth. Kamal, along with other Egyptians of his generation, had begun to envision a new guild to replace the treasure hunters (*mutalibin*): a guild of scholars, inspectors and curators. It would be these men (and this was very clearly a gendered profession) who had rights to the heritage commons, albeit under the authority of sanctioning institutions such as museums and universities, as well as the authorizing discourses of archaeology and science.[23]

For Egyptians of the nineteenth and twentieth centuries, the value of the archaeological past was not limited, however, to the category of treasure and its quixotic promise of life-changing wealth. In some cases, it was much more down-to-earth. Egyptian peasants have long excavated archaeological sites for the nitrogen rich *sibbakh* – the decaying mudbrick of ancient structures, which they spread as fertilizer on their fields. This resource, known more specifically as *sibbakh kufri* (to distinguish it from other fertilizers and animal manures), would even be subjected to scientific investigation by British agronomists researching the farming practices of the *fallahin*. One scholar of Egyptian manure has argued:

> Compared with good farm yard manure, Sebakh Coufri is poorer in nitrogen; but one essential point must be carefully noted […] By examination of the analyses we see that about 40% of the nitrogen in the farm yard manure is soluble, and of that in the Sebakh Coufri 50% is soluble.[24]

The general conclusion drawn by scholars about the efficacy of *sibbakh kufri* was that larger quantities were needed due to the lower nitrogen levels; however, analysis did indicate minor variations in chemical composition across the various regions in the Nile Delta, Fayyum and outskirts of Cairo – some of the most prominent areas of *sibbakh* exploitation. Its use required careful application in small but frequent amounts given the potentially disastrous effect of salinization of the soil.[25] For this reason, it was deemed most suitable for supporting maize cultivation, though this was not exclusively done in practice given the farmer's access to other available fertilizers.[26]

There is no clear documentary evidence for when Egyptian *fallahin* first began to recycle the ancient sites at their disposal to support the growth of their crops. However, by the mid-nineteenth century, the scale of the exploitation of *sibbakh* seems to have increased significantly as large land companies began to organize its extraction.[27] Modernization of agriculture, under Muhammad Ali Pasha and the later khedival administrations, facilitated access to archaeological mounds. The laying of narrow-gauge rail lines allowed for a more industrial-scale removal of *sibbakh*, often destined for the fields of large landowners, including those of the ruler himself and others with access to the capital needed to mount such an operation.[28] The impact of these excavations was not lost on either the Egyptologists or the inspectors of the Antiquities Service. However, given their structural weakness in the face of the more powerful agricultural power brokers of the period, they were largely unable to do more than simply document the destruction. As one inspector for the Fayyum noted in 1904, free access to *sibbakh* was a public utility, provided without charge.[29] In reality, however, it had become far more the province of the wealthy property owners, some of whom sought to enclose whole archaeological mounds that rested in the vicinity of their land holdings or, alternatively, to purchase the rights to them from the government.[30]

Figure 12.3: Mudbrick buildings within the archaeological site of Karanis, Fayyum, Egypt, 2008. Ian Straughn.

Ultimately, the Antiquities Service would look to secure its own rights to the exploited sites and, by 1910, they would be granted supervision of some 545 sites across Egypt. This followed extensive reporting of the exploitation of the *sabbakhin* (not the large land-owners) in various annual reports, paying particular attention to the Fayyum and the area of Cairo around the Mosque of ʿAmr and ʿAyn al-Sira.[31] The focus on the Fayyum was largely in response to numerous foreign scholars who had recognized the area themselves as fertile ground – not for fertilizer, but for papyri. Their consternation at the *sabbakhin*, at sites such as Karanis (Kom Aushim) and Kiman Faris, merits consideration, if only to highlight the less-than-subtle hypocrisy it signals, given the methods employed by some of these early papyrus hunters [Figure 12.3]. Grenfell and Hunt, the first excavators at Karanis at the end of the nineteenth century, described their work as follows:

The gold-seeker follows a vein of quartz, while the papyrus-digger has to follow a stratum […] of what the natives call *afsh* […] The gold-digger does not look for gold where there is no quartz, and similarly the papyrus-seeker may practically disregard any other kind of earth than *afsh*. Objects of stone, wood, or pottery he may find elsewhere, but without *afsh* he will hardly ever find papyrus.[32]

The difference, then, is not in the practice, but in the discourse. The discourse ascribed to the peasant is one of indifference, rooted in a base materialism.

For the 'ignorant' Egyptian farmer, the relics of the past are raw materials, an economic resource that becomes either nutrients for crops or objects for the antiquities market. Ascribed to peasants is a sense of heritage that is devoid of both appreciation and affect for these material traces of a distant history. Such disinterest in the past forecloses even the cultivation of the disposition advocated by al-Mas'udi, and certainly excludes Kamal's modernist advocacy of the professional scholar.

We are, however, never privy to the *fallahin*'s own voices. That absence, that silence, while not surprising, requires recognition and perhaps some speculation. A glimpse into the practices of the *sabbakhin* is afforded by the collecting practices of the Egyptian physician Dr Henri Amin Awad and his patients. As Jere Bacharach details in his introduction to *Fustat Finds*, in 1950 Dr Awad opened a clinic in the area of what was historically the early Islamic urban settlement of Fustat [Figure 12.4].[33] The area had long served as a local reservoir of *sibbakh* for agriculturists working on the margins of the expanding metropolis of modern Cairo. Since many of his clients were poor, he began to accept objects they had collected from their illicit, though largely unimpeded, diggings in the area, in lieu of cash as payment for his services. According to Bacharach's narration, these items were often the 'boxes of unidentified junk' retained by the *sabbakin* 'awaiting some future use'.[34] In general, he argues that these were artefacts that could not find a ready buyer in the local antiquities market that traded in objects from Fustat through the 1970s: lumps of metal, beads and fragmented artefacts deemed otherwise unmarketable.[35] Dr Awad is distinguished from his patients, who seem to merely hoard without insight. We learn that he would later pursue a degree in Islamic archaeology and even author numerous scholarly articles based on his collection. Moreover, he would donate these materials to various institutions to form study collections for future scholars. Both the *sabbakhin* and the good doctor placed a value on these materials. Nevertheless, in Bacharach's telling of this story, the physician received the greater valorization for his efforts in the production and preservation of knowledge about the past (albeit lacking certain elements of scientific rigour given the absence of an *in situ* and stratigraphic context). His peasant patients, we are to assume, were motivated by a crass materialism, given their willingness to exchange these materials for the suturing of a wound or a child's chest exam. Such a reading seeks to assure us that, at the disciplinary and institutional level, there remains a purity of purpose through which the sometimes destructive means seem to justify the preservationist ends. The past should not be left in the hands of those who would simply allow for it to be forgotten, shoe-boxed for some unknown future transaction. As Mohamed Ibrahim suggested in his 2013 *Washington Post* editorial, to imagine such a world would be unthinkably dystopian.[36] Lay individuals can persist in accessing the raw resources of the material past only if they can demonstrate that

Figure 12.4: Archaeological preserve of Fustat, Cairo, Egypt, 2008. Ian Straughn.

their claim to the commons is coupled with a willingness to engage in practices of meaning-making. Just as al-Mas'udi sought to police the boundary of licit and illicit destruction by articulating a particular kind of disposition to the past, so too have the modern disciplines of archaeology and heritage preservation. While the legal and institutional efforts of the state can legislate, and (sometimes) enforce, proscriptions against looting, treasure hunting or the practices of the *sabbakhin*, this enclosure has coincided with a mandate to 'do' heritage.

I want to suggest a possible alternative, and one that does not necessarily retreat to those largely underappreciated 'faculties of forgetting', those conscious efforts to let ruins be ruins, to make peace with decay, which have become sublimated to the imperatives to save and care for our heritage. How might we make space for an ethics of the heritage commons that resists the impulse to find meaning in the past, in order to locate it within a Kantian cosmopolitanism, a philosophical notion that underpins our contemporary universalizing heritage discourse? How might we expand, rather than abandon, the moral claims of heritage discourse, particularly when it speaks to power? Is there a more inclusive response

Figure 12.5: Basalt mortar carved from a Roman-period capital, al-Hadir, Syria (2000). Ian Straughn.

to those forces of enclosure, whether they be powerful state institutions or corporate entities that bring forward all manner of destruction in the name of preservation?

From Commoners to Caretakers

In Syria, primarily in the Hawran region, there was (and perhaps still is, despite the current conflict) something of a cottage industry where column capitals, particularly those made of basalt, were turned into mortars for grinding small amounts of grain or other foodstuffs [Figure 12.5]. These column capitals were circulated widely within the country, and the capital described here is from al-Hadir, a village some 30 kilometres south of Aleppo where I have previously conducted archaeological fieldwork. Households prized these capitals as both high-quality utilitarian objects and as pieces of craftsmanship. In conversations with several owners of such objects, they related to me that they liked them because they were ancient (*rumani*), but none of these informants were specifically aware of their previous architectural function. The stone itself, the raw material and the fact that people of the past knew what kinds of basalt could last, were more important to the villagers than their previous function.

Throughout this town of some 15,000 inhabitants, dwelling in the shadows of a Bronze Age archaeological tell, I recorded numerous instances of architectural fragments in reuse,

Figure 12.6: Carved column drum supporting a bench outside of a resident's home, al-Hadir, Syria, 2000. Ian Straughn.

not as building materials, but as accoutrements in living spaces, in courtyards and even outside of a petrol station. In some cases, significant effort was made to drag a column fragment several kilometres from the surrounding countryside only to leave it somewhat unceremoniously outside a doorway, seemingly without either a significant functional or aesthetic intent [Figure 12.6]. In the case of one undecorated sarcophagus, cash apparently traded hands between neighbours because the purchaser took a fancy to it. Under the then-existing antiquities laws in Syria none of this was legal. In theory, all such items were the property of the state.

In practice, however, the state had little interest in such things. How many such fragments could they reasonably look to house, record, protect and transport? Similarly, for the residents of al-Hadir, the letter of the law was of little consideration when employing spolia in the village cemetery [Figure 12.7]. That simply seemed an appropriate place for many who encountered or acquired these fragments. Why not put them to use there rather than have them carted off to some regional museum, or more likely a storage depot, if not worse. The temptation is to read this appropriation of the past as sacred, as a demarcation of space and time. Perhaps; but it is all a bit more haphazard than such a pronouncement suggests. This is not to say that it lacks intentionality, but simply that it was more prosaic, more reflective of the way one might consider the commons to have functioned before there was the threat or reality of enclosure.

Figure 12.7: Burial in the town cemetery using spolia to delimit the plot, al-Hadir, Syria, 2000. Ian Straughn.

Before we began any excavations in our first full season of fieldwork at al-Hadir, our team was fortunate that village elders organized a town meeting of sorts where we could explain the project, our presence in their lives, and what they might expect over the course of the next eight weeks or so that we had planned. It also served as an opportunity for us to hear about their discoveries and what they understood and had been taught about the various archaeological remains in the area (both Islamic period and earlier), and for them to express what interests they might have in the work that we were undertaking. During this gathering one middle-aged villager brought out an artefact that he had discovered when excavating a foundation. He presented us with a largely intact vessel of geometric-painted Mamluk ware, fragments of which were not uncommon in the excavation materials from our trenches. While not a remarkable find – no golden chalice or hoard of precious metals – a scandal soon erupted. Attending the meeting was our local representative of the Directorate General of Antiquities and Museums – the official in charge of monitoring our activities and authorizing our permission to engage in fieldwork at the site. When the artefact was handed to her to examine after passing through several others on the team, she declared that she would be keeping the object for the museum in Aleppo, informing the farmer that it was in fact state property. This pronouncement did not meet with either the man's or the rest of the villagers' approval. Heated words were exchanged. Large gesticulations ensued. The mood of the gathering swiftly changed from one of curiosity and openness to one of resistance and antipathy. The conversation abruptly came to an end. Was the official right to have made this claim of ownership? Would it result in the item's future preservation, its protection from damage or its falling into the hands of the illicit antiquities trade? Perhaps it would result in all three. However, I can also report that it was a move that undermined our team's efforts to establish dialogue, to get 'buy-in' from the community and, ultimately, to conduct our fieldwork now that we had been painted more vividly with the brush of state officialdom. It took extensive efforts to soften that impression, and it was never fully achieved. The general impression of our presence as little more than an extension of the state and its marginalization of local communities would never fully rub off. To the extent that we did overcome this association and encourage inhabitants to share their relationship to their material past with us, we witnessed how such artefacts were not constrained by our definition of them as 'artefacts'; rather, these practices of care and engagement also sought to embrace what such objects *could be*, in part because material heritage was subsumed within the commons. The perceived threat posed to those local practices by professional archaeologists descending upon the site under official auspices was not without merit. Our presence directly challenged not only their claims of ownership but also their sense of themselves as local caretakers, albeit some more fastidious than others. In these cases it is also important to recognize that the responsibility to preserve the past was not understood as a requirement for appreciation or connection. Nor was it necessary to tell a story, to give life to these objects and to consciously sustain a new chapter in the biography of things. Rather, the goal was to put them to use or even to merely locate them within their presence. This, in itself, constituted a form of respect. In his book *Friends of Interpretable Objects*, Miguel Tamen offers a counterpoint to this form of ethics as he demonstrates how the impulse toward preservation cannot serve as the dialectical resolution to the antagonistic relationship between idolatry and iconoclasm.[37] Preservation, he contends, follows the same logic as iconoclasm because it claims to strip the material thing of that economic ingredient by which form gives way to incarnation. He therefore suggests that form takes precedence and any hopes of veneration are eliminated. However, amongst the inhabitants of al-Hadir, veneration is not even a part of the conversation. Appreciation, or perhaps even more basic, a sense of marking such objects as 'not trash' by incorporating them as common resources worthy of some level of attention, constitutes how one cares for the past. Such practices seem alien to Alfred Gell's assessment of the preservationist's impulse, when he states, 'We have neutralized our idols by reclassifying them as art.'[38] Idolatry is not even a question of how the villagers of al-Hadir repurpose the past. Instead, they, like the *sabbakhin* and treasure hunters before them, indicate an attachment to the commons that has similarly been neutralized, though not totally enclosed, by modern heritage discourses and practices in the Middle East. Despite those institutional and state-directed efforts to save the past, the cultivation of care for old things persists, even when it fails to show the signs of expertise, or to follow the lessons of scholars.

Acknowledgements

This chapter has benefited greatly from valuable comments and questions during presentations of this research at the University of Kansas and University California, Irvine. I would like to thank my colleagues at Brown for spirited conversations on vernacular archaeology. I owe a further debt of gratitude to Mirjam Brusius for her kind invitation to a workshop at Harvard where these ideas had their start. Finally, I am grateful to Stephennie Mulder for her careful engagement with this chapter at many stages and the valuable comments from anonymous reviewers.

Notes

1. Lila Abu-Lughod, 'Do Muslim Women Really Need Saving? Anthropological Reflections on Cultural Relativism and Its Others', *American Anthropologist* 104.3 (2002): 784. This article would later be developed in a monograph of the same title: *Do Muslim Women Need Saving?* (Cambridge, MA: Harvard University Press, 2013).
2. Mohamed Ibrahim, 'Looting Egypt's Heritage', *Washington Post*, October 18, 2013.
3. Finbarr Barry Flood, 'Between Cult and Culture: Bamiyan, Islamic Iconoclasm, and the Museum', *The Art Bulletin* 84.4 (2002): 654.
4. Some prominent examples of this research and critique include Lynn Meskell and Robert W. Preucel, *Companion to Social Archaeology* (Malden, MA: John Wiley & Sons, 2008); Lynn Meskell and Peter Pell, eds, *Embedding Ethics: Shifting the Boundaries of the Anthropological Profession* (London: Berg Press, 2005); Richard Sandell and Eithne Nightingale, *Museums, Equality and Social Justice* (New York: Routledge, 2013).

5. Barbara J. Mills, 'Remembering While Forgetting: Depositional Practices and Social Memory at Chaco', in *Memory Work: Archaeologies of Material Practices*, eds Barbara J. Mills and William H. Walker (Santa Fe: School for Advanced Research Press, 2008), 81–108.
6. Ian Russell, 'Towards an Ethics of Oblivion and Forgetting: The Parallax View', *Heritage & Society* 5.2 (2012): 249–72. See also Katherine Hayes, 'Occulting the Past: Conceptualizing Forgetting in the History and Archaeology of Sylvester Manor', *Archaeological Dialogues* 18.2 (2011): 197–221.
7. Russell, 'Towards an Ethics', 260.
8. Joseph Meri, 'Memorializing the Sacred in the Islamic Civilizational Context', *Islamica* 15 (2006): 69–74.
9. Daniel Howden, 'The Destruction of Mecca: Saudi Hardliners are Wiping Out Their Own Heritage', *The Independent*, August 5, 2005.
10. Joseph Meri, 'Aspects of *Baraka* (Blessing) and Ritual Devotion among Medieval Muslims and Jews', *Medieval Encounters* 5.1 (1999): 46–69.
11. Josef W. Meri, *The Cult of Saints among Muslims and Jews in Medieval Syria* (Oxford: Oxford University Press, 2002); J. W. Meri, 'Relics of Piety and Power in Medieval Islam', *Past & Present* 206.5 (2010): 97–120.
12. Mohamed Zakariya, 'Comment', *Islamica* 15 (2006): 75.
13. Ibid.
14. Georg Stauth and Joska Samuli Schielke, eds, *Dimensions of Locality: Muslim Saints, Their Place and Space* (Bielefeld: Transcript, 2008).
15. Translated and citied in Elliott Colla, *Conflicted Antiquities: Egyptology, Egyptomania, Egyptian Modernity* (Durham, NC: Duke University Press, 2007), 88.
16. Michael Greenhalgh, *Marble Past, Monumental Present: Building with Antiquities in the Mediaeval Mediterranean* (Leiden: Brill, 2009).
17. Ulrich Haarman, 'Medieval Muslim Perceptions of Pharaonic Egypt', in *Ancient Egyptian Literature: History and Forms*, ed. Antonio Loprieno (Leiden: Brill, 1996).
18. Finbarr Barry Flood, 'Image against Nature: Spolia as Apotropaia in Byzantium and the Dar Al-Islam', *The Medieval History Journal* 9.1 (2006): 143–66.
19. Okasha El Daly, *Egyptology: The Missing Millennium: Ancient Egypt in Medieval Arabic Writings* (London: UCL Press, 2005), 31–44.
20. Ibid., 35.
21. Ahmad Kamal, *Livre des perles enfouies et du mystère précieux au sujet des indications des cachettes des trouvailles et des trésors,* vol. 2 (Cairo: Imprimerie de l'Institut français d'archéologie orientale, 1907).
22. Ibid., viii (my translation).
23. For a more detailed discussion of the development of Egyptian professionals and their connections to nationalist policies, see Donald M. Reid, *Whose Pharaohs?: Archaeology, Museums, and Egyptian National Identity from Napoleon to World War I* (Berkeley: University of California Press, 2002).
24. W. Cossar Mackenzie, *Manures in Egypt and Soil Exhaustion* (Cairo: National Printing Office, 1896), 32.

25. George P. Foaden and F. Fletcher, *Text-Book of Egyptian Agriculture*, vol. 1 (Cairo: National Printing Department, 1908).
26. Ibid., 263.
27. Donald M. Bailey, 'Sebakh, Sherds and Survey', *Journal of Egyptian Archaeology* 85 (1999): 211–12.
28. Paola Davoli, 'Papyri, Archaeology, and Modern History', Center for the Tebtunis Papyri, accessed March 17, 2017, http://tebtunis.berkeley.edu/ lecture/arch.
29. Bailey, 'Sebakh, Sherds and Survey', 212.
30. Ibid., 213. It is not clear to what extent such purchases were sweetheart deals greased by bribes or other favours to the relevant bureaucrats.
31. Comité de conservation des monuments de l'art Arabe, *Procès-verbaux des séances, rapports de la Deuxième commission* (Cairo: Lajnat Hifz al-Athar al-'Arabiyah, 1894).
32. Bernard P. Grenfell, *Fayûm Towns and Their Papyri*, eds Arthur S. Hunt, D. G. Hogarth and J. G. Milne (London: Offices of the Egypt Exploration Fund, 1900), 24.
33. Jere L. Bacharach, *Fustat Finds: Beads, Coins, Medical Instruments, Textiles, and Other Artifacts from the Awad Collection* (Cairo: American University in Cairo Press, 2002).
34. Ibid., 3.
35. Ibid., 3.
36. Ibrahim, 'Looting Egypt's Heritage'.
37. Miguel Tamen, *Friends of Interpretable Objects* (Cambridge, MA: Harvard University Press, 2001).
38. Alfred Gell, *Art and Agency: An Anthropological Theory* (Oxford: Clarendon Press, 1998), 97.

Notes on Contributors

Ondřej Beránek is a researcher at the Oriental Institute of the Czech Academy of Sciences. He received his Ph.D. in Arabic and Islamic studies from Charles University, Prague. As part of his education he also studied Arabic in Tunisia and Arabic and Islamic culture at the King Saud University in Riyadh, Saudi Arabia. During 2005–07, he was a fellow at the Center for Middle Eastern Studies, Harvard University and in 2007–09, he was a postdoctoral fellow at the Crown Center for Middle East Studies, Brandeis University. His research studies focus on the modern and contemporary history of the Middle East, the history of Saudi Arabia and Salafism. He is a co-author, with Pavel Ťupek, of *The Temptation of Graves in Salafi Islam: Iconoclasm, Destruction and Idolatry* (Edinburgh University Press, 2018).

Elizabeth Cohen worked at the Ian Potter Museum of Art (University of Melbourne) and the Ashmolean Museum (University of Oxford), before completing her Ph.D. in 2015 in critical heritage studies at the University of Cambridge with a focus on the perception of Greece's Ottoman heritage. Her particular research interests are the interpretation of dissonant pasts, the multilayered nature of national identity formation, as well as the construction of postcolonial landscapes. Now living in Edinburgh, she is interested in the construction of Scottish identity, particularly in relation to how the country is confronting its imperial history and its involvement in the transatlantic slave trade.

Dotan Halevy is a Polonsky postdoctoral fellow in the Van Leer Institute, Jerusalem. His research focuses on the culture, society, and environment of the modern Middle East. His doctoral dissertation, entitled 'Stripped: Ruination, Liminality, and the Making of the Gaza Strip 1840–1950', was completed at Columbia University, and offers a modern history of the Gaza borderland under Ottoman and British rule.

Amanda Herring is assistant professor in the Department of Art and Art History at Loyola Marymount University. She received her BA from Dartmouth College and her MA and Ph.D. from UCLA. Her research examines sculpture and architecture in the Hellenistic period as well the history of archaeology in the Ottoman Empire and the reception of the classical past in the modern world. Her work has been published by the *Journal of the*

Society of Architectural Historians, the *History of Photography*, and the Cotsen Institute of Archaeology Press.

Sarah Cresap Johnson is curator of the Middle East and North Africa collections at the Dutch National Museum of World Cultures. Her research centers on modern and contemporary material culture from the Middle East, with a particular focus on Iraq, as well as on early Islamic objects. She received a Ph.D. from the Freie University in Berlin. Previously, she was a curator of Islamic collections at the British Museum in London and as a researcher in the curatorial department at the National Museum of Asian Art in Washington, D.C.

Santhi Kavuri-Bauer is professor of Islamic and South Asian art at San Francisco State University. Her research focuses on the history of Islamic monuments both in the medieval and modern periods. Her book, *Monumental Matters: The Power, Subjectivity, and Space of India's Mughal Architecture* (Durham and London: Duke University Press, 2011) is a critical examination of the practices of monumental preservation from the colonial period to the present. Her current research investigates the influences of Islamic philosophy and mysticism on the design and forms of Islamic Indian architecture and urban planning.

Daniel Mahoney is a postdoctoral researcher at Ghent University in the Department of Languages and Cultures. In 2014, he completed his Ph.D. thesis at the University of Chicago on the history and archaeology of the central highlands of South Arabia during the medieval and early Ottoman periods.

Muhsin Lufti Martens has worked in different capacities as an educator, researcher, and conservator specializing in Islamic art at various cultural institutions across the Muslim world, including in Malaysia, Morocco, and Saudi Arabia.

Miroslav Mlčák is a research fellow at the Oriental Institute of the Czech Academy of Sciences, Prague. He studied Arabic language and Islamic studies at Charles University, Prague, where he obtained his Ph.D. in 2009. His main research interests include charitable foundations (*awqaf*) in Syria and Egypt and Islamic urbanism of Northern Mesopotamia. Between 2013 and 2015, he was a member of the Czech archaeological mission in Iraqi Kurdistan (project 'Medieval Urban Landscape in Northeastern Mesopotamia'). Currently, he is a research team member of the project 'Monuments of Mosul in Danger', documenting and researching the destroyed heritage of the town.

Stephennie Mulder is associate professor of Islamic art and architecture at the University of Texas at Austin. She is a specialist in Islamic architectural history and archaeology and has worked at numerous archaeological sites throughout the Middle East, including over ten years as the head ceramicist at Balis, a medieval Islamic city in Syria. Dr Mulder has published books and articles on issues related to cultural heritage, the intersections between art, spatiality and sectarian relationships in Islam, anthropological theories of art, material culture studies, theories of ornament and mimesis, and place and landscape studies. Dr Mulder also serves on the board of several cultural heritage organizations and is the founder of UT Antiquities Action. Her book *The Shrines of the 'Alids in Medieval Syria* (Edinburgh University Press, 2014) won the 2015 World Prize for Book of the Year from the Islamic Republic of Iran and was selected as a *Choice* Outstanding Academic Title.

Emily Neumeier (Ph.D., University of Pennsylvania) is Assistant Professor of Islamic Art and Architecture at Temple University. She specializes in the visual and spatial cultures of the Eastern Mediterranean, with a focus on the Ottoman Empire. Her research addresses issues of architecture, cultural heritage, the history of archaeology, and nationalist discourses through art. She is currently preparing a book-length study that will be an alternative history of Ottoman architecture from the view of the provinces during the Age of Revolutions. Her research has been supported by the American Research Institute in Turkey and the Fulbright Program. She is also a former Research Collaborator in the Max Planck Research Group 'Objects in the Contact Zone: The Cross-Cultural Lives of Things' at the Kunsthistorisches Institut in Florence.

Eli Osheroff is a postdoctoral fellow at the Truman Institute for the Advancement of Peace at The Hebrew University. His work focuses on modern Arab intellectual and political history, especially in the context of Jewish-Arab relations.

Virginie Rey (Ph.D.) is a museum anthropologist and a lecturer in cultural heritage and museum studies at Deakin University, Australia. She is the author of *Mediating Museums* (Brill, 2019), the co-editor of *Making Modernity from the Mashriq to the Maghrib* (Arena, 2015) and the editor of *The Art of Minorities: Cultural Representation in Museums of the Middle East and North Africa* (Edinburgh University Press, 2020).

Wendy M. K. Shaw (Ph.D. UCLA, 1999) publishes on the impact of coloniality and Eurocentrism on art-related institutions, heritage and preservation, modern art and pre-modern discourses of perception, and religious thought under secular modernism. Her work focuses on the Ottoman Empire, modern Turkey and regions of Islamic hegemony. She is author of *Possessors and Possessed: Museums, Archaeology, and the Visualization of History in the Late Ottoman Empire* (University of California Press, 2003), *Osmanlı Müzeleri* (İletişim Yayınları, 2006), *Ottoman Painting: Reflections of Western Art from the Ottoman Empire to the Turkish Republic* (IB Tauris, 2011). *What Is 'Islamic' Art: Between Religion and Perception* (Cambridge University Press, 2019, Honorable Mention for the 2020 Albert Hourani Book Award of the Middle East Studies Association and the 2021 Iran Book Award), and *Loving Writing: Techniques for the University and Beyond* (Routledge, 2021). She is currently reinventing the wheel to communicate transcultural thought through aesthetic practices.

Ian B. Straughn (Ph.D. 2005, The University of Chicago) is currently assistant professor of teaching in the Department of Anthropology at UCI and has held several faculty positions at Brown University. Dr Straughn specializes as an archaeologist of the Islamic world having worked in Syria, Jordan, Armenia and Egypt. More recently he has had funding from the British Library to document a collection of Arabic manuscripts from Timbuktu, held in a private collection in Bamako Mali. His recent publications explore aspects of heritage discourse and practice within Muslim societies, past and present. He is currently co-editing a volume on the Islamic textual tradition of West Africa – tentatively titled *Timbuktu Unbound* – and developing new pedagogical tools for teaching archaeology and material culture.

Index

A
Abbasid Empire 23, 37, 258–59
'Abd al-Malik b. Marwan 73–75, 78n31, 259
Abdullah Lutfi 252–54
Abraham (Ibrahim) 75, 259
Abu Sha'ban, Hilmi 208–11, 213–14
Abu Simbel (Wadi Halfa), Egypt 221, 236–38, 242
Académie des Inscriptions et Belles–Lettres 171, 175
Actium, Battle of 141, 143, 153, 155–56
adab (literature) 40, 88, 91
Afghanistan 195–96, 222, 239–41
   Mes Aynak 242
African Tunisian (Black) 297
Ahmed, Shahab 16
'ajab,' ajiba, 'aja'ib(wonder, wonders) 15, 17, 20, 22–23, 58, 83–106
'Ali ibn Abi Talib 68–69, 75, 269
Ali Pasha, Tepedelenli 24, 138–58
   antiquarianism 138–43
   archaeological excavations 143–48
   inscriptions 148–51, 150
Amazigh 25, 295–99, 306
Anatolia 24, 165–80, 235
antiquarianism 115–18, 139–43, 165, 167–71
antiquities laws 167–74
antiquity, idea of 4, 15–18, 21
Aphrodisias/Geyre 221, 233, *234–35*
apotropaic function (of antiquities) 17–20, 23

Arab Spring
   Jasmine Revolution 295–96, 305
al-'Arif, 'Arif 206–08, 211–12
Aristotle 88, 102
al-As'ad, Khaled 3, 7, 26, 222
athar (traces, ruins) 23, 40, 45, 52 *see also* ruins
  and nostalgia 51–53
  in poetry 40–41
Athens, Greece 24, 115–25, *126*
   Acropolis 117–19, 123–25
   Fethiye Mosque *123*, 124
   Parthenon 117–20, 122, *123*, 127, 158
   Temple of Olympian Zeus (Olympieion) 24, 116, 120–26
   Tzisdarakis (Djistaraki) Mosque 124–25
Augustus 143, 152–53
Aurangzeb 240

B
Babylon, Iraq 44–46
Badr al-Din Lulu 269, 271
Baghdad, Iraq 39, 44, 47, 49, 53, 55, 58, 88–90, 94–95, 205
   House of Wisdom 205
Balkans 115, 158
Bamiyan Buddhas, Afghanistan 4, 125, 195–96, 213, 221, 239–41
Bardo Museum, Tunis 293–94, 304–05
   attack on 293

Bassae, Greece
    Temple of Apollo Epicurius 137, *138, 139*, 143
Bedouin 52–53, 226–27, 299
Bedri Bey 176
Beirut, Lebanon 226–27
Bell, Gertrude 228
Ben Ali, Zine El Abidine
    nation-building 296–97
    ousting 295, 299
    patrimonialization 294–95, 299, 301–03
Benndorf, Otto 171
Berber *see* Amazigh
al-Biruni 89–91, 94
Blue Helmets of Culture 221
Bone, Muirhead 200
Book of Strangers (al-Isfahani) 37, 46, 49, 51, 57–58
Borges, Jorge Luís 214
Borra, Giovanni Battista 224, *225*
Bouazizi, Mohammed 295–96
Bourguiba, Habib
    and heritage 298, 300, 302
    nation-building 295–97, 304
British Empire 198, 206, 236
    army 197–203, 214
British Mandate for Palestine 206, 208–09
British Museum 138, 158, 168, 171
Brøndsted, Peter 137, 142, 143–45
de Bruijn, Cornelius 223, *224*
al-Buhturi 53–56, 58
al-Bustani, Salim 226
Byzantine Empire 6, 7, 18–19, 116

C

Cairo 20, 314, 237, 314, 319–23
    Wikala of Qawsun 20, *21*
Centre des Arts et Traditions Populaires 303
de Certeau, Michel 306
Chamonard, Joseph 171, 174–78, 180
Chandler, Richard 118–19, 122, 124, 168
Charlie Hebdo 4, 28, 304–05
Christianity
    in Ottoman Athens 119–21, 125–28
    in Mosul 267
    in Palmyra 6–8, 21–22
Clermont-Ganneau, Charles 208, 210
Colla, Elliot 14–15
collective memory *see* memory
commons, the 319–29
Constantinople 19–20 Istanbul
    serpent column in hippodrome 19–20
Cousin, Georges 171
Ctesiphon, Iraq 15, 41
    Qasr bint al-Qadi 42, *43*
    Taq–i Kisra 41, 53–56
    White Palace 41–44

D

Da'esh *see* ISIS
Damascus, Syria 21–22
    Bimaristan (hospital) of Nur al-Din 18–19
    Umayyad Mosque 22, 258
Dawkins, James 28, 224, *225*, 229
Delhi, India
    Ashokan pillar 83, *84*, 85–86, 100, 102, 103, 104–05
    Firuzabad 83
    Firuz Shah Kotla Fort 23, *83, 101*
    iron pillar 86, *87*, 95–99, 100
    Qutb Minar 91, *93*, 94–96
    Quwwat al-Islam Mosque 90–92, 94–96, 98–99
Delhi Sultanate 86–100
destruction *see* heritage, destruction of
Djerba
    Association pour la Sauvegarde de l'Ile de 299–301
    Judaism in 297–98
    Synagogue of 299
dreams, as generative of heritage 22, 269
Duncan, Carol 14

E

École française d'Athènes 171, 175
Edhem, Halil 180–81

Egypt 17, 19, 26, 88, 94, 221, 236–38, 314, 320–24
   pyramids 15, 88, 94
Egyptology 77n17, 320–21
Elgin, Lord Thomas 118, 124, 138, 143, 158
   Elgin Marbles *see* Parthenon Marbles
enclosure 328–29
Enlightenment 137, 224, 228, 293, *see also* al-Nahda
   Greek 142, 152
   Arab *see* al-Nahda
Ennahda Party 296, 305
Epirus, Greece and Albania 148, 150–52, 158
ethnography 301–04
Evliya Çelebi 119, 121–23, 153

F
fada'il (virtues) 15, 17
Fayyum, Egypt 321, 322
Firuz Shah Tughluq 23, 83, 85–86, 101–06
Flood, Finbarr Barry 14, 85, 195, 315
folk songs 151–52
forgetting 315, 324
Fowden, Elizabeth Key 119–20, 127
France 230, 305
Fustat, Egypt 319, 322–25

G
Gaza, Palestine
   candelabrum in mosque 206, 209–12
   Great Mosque 24, 195–214
   library 198, 204–05
   occupation by Israel 212–13
geographical treatises (Arabic) 40, 86–88, 91
geography 23, 44–45, 66, 141
Ghannouchi, Rached 296
al-Ghazali 91, 317
Ghurid Dynasty 91
graffiti 49–51, 57–58
Greece 24, 115–25, 137–43
Greek Enlightenment 142–43, 152
Güler, Ara 233, *234–35*
Gupta Empire 23, 86, *97*

H
al-Hadir, Syria 325–29
Hajj (pilgrimage) 254–56, 259–60
al-Hamdani 23, 71–75
Hamilton, Gavin 224, *225*, 226
Hazara people 240–42
Hebrew 206, *207*, 208, 210, 212
Hegelianism 223, 228
heritage 13–16
   Authorized Heritage Discourse 14, 128
   cosmopolitan/global/world 14, 25–26, 158, 221, 221–22, 231, 236–38, 238–39, 240, 242, 242–43, 313, 324
   destruction of 117–18, 195–208, 213–14, 251–59, 274, 276–80
   as faith, religious attributes of 14–15
   Islamic conceptualizations of 15–23, 222–23, 251–61, 317
   local 13–16, 25–26, 127–28, 141, 222–23, 242, 279, 300–04, 313, 317, 328
   nonconforming 24, 26, 128
   patrimonialization 294–95, 299, 301–03
Hinkel, Friedrich W. 238, *239*
al-Hira, Iraq 40, 49
history, historical writing 40–44, 65–69
History of Gaza ('Arif al-'Arif) 206, *207*, 208
Hoelscher, Steven 14
Holy Land (*ard al-muqaddisa*) 22
Homolle, Théophile 175–76

I
Ibadism
   faith 295, 304
   mosques 299–301
'ibar (lessons [of the past]) 17, 22–23, 319
Ibn Battuta 99
Ibn Jubayr 257
Ibn Hawqal 40–41, 44
Ibn Khaldun 47, 258
Ibn Taymiyya 277, 317

Ibn al-Zubayr 258–59
iconoclasm 4, 12–13, 15–16, 18, 20, 25, 125, 196–97, 258, 313–15, 328–29 *see also* taswiyat al-qubur
identity 23, 116, 123–25, 151, 223, 230, 258, 297, 305
   archaeology and 172–76
   Islamic 299, 301
   national *see* nationalism
idolatry 14, 41, 89–90, 196, 258, 277–78, 318, 328–29
al-Iklil (The Crown) 23, 65–75
Iltutmish 91, 94–95, 98, 106
Ioannina, Greece 138, 142–43, 148–52, 150
imperialism (European)
   British 236, 240
   French 230, 240
Imru' al-Qays 37, 52, 204
India 23, 83–107
Institute National D'Archéologie et d'Art 302
Iraq 37–58, 222
al-Isfahani 37
ISIS (Islamic State of Iraq and Syria) 4–5, 12–15, 25, 195–97, 213, 222, 239, 241, 313–15
   in Mosul 267, 268, 278–80
Islamization 115, 125
Istanbul, Turkey 143, 152, 174
   Imperial Museum 166, 172–73, 174, 175, 179–80, 181

J

Jasmine Revolution 26, 295–96, 305
Jerusalem 21, 198, 212, 258
   Dome of the Rock 21, 212
Johnson, Boris 238–39
Judaism 24, 206, 295, 296, 297–98, 306
   history and material traces in Gaza 206–08, 210–11
   in museums in Tunisia 297–98
   Spring Festival in Tunisia 299
   Synagogue of Djerba in Tunisia 299

K

Ka'ba *see also* Mecca 251–60
   images of 254
Kamal, Ahmad 320–22
Karanis (Kom Aushim), Egypt 322
kingship 23, 85, 100, 106 *see also* sovereignty
Knackfuss, Hubert 180–81

L

Lagina, Anatolia 24, 165–89, 166, 169, 170, 177–80
landscape, sacred 22, 67, 69, 77n16, 78n22, 79n37, 80n52
Leake, William Martin 155, 183n14
Leaning Virgin of Albert 200, 202
Legrand, Philippe 151–52, 171
local identity 141–42, 328 *see also* heritage, local
London, England
   Trafalgar Square 221–22, 238

M

al-Mada'in, Iraq 39–41, 47, 53, 55–58
Magnesia on the Meander 181
al-Mahdi 259
Mahmud Efendi 119, 127
manaqib 104
al-Mansur 259
al-Mas'udi 45, 49, 319
McBey, James 202–03, 214
Mecca, Saudi Arabia 25, 201, 251–61, 316–19
   Ka'ba 251–60
   al-Masjid al-Haram (Great Mosque) 25, 251–61
   modern renovations to portico 253–54, 259–61, 261
   Ottoman renovations to portico 252, *253*, *254*, 260
Medina, Saudi Arabia 257
   al-Masjid al-Nabawi (Prophet's Mosque) 257
Mehmet Aga 251

Index

memory 41–43, 125, 228
   collective 23–24, 66–71
   historical 213, 269, 296
Mesopotamia 17, *39*
Midhat Pasha, Ahmet 173
Mosul, Iraq 3, 25, *45*
   Christian monuments 274, 276
   destruction by ISIS 267, 268, 271, 274, 276–80, 287n4, 287n5, 289n23, 290n34
   ISIS in 267–68, 278–80
   mosques, destruction 269
   shrines 268, 269, 271, 277, 288n10, 288n12
   wathiqat al-madina ("Charter of the City") 278
al-Muʿallaqat (Imruʾ al-Qays) 37, 52
Muhammad (prophet) 15, 73, 268–69, 277–78, 316–17
   heritage destruction 65, 75, 213
   heritage preservation 68, 256
   light of, in Parthenon 120
   memory of, in Mecca and Medina 256–58
Muʿjam al-buldan(Yaqut) 256
al-Muqaddasi 46, 49, 58
Murray, Archibald 198, 201

N

Nadir Shah 240
al-Nahda (modern Arab Enlightenment) 205
Napoleon 152–56, *156*
nationalism 151, 158, 166–67, 172–73, 181–82, 196, 212, 258
   national identity 23, 115, 125, 186n44, 230, 236, 238, 293, 295–97, 304–05
Nemrud Dağı (Mt. Nimrod) 24, 165, 173, 174, 181
Neoplatonism 23, 88
Newton, Charles 168–71
Niemann, George 171
Nikopolis 143–48, *144*, 152–57
Nineveh, Iraq 44, *45*, 269, 277
nostalgia 51–53

Nubian people 236, *239*, 241
Nur al-Din 18, 271

O

Osgan Efendi 174
Osman Hamdi Bey 165–66, 172–82
Ottoman Empire 23–24, 115–28, 226, 228, 233, 251
   archaeology 143, 165, 172–82
   army 202, 204–06
   cosmopolitanism 206, 208, 212, 214
   national identity 166, 172, 173, 181–82
   program of modernization 172, 173
   provincial power-holders in 138
Ottomanization 115–17, 125, 127–28

P

Palestine 24, 37, 198, 202, 206–08, 212
Palmyra, Syria 3–13, 21–22, 26, 37–39, 221–33, 238, 240 *see also* Tadmur
   Byzantine Church 6–7, 12
   Christianity in, *see* Christianity
   conservation of 4–5, 8
   destruction by French archaeolgists 4–5, 8–13, 230–31
   destruction by ISIS 3–4, 125, 195–96
   Mosque of Tadmur 7–12
   prison 222
   Shiʾi shrines 222, 233
   Temple of Bel 4–12, 222, 228
Pars, William 168
Parthenon *see* Athens
Parthenon Marbles 118–19, 124–25
Peacock, Thomas Love 226
Peloponnese (Morea), Greece 137, 143
Perfect Man 104, 106, 109
Petra 315, *316*
philhellenism 115, 167
pilgrimage 67–69, 75, 120, 242 *see also* Hajj
pillars 23, 83–107, 206–08, 251–54
Plato 102, 119
Pococke, Richard 168
poetry 17, 40, 51–53, 56–57, 91, 204, 298

preservation, preservationism 4–5, 8, 17–18, 21–24, 251, 255, 257, 315, 328–29
Preveza, Greece 145–48, 153
Pyrrhus 148–52

Q
Qasr al-Hayr al-Gharbi, Syria 38
Qur'an 17, 42–45, 68–69, 71–72, 88, 91, 201–11, 257, 319

R
Raqqa, Syria 51, 58, 226
redevelopment 251–53, 255, 257
reuse 118, 252 *see also* spolia
Revett, Nicholas 123, 168
ruins, concept or idea of 13, 37–38, 46–49, 319 *see also* athar
   apotropaic use of 18
   Islamic idea of 16–18, 66, 75
   in literature 46–49
   nostalgia and 51–53
   royal power and 45, 49–50

S
sabbakhin 321–25
sacred histories 21–22
sacred landscape 22, 67–69
Salafism 26, 267, 277–78, 289n24, 295–96, 299, 301, 305, 317–18
Samarra, Iraq 39–40, 51, *57*, 58
Seljuk Sultanate 37
Service des Antiquités de Syrie et du Liban (French Antiquities Service) 4–5
Seyahatname (Evliya Çelebi) 119
Seyrig, Henri 5, 13, 15, 230
Shi'ism 97, 222, 269, 276–77, 317
shirk see idolatry
shrines
   destruction (by ISIS) 267
   of Prophet Muhammad's family in Mecca 268–71
   visitation of 3, 16, 258, 316
Sidon, Lebanon 24, 165, 173–81

Sinan 252–54, 258–59
Sirat-i Firozshahi (anonymous) 83
Smith, Laurajane 14, 294
Smith, Robert Murdoch 168, 171
Society of the Dilettanti 168
Socrates 119
Solomon (prophet) 22, 119–20
South Arabia 23, 65–75
sovereignty 51, 89, 91, 142, 207, 258 *see also* kingship
Spivak, Gayatri 232
spolia 38, 46–49, 145–48, 252 *see also* reuse
Stratonikeia (Eskihisar), Turkey 166, 168
Sudan 236–38
Suleyman the Magnificent 25, 251
Sunnism 97, 269, 317
Syria 3–13, 18, *19*, 20–22, 37, 55, *56*, 72, 106, 198
   war 3–4, 222–23, 238

T
al-Tabari 40–42, 44, 71, 256–57
al-Tabba', 'Uthman Mustafa 204–05, 211, 214
Tadmur, Syria 4–14, 26, 38, 72–73, 195, 222–29, 234, 238 *see also* Palmyra
   Mosque of *see* Palmyra, Mosque of Tadmur
Taliban 4, 195–96, 213, 221, 239, 241, 314
Tarih-i Medinetü'l-Hukema ('History of the City of the Philosophers') 119
taswiyat al-qubur (leveling of graves) 267, 277–78, 287n4
Todd, Emmanuel 305
travel 51, 53, 57–58, 141–42
travellers' accounts 115–24
   European 115–17, 122–24, 128
   Ottoman 117–19, 128
treasure hunting 319–22
Tournaire, Joseph-Albert 179
Trysa (Gölbaşı), Turkey 171

Tunis, Tunisia
    Bardo Museum 26, 293–94, 305
Tunisia 25, 293–306
    French Protectorate 295, 297, 303
Turkey 165, 221, 242 *see also* Anatolia

U
'Uthman ibn 'Affan 256–57, 260
'Umar Ibn al-Khattab 46, 68–70, 74, 198, 256–57
Umayyad Empire 7, 38–39, 73, 228, 255–59
UNESCO 14, 25, 222, 241
    World Heritage 222, 231, 236–38, 240, 242

V
Veli Pasha 143
Vilnay, Ze'ev 206, 208, 212

W
Wahhabism 257–58, 316
    Ibn 'Abd al-Wahhab, Muhammad 277, 278
Wiegand, Theodor 180–81
Wingate, Reginald 201
wonder *see* 'ajab
Wood, Robert 28, 224, *225*

Y
Yakovlev, Alexander Evgenevich 232, *233*
al-Yaqubi 257
Yaqut al-Hamawi 7, 240, 256
Yemen 3, 65–75, 95, 278 *see also* South Arabia

Z
Zenobia 14, 223
Zionism 206, 208–09, 211
ziyara (visitation of tombs) 277, 317